PRESIDENTIAL CONTROL OVER ADMINISTRATION

STUDIES IN GOVERNMENT AND
PUBLIC POLICY

PRESIDENTIAL CONTROL OVER ADMINISTRATION

A New Historical Analysis of Public Finance Policymaking, 1929–2018

Patrick R. O'Brien

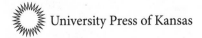 University Press of Kansas

Published by the University Press of Kansas (Lawrence, Kansas 66045), which was organized by the Kansas Board of Regents and is operated and funded by Emporia State University, Fort Hays State University, Kansas State University, Pittsburg State University, the University of Kansas, and Wichita State University.

Library of Congress Cataloging-in-Publication Data

Names: O'Brien, Patrick R., author.
Title: Presidential control over administration : a new historical analysis
   of public finance policymaking, 1929–2018 / Patrick R. O'Brien.
Description: Lawrence, Kansas : University Press of Kansas, 2022. | Series:
   Studies in Government and Public Policy | Includes index.
Identifiers: LCCN 2021026160
   ISBN 9780700632961 (Cloth)
   ISBN 9780700632978 (eBook)
Subjects: LCSH: Presidents—United States—History. | Executive
   power—United States—History. | Executive-legislative relations—United
   States. | Finance, Public—United States—History.
Classification: LCC JK511 .O27 2022 | DDC 352.230973—dc23/eng/20211210
LC record available at https://lccn.loc.gov/2021026160.

British Library Cataloguing-in-Publication Data is available.

Printed in the United States of America

10 9 8 7 6 5 4 3 2 1

The paper used in this publication is acid free and meets the minimum requirements of the American National Standard for Permanence of Paper for Printed Library Materials Z39.48-1992.

To Caitlin, Graham, and Molly

CONTENTS

V. Historical Variation in Presidential Control during the Great Recession and Beyond

PREFACE AND ACKNOWLEDGMENTS

This project began nearly a decade ago with the aim of answering an important question regarding a single president: Why did Barack Obama fail to restructure the domain of public finance in response to the Great Recession? Obama's failure on this front was especially puzzling at the time when taking into account several key dynamics: he ran on an explicit platform of "change" and succeeded an opposition-party president; he inherited, in his own words, the "greatest economic crisis since the Great Depression"; and he assumed office with unified party control of the government and substantial popular support.

In the process of developing a satisfactory answer, the research question began to broaden: Which presidents throughout US history did in fact oversee the restructuring of the domain of public finance, and why and how did that occur? This broader question required reading a wide range of material: at least a single biography on every president (and in most cases multiple biographies); the memoirs and relevant letters and speeches of the presidents; biographies on the major public-finance principals; the memoirs, oral histories, and relevant letters and government publications of the major public-finance principals; historical accounts on the most important public-finance policies and problems, beginning with the collapse of the public credit during the 1780s; and historical accounts on the most important public-finance institutions, beginning with the creation of the Treasury Department in 1789. I also closely examined a wide range of quantitative data using annual reports from the Treasury Department for the early and middle periods of US history and multiple sources for the modern period.

Based on that extensive qualitative and quantitative research, I uncovered a recurring development. Specifically, I found that in response to an exceptionally severe and highly prioritized problem, some presidents increase their control by restructuring both the public-finance apparatus and the key parameters of public-finance policy. Equally important, I found that as the problem in the policy domain and the prioritization of that problem decline, the restructured public-finance apparatus and its principals continue to structure the policymaking process for subsequent incumbents, thereby securing the restructured policy parameters in the process of limiting presidential control. Put simply, I found that presidential control over administration operates as a key historical variable in policymaking.

Returning to the original research question, Barack Obama failed to take the lead in restructuring the domain of public finance in large part because the Great Recession was, in relative terms, neither an exceptionally severe problem nor a highly prioritized problem for a sustained period, all of which limited the president's control over public-finance administration and in turn his ability to shift public-finance policy in a substantial and durable way.

Regarding the broader research question, two presidents oversaw the restructuring of the domain of public finance during the early period of US history: George Washington in response to the collapse of the public credit and Andrew Jackson in response to the elimination of the national debt. Two presidents then oversaw a similar process during the modern period: Franklin Roosevelt in response to the Great Depression and Ronald Reagan in response to the Great Inflation. The policy domain was also restructured during the middle period of US history, but the initial process was especially unique due to the Civil War, and several dynamics complicated the subsequent process, which occurred in partial steps, primarily under Grover Cleveland and Woodrow Wilson, the only two Democrats elected to office during the roughly seven decades of Republican rule. To be clear, the empirical analysis that follows in this book focuses on the modern period—which was essential to make the analysis a manageable length—but I use examples from the early and middle periods to develop the argument.

Finally, while examining the dynamics of presidential control in the domain of public finance across more than two centuries, key limitations of the leading approaches to studying the presidency and policymaking became increasingly apparent, and therefore the central research question became even broader: What role does presidential control over administration play in policymaking, especially given that the Constitution has made each president throughout US history the sole legal head of the executive branch? To answer that question, this book develops a new historical approach for studying the presidency and policymaking in general and helps to explain in particular why most presidents do not oversee the restructuring of the key domain of public finance as well as why on occasion some presidents do in fact oversee its restructuring.

* * *

I owe thanks to many people who provided support for this project. My greatest debt is to Stephen Skowronek. Throughout my time at Yale, Steve provided invaluable feedback on countless drafts of chapters and consistent encouragement more generally. I could not have asked for a more thoughtful and engaged advisor. I also especially thank David Mayhew and Jacob Hacker for their considerable support and advice.

Others provided support along the way as well. I thank Brian Balogh, who oversaw my appointment to the National Fellowship Program at the University of Virginia's Miller Center, and Andrew Rudalevige, who served as my mentor through the program. I thank Matt Bettinger, John Dearnbon, Sam DeCanio, Charles Decker, Richard Ellis, William Howell, Sidney Milkis, Bruce Miroff, and Susan Rose-Ackerman for helpful feedback. I thank Kevin McMahon, who oversaw my appointment as a postdoctoral fellow at Trinity College and provided at times much needed encouragement to get this project across the finish line. I thank David Congdon at the University Press of Kansas and the anonymous reviewers, all of whom helped to make this a more accessible book. I thank Emily Byrne and the staff at Connecticut Voices for Children, a state-level think tank and member of both the State Priorities Partnership (overseen by the Center on Budget and Policy Priorities) and the Economic Analysis and Research Network (overseen by the Economic Policy Institute). As I revised the book, my position as a research and policy fellow at CT Voices provided an invaluable opportunity to continue to develop my knowledge of public-finance policy.

Last but not least, I thank my family, to whom this book is dedicated. I am particularly grateful to my wife, Caitlin, whose endless support at each step truly made this book possible.

Part I
A New Historical Approach for Studying the Presidency and Policymaking

1. Introduction

In 1933, Franklin Roosevelt's public-finance principals repeatedly opposed his efforts to create a "managed currency" to support the economy during the Great Depression. For example, one principal explained that the "first plan of [international currency] stabilization put up to the President was far-reaching in character and would have required renunciation of *his* monetary policy."[1] Making clear the president's frustration with the substantial and sustained opposition from within his own administration that year, Roosevelt complained that his public-finance principals have "failed to take into consideration the United States, and look at things, I fear, from the point of view of New York and banking."[2] Going further, the president actively worked to defeat an international currency stabilization agreement that would have undercut the creation of a managed currency. As Roosevelt explained in a bombshell message to the conference at which his principals were employed, "The world will not be lulled by the specious fallacy of achieving . . . an artificial stability in foreign exchange. . . . The sound internal economic system of a Nation is a greater factor in its well-being than the price of its currency in changing terms of the currencies of other Nations." For this reason, he added, the "old-fetishes of so-called international bankers are being replaced by efforts to plan national currencies."[3] Underscoring the impact of the president's declaration in direct opposition to the work of his own principals, the *New York Times* reported, "No international gathering has ever met a harder blow than that dealt by President Roosevelt to the World Economic Conference today."[4]

Later that year, Treasury Secretary Dean Acheson opposed the gold-purchase program that the president supported in a continued effort to create a managed currency. As Acheson explained following the president's decision to move forward, "The battle was on. I said that the time for argument was not over; it had only just begun, for I was the official who under the plan would have to authorize the payment of government funds without, as I believed, legal authority" and "I would not violate the law."[5] In response to the Treasury secretary's opposition, the president turned elsewhere for support, remarking, "I have a method of my own to break the law."[6] Moreover, after ultimately firing the unresponsive Treasury secretary, after forcing the resignation of other unresponsive principals through a sustained effort to create a managed currency, and after appointing more responsive principals to implement his preferred policy, the president made clear the importance of these moves, declaring, "I have had the shackles on my hands for months now and I feel for the first time as though I [have] thrown them off."[7]

Equally revealing, Roosevelt's predecessor, Herbert Hoover, had complained during his own time in office that "I cannot run the Federal Reserve Banks, much as . . . I might like to have it that way."[8] Hoover then confirmed that the "march toward 'managed currency' came quickly . . . following Roosevelt's inauguration," and in the process, which involved a heated battle within the administration, Roosevelt acquired "legal authority over money as absolute as that of Tiberius Caesar or Henry VIII, Stalin or Hitler. It consummated the dreams and promises of every American tinkerer with the currency since the foundation of the Republic."[9] Also notable, even in the case when the Federal Reserve chair retained legal authority to act independent of the president in managing monetary policy, Roosevelt's new appointee later confirmed that he had sought the president's approval because he "felt the country would hold [the president] responsible."[10]

In contrast to Roosevelt, and similar to Hoover, Barack Obama largely failed to gain control over administration. For example, in the first annual review of the Obama presidency, Pete Rouse, a senior advisor to the president, observed, "When the economic team does not like a decision by the President, they have on occasion worked to re-litigate the overall policy." In particular, Rouse singled out Larry Summers, the director of the National Economic Council (NEC), as a major source of internal resistance, noting "deep dissatisfaction within the economic team with what is perceived to be Larry's imperious and heavy-handed direction." Rouse also observed that "once a decision is made, implementation by the Department of the Treasury has at times been slow and uneven," and all of these factors "adversely affect execution of the policy process."[11]

Further confirming the president's limited control, Obama himself acknowledged near the end of his second term that when it comes to managing the economy and monetary policy in particular, "I've got the Federal Reserve," one of many federal agencies that "technically is independent, so I can't tell them what to do" and "I'm hoping that they do the right thing."[12]

Lastly, and similar to Hoover and Obama, Donald Trump largely failed to gain control over administration, especially during his first two years in office. For example, Peter Navarro, a senior advisor, explained to the new president, "It is impossible to get a trade action to your desk for consideration in a timely manner" due to three key administrative obstacles. First, "any proposed executive action on trade that moves through the Staff Secretary process is highly vulnerable to dilution, delay or derailment." Second, Gary Cohn, the director of the NEC, "has amassed a large power base in the West Wing" and is "fundamentally opposed to the Trump trade agenda." Third, "Treasury Secretary Mnuchin is part of Cohn's 'Wall Street Wing,' which has effectively blocked or delayed every proposed action on trade."[13]

Even more revealing, Trump himself confessed, "I hired the wrong guy for Treasury secretary"; after appointing Cohn as director of the NEC, Trump complained, "I made a huge mistake giving [that position] to you"; and after appointing Jerome Powell as Federal Reserve chair, Trump conceded that it was "one of the worst choices I've ever made."[14] Going further, the president remarked after appointing four of the five sitting members to the Federal Reserve Board, "We have people on the Fed that really weren't . . . my people" and "certainly didn't listen to me." He then added, "The only problem our economy has is the Fed."[15]

The above illustrations frame the central question of this book: What role does presidential control over administration play in policymaking, especially given that the Constitution has made each president throughout US history the sole legal head of the executive branch?

The central argument of this book is that *presidential control over administration is a foundational component of policymaking and operates as a historical variable.* By "foundational component of policymaking," I mean that control over administration is often one of the first and most important requirements for the president to shift policy in a substantial and durable way, even in cases when the president has significant congressional support and popular support. By "operates as a historical variable," I mean that although the Constitution vests the "executive power" in a single "President of the United States," control over the administrative apparatus for a given policy domain often varies significantly in practice from one president to the next.

To explain the different configurations of presidential control over administration that recur throughout history and to test the argument, this book develops a new theory and then traces the policymaking process in the domain of public finance across nearly a century of history, beginning with Herbert Hoover during the Great Depression and ending with the first two years of the Trump presidency. Although the focus here is on historical variation in presidential control over administration in the domain of public finance—broadly defined to include fiscal policy, monetary policy, and the effect of both on economic policy—the theory and empirical analysis are highly relevant for recent incumbents. As illustrated, the initial efforts of Obama and Trump to change the established course during a period of unified party control of the government were largely undercut—or "adversely affect[ed]" and "effectively blocked," respectively—by their own limited control over administration.

Before developing and testing the theory, the first step is to explain the relationship between this new historical approach and the current leading approaches to studying the presidency and policymaking. The next three sections address those approaches: the unitary executive framework, the principal-agent framework, and the political time framework.

THE UNITARY EXECUTIVE FRAMEWORK

For several decades, research on the presidency was criticized for being too descriptive, atheoretical, and poorly designed.[16] Accordingly, Richard Neustadt's book, *Presidential Power*—the leading work in the field and one that emphasizes the complexities of the modern president's leadership position—came under attack as the main target of this critique.[17] As Terry Moe puts it, the problem is that "Neustadt did not offer a coherent, well-developed theory, but rather a loose set of ideas . . . that were not formulated with much precision."[18]

Taking direct aim at the perceived shortcomings of Neustadt's work, the so-called rational choice "revolution" has proceeded, in Moe's words, to bring "simplicity, clarity, logical rigor, and deductive power" to the study of the presidency.[19] Although each contribution is unique in its approach, this line of research as a whole elaborates a set of structural claims that allegedly follow from executive unity. Most notably, scholars contend that the Constitution endows the president with a *first-mover advantage*,[20] a *collective-action advantage*,[21] and an *informational advantage*[22] relative to the other branches. For example, Kenneth Mayer emphasizes that the president can take "advantage of his ability to move first."[23] David Lewis and Terry Moe stress that "presidents are not hobbled by collective action problems" for "within their own institutions they can simply make authoritative decisions about what to do and then do it."[24] And Jeffrey Cohen highlights the "informational advantages that accrue to the president."[25]

With these structural advantages in hand, this literature cuts through much of the important complexity that earlier research dwelled upon. In particular, the unitary executive framework reduces the executive branch to a single actor—the president—operating in relation to Congress or the courts; it models the policymaking process as an iterated game, starting over each year or congressional term; and it assumes that the parameters of the policy domain of interest, including administrative operations and presidential control, all remain impervious to change from one period to the next. Then, with the policymaking model stripped down in this way, the focus is on the president's ability to use one fixed structural advantage or another to shift the policy status quo, and variation is accounted for with reference to conventional political variables, such as congressional support and popular support.

Consider William Howell's prominent work, *Power Without Persuasion*, which applies the unitary executive framework to unilateral policymaking and stresses all three of the president's structural advantages. In Howell's words, "The most important [advantage] is that the president moves policy first and thereby places upon Congress . . . the burden of revising a new political landscape." Second, "the president acts alone," unconstrained by Congress's collective-action problems. Third, "the president often knows more about policy matters than do members of Congress, and he uses this fact to his advantage when deciding to act unilaterally." Based largely on these structural advantages, "presidents just act." They "need not secure the formal consent of Congress" or "the active support of bureaucrats. . . . Instead, presidents simply set public policy" and "as long as Congress lacks the votes . . . to overturn him, the president can be confident that his policy will stand."[26]

To demonstrate the successful application of the unitary executive framework in this case, Howell's work calls attention to a correlation between several conventional political variables and the number of "significant" executive orders issued each congressional term for thirteen categories, including "government intervention into the domestic economy." Summarizing the key findings, Howell explains that "presidents issue fewer significant executive orders" when "majority parties grow and become increasingly unified." Likewise, divided party control of the government "has a statistically significant and negative impact on the number of significant executive orders issued."[27]

To take another example, consider Brandice Canes-Wrone's prominent work, *Who Leads Whom*, which applies the unitary executive framework to legislative policymaking and stresses two of the president's structural advantages. Implicitly stressing the first-mover advantage—and highlighting the fixed sequence of play—Canes-Wrone explains that the "Public Appeals Theory involves three actions," the first being the president's ability to "appeal to the public" concerning his legislative proposal. Moreover, Canes-Wrone explicitly stresses the informational advantage, explaining that the "president has better information than the other actors" and can "utilize this informational advantage to try to convince the Congress and electorate that his preferred policy is the one that will advance their interests."[28]

To demonstrate the successful application of the unitary executive framework in this case, Canes-Wrone's work highlights a correlation between a "public appeals" variable, which accounts for whether the president made an appeal to the public about his budgetary proposal, and a "presidential budgetary success" variable, which "equals the absolute difference between the percentage change in appropriations requested by the president and the percentage change enacted." Summarizing the key findings, Canes-Wrone explains that "the effect of a domestic policy appeal is positive and solidly significant" and that "a president's ability to enact a proposal is greater the more popular is the proposal," all of which "contradict[s] research that suggests public appeals only rarely affect policymaking."[29]

In simple terms, Howell's work largely focuses on variation in congressional support that reinforces or weakens the president's fixed structural advantages relative to the other branches in unilateral policymaking, and Canes-Wrone's work largely focuses on variation in popular support that reinforces or weakens the president's fixed structural advantages relative to the other branches in legislative policymaking. To be sure, both works contribute significantly to our understanding of the presidency and policymaking, especially in highlighting the importance of the first-mover advantage. Yet, these works also have a significant limitation in assuming that the first-mover advantage is a fixed part of the policymaking process rather than a historical variable that turns on the president's control over the administrative apparatus and principals working to structure the policymaking process.

To demonstrate this limitation, consider the variation in presidential control over administration for two incumbents during the early period of US history: Thomas Jefferson, who assumed office with unified party control of the government and substantial popular support as the founder of the Democratic-Republican Party; and Andrew Jackson, who assumed office with unified party control of the government and substantial popular support as the founder of the Democratic Party.

In 1804 Thomas Jefferson signed a bill that authorized the Bank of the United States—essentially the central bank of its day—to create a branch in New Orleans despite the fact that he opposed the powerful financial institution on constitutional grounds.[30] For example, a decade earlier Jefferson fought the creation of the Bank, recommending that George Washington veto the bill, as "the negative of the President is the shield provided by the constitution."[31] Moreover, two years into his own administration, Jefferson suggested to Treasury Secretary Albert Gallatin—his party's leading expert on matters of public finance—that they should attempt to prevent the Bank from obtaining an "exclusive monopoly" of the government's deposits. Yet, relying on the financial institution to carry out his own departmental responsibilities, Gallatin informed the president in no uncertain terms that it was "not proper to displease" the directors of the Bank "because they place our money where we may want it, from one end of the Union to the other."[32]

After this initial setback Jefferson turned to the idea of the national welfare to make his case. "It is certainly for the public good to keep all the banks competitors for our favors by a judicious distribution of [the government's deposits]," he informed the Treasury secretary, and so it is essential "to engage the individuals who belong to [the various banks] in the support of the reformed order of things, or at least in an acquiescence under it."[33] Yet, continuing to rely on the Bank's services, and operating with a substantial degree of independence, Gallatin simply ignored the president's recommendation. Jefferson therefore tried a more political approach the following year. "I am decidedly in favor," he explained, "of making all the banks Republican, by sharing deposits among them in proportion to the dispositions they show; if the law now forbids it, we should not permit another session of Congress to pass without amending it."[34] However, once again, Gallatin simply ignored the president's recommendation.

Finally, in late 1803—just four months before signing the law to expand the Bank—Jefferson exploded, writing to Gallatin, "This institution is one of the most deadly hostility existing against the principles [and] form of our constitution. . . . Now, while we are strong, it is the greatest duty we owe . . . to bring this powerful enemy to a perfect subordination." Yet, not an expert himself, and revealing a key source of the Treasury secretary's independence, Jefferson concluded the letter by adding, "I pray for you to turn this subject in your mind, and to give it the benefit of your knowledge of details; whereas, I have only very general views of the subject."[35]

In the end Jefferson's strong preference to dismantle or reform the Bank did not falter due to a lack of support in Congress or from the public. Rather, his recommendations simply failed to move beyond his own Treasury secretary. In particular, the president failed to act unilaterally by not removing the government's deposits, and he failed to act legislatively by not vetoing the bill to expand the Bank's branches, all of which were within his legal and constitutional powers and would have helped to bring that "powerful enemy to a perfect subordination." As a result, the Bank not only survived the "revolution of 1800" but also expanded its reach from Philadelphia to the new capital in Washington and outward to the Louisiana territory, the great legacy of Jefferson's presidency.

Further underscoring his failure to restructure the domain of public finance, Jefferson himself all but admitted that he had no meaningful first-mover advantage due to the administrative apparatus and policies that George Washington and Treasury Secretary Alexander Hamilton had worked to put into place a decade earlier. As Jefferson put it, "When this government was first established it was possible to have kept it going on true principles, but the . . . ideas of Hamilton destroyed that hope in the bud. . . . It mortifies me to be strengthening principles which I deem radically vicious, but this vice is entailed on us by the *first error*."[36]

In stark contrast to Jefferson, who pleaded in vain for his Treasury secretary to act, Andrew Jackson swept aside the opposition within his administration nearly three decades later.[37] Notably, like Jefferson, Jackson initially appointed a Treasury secretary, Louis McLane, who supported the Second Bank of the United States, the expanded successor to the First Bank, whose twenty-year charter had expired in 1811. For example, in the annual report on the finances in 1831, McLane defended both "the authority of the present Government to create [the Bank]" and its "indispensable necessity."[38] Unlike Jefferson, Jackson pushed back, turning to Roger Taney, the loyal attorney general. In particular, while the Treasury secretary and nearly all the other department heads advised Jackson to sign a bill in 1832 renewing the charter for the Bank, the attorney general developed a lengthy argument for a veto on the grounds that the Bank was inexpedient and unconstitutional. Underscoring the substantial opposition within his own administration, Jackson remarked, "The coalition are determined to press upon me at this session" the issue of the recharter, and even my "able heads of Departments, except Woodbury and the attorney General, are all in favor of the Bank." The president then made clear his own position on the Bank, vetoing the recharter and declaring that the "monster, as it stands, [and] as administered, must be put down."[39]

After Jackson's veto the attorney general continued the attack on the Bank, submitting an extensive report that recommended removing the government's deposits in order to destroy the institution once and for all. Again Jackson concurred, explaining that if the Bank retained the government's deposits, it would have the "power to distress the community, destroy the state banks, and if possible . . . corrupt congress and obtain two thirds to recharter."[40] The problem, however, was that the Second Bank's charter—unlike the First Bank's charter— explicitly vested authority over the government's deposits with the Treasury secretary, not the president. Moreover, in line with his opposition to the veto, McLane opposed the removal decision.[41] Jackson therefore reshuffled his cabinet in 1833, transferring McLane to the State Department and appointing William Duane, a known critic of the Bank, to head the Treasury. Yet, it was soon evident that Duane also opposed removing the government's deposits, which quickly led Jackson to replace Duane with Taney, who began to carry out the removal order as a recess appointee. Making clear the importance of this rapid replacement of the top public-finance principal, the president remarked that the new Treasury secretary "unites with me heart in hand to meet the crisis. Mr. Taney is commissioned, sworn into office, and the business of the Treasury is progressing as though Mr. Duane had never been born."[42]

In the end—and notwithstanding the same strong preference of many earlier incumbents, especially Jefferson—Jackson succeeded in permanently destroying the Bank. In particular, he acted legislatively by vetoing the bill to recharter the Bank, and he acted unilaterally by directing the Treasury secretary to remove the government's deposits, all of which finally brought that "powerful enemy to a perfect subordination."[43]

Viewing presidential control over administration as a foundational component of policymaking that operates as a *historical variable*, Jefferson relied upon a conventional Treasury secretary, which significantly limited his ability to destroy the Bank and shift public-finance policy in a substantial and durable way; in contrast, Jackson bypassed two Treasury secretaries and appointed a new, highly responsive secretary, which significantly strengthened his ability to destroy the Bank and shift public-finance policy in a substantial and durable way. Put in terms common to the unitary executive framework, Jefferson relied upon a conventional Treasury secretary, the primary source of the collective-action and informational advantage relative to the other branches of government, which in turn significantly limited the president's first-mover advantage in the policymaking process; conversely, in bypassing two Treasury secretaries and in appointing a new, highly responsive secretary, all of which worked to restructure the primary source of the collective-action and informational advantage relative to the other branches of government, Jackson significantly strengthened his first-mover advantage.

THE PRINCIPAL-AGENT FRAMEWORK

Unlike the unitary executive framework, which excludes the issue of administration, the principal-agent framework focuses on the ways in which a political principal—in this case, the president—uses various instruments to exercise control over an administrative agent. The most prominent instruments include the president's use of *appointments*, *directives*, and *oversight* and his ability to influence *organizational design*.[44] For example, David Lewis argues that the president works with Congress "to jointly create the administrative state" and his "calculations about the 'proper' design of administrative agencies [is] shaped less by concerns for efficiency or effectiveness than by concerns about reelection, political control, and, ultimately, policy outcomes."[45] Richard Nathan stresses that the president's "appointment of the right people . . . is fundamental to management control."[46] And B. Dan Wood and Richard Waterman contend that the president can work through the Office of Management and Budget to control "the resources of most agencies" and monitor "the activities of bureaucracies," especially "their compatibility with the president's program."[47]

Although the principal-agent framework has been used effectively to show that presidential control over administration is a foundational component of policymaking, studies that apply this approach tend to cut through important complexity, much like the application of the unitary executive framework. In particular, the standard application of the principal-agent framework examines the dynamics of political control over either a single administrative agent or multiple administrative agents that are presumed to operate independent of one another.

Consider Terry Moe's prominent work "The Politicized Presidency," which focuses on the ways in which the president acts "to take hold of the administrative machinery of government," especially through the use of the appointment power. In Moe's words, "A president who finds institutional arrangements inadequate to his needs has incentives to pursue reform, but the reforms he actually pursues are determined by the resources he can marshal and his flexibility in putting them to use. In these respects, the president is severely constrained. Many reforms may seem well designed to enhance executive leadership, but few are in fact attainable."[48]

This dynamic, Moe continues, "encourages two basic developmental thrusts. The first is the increasing centralization of the institutional presidency in the White House" because "the president can count on unequaled responsiveness from his own people." The other development "is the increasing politicization of the institutional system. This approach to responsive competence is particularly attractive because it is anchored in a formal presidential power . . . the power of appointment. By appointing individuals on the basis of loyalty, ideology, or programmatic support, [the president] can take direct action to enhance responsiveness throughout the administration."[49]

To demonstrate the successful application of the principal-agent framework in this case, Moe's work traces the growing politicization of the Office of Management and Budget, one of the key administrative institutions in the domain of public finance. As Moe explains, "The sphere of politicization" during the Reagan administration

> naturally included the Office of Management and Budget. In part because so many of the Reagan policy initiatives during the crucial first year were purposely intertwined with its budgetary strategy, the OMB quickly became a central participant in policymaking and political action. From Reagan's standpoint, its critical role on the team only underlined the absolute need for responsiveness. Budget Director David Stockman and his principal subordinates were everywhere: at high-level White House policy meetings, at lower level meetings with agency representatives, at congressional hearings, at press conferences. Stockman became a nationally recognized political figure.[50]

Based in large part on this effective use of the appointment power, Moe concludes that Reagan "more than any other modern president . . . moved with dedication and comprehensiveness to take hold of the administrative machinery of government" and "got essentially what he wanted: the mobilization of OMB resources toward presidential ends."[51]

Without question, Moe's work contributes significantly to our understanding of the presidency and policymaking. Yet, it also has a significant limitation in focusing on presidential control over a single administrative institution operating within the domain of public finance rather than the multiple administrative institutions—often with overlapping jurisdictions—that comprise the public-finance apparatus.

By "public finance apparatus," I mean, as Alexander Hamilton explained in *The Federalist*, the administrative institutions—or "system of administration"—primarily responsible for the "preparatory plans of finance" and implementation. Moreover, since at least the Great Depression, the public-finance apparatus has expanded to include administrative institutions overseeing the use of public finance to manage the economy. Also important, although Hamilton reasoned that the principals "to whose immediate management these different matters are committed ought to be considered as the assistants or deputies of the Chief Magistrate, and on this account they ought to derive their offices from his appointment" and "be subject to his superintendence," that has not always been the case.[52] For example, the public-finance apparatus included the independent Bank during the early period—which Hamilton himself took the lead in creating—and the public-finance apparatus currently includes several types of agencies that operate with varying degrees of independence from the president.

To demonstrate the limitations of Moe's approach, consider the related development of three current public-finance institutions: (1) the Office of Management and Budget (OMB), which is an executive agency headed by a director whom the president has the legal power to appoint and remove; (2) the Federal Reserve (Fed), which is an independent agency headed by a chair whom the president has the legal power to appoint but not to remove; and (3) the Congressional Budget Office (CBO), which is a legislative agency headed by a director whom the president has neither the legal power to appoint nor remove.

As Moe shows in his prominent work, David Stockman, a president-appointed public-finance principal, played a key role in implementing Reagan's program in 1981. In particular, the responsive OMB director took the lead in manipulating the administration's economic forecast, manipulating the administration's budget proposal, and repurposing the budget reconciliation process, all in order to pass a budget that year that made the president's historic tax cut and top priority appear affordable. Equally important, the politicization of the budget process and accompanying rise in the budget deficit played a key role in two major administrative developments beyond the scope of Moe's analysis.

The first major development is that control over economic forecasting and budget scoring began to shift from the OMB to the CBO. For example, in 1982 the Republican-controlled Senate Budget Committee unanimously declared the Reagan administration's new budget "dead on arrival," notwithstanding Stockman's attempt to repeat, in part, his earlier approach. As the budget director acknowledged, "Since no one in the White House wanted to propose the first triple-digit budget deficit in history . . . I out-and-out cooked the books, inventing $15 billion per year of utterly phony cuts."[53] This time, however, the CBO effectively checked the OMB, projecting the deficit more accurately at $132 billion. "That was our finest hour in some ways," CBO Director Alice Rivlin later explained, adding, "By then CBO's right" to check the OMB "was not questioned in the Congress."[54]

The second major development is that the rise of large budget deficits following the 1981 program diminished the role of fiscal policy relative to monetary policy in managing the economy, the latter of which operates under the direction of the independent Fed. Making clear the rise of the Fed's influence, due in large part to the shackling of fiscal policy after the 1981 program, Stockman explained, "The effect of the triple-digit deficits was that it really forestalled or dulled what might have been the usual attacks on the Fed. . . . Because [the politicians] were out of line so far on fiscal policy, they couldn't attack the Fed. It really produced a window of maneuverability for the Fed."[55]

These related developments—the decreasing influence of the OMB and the increasing influence of the CBO and the Fed—significantly limited presidential control over administration for Reagan's successor, George H. W. Bush. First, unlike Reagan, Bush could not simply rely upon the appointment power and the "mobilization of OMB resources" to set the direction for fiscal policy. For example, OMB Director Richard Darman explained that Alan Greenspan, the Reagan-appointed Fed chair, "would not allow higher money supply growth or higher real economic growth without our first achieving a legislative solution to the deficit problem."[56] Second, the CBO, not the OMB, now played the key role in economic forecasting and budget scoring within the newly shackled fiscal policymaking process. For example, the OMB director conceded, "I felt like the director of nothing."[57] In contrast, CBO Director Robert Reischauer—whom congressional leaders had appointed and whom the president had no power to remove—explained that the CBO's rise is "one of the great success stories of American government. . . . This hasn't been recognized enough, but it's an important institution that plays a very important role," one that was "greatly enhanced by the fact that . . . the Reagan administration . . . doctored the evidence."[58]

The same administrative developments also significantly limited presidential control for Bush's successor, Bill Clinton. However, unlike Bush, who had declared from the start, "I don't propose to reverse direction," Clinton assumed office on a platform of "change," meaning the increasing influence of the Fed and the CBO was even more problematic.[59] In particular, the Reagan-appointed Fed chair used his control over monetary policy to compel Clinton to propose a fiscal-policy program in 1993 that went against the new president's major campaign promises. Underscoring his limited control over the policymaking process, Clinton remarked in a near state of disbelief, "You mean to tell me that the success of the [budget] program and my reelection hinges on the Federal Reserve and a bunch of fucking bond traders?"[60] Moreover, once the Fed set the direction for fiscal policy, the CBO played the key role in economic forecasting and budget scoring, which continued to undercut the president's control. Making clear the considerable influence of this public-finance principal that the president had not appointed and had no power to remove, Clinton complained, "We've gutted our investment program by turning the government over to [CBO Director] Reischauer!"[61]

Viewing presidential control over administration as a foundational component of policymaking that operates as a historical variable and includes the *interaction of multiple administrative institutions*, "Reagan got essentially what he wanted" in the domain of public finance through, in part, the "increasing centralization of the institutional presidency." But that process made the public-finance apparatus as a whole more *decentralized* moving forward, which significantly diminished presidential control over administration for Reagan's successors and therefore made it much harder for them to get what they wanted, even with the advantage of greater conventional congressional support. Most notably, unlike Reagan, Clinton assumed office with unified party control of the government but failed to shift the established policy parameters in a substantial and durable way. As Clinton later conceded, "I had underestimated how hard it would be to turn Washington around after 12 years on a very different course."[62] Likewise, Barack Obama assumed office with unified party control of the government but failed to shift the established course in the domain of public finance. Making clear his surprise at the difficulty of governing following Reagan's restructuring of the policy domain, Obama confessed, "What I didn't fully appreciate, and nobody can appreciate until they're in the position, is how decentralized power is in this system."[63]

THE POLITICAL TIME FRAMEWORK

The third leading approach to studying the presidency and policymaking is the political time framework, which Stephen Skowronek developed in his classic work, *The Politics Presidents Make.*[64] This framework focuses on the varying leadership roles of presidents. In Skowronek's words,

> A president's political authority turns on his identity vis-à-vis the established regime; warrants for exercising the powers of the office vary depending on the incumbent's political relationship to the commitments of ideology and interest embodied in preexisting institutional arrangements. Presidents attempt to build all sorts of nuance and subtlety into this relationship, but stripped to essentials, it comes in two forms: opposed and affiliated. Leaders either come to power from the opposition to the pre-established regime, or they come to power affiliated with its basic commitments. Corresponding to these two identities are the two generic projects for political action: the leadership project of the opposition leader is to challenge the received agenda, perhaps to displace it completely with another; the leadership project of the affiliated leader is to continue, perhaps to complete, the work on that agenda.[65]

In particular, Skowronek identifies four structures of "presidential leadership in political time" based on the combination of two components: the president's political identity to established commitments and the current status of those commitments. First, in the "politics of disjunction," the president is "affiliated with a set of established commitments that have . . . been called into question as failed or irrelevant responses to the problems of the day." These presidents are "often singled out as political incompetents." Second, in the "politics of reconstruction," the "president heralds from the opposition to the previously established regime, and pre-established commitments of ideology and interest have . . . become vulnerable to direct repudiation as failed or irrelevant responses to the problems of the day." These presidents are often able "to reformulate the nation's political agenda altogether" and recapture "the authority of being first, and with it a rare opportunity to recast the foundations of American government and politics." Third, in the "politics of articulation," the president is affiliated with the "established commitments of ideology and interest" that "are relatively resilient, providing solutions . . . to the governing problems of the day." These presidents often "stand in national politics as ministers to the faithful," casting "their leadership as wholly constructive rearticulations of the received orthodoxy." Fourth, in the "politics of preemption," opposition "presidents have the freedom of their independence from established commitments, but unlike presidents in a politics of reconstruction, their repudiative authority is manifestly limited by the political, institutional, and ideological supports" of the resilient regime. These presidents often "interrupt a still vital political discourse and try to preempt its agenda by playing upon the political divisions within the establishment that affiliated presidents instinctively seek to assuage."[66]

To demonstrate the successful application of the political time framework, Skowronek uses case studies to trace throughout history three of the four recurring leadership roles. This includes the reconstructions of Thomas Jefferson, Andrew Jackson, Abraham Lincoln, Franklin Roosevelt, and Ronald Reagan; the articulations of James Monroe, James Polk, Theodore Roosevelt, Lyndon Johnson, and George H. W. Bush; and the disjunctions of John Quincy Adams, Franklin Pierce, Herbert Hoover, and Jimmy Carter.

Undoubtedly, Skowronek's groundbreaking work contributes significantly to study of the presidency and policymaking. Yet, it also has a significant limitation in examining the ability of presidents to "reconstruct" the "established regime" due to variation in the "problems of the day," as that sweeping approach tends to overlook considerable variation in the ability of presidents to—in the terms used in this book—restructure the established administrative apparatus for individual policy domains. To demonstrate this limitation, consider once again the example of variation in presidential control over administration during the early period of US history.

In the first two case studies on the "politics of reconstruction," Skowronek concludes, respectively, that "Thomas Jefferson shows us the reconstructive authority at its most expansive" and that "Andrew Jackson wielded reconstructive authority for the first time since Thomas Jefferson."[67] Yet, even if Jefferson and Jackson both largely succeeded in "reconstructing" the "established regime"— and the evidence is strong—Jefferson, unlike Jackson, failed to restructure the domain of public finance in particular.

As previously addressed, Treasury Secretary Albert Gallatin significantly limited Jefferson's control. Most notably, after overseeing the expansion of the Bank of the United States in 1804, Gallatin went even further in recommending on the last full day of the Jefferson administration that Congress renew the Bank's charter and enlarge its capital stock from $10 million to $30 million.[68] Gallatin's successors also limited presidential control throughout the founding era in the process of supporting public-finance policies set into motion during the Washington administration. For example, Treasury Secretary Alexander Dallas supported the creation of the Second Bank even though James Madison, like Jefferson, had initially opposed a national bank.[69] Moreover, in 1828—nearly three decades after the "revolution of 1800"—Treasury Secretary Richard Rush wrote in the annual report on finances that Alexander Hamilton's policies and procedures still "throw a guiding light over the path of his successors."[70] This continuity in the orientation of the Treasury secretaries throughout the founding era meant that shifting public-finance policy in a substantial and durable way in general and destroying the Bank in particular required the president to take the lead in restructuring the role of the top public-finance principal, a course that Jackson pursued, not Jefferson.

Variation in presidential control during the Jefferson and Jackson administrations was due in large part to variation in the "problems of the day" in the domain of public finance. To start, Treasury Secretary Alexander Hamilton took the lead both in consolidating and funding the national debt in 1790 and in overseeing the creation of the First Bank the following year, all of which significantly improved the public credit and provided a long-term foundation for the policy domain—or Rush's words, threw "a guiding light over the path of his successors."[71] When Jefferson assumed office a decade later, his Treasury secretary largely supported Hamilton's public-finance program in order to maintain stability in the policy domain. For example, Gallatin made clear not only his opposition to changing the established course but also the reason for it, explaining, "The banking system is now firmly established" and any failure to maintain the Bank "will be attended with much individual, and probably with no inconsiderable public injury."[72] Likewise, as noted, Jefferson himself conceded that earlier developments impeded his ability to change course. "It mortifies me to be strengthening principles which I deem radically vicious," he explained, "but this vice is entailed on us by the first error." Equally revealing, Jefferson added, "*In other parts of our government* I hope we shall be able by degrees to introduce sound principles and make them habitual."[73]

In contrast to Jefferson, Jackson took the lead in restructuring the domain of public finance in response to new "problems of the day." To begin with, the Second Bank had played a key role in precipitating the Panic of 1819, which showed for the first time that the Bank's own operations could produce considerable instability, thereby undercutting Gallatin's earlier argument that it was necessary to maintain the established system in order to prevent "public injury." Making clear the considerable impact of the Panic of 1819, Jefferson wrote that year, "The paper [money] bubble is . . . burst. This is what you and I, and every reasoning man, seduced by no obliquity of mind or interest, have long foreseen; yet its disastrous effects are not the less for having been foreseen."[74]

Adding to the situation, the Bank began to play a less important role in "plac[ing] our money where we may want it, from one end of the Union to the other" due to the impending elimination of the national debt, which had declined from the equivalent of 38 percent of the size of the US economy in 1790 to 2 percent in 1832. In response, the Bank worked to prevent the elimination of the debt until it could secure a new charter. As Jackson explained, "Although [the Bank] was well aware that the government designed shortly to call out nearly all the large [deposit] it then had in [the Bank], for the purpose of paying the public debt, and that its charter would expire in a few years, it nevertheless proceeded to increase its loans in such profusion." Jackson then added, "The motive of this enormous extension of loans can no longer be doubted. It was unquestionably to gain power in the country, and force the government through the influence of debtors, to grant it a new charter."[75]

Following the Bank's efforts to slow the retirement of the debt, Jackson directed his Treasury secretary to remove the government's deposits from the financial institution. This in turn spurred Nicholas Biddle, the president of the Bank, to call in a large portion of the institution's loans as quickly as possible in order to trigger a panic that would force the president to back down. As Biddle put it, "Nothing but the evidence of suffering . . . will produce any effect. . . . Our only safety is in pursuing a steady course of firm restriction—and I have no doubt that such a course will ultimately lead to restoration of the currency and the recharter of the Bank."[76] Yet, this intentional monetary shock largely mirrored the contraction that had triggered the Panic of 1819 and now only intensified the president's efforts to restructure the unstable policy domain, which included first and foremost destroying the Bank. "Created for the convenience of the Government," Jackson declared, "[the Bank] has become the scourge of the people" both in interfering "to postpone the payment of . . . the national debt" and in directing an "extraordinary extension and contraction of its accommodations to the community."[77]

Viewing presidential control over administration as a foundational component of policymaking that operates as a historical variable within *individual policy domains*, Jefferson relied upon a conventional Treasury secretary during a period of stability in the domain of public finance, which significantly limited the president's ability to destroy the Bank and shift the established public-finance policy parameters in a substantial and durable way, even as he succeeded in restructuring "other parts of our government"; in contrast, Jackson bypassed two Treasury secretaries and appointed a new, highly responsive secretary during a period of instability in the domain of public finance, which significantly strengthened the president's ability to destroy the Bank and shift the established public-finance policy parameters.

A NEW FRAMEWORK: PRESIDENTIAL CONTROL OVER ADMINISTRATION AS A HISTORICAL VARIABLE

The preceding sections addressed key limitations in the three leading approaches for studying the presidency and policymaking. Specifically, the standard application of the unitary executive framework overlooks the fact that presidential control over administration often operates as a *historical variable*; the standard application of the principle-agent framework overlooks the fact that presidential control over administration often operates as a historical variable that incorporates the *interaction of multiple administrative institutions*; and the standard application of the political time framework overlooks the fact that presidential control over administration often operates as a historical variable within *individual policy domains*.

To further demonstrate the key limitations of the three leading approaches and to test a new historical approach, this book examines the policymaking process in the domain of public finance, broadly defined to include government spending and taxing, the government's management of the currency and interest rates, and the government's management of the economy through both instruments—or, in modern terms, fiscal policy, monetary policy, and the effect of both on economic policy. At least five features make this policy domain an ideal choice.

First, all three leading frameworks reviewed here have been applied, at least in part, to the domain of public finance. Recall that Howell's work examines "government intervention into the domestic economy"; Canes-Wrone's work examines "presidential budgetary success"; Moe's work examines the OMB; and Skowronek's work examines Jackson's destruction of the Bank and more.

Second, the domain of public finance allows for a parallel examination of presidential control over administration in the subdomains of fiscal policy and monetary policy, which not only doubles the number of cases used to test the new approach but also reveals important policymaking dynamics at play that are often missed by studies that examine only one subdomain or the other.

Third, the domain of public finance allows for a quantitative and qualitative—or multimethod—examination of presidential control over administration in the subdomains of fiscal policy and monetary policy. This further expands the evidence used both to test the new approach and to demonstrate the limitations of the three leading approaches, which generally rely upon either quantitative evidence or qualitative evidence but not a combination of the two.

Fourth, the domain of public finance allows for an examination of presidential control over administration in both unilateral policymaking and legislative policymaking, as monetary policy primarily involves unilateral policymaking on the part of one or more administrative institutions, and fiscal policy primarily involves legislative policymaking; yet at times each subdomain incorporates both policymaking processes.

Fifth, public finance is one of the central issues in American politics. For example, Thomas Jefferson made clear the importance of the political divide over public finance shortly after the creation of the US constitutional system, writing to George Washington in 1792, "I was duped . . . by the Secretary of the Treasury and made a tool for forwarding his schemes, not then sufficiently understood by me; and of all the errors of my political life, this has occasioned me the deepest regret." Going further, Jefferson explained, "That I have utterly . . . disapproved of the system of the Secretary of the Treasury, I [acknowledge] and avow: and this was not merely a speculative difference. His system flowed from principles adverse to liberty, and was calculated to undermine and demolish the republic."[78]

THE LAYOUT OF THE BOOK

To explain the different configurations of presidential control over administration that recur throughout history and to test the theory, the book proceeds in five parts:

In Part I, chapter 2 presents a new theory of historical variation in presidential control. In particular, it explains why several key restrictions (time, knowledge, and the structure of government) and two key incentives (maintaining acceptable performance and implementing preferred policies) vary in response to the severity of the problem in the policy domain and the prioritization of that problem. These factors in turn largely determine whether the president accepts the established approach in managing the policy domain or works to restructure that approach. The theory also addresses two intermediary processes: overseeing the gradually failing approach or working to secure the newly established approach, the latter of which tends to incorporate an additional key restriction (party continuity) and an additional key incentive (implementing a predecessor's preferred policies). The chapter then reviews the four configurations of presidential control that recur in succession: collapse, innovation, stabilization, and constraint.

In Part II, chapter 3 presents a quantitative overview of historical variation in public-finance problems, prioritization, administration, and policy. This provides an initial test of the theory of historical variation in presidential control by showing that public-finance administration and policy are closely connected and change in relation to historical variation in public-finance problems and prioritization. In particular, the quantitative overview provides evidence that Franklin Roosevelt and Ronald Reagan oversaw the most comprehensive restructuring of public-finance administration and policy in response to the two most exceptionally severe and highly prioritized problems, the Great Depression and the Great Inflation, respectively. The quantitative overview also provides evidence that relative to the Great Depression and the Great Inflation, the Great Recession was neither an exceptionally severe problem nor a highly prioritized problem for a sustained period, which prevented the restructuring of the policy domain.

Part III presents case studies that trace the historical variation in presidential control during the New Deal era. The analysis proceeds in four steps. Chapter 4 initially traces the creation of the decentralized New Era apparatus, and it then traces the process of the established, gradually failing New Era apparatus and its principals in limiting Herbert Hoover's control. Chapter 5 traces the process of Franklin Roosevelt strengthening his control in restructuring the policy domain in response to the Great Depression. Chapter 6 traces the process of Harry Truman relinquishing much of his control to Roosevelt in working to secure the newly restructured policy domain. And chapter 7 traces the process of the established, relatively stable New Deal–era apparatus and its principals in limiting Dwight Eisenhower's control.

Part IV presents case studies that trace the historical variation in presidential control during the Reagan era. The analysis proceeds in four steps. Chapter 8 initially traces the preliminary collapse of the New Deal–era apparatus under Richard Nixon and Gerald Ford, and it then traces the process of the gradually failing New Deal–era apparatus and its principals in limiting Jimmy Carter's control. Chapter 9 traces the process of Ronald Reagan strengthening his control in restructuring the policy domain in response to the Great Inflation. Chapter 10 traces the process of George H. W. Bush relinquishing much of his control to Reagan in working to secure the newly restructured policy domain. And chapter 11 traces the process of the established, relatively stable Reagan-era apparatus and its principals in limiting Bill Clinton's control.

Part V presents case studies that trace the historical variation in presidential control during the Great Recession and beyond. The analysis proceeds in three steps. Chapter 12 traces the process of the established Reagan-era apparatus and its principals in supporting a mix of inadequate New Deal–era approaches and traditional Reagan-era approaches, all of which limited Barack Obama's control in managing the Great Recession and its aftermath. Chapter 13 traces the process of the established, gradually failing Reagan-era apparatus and its principals in limiting Trump's control during the first two years of his presidency. Chapter 14 concludes the book by providing an overview and final thoughts on presidential control moving forward.

2. A Theory of Historical Variation in Presidential Control

Although the Constitution vests the "executive power" in a single "President of the United States," the support of an administrative apparatus and its principals proves critical, as it is impossible in practice for any single president to completely control the executive power. This is a formative dilemma for the Constitution and the presidency alike. It is therefore no surprise that George Washington addressed the matter in 1789, less than a month after assuming office. As Washington explained,

> The impossibility that one man should be able to perform all the great business of the state, I take to have been the reason for instituting the great departments, and appointing officers therein, to assist the supreme magistrate in discharging the duties of his trust. And perhaps I may be allowed to say of myself, that the supreme magistrate of no state can have a greater variety of important business to perform in person than I have at this moment.[1]

Likewise, Alexander Hamilton addressed the important role of administration a year earlier in *The Federalist*, writing,

> The administration of government, in its largest sense, comprehends all the operations of the body politic, whether legislative, executive, or judiciary; but in its most usual, and perhaps its most precise signification, it is limited to executive details, and falls peculiarly within the province of the executive department. The actual conduct of foreign negotiations, the preparatory plans of finance, the application and disbursement of the public moneys in conformity to the general appropriations of the legislature, the arrangement of the army and navy, the directions of the operations of war, these, and other matters of a like nature, constitute what seems to be most properly understood by the administration of government. The persons, therefore, to whose immediate management these different matters are committed, ought to be considered as the assistants or deputies of the chief magistrate, and on this account, they ought to derive their offices from his appointment, at least from his nomination, and ought to be subject to his superintendence. This view of the subject will at once suggest to us the intimate connection between the duration of the executive magistrate in office and the stability of the system of administration.[2]

Although Hamilton provided one of the first formal definitions of the administrative apparatus—or "system of administration"—that supports the president, it is notable that he never reconciled it with the other element in his broader "definition of good government"—unity in the executive. "That unity is conducive to energy will not be disputed," Hamilton reasoned. "Decision, activity, secrecy, and dispatch will generally characterize the proceedings of one man in a much more eminent degree than the proceedings of any greater number; and in proportion as the number is increased, these qualities will be diminished." Going further, Hamilton explained, "Unity may be destroyed in two ways: either by vesting the [executive] power in two or more magistrates of equal dignity and authority, or by vesting it ostensibly in one man, subject in whole or in part to the control and cooperation of others, in the capacity of counselors to him."[3]

Both of Hamilton's ideas are central to understanding the presidency, and yet there is an inherent tension. Specifically, the president requires the support of the "system of administration" to manage the executive power, but "unity" is destroyed by vesting the executive power in the president and the system of administration—or, that is, "ostensibly in one man, subject in whole or in part to the control and cooperation of others, in the capacity of counselors to him." Moreover, if the system of administration is always necessary due to the "impossibility that one man should be able to perform all the great business of the state," which Washington confirmed shortly after assuming office, then unity in the executive is always imperfect.

Herbert Simon described this same problem more generally in his classic work, *Administrative Behavior*. As Simon put it, the principle of "unity of command" is "incompatible with the principle of specialization." Furthermore, like Washington, Simon observed that "actual administrative practice would seem to indicate that the need for specialization is to a very large degree given priority over the need for unity of command."[4]

Although the tension in Hamilton's constitutional theory and the application of Simon's general theory are both effective starting points for thinking about presidential control over administration or unity in the executive—I use the two terms interchangeably—history reveals a more dynamic process at play, meaning that even if control is always imperfect, significant variation can be observed over time in the relationship between the president and the system of administration. Control, I propose, is at its maximum when and to the extent that the president restructures the established administrative apparatus in order to implement his preferred policy parameters. Conversely, control is at its minimum when and to the extent that the president accepts the established administrative apparatus that is oriented toward supporting the established policy parameters. This conditional control is especially pronounced when the president's preferences run contrary to the established policy parameters.

THE KEY RESTRICTIONS AND INCENTIVES LIMITING PRESIDENTIAL CONTROL

I account for the limits on presidential control with reference to several key restrictions and incentives that prevent each new incumbent from routinely restructuring the established administrative apparatus and policy parameters for a given domain. Three sets of sources primarily support this theorizing: Herbert Simon's general theory of administration, several leading works on the presidency and policymaking, and the firsthand observations of several presidents and principals.

The first key restriction is *time*.[5] As Herbert Simon explained more generally, "We must share our time among . . . many agenda items, some requiring prompt attention, some allowing more flexibility."[6] In particular, the vast responsibilities of the office require the president to manage multiple issues on any given day. The president therefore tends to accept the established administrative apparatus, and if at all, he tends to work toward shifting policy within the established parameters rather than take time first to consider the role of the established administrative apparatus in structuring those parameters and then work to restructure the policy domain. For example, Harry Truman stressed the time restriction, explaining, "The conduct of the war and the management of foreign affairs had crowded into my life with such speed and insistence that I could not find all the time I needed to devote to domestic matters."[7] Likewise, Gerald Ford acknowledged that he managed the time restriction by relying upon his principals. As Ford put it, "I would leave the details of administration to [Cabinet members] . . . . I wanted men and women who would give me unvarnished truth, then lay out the options for decisions that I would have to make."[8]

Equally revealing, the time restriction is not exclusive to the modern era or a wartime period. For example, even Calvin Coolidge, who believed in limited government and in "never doing anything that someone else can do for you," explained, "Every day of Presidential life is crowded with activities. When people not accustomed to Washington came to the office . . . they often remarked that it seemed to be my busy day, to which my stock reply came to be that all days were busy and there was little difference among them."[9] Similarly, Herbert Hoover complained of the "useless [exhaustion]" due to "signing routine papers. No man could read them even on a twenty-four-hour shift." In operation, "the president could only sign on the dotted line and trust to Heaven and his Cabinet officers that they were all right. The Cabinet officers, in turn, trusted [the] Bureau heads." Worse still, Hoover added, "with the depression the demands upon the White House increased to war dimensions. Telephone calls, telegrams, and mail were a sort of index. They quadrupled Mr. Coolidge's stint."[10]

Building on the time restriction, the second key restriction is *knowledge.*[11] As Herbert Simon explained more generally,

> It is impossible for the behavior of a single, isolated individual to reach any high degree of rationality. The number of alternatives he must explore is so great, the information he would need to evaluate them so vast that even an approximation to objective rationality is hard to conceive. Individual choice takes place in an environment of "givens"—premises that are accepted by the subject as bases for his choice; and behavior is adaptive only within the limits set by these "givens."[12]

In particular, the vast responsibilities of the office require the president to manage not only multiple issues on any given day but also complex issues, many of which he is unlikely to understand in great detail, if at all. This further reinforces the president's reliance upon the established administrative apparatus and its principals in structuring the policymaking process. For example, Theodore Sorensen, special counsel to the president, revealed John Kennedy's limited understanding of public finance, writing,

> [The president] never mastered the technical mysteries of debt management and money supply. He once confided in his pre-Presidential days that he could remember the difference between fiscal policy, dealing with budgets and taxes, and monetary policy, dealing with money and credit, only by reminding himself that the name of the man most in charge of monetary policy, Federal Reserve Board Chairman William McChesney Martin, Jr., began with an "M" as in "monetary." But as President he more than compensated for his limited background in economics by his superb ability to absorb information and to ask the right questions. He was surrounded with probably the most knowledgeable group of articulate economists in U.S. history.[13]

Although the president tends to rely upon the established administrative apparatus and its principals for support, the established administrative apparatus and its principals are not necessarily responsive to the president's preferences. As Herbert Simon explained more generally, "Most organizations are oriented around some goal or objective which provides the purpose toward which [their] decisions and activities are directed."[14] In other words, the policy orientation of the established administrative apparatus supporting the president does not automatically change each time a new incumbent assumes office. For example, Harry Truman explained, "From the time I first sat down in the President's chair I found myself part of an immense administrative operation. There had been a change of executives, but the machinery kept going on in its customary routine manner, and properly so. It would have been sheer nonsense to expect anything else."[15] Similarly, Gerald Ford observed, "One of the enduring truths of the nation's capital is that bureaucrats *survive*. Agencies don't fold their tents and quietly fade away."[16]

This leaves the president with two basic options: create a new administrative apparatus that is supportive of his preferred policy parameters, or attempt to exercise control over the established administrative apparatus. However, the first option is generally too challenging, due in part to limited time and limited knowledge. The president therefore often attempts to appoint principals that he believes provide an optimal combination of responsiveness to his preferences and knowledge of the established administrative apparatus and policy parameters.

Further revealing the limits of control in practice, the president often fails in the execution of even this more restricted approach because he simply does not have the time and knowledge necessary to make optimal appointments in most cases. For example, Rutherford Hayes confessed, "The President has neither time nor authority, neither means nor men, to gather the information required to make appointments and removals. In my last message I may frankly admit my own shortcomings."[17] Moreover, Raymond Moley, the architect of the "Brain Trust" and one of Franklin Roosevelt's most influential advisers at the start of the New Deal, confirmed that this shortcoming is not limited to lower-level appointments. It is worth quoting Moley at length:

> [Roosevelt] considered himself under direct obligations to no man so far as Cabinet appointments were concerned. Neither recognized party leadership nor active campaign support figured heavily in his calculations.
>
> This might have suggested to a logical mind that he wanted to surround himself with the best possible advisers he could get, whether they were "big names" or relatively obscure men. But nothing in his conversation indicated any such desire. Certainly the Cabinet as it finally took shape did not even remotely hint of it.
>
> There was another possibility—the chance that he might want a Cabinet which, regardless of ability or political status, would be wholeheartedly sympathetic to his policies. *But except in the consideration of the Treasury appointment,*

the question of general sympathies was never brought up. Nor was there, on the other hand, any extensive attempt to balance the political and economic philosophies of the Cabinet members.

So far as I could see, there was neither a well-defined purpose nor underlying principle in the selection of the Roosevelt Cabinet. It was shaped by a score of unrelated factors.[18]

In the following section I will come back to the exception that Moley identified in Roosevelt's consideration of the Treasury appointment. It is enough here, however, to suggest that the president's appointment power alone is often insufficient to ensure responsiveness, as the time and knowledge restrictions tend to promote either appointments with no "underlying principle" or the appointment of those with previous experience in a policy domain. In particular, it is common for the president to appoint as a top principal either an official with experience in a related, lower-level position in a previous administration or a congressperson with experience on a related committee. This practice in turn tends to reinforce the established administrative apparatus and policy parameters because either type of experienced appointee is likely already indoctrinated with the governing objective in the policy domain. As Herbert Simon explained more generally,

When persons with particular educational qualifications are recruited for certain jobs, the organization is depending upon . . . pre-training as a principal means of assuring correct decisions in their work. . . . Training may supply the trainee with the facts necessary in dealing with . . . decisions; it may provide him a frame of reference for his thinking; it may teach him "approved" solutions; or it may indoctrinate him with the values in terms of which his decisions are to be made.[19]

Even if the new principal does not have previous experience—or, in Moley's words, there appears to be no "underlying principle" in his selection—he is still likely to support the established governing objective in the policy domain due to his own time and knowledge restrictions. For example, Charles Dawes, the founding director of the Bureau of the Budget, explained,

How is it possible for these Cabinet members, occupying their positions for much less than four years on the average, as experience shows, brought suddenly into control of a business of enormous magnitude, with which they have had no previous familiarity, consisting of unrelated activities, engaging the services of tens of thousands of people occupied in technical activities of the most diversified kind—how can these Cabinet members really be very efficient in connection with discerning control of the routine working of their departments? . . . We might as well get down to brass tacks and face facts. These Cabinet members, to enable them to intelligently perform their duties, have to have the help of men who have been connected with the business for years not only inside their departments but through these co-ordinating agencies of ours outside the departments.[20]

Further confirming the often limited responsiveness of the president's top appointees, John Ehrlichman, assistant to the president for domestic affairs under Richard Nixon, observed that many of the key officials in an administration "go off and marry the natives" in their departments.[21] Likewise, Martin Anderson, the chief domestic policy adviser under Ronald Reagan, explained, "The problem every winning campaign faces is how to ensure that those with more distinguished reputations who will be chosen for the cabinet posts do not betray the policies the campaign was fought on."[22]

Limiting presidential control further still, the third key restriction is the *structure of government*.[23] Most notably, multiple veto points across the branches of government often make it difficult to change the established administrative apparatus and policy parameters. For example, the Senate might filibuster the president's proposal or block a preferred nominee to a top post. Moreover, the established administrative institutions often work to protect their independence. As Calvin Coolidge explained, "Different departments and bureaus are frequently supporting measures that would make them self-perpetuating bodies to which no appointments could be made that they did not originate."[24] Similarly, Richard Nixon observed, "During my first term, all my attempts at reorganizing or reforming the federal government along more efficient and effective lines had been resisted by the combined and determined inertia of Congress and the bureaucracy."[25]

Although the "combined and determined inertia of Congress and the bureaucracy" is challenging enough, the time and knowledge restrictions further reinforce the structure of government restriction. In particular, the president tends to have maximum political support to overcome the structure of government restriction when he first assumes office, which is also when his time is most valuable and his knowledge is most limited. Conversely, when the president has more time and knowledge to change the established administrative apparatus and policy parameters, he generally lacks the necessary political support and, in some cases, the energy to do so.[26] For example, William Howard Taft explained, "Even in the case of the most popular President, his prestige wanes with Congress as the term wears on."[27] To take another example, during his final month in office, and six years after losing unified party control of the government, Barack Obama acknowledged, "There is no doubt I'm a better president now than I was when I start[ed]. . . . But what is also true is that . . . this is grueling. And sustaining the energy and focus involved in doing a good job . . . starts to get tougher the longer you do it."[28]

In addition to the three key restrictions, there are two key electoral and historical incentives to consider. First, as the only elected representative of the entire nation and the individual historically assigned much of the credit or blame for the handling of important issues—whether rightly or wrongly deserved—the president has an electoral and historical incentive to provide *acceptable performance* in each policy domain. Second, as the representative of a particular political coalition and the individual best positioned to make a mark on history, the president has an electoral and historical incentive to implement his *preferred policies*.[29]

Although there may be little or no conflict in the long run, implementing new policies can be a disruptive process that threatens to weaken performance significantly in the short run. For example, Treasury Secretary William Mc-Adoo explained that Woodrow Wilson preferred a "downward revision" in the tariff, "but in dealing with it as a practical problem," the president "realized that the American high tariff system had existed so long that it had become an accepted part of our industrial life," meaning "a drastic reduction in tariff schedules, if put into effect all at once, would dislocate the entire structure of American commercial enterprise."[30]

The potential conflict between the two electoral and historical incentives often requires the president to make a tradeoff. Specifically, if the president's resources were unlimited, he would likely aim to ensure some optimal combination of acceptable performance and preferred policies, but the president's resources are not unlimited. Therefore, in order to protect his prospects for reelection, his standing in history, or both, the president sometimes accepts undesirable policies that maintain or improve performance in the short run.

Consider the situation that Richard Nixon faced in 1971, a year before his reelection. "Vietnam and other foreign problems dominated most of [the year]," Nixon explained.[31] This meant that when it came to managing domestic problems, especially inflation, the president relied upon his public-finance principals and ultimately accepted the implementation of wage and price controls that they supported and that he opposed. As Nixon conceded, "Having talked until only recently about the evils of wage and price controls, I knew I had opened myself to the charge that I had either betrayed my own principles or concealed my real intentions." Yet, the controls were implemented, he added, because it "was politically necessary . . . in the short run."[32]

A similar situation occurred during the financial crisis in 2008—though in this case George W. Bush was concerned more with his standing in history than electoral incentives. As the president explained, "If we're really looking at another Great Depression, you can be damn sure I'm going to be Roosevelt, not Hoover."[33] Notably, however, Bush himself remained focused on foreign affairs, particularly with regard to whether the "surge" would succeed in "[putting] Iraq policy onto a stable footing" for his successor.[34] The president therefore delegated the management of the financial crisis to the Treasury secretary and Fed chair. Making clear his limited involvement, Bush remarked, "Someday you guys are going to have to tell me how we ended up with a system like this and what we need to do to fix it."[35] With the public finance principals taking the lead, the president then accepted the implementation of several policies that they supported and he opposed. For example, Bush confessed that the Troubled Asset Relief Program "was a breathtaking intervention in the free market. It flew against all my instincts. But it was necessary to pull the country out of the panic."[36]

Incorporating all these key restrictions and incentives at play—time, knowledge, and the structure of government, and, in certain situations, prioritizing short-run performance over preferred policies—the president tends to rely upon the established administrative apparatus and its principals, which often limits the president's control in the process of supporting the established policy parameters. In particular—and further applying some of Herbert Simon's general terms—the administrative apparatus for a policy domain "establishes standard practices," it "provides channels of communication running in all directions through which information for decision-making flows," and it "trains and indoctrinates" the principals in support of a specific governing objective.[37] All this works to support a narrow set of policy alternatives in order to assist the president in managing complex problems in multiple policy domains simultaneously. Yet, in assisting the president, the established administrative apparatus and its principals also routinely limit his control.[38]

In contrast to some of the leading views on the presidency and policymaking, the picture presented here suggests that the president's prospects for maximizing control are rather bleak. Nevertheless, presidents do take the lead in restructuring the established administrative apparatus and policy parameters from time to time. A complete theory therefore needs to explain variation in presidential control in addition to the often significant limits in practice.

VARIATION IN THE KEY RESTRICTIONS AND INCENTIVES

Although presidential control is always imperfect due to several key restrictions and incentives that prevent each new incumbent from routinely restructuring the established administrative apparatus and policy parameters for a given do-main, significant variation in presidential control can be observed from one incumbent to the next due to variation in the key restrictions and incentives.

First, the management of the *time* restriction varies. As Jimmy Carter ex-plained, "When he can concentrate his attention on one major thrust to the exclusion of other matters, the President can usually prevail, but such an op-portunity seldom arises."[39] Although the president's ability to focus exclusively on one issue "seldom arises," there are occasions when that kind of attention is compelled. For example, George W. Bush admitted, "The summer of 2006 was the worst period of my presidency. I thought about the war constantly." It "had stretched to more than three years and we had lost more than 2,500 Americans. . . . For the first time, I worried we might not succeed."[40] In this case, the president focused "constantly" on a single policy domain for an extended period; this was also a domain that his predecessor had spent much less time addressing, as foreign affairs played a relatively limited role during the Clinton administration.

To account more generally for variation in this key restriction, I propose that the president tends to spend more time addressing a problem in a policy domain as it increases in severity overall and relative to problems in other do-mains.[41] The obvious reason is that the issue inevitably moves higher on the government's agenda, crowding into the president's life with speed and insist-ence—to paraphrase Harry Truman—and pushing other matters aside.

Second, the management of the *knowledge* restriction varies. As discussed, the president can appoint either experienced or inexperienced principals, and due to his time and knowledge limitations, the president often appoints expe-rienced principals who support the established approach in a policy domain. Moreover, even when the president appoints inexperienced principals, they of-ten support the established approach due to their own time and knowledge limitations and eventual indoctrination. However, there is little reason to ap-point experienced principals when a severe and prioritized problem discredits the established approach in a policy domain. In such a case, the president is inclined to appoint inexperienced principals who are more responsive to his preferences and more supportive of restructuring the established approach. Re-inforcing this move, the ability of the established administrative apparatus to indoctrinate the inexperienced principals is diminished. For example, the "gen-eral sympathies" of the cabinet members at the start of the Roosevelt adminis-tration was discussed only "in the consideration of the Treasury appointment."[42] This was due to the Great Depression, which discredited the established ap-proach to public finance.

To account more generally for variation in this key restriction, I propose that as a problem becomes more severe overall and relative to problems in other domains, it becomes more practical for the president to supplement his knowledge limitations by relying upon inexperienced principals who are more responsive to his preferences and more supportive of restructuring the established administrative apparatus and policy parameters.

Third, the effectiveness of the *structure of government* restriction varies. By design, the constitutional system divides power among the three branches, frequently impeding the president's ability to take the lead in restructuring the established approach in a policy domain. As James Madison explained in *The Federalist*, the "structure of the government" is meant to ensure "that its several constituent parts may, by their mutual relations, be the means of keeping each other in their proper places."[43] However, the effectiveness of the structure of government restriction is diminished when a severe and prioritized problem puts pressure on each branch simultaneously. For example, Lyndon Johnson explained, "A sense of national urgency is perhaps the most important source of cooperation. When the national interest is clear and the need for action compelling, the separate constituencies of the President and the Congress come together."[44]

Further accounting for variation in this key restriction, the president is inclined to proceed unilaterally if Congress fails to act in response to a severe and prioritized problem or if Congress's actions prove insufficient. The reason is that the severe and prioritized problem weakens the legislative branch's ability to block or reverse the president's actions—even if he lacks the support of a majority in Congress—and it also weakens the independence of the established administrative apparatus and its principals. For example, Grover Cleveland acted unilaterally in order to maintain the gold standard during and after the Panic of 1893. This occurred at a time when both Congress failed to act and Treasury Secretary John Carlisle believed that the sole authority to address the matter rested with the legislative branch. As the Treasury secretary explained in the report on the finances in 1893, "Congress alone has the power to adopt such measures as will relieve the present situation and enable the Treasury to continue the punctual payment of all legitimate demands upon it."[45] In contrast, Cleveland was near defiant, declaring in his annual message the following year, "Congress has not only thus far declined to authorize the issue of bonds, . . . there seems a disposition in some quarters to deny both the necessity and power for the issue of bonds at all." Then, regarding the Resumption Act of 1875, the scope of which the president had reinterpreted in order to act unilaterally, Cleveland added, "As long as no better authority for bond issues is allowed than at present exists, such authority will be utilized whenever and as often as it becomes necessary to maintain a sufficient gold reserve."[46]

To account more generally for variation in this key restriction, I propose that as a problem becomes more severe overall and relative to problems in other domains, the president's ability to navigate the structure of government restriction increases.

Lastly, the balance of the electoral and historical incentives to provide *acceptable performance* and to implement *preferred policies* varies. In practice, the president can either prioritize performance, preferred policies, or some combination of the two. Recall that Richard Nixon and George W. Bush prioritized short-run performance over preferred policies in the cases considered in the previous section. Although several factors account for those decisions, one common, overriding factor is apparent: each president viewed a problem in another policy domain as more important than the problem in the domain of public finance. In particular, Nixon prioritized the Vietnam War and Bush prioritized the Iraq War, which he feared was headed toward a "repeat of Vietnam."[47] Both presidents therefore accepted the implementation of undesirable policies in the domain of public finance largely because they had delegated responsibility to the public-finance principals and then focused on another policy domain with a more severe and prioritized problem.

To demonstrate the variation in the balance of the key electoral and historical incentives, consider Bush's actions in the policy domain that he prioritized. In late 2006 the Democratic Party swept the midterm election, gaining control of the House and Senate, and the political consensus at the time was that the president should end the war in Iraq and bring the troops home. Moreover, the president's own national-security principals—including Secretary of Defense Donald Rumsfeld, Secretary of State Condoleezza Rice, General George Casey, and General John Abizaid—all supported some commitment of a drawdown in troops.[48] However, rather than rely upon his national-security principals and select from among the two recommended alternatives at the time—accelerating the existing strategy of training Iraqi forces and withdrawing US troops, or pulling US troops back from Baghdad until the violence subsided—the president informed his national-security adviser, "We need to take another look at the whole strategy. I need to see some new options."[49] In response, the government eventually deployed 20,000 additional US troops to Iraq. Equally notable, the president appointed new principals—Secretary of Defense Robert Gates and General David Petraeus—to implement the new plan, and he then defeated the efforts of the new Democratic-controlled Congress to reverse it, signing a bill in May 2007 that fully funded the deployment of troops without a schedule for withdrawal. Underscoring the opposition that he overcame in the policy domain, Bush explained, "Years from now, historians may look back and see the surge as a forgone conclusion," yet "nothing about the surge felt inevitable at the time."[50]

The comparison of Bush's handling of the financial crisis and the Iraq war side by side suggests that the president prioritized short-run performance over preferred policies in the domain of public finance, the management of which he delegated to the public-finance principals. In contrast, Bush applied his limited resources toward appointing new, more responsive national-defense principals in order to develop and implement preferred policies that he believed would ultimately produce the best performance in the case of Iraq, the greater problem from his perspective.

To account more generally for variation in the key electoral and historical incentives, I propose that as a problem becomes more severe overall and relative to problems in other domains, the president becomes more likely to implement his preferred policies in an effort to improve performance rather than prioritize short-run performance at the expense of his preferred policies. The reason is that as the problem becomes more severe overall, the conflict between the two incentives weakens. In other words, the very existence of the problem signifies that performance is already inadequate and so there is less concern that implementing preferred policies will be disruptive. For example, this was one of the key dynamics at play when Rahm Emanuel, the chief of staff during the Obama administration, remarked, "You never want a serious crisis to go to waste. And what I mean by that is an opportunity to do things that you think you could not do before."[51] Moreover, as the problem becomes more severe relative to other problems, the president becomes more likely to apply his limited resources to it—or, in Emanuel's terms, if simultaneous crises exist, the more severe one is less likely to "go to waste."

THE TWO PRIMARY CONFIGURATIONS OF PRESIDENTIAL CONTROL: CONSTRAINT AND INNOVATION

Incorporating the preceding variation in the key restrictions and incentives, I propose that presidential control comes in two primary configurations: *constraint* and *innovation*.

For the configuration of constraint, I propose that due largely to the absence of an exceptionally severe and highly prioritized problem—which strengthens the average restrictions on presidential control and weakens the average incentive to maximize control—some presidents rely upon the established, relatively stable administrative apparatus and its principals, which supports the established policy parameters and significantly limits the control of those presidents. This conditional control is especially pronounced when the president opposes the established policy parameters.

For the configuration of innovation, I propose that due largely to an exceptionally severe and highly prioritized problem—which weakens the average restrictions on presidential control and strengthens the average incentive to maximize control—some presidents significantly strengthen their control in working to restructure both the established administrative apparatus and the established policy parameters.

To be clear, restructuring the established administrative apparatus proves critical not only during the initial process of restructuring the established policy parameters but also in supporting those policy parameters moving forward. In particular—and continuing to apply some of Herbert Simon's general terms— the restructured administrative apparatus for a policy domain "establishes [new] standard practices," it "provides [new] channels of communication running in all directions through which information for decision-making flows," and it "trains and indoctrinates" the principals in support of a new governing objective. All of this works to structure a new, narrow set of policy alternatives in order to assist the president and his successors in managing complex problems in multiple policy domains simultaneously.

By "restructure the established administrative apparatus and policy parameters," I mean that the president oversees a substantial and durable shift in the administrative apparatus and key policy parameters.[52] On the administrative front, four approaches are discernable.

The first approach is to restructure the administrative apparatus through *direct legislative action*. This primarily includes creating an institution, destroying an institution, or significantly modifying an institution. For example, George Washington and his principals played a key role in developing and passing the act of February 25, 1791, which created the First Bank of the United States; Andrew Jackson and his principals played a key role in vetoing the charter for the Second Bank of the United States, which led to the destruction of that institution; and Franklin Roosevelt and his principals played a key role in developing and passing the Banking Act of 1935, which significantly modified the Federal Reserve System.

The second approach is to restructure the administrative apparatus through *indirect legislative action*. This includes unplanned developments based on legislation primarily for other purposes. For example, the increase in the national debt during the Second World War and the rise in national defense spending during the Cold War both weakened the independence of the Federal Reserve throughout much of the New Deal era. In particular, those budgetary develop-

ments put increased pressure on the Fed to assist the Treasury in the management of the debt, which in turn weakened the Fed's independence in managing
monetary policy.

The third approach is to restructure the administrative apparatus through
direct executive action. This primarily includes the president's appointment and
removal power, executive directives, and executive oversight. For example, Andrew Jackson weakened the independence of the Treasury secretary through
the increased use of the appointment and removal power; he also weakened
the influence of the Second Bank in directing the Treasury secretary to remove the government's deposits; and Ronald Reagan strengthened the independence of the Fed by ending the practice of commenting publicly on monetary policy, which significantly weakened executive oversight.

The fourth approach is to restructure the administrative apparatus through
indirect executive action. This includes unplanned developments based on executive action primarily for other purposes. For example, Ronald Reagan used the
appointment power to strengthen his control over the Office of Management
and Budget. However, the politicization of the OMB ultimately strengthened
the influence of the nonpartisan Congressional Budget Office.

To be sure, in incorporating multiple approaches, two of which include
indirect—or largely unplanned—action, the complex process of restructuring
the administrative apparatus is unlikely to proceed entirely as intended. Nevertheless, the presidents who take the lead in this process are generally the most
successful in ensuring that the new administrative apparatus supports their preferred policy parameters, both in implementing those policy parameters and in
making it more difficult for subsequent incumbents to change course.

Finally, the process of restructuring the administrative apparatus for a policy domain incorporates not only multiple approaches but also multiple institutions. In particular, presidential control over administration always includes
at least two components, the president and the department or agency directly
overseeing the policy domain, and rarely, if ever, does a single department or
agency maintain a monopoly. For example, Council of Economic Advisers
Chair Herbert Stein explained, "Something that I didn't really appreciate before" serving in office "is the fact that [the CEA] participates in so many inter-agency arrangements, committees, and task forces. Hardly any important
matter decided in the government isn't the subject of some inter-agency consultations because all the important matters involve more than one agency."[53]

Additionally, the different administrative institutions working together often operate with varying degrees of independence from the president.[54] For
example, even during the early period of US history, public-finance administration involved, at times, three key components: a mix of formal and informal

advisors to the president; the Treasury Department, headed by a president-appointed, Senate-confirmed principal; and the independent Bank of the United States, headed by a principal not appointed by the president.

Taking into account the multiple approaches to restructuring an administrative apparatus for a policy domain and the multiple institutions comprising the administrative apparatus, an effective study of historical variation in presidential control over administration requires examining, in the words of Karen Orren and Stephen Skowronek, "multiple orderings of authority."[55]

TWO INTERMEDIARY CONFIGURATIONS OF PRESIDENTIAL CONTROL: COLLAPSE AND STABILIZATION

At its core presidential control comes in two configurations: constraint and innovation. But this division is often too stark, as it overlooks two intermediary configurations of presidential control that recur throughout history: *collapse*, which bridges the transition from constraint to innovation; and *stabilization*, which bridges the transition from innovation to constraint.

As theorized, when the severity and prioritization of a new problem begins to increase, this begins to increase the president's ability to spend time on the policy domain, his ability to ensure responsiveness in supplementing his knowledge limitations, his ability to effectively navigate the structure of government, and his incentive to maximize control. However, it can take several years for a new problem to become sufficiently severe and prioritized to support the restructuring of a policy domain. This means that some presidents rely upon the established, gradually failing administrative apparatus to manage a new problem rather than work to restructure the established approach, especially if the policy domain is relatively stable when the president first assumes office and sets the course for his administration.

For the configuration of collapse, I propose that due largely to an increasingly severe and increasingly prioritized new problem—which only begins to weaken the average restrictions on presidential control and only begins to strengthen the average incentive to maximize control—some presidents rely upon the established, gradually failing administrative apparatus and its principals, which allows those presidents to strengthen their control to a degree but, for the most part, limits their control in the process of supporting the established policy parameters. This conditional control is especially pronounced when the president opposes the established policy parameters.

Continuing to apply Herbert Simon's general terms, in this situation the old "standard practices" largely remain in place, the old "channels of communication running in all directions through which information for decision-making flows" largely remain in place, and the "train[ed] and indoctrinate[d]" principals largely continue to operate in support of the old governing objective. All of this largely continues to support a narrow set of policy alternatives in order to assist the president in managing complex problems in multiple policy domains simultaneously. Yet, in assisting the president, the established, gradually failing administrative apparatus and its principals also largely limit his control.

The inverse of this process unfolds for the transition from innovation to constraint. As theorized, when the severity and prioritization of a problem begin to decrease, this begins to decrease the president's ability to spend time on the policy domain, his ability to ensure responsiveness in supplementing his knowledge limitations, his ability to effectively navigate the structure of government, and his incentive to maximize control. Like its counterpart, this process can take several years to unfold and—no doubt due in part to the prominence of public finance as a political issue—it often occurs under presidents of the same party as the incumbent who oversaw the restructuring of the policy domain, which introduces a new key restriction and a new key incentive.

First, *party continuity* is a restriction.[56] As Alexander Hamilton reasoned in *The Federalist*, "To reverse and undo what has been done by a predecessor is very often considered by a successor as the best proof he can give of his own capacity and desert."[57] Yet, in this situation, the president has to prove "his own capacity and desert" while reaffirming and resolving what his predecessor began, a more challenging charge. For example, Herbert Hoover explained, "It is a handicap to any man to succeed a member of his own party as President." The problem is that the "new President cannot blame his predecessor for inevitable mistakes, and therefore he must keep quiet and inherit responsibility for them."[58]

Adding to this new, inherited responsibility, the president in this situation is more likely to retain his predecessor's principals or appoint principals whom his predecessor finds acceptable in order to prevent a division from forming within the party. For example, John Adams retained his predecessor's entire cabinet, explaining, "Washington had appointed them and I knew it would turn the world upside down if I removed any one of them."[59]

Second, party continuity introduces a new incentive. Rather than either prioritize his preferred policies in an effort to improve performance, or prioritize performance at the expense of his preferred policies, the president in this situation has an incentive to support his *predecessor's preferred policies*, as those policies—which may or may not match his own preferred policies—have a proven record of electoral success and are viewed as more representative of the faithful party position in the restructured domain.[60] For example, William Howard Taft pledged at the start of his presidency to support the policies of his predecessor, Theodore Roosevelt. As Taft explained in his inaugural address,

> I have had the honor to be one of the advisers of my distinguished predecessor, and, as such, to hold up his hands in the reforms *he has initiated*. I should be untrue to myself, to my promises, and to the declarations of the party platform upon which I was elected to office, if I did not make the maintenance and enforcement of those reforms a most important feature of my administration.[61]

The distinct combination of the key restrictions and incentives in this situation—the middling severity and prioritization of the problem, the president's inability to repudiate his predecessor, the tendency to retain his predecessor's principals or appoint principals whom his predecessor finds acceptable, and the electoral incentive to support his predecessor's preferred policies—accounts for further variation in presidential control that can be observed from one incumbent to the next. Specifically, for the configuration of stabilization, I propose that due largely to party continuity and a decreasingly severe and decreasingly prioritized problem—all of which begin to strengthen the average restrictions on presidential control and begin to weaken the average incentive to maximize control—some presidents relinquish much of their control to their predecessor in working to secure both the newly established administrative apparatus and the newly established policy parameters.

Continuing to apply Herbert Simon's general terms, in this situation the newly established "standard practices" are secured, the newly established "channels of communication" are secured, and the "train[ing] and indoctrinat[ion]" of the principals in support of the newly established governing objective are secured. All of this works to secure the newly established administrative apparatus and narrow set of policy alternatives, making it more difficult for subsequent presidents to change course.

AN OVERVIEW OF THE FOUR CONFIGURATIONS OF PRESIDENTIAL CONTROL

The following is an overview of the four configurations of presidential control that have recurred in succession throughout much of US history: collapse, innovation, stabilization, and constraint.

Collapse. Due largely to an increasingly severe and increasingly prioritized new problem, some presidents rely upon the established, gradually failing administrative apparatus and its principals, which allows those presidents to strengthen their control to a degree but, for the most part, limits their control in the process of supporting the established policy parameters. For this configuration, *the average restrictions on presidential control are transitioning from strong to weak*: specifically, the increasingly severe and increasingly prioritized new problem begins to increase the president's ability to spend time on the policy domain, his ability to ensure responsiveness in supplementing his knowledge limitations, and his ability to effectively navigate the structure of government, but the initial weakening of the average restrictions is insufficient for the president to take the lead in restructuring the policy domain, especially when he first assumes office and sets the course for his administration. At the same time, *the average incentive to maximize presidential control is transitioning from weak to strong*: specifically, the increasingly severe and increasingly prioritized new problem begins to strengthen the president's incentive to implement new, preferred policies in an effort to improve performance, yet the initial strengthening of the average incentive to maximize presidential control is insufficient for the president to take the lead in restructuring the policy domain, especially when he first assumes office and sets the course for his administration.

Innovation. Due largely to an exceptionally severe and highly prioritized new problem, some presidents significantly strengthen their control in working to restructure both the established administrative apparatus and the established policy parameters. For this configuration, *the average restrictions on presidential control are weak*: specifically, the exceptionally severe and highly prioritized new problem increases the president's ability to spend time on the policy domain, his ability to ensure responsiveness in supplementing his knowledge limitations, and his ability to effectively navigate the structure of government. At the same time, *the average incentive to maximize presidential control is strong*: specifically, the exceptionally severe and highly prioritized new problem strengthens the president's incentive to implement new, preferred policies in an effort to improve performance.

Stabilization. Due largely to party continuity and a decreasingly severe and decreasingly prioritized problem, some presidents relinquish much of their control to their predecessor in working to secure both the newly established administrative apparatus and the newly established policy parameters. For this configuration, *the average restrictions on presidential control are transitioning from weak to strong*: specifically, even if the decreasingly severe and decreasingly prioritized problem continues to weaken the time and structure of government restrictions, party continuity limits the president's ability both to repudiate his predecessor and to appoint responsive principals to supplement his knowledge limitations. At the same time, *the average incentive to maximize presidential control is transitioning from strong to weak*: specifically, even if the decreasingly severe and decreasingly prioritized problem continues to strengthen the president's incentive to implement new, preferred policies in an effort to improve performance, party continuity induces the president to promote his predecessor's preferred policies, which may or may not be the same as his own preferred policies.

Constraint. Due largely to the absence of an exceptionally severe and highly prioritized problem, some presidents rely upon the established, relatively stable administrative apparatus and its principals, which supports the established policy parameters and significantly limits the control of those presidents. For this configuration, *the average restrictions on presidential control are strong*: specifically, the absence of an exceptionally severe and highly prioritized problem decreases the president's ability to spend time on the policy domain, his ability to ensure responsiveness in supplementing his knowledge limitations, and his ability to effectively navigate the structure of government. At the same time, *the average incentive to maximize presidential control is weak*: specifically, the absence of an exceptionally severe and highly prioritized problem weakens the president's incentive to implement new, preferred policies in an effort to improve performance.

TESTING THE THEORY

As discussed in the previous chapter, this book tests the theory of historical variation in presidential control using a multimethod examination of public-finance policymaking, which includes the subdomains of fiscal policy and monetary policy. In particular, part II presents a quantitative overview of historical variation in public-finance policymaking. Part III presents a case study analysis that initially traces the creation of the New Era apparatus and its collapse while assisting Herbert Hoover, and it then traces the historical variation in presidential control for the first three incumbents of the New Deal era: Franklin Roosevelt, Harry Truman, and Dwight Eisenhower. Part IV presents a case study analysis that initially traces the collapse of the New Deal–era apparatus while assisting Richard Nixon, Gerald Ford, and Jimmy Carter, and it then traces the historical variation in presidential control for the first three incumbents of the Reagan era: Ronald Reagan, George H. W. Bush, and Bill Clinton. Part V presents a case study analysis that traces the historical variation in presidential control for two recent incumbents during the Great Recession and beyond: Barack Obama and Donald Trump.

Part II
A Quantitative Overview of Historical Variation in Public-Finance Policymaking

3. Public-Finance Problems, Prioritization, Administration, and Policy

This chapter presents a quantitative overview of historical variation in public-finance policymaking for two primary purposes. First, it provides an initial test of the theory of historical variation in presidential control by showing that public-finance administration and policy are closely connected and change in relation to variation in public-finance problems and prioritization. Second, it provides an extensive empirical foundation for the case studies that follow. To that end, the analysis proceeds in three sections. The first section provides a quantitative overview of historical variation in public-finance problems and prioritization. The second section provides a quantitative overview of historical variation in public-finance administration. The third section provides a quantitative overview of historical variation in public-finance policy, which includes both fiscal policy and monetary policy.

HISTORICAL VARIATION IN PUBLIC-FINANCE PROBLEMS AND PRIORITIZATION

The first section of the analysis provides a quantitative overview of historical variation in public-finance problems and prioritization. It includes three parts: a quantitative overview of historical variation in public-finance problems, a quantitative overview of historical variation in public-finance prioritization, and a review of both.

For part one, figure 3.1 shows the public-finance problem index, measured as the sum of two components: the unemployment rate and the absolute value of the inflation or deflation rate. The unemployment rate measures "the number of unemployed individuals as a percentage of the entire labor force." The inflation or deflation rate measures "changes in the average price of a consistent set of goods and services, often referred to as a market basket." In particular, inflation is "a general increase in the price of goods and services across the economy" and deflation is "a general decrease in the price of goods and services."[1]

Underscoring the importance of the first problem indicator, the nonpartisan Congressional Research Service (CRS), the US Congress's public policy research institute, explains, "The unemployment rate is most often used as a measure of labor market strength, but it is also a useful indicator and predictor of the broader state of the economy." Most importantly, "gross domestic product (GDP) and the unemployment rate have a negative long-run relationship. In general, for economic production to increase, the number of individuals who work must increase. Therefore, as economic growth increases, unemployment tends to decrease, and vice versa."[2]

Regarding the second problem indicator, the CRS explains, "Inflation tends to interfere with pricing mechanisms in the economy, resulting in individuals and businesses making less than optimal spending, saving, and investment decisions," which then works to "reduce incomes, economic growth, and living standards."[3]

The CRS also addresses the important relationship between the two problem indicators, explaining, "In general, economists have found that when the unemployment rate drops below a certain level, referred to as the natural rate, the inflation rate will tend to increase and continue to rise until the unemployment rate returns to its natural rate. Alternatively, when the unemployment rate rises above the natural rate, the inflation rate will tend to decelerate."[4]

Although many factors impact the domain of public finance, unemployment and inflation operate as the two primary problem indicators. Most notably, the Employment Act of 1946 made it the "continuing policy and responsibility of the Federal Government . . . to promote maximum employment"; and the Full Employment and Balanced Growth Act of 1978 established the dual governing objective of promoting "full employment" and reasonable "price stability."[5]

Looking now at the historical variation in what I label here the public-finance problem index—or, by its more popular label, the "misery index"—a visual examination reveals two exceptionally severe problems since the late 1920s: the Great Depression and the Great Inflation.

Consider the Great Depression. This historic episode incorporated two major economic downturns, the Great Depression proper of 1929–1933 and the Recession of 1937–1938. In particular, the problem index remained in double digits from 1930 through 1942, a total of thirteen years; the index peaked at 33.5 during the former downturn and 21.1 during the latter; and in the aftermath of this historic episode, the government generally prioritized the problem of unemployment, as evidenced by the Employment Act and the fact that on occasion the inflation rate surpassed the unemployment rate as the government worked to lower the latter.

In terms of variation in the key restrictions and incentives discussed in the

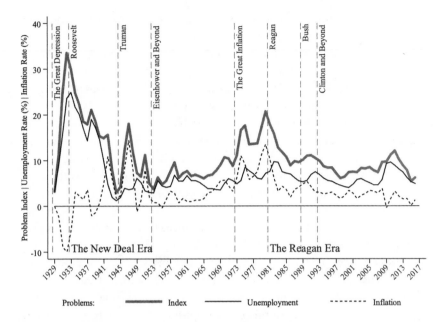

Figure 3.1   Historical Variation in Public-Finance Problems

Sources: Unemployment data for 1929–1947 from Stanley Lebergott, "Annual Estimates of Unemployment in the United States," in *The Measurement and Behavior of Unemployment* (Princeton, NJ: Princeton University Press, 1957), 215–216, percent of civilian labor force. Unemployment data for 1948–2016 from the US Bureau of Labor Statistics, Series ID LNS14000000, annual average. Inflation data from the US Bureau of Labor Statistics, Historical Consumer Price Index for All Urban Consumers (CPI-U), percent change from previous, annual average. Data accessed in 2017.

theory chapter, the Great Depression and its aftermath unfolded in four key problem stages:

First, the Great Depression started during the Hoover administration. This began to weaken the average restrictions on presidential control and began to strengthen the average incentive to maximize control. Importantly, however, the Great Depression was not exceptionally severe when Herbert Hoover assumed office and set the course for his administration. In particular, the problem index stood at 3.2 in 1929, and party continuity further limited the president's control.

Second, the Great Depression was exceptionally severe during the start of the Roosevelt administration. This weakened the average restrictions on presidential control and strengthened the average incentive to maximize control. In particular, the problem index peaked at 33.5 in 1932, the year Franklin Roosevelt was elected president, and it stood at 30.0 in 1933, Roosevelt's first year in office.

Third, the Great Depression was over by the start of the Truman administration. Together with party continuity, this began to strengthen the average restrictions on presidential control and began to weaken the average incentive to maximize control. In particular, the problem index stood at 4.2 in 1945, Harry Truman's first year in office. Moreover, although there were two brief spikes in the problem index—one following the end of the Second World War in 1945 and the other following the start of the Korean War in 1950—these problems were significantly less severe and less sustained than the Great Depression.

Fourth, the policy domain was relatively stable by the start of the Eisenhower administration. This strengthened the average restrictions on presidential control and weakened the average incentive to maximize control. In particular, the problem index stood at 3.7 in 1953, Dwight Eisenhower's first year in office, and it remained in single digits through the end of the Eisenhower administration and for several years beyond.

Next, consider the Great Inflation. Like its predecessor, this historic episode incorporated multiple economic downturns: the Recession of 1973–1975, the Recession of 1980, and the Recession of 1981–1982. In particular, the problem index remained in double digits from 1973 through 1985, a total of thirteen years; the index peaked at 20.7 during the middle downturn, the highest level since 1938; and in the aftermath of this historic episode, the government generally prioritized the problem of inflation, as evidenced by the Full Employment and Balanced Growth Act and the fact that the average annual inflation rate has not surpassed the average annual unemployment rate since 1981.

In terms of variation in the key restrictions and incentives discussed in the theory chapter, the Great Inflation and its aftermath unfolded in four key problem stages:

First, the Great Inflation started during the second term of the Nixon administration and its initial phase continued through the Ford and Carter administrations. This began to weaken the average restrictions on presidential control and began to strengthen the average incentive to maximize control. Importantly, however, the Great Inflation was not exceptionally severe when Richard Nixon assumed office and set the course for his administration. Moreover, although the severity of the Great Inflation increased by the time that Gerald Ford assumed office, party continuity and the unusual transition following Nixon's resignation limited the new president's control. Also important, the severity of the Great Inflation temporarily decreased by the time that Jimmy Carter assumed office. Overall, the problem index stood at 9.0 in 1969, Nixon's first year in office; it increased to 16.6 in 1974, Ford's first year in office; and it decreased to 13.6 in 1977, Carter's first year in office.

Second, the Great Inflation was exceptionally severe during the start of the Reagan administration. This weakened the average restrictions on presidential control and strengthened the average incentive to maximize control. In particular, the problem index peaked at 20.7 in 1980, the year Ronald Reagan was elected president, and it stood at 17.9 in 1981, Reagan's first year in office.

Third, the Great Inflation was over by the start of the Bush administration. Together with party continuity, this began to strengthen the average restrictions on presidential control and began to weaken the average incentive to maximize control. In particular, the problem index had fallen to single digits by 1988, the year George Bush was elected president, and it stood at 10.1 in 1989, Bush's first year in office. Moreover, although the problem index continued in low double digits due to the Recession of 1990–1991, this problem was significantly less severe and less sustained than the Great Inflation.

Fourth, the policy domain was relatively stable by the start of the Clinton administration. This strengthened the average restrictions on presidential control and weakened the average incentive to maximize control. In particular, the problem index fell to 9.9 in 1993, Bill Clinton's first year in office, and it remained in single digits through the end of the Clinton administration and for several years beyond.

Lastly, consider the Great Recession of 2007–2009. Using the Great Depression and the Great Inflation as historical baselines, the Great Recession was not an exceptionally severe problem. This means that the average restrictions on presidential control during the Obama administration were relatively strong and the average incentive to maximize control was relatively weak. In particular, the problem index stood at 9.7 in 2009, Barack Obama's first year in office, and it peaked at 12.1 in 2011, which is only roughly half the peak during the Great Inflation and only roughly one-third of the peak during the Great Depression. Also, the problem index only remained in double digits for three years during the Great Recession, compared to thirteen years during the Great Depression and the Great Inflation.

* * *

For part two, figure 3.2 shows the public-finance prioritization level in two forms: (1) an annual prioritization level, measured as the percentage of articles in the *New York Times* referencing both the president and the Treasury within the universe of articles referencing the president; and (2) a weighted presidential term prioritization level, with the greatest weight placed on the earliest years. The aim is to gauge which presidential administrations came into office most focused on addressing the problem in the domain of public finance relative to other problems. The measure used here includes the Treasury because that is the foundational—and for most of US history, the most prominent—administrative institution in the policy domain.

Looking now at the historical variation in both measures, a visual exami-

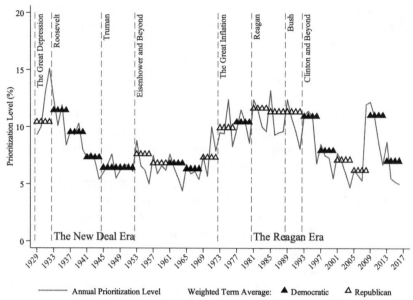

Figure 3.2   Historical Variation in Public-Finance Prioritization

Sources: Search results are from the *New York Times* through the ProQuest Historical Newspapers database for the years 1929–2008 and the ProQuest Newspapers database for the years 2009–2016. Annual prioritization level is the percentage of newspaper articles referencing both the president and the Treasury within the universe of newspaper articles referencing the president. Weighted-term average applies a 50 percent weight for the first year, 30 percent for the second year, 15 percent for the third year, and 5 percent for the fourth year. Data accessed in 2017.

nation reveals two sustained episodes since the late 1920s during which public-finance problems were highly prioritized: the Great Depression and the Great Inflation.

Consider the Great Depression. First, the public-finance prioritization level started to increase during the Hoover administration. Second, the average public-finance prioritization level peaked during the first term of the Roosevelt administration. The average prioritization level also remained relatively high during the second term—due to the enduring effect of the Great Depression proper of 1929–1933 and the new effect of the Recession of 1937–1938—but it then fell substantially during the third term, as attention shifted to national defense. Third, the public-finance prioritization level remained low during the whole of the Truman administration despite the brief spikes in the problem index, as other policy domains required greater attention at the time, especially national defense. Fourth, as the first Republican administration in two decades, and one with a strong desire to reverse many of the changes in public finance, the average prioritization level ticked up during the first term of the Eisenhower administration, but there was not an exceptionally severe problem to support this shift in prioritization at the time or to sustain it moving forward. Accordingly, the prioritization level decreased during the second half of the 1950s, and it essentially remained at that low level for the whole of the 1960s and early 1970s.

Next, consider the Great Inflation. First, the prioritization level started to increase during the second term of the Nixon administration, and it continued to do so during the Ford and Carter administrations. Second, the average public-finance prioritization level peaked during the first term of the Reagan administration, and it remained high during the second term. Third, and unlike the earlier transition to the Truman administration, the average prioritization level remained high during the Bush administration, due in part to the less resolved problem in the policy domain—the problem index averaged 9.5 under Truman versus 10.7 under Bush. Fourth, as the first Democratic administration in over a decade, and one with a strong desire to reverse many changes in public finance, the prioritization level remained high at the start of the Clinton administration, but the problem index had already declined, meaning there was not an exceptionally severe problem to support the high level of prioritization at the time or to sustain it moving forward. Accordingly, the prioritization level decreased by the start of Clinton's second term, and it remained low for the next decade.

Lastly, consider the Great Recession of 2007–2009. Using the Great Depression and the Great Inflation as historical baselines, the Great Recession was not a highly prioritized problem for a sustained period. To be sure, the annual prioritization level peaked at 12.2 percent during the first year of the Obama administration, nearly matching the first-year level of 12.4 percent for the Roosevelt and Reagan administrations. Likewise, the average prioritization level peaked at 11 percent during the first term of the Obama administration, nearly matching the first term average of 11.4 percent and 11.6 percent for the same two earlier administrations respectively. However, unlike the earlier administrations, there was no equivalent level of sustained prioritization. In particular, whereas the average prioritization level increased before the start of the Roosevelt and Reagan administrations, which contributed to the gradual weakening of the average restrictions on presidential control and the gradual strengthening of the average incentive to maximize control, the average prioritization level remained low for the three terms preceding the Obama administration. Also, whereas the average prioritization level remained high during the second term of the Roosevelt and Reagan administrations, it decreased considerably during the second term of the Obama administration.

* * *

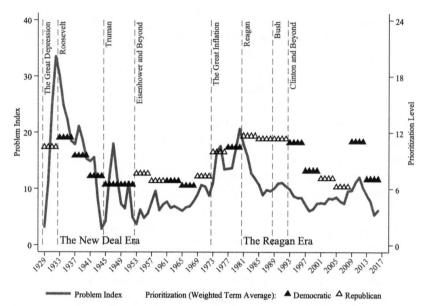

Figure 3.3   Historical Variation in Public-Finance Problems and Prioritization
Sources: Lebergott, "Annual Estimates of Unemployment in the United States." US Bureau of Labor Statistics, Series ID LNS14000000. US Bureau of Labor Statistics, Historical Consumer Price Index for All Urban Consumers (CPI-U). ProQuest Historical Newspapers database. ProQuest Newspapers database. Data accessed in 2017.

For part three, figure 3.3 shows the public-finance problem index and the average prioritization level together in order to review three key findings from the preceding examination of both components.

First, the Great Depression was an exceptionally severe and highly prioritized problem that peaked in severity in 1932, the year Franklin Roosevelt was elected president, and it remained exceptionally severe and peaked in prioritization during the first term of the Roosevelt administration, all of which weakened the average restrictions on presidential control and strengthened the average incentive to maximize control.

Second, the Great Inflation was an exceptionally severe and highly prioritized problem that peaked in severity in 1980, the year that Ronald Reagan was elected president, and it remained exceptionally severe and peaked in prioritization during the first term of the Reagan administration, all of which weakened the average restrictions on presidential control and strengthened the average incentive to maximize control.

Third, relative to the Great Depression and the Great Inflation, the Great Recession was neither an exceptionally severe problem nor a highly prioritized problem for a sustained period, meaning the average restrictions on presidential control remained relatively strong during the Obama administration and the average incentive to maximize control remained relatively weak.

HISTORICAL VARIATION IN PUBLIC-FINANCE ADMINISTRATION

The second section of the analysis provides a quantitative overview of historical variation in public-finance administration. It includes two parts: a quantitative overview of historical variation in the relative influence of the individual administrative institutions and a quantitative overview of historical variation in the level of centralization for the public-finance apparatus as a whole.

For part one, figure 3.4 shows the relative influence of the six primary administrative institutions that comprise the public-finance apparatus:

First, the Treasury Department was created in 1789, and it is currently an executive department that "operates and maintains systems that are critical to the nation's financial infrastructure, such as the production of coin and currency, the disbursement of payments to the American public, revenue collection, and the borrowing of funds necessary to run the federal government."[6]

Second, the Federal Reserve System (Fed) was created in 1913, and it is currently an independent agency that "conducts the nation's monetary policy to promote maximum employment" and "stable prices."[7]

Third, the Office of Management and Budget (OMB) was created as the Bureau of the Budget in 1921 and renamed in 1970. The OMB is currently an agency in the Executive Office of the President (EOP) that works "to assist the President in meeting his policy, budget, management and regulatory objectives."[8]

Fourth, the Council of Economic Advisers (CEA) was created in 1946, and it is currently an agency in the EOP "charged with offering the President objective economic advice on the formulation of both domestic and international economic policy."[9]

Fifth, the Congressional Budget Office (CBO) was created in 1974, and it is currently a legislative agency that produces "independent analyses of budgetary and economic issues to support the Congressional budget process."[10]

Sixth, the National Economic Council (NEC) was created in 1993, and it is currently an agency in the EOP that works "to coordinate economic policy advice for the President, to ensure that policy decisions and programs are consistent with the President's economic goals, and to monitor implementation of the President's economic policy agenda."[11]

Recall that by "public-finance apparatus," I mean, as Alexander Hamilton discussed in *The Federalist*, the administrative institutions—or "system of administration"—primarily responsible for the "preparatory plans of finance" and implementation. Moreover, since at least the Great Depression, the public-finance apparatus has expanded to include administrative institutions overseeing the use of public finance to manage the economy. Also important, although Hamilton reasoned that the principals "to whose immediate management these different matters are committed ought to be considered as the assistants or deputies of the Chief Magistrate, and on this account they ought to derive their offices from his appointment" and "be subject to his superintendence," that has not always been the case.[12] In particular, the public-finance apparatus during the early period included the independent Bank of the United States—which Hamilton himself took the lead in creating—and the public-finance apparatus currently includes several types of agencies that operate with varying degrees of independence from the president.

The relative annual influence of the six primary administrative institutions is measured here as the percentage of articles per year in the *New York Times* referencing each institution within the universe of articles per year in the *Times* referencing any one or more of the institutions comprising the public-finance apparatus.

Measuring the influence of administrative institutions precisely is undoubtedly difficult, but there is reason to believe that the use of the *Times* is reasonably effective here because the primary objective is to capture the variation in two key dynamics: the importance of fiscal policymaking relative to monetary policymaking, and the relative influence of the individual administrative institutions within these subdomains. Consider two examples. First, if the *Times* begins to report more on the Fed compared to the other public finance institutions, this suggests that the role of monetary policy within the domain of public finance has increased relative to the role of fiscal policy. Second, if the *Times* begins to report more on the CBO compared to the OMB and the CEA, this suggests that the role of the CBO within the subdomain of fiscal policy has increased relative to the other institutions. Put together, these shifts in reporting provide an important measure of historical variation in the public-finance apparatus that both assists and constrains the president.

To be sure, it is possible for an institution to exercise substantial influence behind the scenes in individual cases that the *Times* fails to report. However, the purpose of this measure is to identify substantial and durable shifts in the policymaking process, and the *Times* is likely to increase its coverage of any institution that continually exercises substantial influence in the relatively well-documented domain of public finance.[13]

For part two, figure 3.5 shows the level of centralization for the public fi-

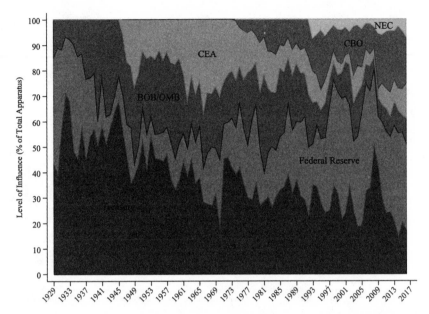

Figure 3.4   Historical Variation in Public-Finance Administration: Level of Influence
Sources: Search results are from the *New York Times* through the ProQuest Historical Newspapers database for the years 1929–2008 and the ProQuest Newspapers database for the years 2009–2016. Search results are based on the title and last name of the principals for the Treasury and the Federal Reserve—the two largest institutions and best-known principals—and only the name of the institution for the other four institutions. Data accessed in 2017.

nance apparatus as a whole along a four-point continuum based on the different types of institutions that currently comprise the apparatus: (1) congressional agencies; (2) independent agencies; (3) executive departments; and (4) agencies in the Executive Office of the President. By "level of centralization," I mean the average degree to which the public-finance apparatus as a whole operates under the president's legal control. The level of centralization is measured here by multiplying each institution's centralization score (ranging from one to four) and its annual level of influence (ranging from 0 to 100 percent) and then totaling the calculation for all six institutions. This approach builds upon Andrew Rudalevige's prominent work in *Managing the President's Program*.[14]

The centralization scoring is based as follows: (1) The CBO is scored as the least centralized administrative institution because the bureaucracy is removed from the president's supervision, and the president has no legal power to appoint or remove the director. (2) The Fed is scored as the second least centralized administrative institution because the bureaucracy is removed from the president's supervision, and although the president has the legal power to

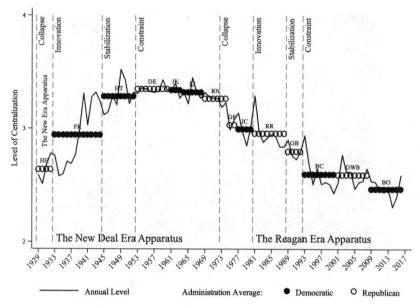

Figure 3.5   Historical Variation in Public-Finance Administration: Level of Centralization

Sources: ProQuest Historical Newspapers database and ProQuest Newspapers database. Annual level of centralization is measured by multiplying each institution's centralization score (ranging from one to four) and its annual level of influence, then totaling the calculation for all six institutions. Data accessed in 2017.

appoint the chair and other members of the Board, he has no legal power to remove them. (3) The Treasury is scored as the second most centralized administrative institution because much of the bureaucracy operates under the president's supervision, but some parts of it are removed from the president's control. For example, the president has the legal power to appoint and remove the Treasury secretary, but the president only has the legal power to appoint—not remove—the head of the independent Office of the Comptroller of the Currency within the Treasury. (4) The OMB, CEA, and NEC are all scored as the most centralized administrative institutions because these relatively small bureaucracies operate under the president's supervision, and the president has the legal power to appoint and remove the top principals.[15]

While the centralization framework is useful for identifying variation in the president's legal control over the public-finance apparatus as a whole, this is only one of two functions that it serves. The other function is that it shows whether the president governed with the support of the established public-finance apparatus or whether he oversaw the restructuring of the established apparatus, adding to the analysis the issue of variation in the president's actual control. This is equally important because—as theorized in the preceding chapter—administrative institutions structure decision-making and narrow the choice of policy alternatives by design, meaning that they simultaneously assist and constrain the president. Moreover, although the least centralized institutions are generally the most effective at limiting presidential control, highly centralized institutions often limit presidential control in practice due to a combination of key restrictions and incentives that prevent each incumbent from routinely restructuring established administrative arrangements in order to implement preferred policies.

Looking now at the historical variation in both figures—the influence of the individual institutions and the level of centralization for the public-finance apparatus as a whole—a visual examination reveals that public-finance administration has changed in substantial and durable ways since the late 1920s. For example, Dwight Eisenhower governed with the assistance of a relatively centralized public-finance apparatus that included among its various components a relatively influential BOB and CEA. In contrast, Bill Clinton governed with the assistance of a relatively decentralized public-finance apparatus that included among its various components a relatively influential Fed and CBO. To address the historical variation in public finance administration more systematically, I divide the modern period into two eras: the New Deal era and the Reagan era.

Consider the New Deal era, which—in line with the four-stage, problem- and prioritization-driven variation in the key restrictions and incentives reviewed in the previous section—unfolded in four key administrative stages: collapse, innovation, stabilization, and constraint.

Collapse: Due largely to party continuity and the initial limited severity and limited prioritization of the Great Depression, which only began to weaken the average restrictions on presidential control and only began to strengthen the average incentive to maximize control, especially when he first assumed office and set the course for his administration, Herbert Hoover relied upon the established, gradually failing New Era apparatus, which allowed him to strengthen his control to a degree but, for the most part, limited his control.

Innovation: Due largely to the full impact of the Great Depression, an exceptionally severe and highly prioritized problem that weakened the average restrictions on presidential control and strengthened the average incentive to maximize control, Franklin Roosevelt significantly strengthened his control in working to create the centralized New Deal–era apparatus. In particular, the restructuring of the public-finance apparatus was substantial in that it shifted from relatively decentralized to relatively centralized over the course of the Roosevelt administration; and it was durable in that the restructured apparatus remained relatively centralized until 1979, the first year that the level of central-ization fell below the average for the Roosevelt administration, which operated as the New Deal–era's administrative floor.

Stabilization: Due largely to party continuity and a decreasingly severe and decreasingly prioritized problem, all of which began to strengthen the average restrictions on presidential control and began to weaken the average incentive to maximize control, Harry Truman relinquished much of his control to Frank-lin Roosevelt in working to secure the New Deal–era apparatus.

Constraint: Due largely to the absence of an exceptionally severe and highly prioritized problem that strengthened the average restrictions on presidential control and weakened the average incentive to maximize control, Dwight Ei-senhower, John Kennedy, Lyndon Johnson, and (during his first term) Richard Nixon all governed with the support of the established, relatively stable New Deal–era apparatus, which significantly limited their control. This conditional control was especially pronounced when the president opposed the established policy parameters.

Next, consider the Reagan era, which—in line with the four-stage, prob-lem- and prioritization-driven variation in the key restrictions and incentives reviewed in the previous section—also unfolded in four key administrative stages: collapse, innovation, stabilization, and constraint.

Collapse: Due largely to the initial limited severity and prioritization of the Great Inflation, which only began to weaken the average restrictions on pres-idential control and only began to strengthen the average incentive to maxi-mize control, Richard Nixon (during his second term), Gerald Ford, and Jimmy Carter all relied upon the established, gradually failing New Deal–era appara-tus, which allowed them to strengthen their control to a degree but, for the most part, limited their control.

Innovation: Due largely to the full impact of the Great Inflation, an ex-ceptionally severe and highly prioritized problem that weakened the average restrictions on presidential control and strengthened the average incentive to maximize control, Ronald Reagan significantly strengthened his control in working to create the decentralized Reagan-era apparatus. In particular, the restructuring of the public-finance apparatus was substantial in that it shifted from relatively centralized to relatively decentralized over the course of the Reagan administration; and it was durable in that, after three decades, the re-structured apparatus has not exceeded the average level of centralization for the Reagan administration, which has operated as the Reagan era's administrative ceiling. To be clear, the level of centralization first fell below the New Deal–era floor in 1979, but the apparatus quickly become relatively centralized once again in 1980 and 1981, meaning that the New Deal–era apparatus was not restructured until the Reagan administration.

Stabilization: Due largely to party continuity and the decreasingly severe and decreasingly prioritized problem, both of which began to strengthen the average restrictions on presidential control and began to weaken the average incentive to maximize control, George H. W. Bush relinquished much of his control to Ronald Reagan in working to secure the Reagan-era apparatus.

Constraint: Due largely to the absence of an exceptionally severe and highly prioritized problem that strengthened the average restrictions on presidential control and weakened the average incentive to maximize control, Bill Clinton, George W. Bush, and Barack Obama all governed with the support of the established, relatively stable Reagan-era apparatus, which significantly limited their control. This conditional control was especially pronounced when the president opposed the established policy parameters.

HISTORICAL VARIATION IN PUBLIC-FINANCE POLICY

The third section of the analysis provides a quantitative overview of historical variation in public-finance policy. It includes two parts: a quantitative overview of historical variation in fiscal policy and a quantitative overview of historical variation in monetary policy.

As defined here, public-finance policy incorporates two components: fiscal policy, which is the use of government spending and taxes to manage the economy; and monetary policy, which is the use of interest rates and the money supply to manage the economy.

An expansionary (or stimulative) fiscal policy includes an increase in spending, a decrease in taxes, or some combination of the two, and it works to boost the economy, especially during a recession. Conversely, a contractionary fiscal policy includes a decrease in spending, an increase in taxes, or some combination of the two, and it works to slow the economy.

An expansionary (or stimulative) monetary policy includes a decrease in interest rates, an increase in the money supply, or some combination of the two, and it works to boost the economy, especially during a recession. Conversely, a contractionary monetary policy includes an increase in interest rates, a decrease in the money supply, or some combination of the two, and it works to slow the economy.

The relationship between the government's two primary economic stabilization instruments is also important. As the Congressional Research Service explains,

Using monetary and fiscal policy to stabilize the economy are not mutually exclusive policy options. But because of the Fed's independence from Congress and the [president], the two policy options are not always coordinated. If Congress and the Fed were to choose compatible fiscal and monetary policies, respectively, then the economic effects would be more powerful than if either policy were implemented in isolation. For example, if stimulative monetary and fiscal policies were implemented, the resulting economic stimulus would be larger than if one policy were stimulative and the other were neutral. Alternatively, if Congress and the Fed were to select incompatible policies, these policies could partially negate each other. For example, a stimulative fiscal policy and contractionary monetary policy may end up having little net effect on aggregate demand (although there may be considerable distributional effects). Thus, when fiscal and monetary policymakers disagree in the current system, they can potentially choose policies with the intent of offsetting each other's actions. Whether this arrangement is better or worse for the economy depends on what policies are chosen. If one actor chooses inappropriate policies, then the lack of coordination allows the other actor to try to negate its effects.[16]

In addition to considering the use of fiscal policy and monetary policy as economic stabilization instruments, this section examines several of the most important and contested components of fiscal policy and monetary policy in order to identify the most substantial and durable shifts in public-finance policy—or, to quote Harold Laswell, in "who gets what, when, how."[17]

For part one, figure 3.6 provides a quantitative overview of five key components of fiscal policy, some of which contain multiple subcomponents. The overview is divided into two eras: the New Deal era and the Reagan era.

For the New Deal era, the examination of each key component proceeds in three parts corresponding to the key administrative stages following the collapse of the policy domain during the Hoover administration: (1) the restructuring of the fiscal-policy parameters during the Roosevelt administration; (2) the securing of the newly established fiscal-policy parameters during the Truman administration; and (3) the continuation of the established fiscal-policy parameters during the Eisenhower administration and beyond.

Likewise, for the Reagan era, the examination of each component proceeds in three parts corresponding to the key administrative stages following the collapse of the policy domain during the Nixon, Ford, and Carter administrations: (1) the restructuring of the fiscal-policy parameters during the Reagan administration; (2) the securing of the newly established fiscal-policy parameters during the Bush administration; and (3) the continuation of the established fiscal-policy parameters during the Clinton administration and beyond.

The following is an overview of the five key fiscal policy components during the New Deal era and the Reagan era:

The first key component is the size and balance of the budget, and it includes two subcomponents—the first is the size of the budget, measured here as the average of spending and taxes as a percentage of gross domestic product (GDP), which is a measure of the total size of the US economy; the second subcomponent is the debt, which represents the accumulation of government borrowing based primarily on budget deficits (the amount by which spending exceeds taxes) and budget surpluses (the amount by which taxes exceed spending), and it is measured here as the public debt as a percentage of GDP. The size and balance of the budget provide the broadest overview of the government's fiscal responsibilities and its use of fiscal policy to manage the economy.

The New Deal–era parameters: (1.1) The budget began to increase steadily during the Roosevelt administration, climbing from 4.8 percent of GDP in 1932, the last year of the Hoover administration, to a prewar high of 8.6 percent in 1939, and the debt increased substantially in relation to the size of the economy to large annual deficits. (1.2) The budget increased considerably during the Truman administration due to the Second World War and the Korean War, but unlike the Great Depression-induced growth, both of the wartime surges were followed by sharp contractions, resulting in peacetime budgets of between 13 and 15 percent of GDP. Moreover, the debt began to decrease in relation to the size of the economy due to a mix of small annual deficits and surpluses. (1.3) The budget continued to grow during the Eisenhower administration and beyond, never again falling below 15 percent of GDP, and the debt continued to decrease in relation to the size of the economy on average due to a mix of small annual deficits and surpluses.

The Reagan-era parameters: (1.1) After reaching peacetime highs of 20.4 percent of GDP in 1981 and 20.6 percent in 1982, the budget stopped growing during the Reagan administration and fell to 19.1 percent in 1988. Moreover, the debt increased substantially in relation to the size of the economy due to large annual deficits. (1.2) The budget maintained its new trajectory during the Bush administration, staying below 20 percent of GDP, and the debt continued to increase in relation to the size of the economy due to large annual deficits. (1.3) The budget never again exceeded 20 percent of GDP during the Clinton administration and beyond, and the debt continued to increase on average in relation to the size of the economy due to large annual deficits.

The second key component, which includes multiple subcomponents, is tax revenue sources, measured here as the percentage composition of total tax revenue by source. At the broadest level there are two types of taxes. Progressive taxes (such as the individual income tax, the corporate income tax, and the

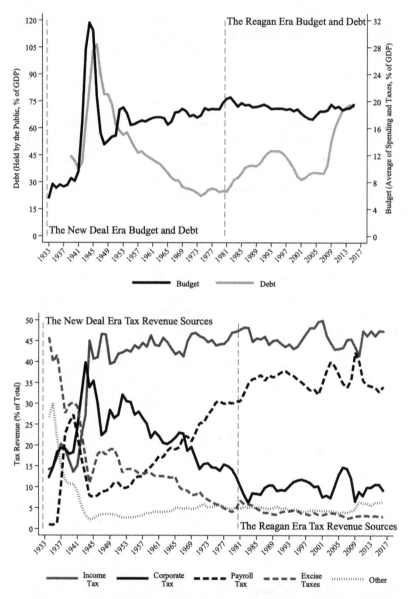

Figure 3.6 Historical Variation in Public-Finance Policy: Key Fiscal-Policy Parameters
Sources: Budget data from the Office of Management and Budget (OMB) Historical Tables, Table
1.2. Debt data from Federal Reserve Economic Data (FRED), Series ID FYPUGDA188S. Tax revenue sources data from the OMB Historical Tables, Table 2.2. Top individual and corporate income
tax rates data from the Tax Policy Center, "Historical Individual Income Tax Parameters" and "Corporate Top Tax Rate and Bracket." Top estate tax rate data from the US Internal Revenue Service,
"The Estate Tax: Ninety Years and Counting." Statutory spending restrictions data from Megan S.

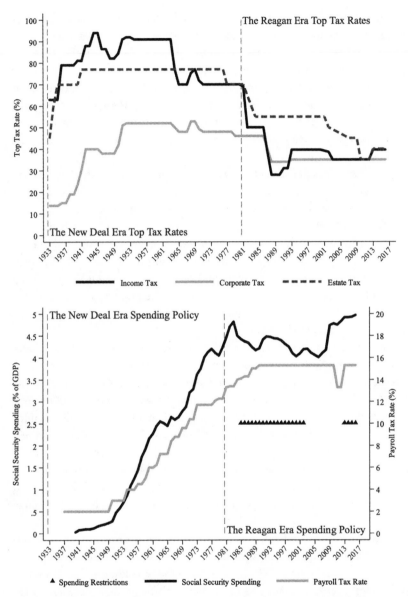

Lynch, "Statutory Budget Controls in Effect Between 1985 and 2002," Congressional Research Service R41901 (2011), https://fas.org/sgp/crs/misc/R41901.pdf; Grant A. Driessen and Megan S. Lynch, "The Budget Control Act: Frequently Asked Questions," Congressional Research Service R44874 (2018), https://fas.org/sgp/crs/misc/R44874.pdf. Social Security spending data from the OMB Historical Tables, Table 3.1. Payroll tax rate data from the Tax Policy Center, "Payroll Tax Rates." Data accessed in 2017 and 2018.

estate tax) tend to reduce income and/or wealth inequality because the effective tax rate—the total amount of taxes paid as a percentage of taxable income and/or wealth—increases as income and/or wealth levels increase. In contrast, regressive taxes (such as tariffs, excise taxes, and payroll taxes) tend to increase income and/or wealth inequality because the effective tax rate decreases as income and/or wealth levels increase. By highlighting the type of taxes used to fund spending, this key component of fiscal policy provides a broad overview of the government's commitment to combating or supporting economic inequality.[18]

The New Deal–era parameters: (2.1) The progressive individual income tax and the progressive corporate income tax became the two highest tax revenue sources during the Roosevelt administration, replacing regressive excise taxes and other taxes, which included regressive tariffs. (2.2) The progressive individual income tax and the progressive corporate income tax remained the two highest tax revenue sources during the Truman administration. (2.3) The progressive individual income tax remained the highest tax revenue source during the Eisenhower administration and beyond, and the progressive corporate income tax remained the second highest tax revenue source on average, but its total share continued to decrease.

The Reagan-era parameters: (2.1) The progressive individual income tax remained the highest tax revenue source during the Reagan administration. Moreover, after becoming the second highest tax revenue source during the late 1960s, the regressive payroll tax remained the second highest tax revenue source during the Reagan administration. (2.2) The progressive individual income tax remained the highest tax revenue source during the Bush administration, and the regressive payroll tax remained steady as the second highest tax revenue source. (2.3) The progressive individual income tax remained the highest tax revenue source during the Clinton administration and beyond, and the regressive payroll tax remained steady as the second highest tax revenue source.

The third key component, which includes multiple subcomponents, is top tax rates, measured here as the top individual income tax rate, the top corporate income tax rate, and the top estate tax rate. At the broadest level there are two primary approaches to managing the economy through the adjustment of tax rates. Demand-side economics maintains that a strong economy is most effectively supported through high levels of government and consumer spending that leads to business expansion. From this perspective it is effective to maintain high tax rates on the wealthy in order both to fund government spending and to combat income and wealth inequality and thereby increase broad-based consumer spending. In contrast, supply-side economics maintains that a strong economy is most effectively supported through lowering taxes, especially the top tax rates on the wealthy, in order to boost savings and investment and thereby increase the productive capacity of the economy. Although the political debate over the effectiveness of the two approaches continues, it is notable that a study of the individual income tax by the nonpartisan Congressional Research Service found little support for supply-side economics, explaining that a "reduction in the top tax rates has had little association with saving, investment, or productivity growth. It is reasonable to assume that a tax rate change limited to a small group of taxpayers at the top of the income distribution would have a negligible effect on economic growth."[19] A subsequent CRS study on the effect of cutting the top corporate income tax rate also found little support for supply-side economics, explaining, "On the whole, the growth effects tend to show a relatively small (if any) first-year effect on the economy" and "tend to rule out very large effects in the near term."[20] Along with the analysis of tax revenue sources, this analysis of top tax rates provides an overview of the government's commitment to combating or supporting economic inequality by identifying the statutory tax rates in place for the wealthiest taxpayers.

The New Deal–era parameters: (3.1) The top individual income tax rate, the top corporate income tax rate, and the top estate tax rate all increased during the Roosevelt administration. (3.2) The top individual income tax rate, the top corporate income tax rate, and the top estate tax rate all remained relatively high during the Truman administration. (3.3) The top individual income tax rate, the top corporate income tax rate, and the top estate tax rate all remained relatively high during the Eisenhower administration and beyond. In particular, the top individual income tax rate remained at 70 percent or higher, the top corporate income tax rate remained at 46 percent or higher, and the top estate tax rate remained at 70 percent or higher.

The Reagan-era parameters: (3.1) The top individual income tax rate, the top corporate income tax rate, and the top estate tax rate all decreased during the Reagan administration. (3.2) The top individual income tax rate, the top corporate income tax rate, and the top estate tax rate all remained relatively low during the Bush administration. (3.3) The top individual income tax rate, the top corporate income tax rate, and the top estate tax rate all remained relatively low during the Clinton administration and beyond. In particular, the top individual income tax rate remained below 40 percent, the top corporate income tax rate remained at or below 35 percent, and the top estate tax rate remained at or below 55 percent.

The fourth key component is statutory spending restrictions, measured here simply as the use or absence of such restrictions. As the Congressional Research Service explains, beginning in 1985, "several statutory budget controls were enacted to reduce the budget deficit. . . . The mechanisms included in these acts sought to supplement and modify the existing budget process, and also added statutory budget controls, in some cases seeking to require future deficit reduction." Addressing the means of deficit reduction, the CRS further explains that some of these laws "set forth a specific process for the cancellation of spending by executive order, known as a sequester order. . . . In the event of sequestration, the funding reduction necessary to achieve the specified target was to be equally divided between defense and non-defense spending."[21] This key component of fiscal policymaking provides an overview of the government's flexibility to increase spending and, relatedly, its ability to use fiscal policy to manage the economy.

The New Deal–era parameters: (4.1) Statutory spending restrictions were not used during the Roosevelt administration. (4.2) Statutory spending restrictions were not used during the Truman administration. (4.3) Statutory spending restrictions were not used during the Eisenhower administration and beyond.

The Reagan-era parameters: (4.1) Statutory spending restrictions were used during the Reagan administration. (4.2) Statutory spending restrictions were used during the Bush administration. (4.3) Statutory spending restrictions were often used during the Clinton administration and beyond.

The fifth key component is Social Security spending, which is the welfare system's foundational progressive spending program and is measured here as a percentage of GDP. The analysis here also includes the rate for the payroll tax, which was created to fund Social Security and later provided funding for other social insurance programs. Although the payroll tax, as noted, is regressive, Social Security has a progressive benefit distribution. As the nonpartisan Congressional Budget Office explains, "Social Security can have a significant effect on the economic well-being of workers and their families. One key to understanding that effect . . . is to measure how Social Security benefits and the burden of the Social Security payroll tax are distributed among different groups of participants." The CBO adds, "For people with lower than average earnings, the ratio of the lifetime benefits they receive from Social Security to the lifetime payroll taxes they pay for the program is higher than it is for people with higher average earnings. In that sense, the Social Security system is progressive."[22] Along with the analysis of tax revenue sources and top tax rates, this key component of fiscal policy provides a further overview of the government's commitment to combating economic inequality.

The New Deal–era parameters: (5.1) A 2 percent payroll tax was created during the Roosevelt administration to fund the new Social Security program. (5.2) The payroll tax rate increased to 3 percent during the Truman administration, and Social Security spending increased from 0.2 percent of GDP to

0.7 percent, making it one of the largest government programs. (5.3) The payroll tax rate continued to increase during the Eisenhower administration and beyond, and Social Security spending continued to increase, making it the largest nondefense program by the end of the 1950s.

The Reagan-era parameters: (5.1) The Social Security Act Amendments of 1983 during the Reagan administration raised the total payroll tax rate to 15.3 percent, which went into effect in 1990, and the law also included the first significant reductions for beneficiaries in the history of the program. Accordingly, Social Security spending stopped increasing after reaching nearly 5 percent of GDP in 1983. (5.2) The earlier payroll tax rate increase went into effect during the Bush administration, and Social Security spending remained below 5 percent of GDP. (5.3) The payroll tax rate remained at 15.3 percent during the Clinton administration and beyond, with the exception of a temporary reduction during the Obama administration, and Social Security spending remained below 5 percent of GDP.

Putting together the individual components in this section—and building upon the analysis in the preceding sections—the quantitative overview provides evidence that Franklin Roosevelt and Harry Truman worked to create and secure, respectively, both the centralized New Deal–era apparatus in response to the Great Depression (and, in some cases, the Second World War) and the New Deal–era fiscal-policy parameters. In particular, Roosevelt and Truman worked to create and secure the following: (1) *A growing and structurally balanced budget that generally operated as the primary economic stabilization instrument.* The evidence here includes the consistent growth in the average size of the budget (spending and taxes) and the decreasing size of the debt due to relatively small deficits and surpluses. (2) *A highly progressive tax system.* The evidence here includes the rise of the progressive individual income tax and the progressive corporate income tax as the two largest tax revenue sources, the decline of other taxes (including the regressive tariff) as a major tax revenue source, and the rise of the top tax rates for the individual income tax, the corporate income tax, and the estate tax. (3) *An unrestricted general spending system and growing Social Security spending.* The evidence here includes the absence of statutory spending restrictions and the consistent growth in Social Security spending.

The quantitative overview also provides evidence that Ronald Reagan and George H. W. Bush worked to create and secure, respectively, both the decentralized Reagan-era apparatus in response to the Great Inflation and the Reagan-era fiscal-policy parameters. In particular, Reagan and Bush worked to create and secure the following: (1) *A steady and structurally unbalanced budget that generally operated as a secondary economic stabilization instrument.* The evidence here includes the end of the growth in the average size of the budget (spending and taxes) and the increasing debt due to relatively large deficits. (2) *A supply-side (or less progressive) tax system.* The evidence here includes the relatively low top tax rates for the individual income tax, the corporate income tax, and the estate tax. (3) *A restricted general spending system and steady Social Security spending.* The evidence here includes the use of statutory spending restrictions and the end of the growth in Social Security spending.

To further demonstrate the differences between the New Deal–era approach and the Reagan-era approach to fiscal policy, especially in managing the economy, figure 3.7 shows two key economic distribution variables: the income share for the top 1 percent of taxpayers and the wealth share for the top 0.1 percent of taxpayers. This analysis provides evidence that the New Deal–era public-finance apparatus and policy parameters worked to create and maintain a more equitable distribution of income and wealth. The income share for the top 1 percent of taxpayers fell from 16.1 percent in 1933 (the first year of the Roosevelt administration) to 10.1 percent in 1952 (the last full year of the Truman administration), and it stood at 8.9 percent in 1981 (the first year of the Reagan administration). Likewise, the wealth share for the top 0.1 percent of taxpayers fell from 18.2 percent in 1933 to 9.1 percent in 1952, and it stood at 8.3 percent in 1981.

This analysis also provides evidence that the Reagan-era public-finance apparatus and policy parameters worked to create and maintain rising income and wealth inequality. The income share for the top 1 percent of taxpayers increased from 8.9 percent in 1981 (the first year of the Reagan administration) to 14.2 percent in 1992 (the last full year of the George H. W. Bush administration), and it then increased to 19.3 percent by 2016 (the last full year of the Obama administration). Likewise, the wealth share for the top 0.1 percent of taxpayers increased from 8.3 percent in 1981 to 11.9 percent in 1992, and it then increased to 20 percent by 2016.

Although the exact estimates and time frame vary depending on the data used, the federal government's own leading analyses of economic inequality show a similar dynamic. The CBO provides the leading analysis of income inequality and finds that "income inequality was greater in 2016 than it was in 1979," the full time frame of the analysis.[23] The Fed provides the leading analysis of wealth inequality and finds that the share of "wealth held by affluent families [has] reached historically high levels," whereas "the wealth share of the bottom 90 percent of families has been falling over most of the past 25 years," the full time frame of the analysis.[24]

To be sure, fiscal policy is not the only thing that affects income and wealth inequality, but it is one of the most important public-policy instruments. Most obviously, a high top individual income tax rate can reduce post-tax income

Figure 3.7   Historical Variation in the Distribution of Income and Wealth
Sources: Top 1 percent (including capital gains) income share data from Thomas Piketty and Em-manuel Saez, "Income Inequality in the United States, 1913–1998," *Quarterly Journal of Economics* no. 1 (2003): 1–39, updated to 2018. Top 0.1 percent (tax units) wealth share data from Gabriel Zucman, "Global Wealth Inequality," *Annual Review of Economics* (2019):109–138. Data accessed in 2020.

inequality through the tax and transfer process. Less obvious but no less im-portant, a high top individual income tax rate can also reduce pretax income inequality by limiting the return to bargaining for a higher share of income. As the CRS explains, research shows that "pre-tax incomes tend to be more equally distributed and labor's share of income larger when the top tax rates are higher." This is because in the past "high top tax rates were part of the institutional structure that restrained top income[s] by reducing gains from bargaining or rent extraction by CEOs and managers. For example, a CEO has less incentive to bargain hard over additional compensation when he keeps 9 cents of every additional dollar (a 91 percent top tax rate) than when he keeps 65 cents of every additional dollar (a 35 percent top tax rate)."[25]

* * *

For part two, figure 3.8 provides a quantitative overview of four key components of monetary policy. The overview is divided into two eras: the New Deal era and the Reagan era.

For the New Deal era, the examination of each key component proceeds in three parts corresponding to the key administrative stages following the collapse of the policy domain during the Hoover administration: (1) the restructuring of the monetary policy parameters during the Roosevelt administration; (2) the securing of the newly established monetary policy parameters during the Truman administration; and (3) the continuation of the established monetary policy parameters during the Eisenhower administration and beyond.

Likewise, for the Reagan era, the examination of each component proceeds in three parts corresponding to the key administrative stages following the collapse of the policy domain during the Nixon, Ford, and Carter administrations: (1) the restructuring of the monetary policy parameters during the Reagan administration; (2) the securing of the newly established monetary policy parameters during the Bush administration; and (3) the continuation of the established monetary policy parameters during the Clinton administration and beyond.

The following is an overview of the four key monetary policy components during the New Deal era and the Reagan era:

The first key component is money supply growth, measured as the quarterly growth rate of M1 currency, which is the currency in circulation outside the Treasury and the Federal Reserve. As the Congressional Research Service explains, "In conducting monetary policy, the Fed has a choice of a target. Since money spending involves money, it could buy and sell U.S. Treasury securities with the objective of targeting the growth of the money supply. Alternatively, since changes in money and credit affect spending largely through changes in interest rates, it could target one or more of those rates directly simply by supplying whatever reserves are needed to meet its target." Addressing the importance of the money supply target at times, the CRS adds, "As inflation during the 1970s accelerated into double digits, the Federal Reserve . . . announced in October 1979 new operating procedures emphasizing the growth of nonborrowed reserves as a means for controlling the growth of M1."[26] Also important, the CRS explains that "changes in inflation expectations can . . . cause changes in actual inflation."[27] Applied to the money supply, this means, for example, that if the growth rate continuously increases on average, the expectation that that process will continue can cause an increase in inflation. Conversely, if the growth rate of the money supply remains steady on average, even if at a relatively high level, the expectation that the growth rate will remain steady can cause a decrease in inflation.

The New Deal–era parameters: (1.1) After averaging -0.2 percent during the 1920s, the growth rate of the money supply became highly unstable and increased substantially during the Roosevelt administration. (1.2) The average growth rate of the money supply remained positive during the Truman administration rather than—as occurred following the First World War—turning negative for an extended period in order to reverse the rise in inflation during the Second World War. (1.3) The average growth rate of the money supply remained positive during the Eisenhower administration rather than turning negative for an extended period in order to reverse the rise in inflation during the Korean War, and the money supply growth rate continuously increased after the Eisenhower administration.

The Reagan-era parameters: (1.1) After remaining positive and continuously increasing for decades, the average growth rate of the money supply decreased and stabilized during the Reagan administration. (1.2) The average growth rate of the money supply remained steady during the Bush administration. (1.3) The average growth rate of the money supply generally remained steady during the Clinton administration and beyond.

The second key component is interest rates, measured here as the discount rate for the Federal Reserve Bank of New York. As the Fed explains, "The discount rate is the interest rate charged to commercial banks and other depository institutions on loans they receive from their regional Federal Reserve Bank's lending facility—the discount window." This "lending to depository institutions . . . plays an important role in supporting the liquidity and stability of the banking system and the effective implementation of monetary policy."[28] To be clear, the Fed has targeted different short- and long-term interest rates throughout its history, including the federal funds rate, which is the rate that depository institutions charge each other for overnight loans of funds. However, unlike the federal funds rates, which closely tracks the discount rate and has operated as the Fed's primary short-term interest rate target for several decades, the discount rate is the Fed's founding interest rate instrument and one that it controls directly.

The New Deal–era parameters: (2.1) The average level of the discount rate declined during the Roosevelt administration, the use of the discount rate declined substantially, and the average size of the relatively infrequent rate changes was small. (2.2) The average level of the discount rate began to increase during the Truman administration, the use of the discount rate remained limited, and the average size of the relatively infrequent rate changes remained small. (2.3) The average level of the discount rate increased during the Eisenhower administration and beyond; the use of the discount rate remained relatively limited on average, especially before the 1970s; and the average size of the relatively infrequent rate changes generally remained small, especially before the 1970s.

The Reagan-era parameters: (2.1) The discount rate reached its highest level in history during the first year of the Reagan administration, the use of the discount rate remained relatively great after increasing during the 1970s, and the

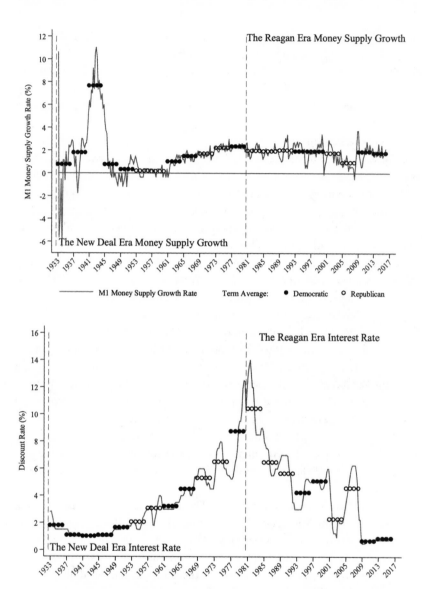

Figure 3.8   Historical Variation in Public-Finance Policy: Key Monetary-Policy Parameters

Sources: Money supply growth rate data for 1933–1946 from Federal Reserve Economic Data (FRED), Series ID M1425AUSM144SNBR, quarterly. Data for 1947–2016 from FRED, Series ID CURRSL, quarterly. Interest rate data for 1933–1968 from FRED, Series ID M13009USM156NNBR, quarterly. Data for 1969–2016 from FRED, Series ID INTDSRUSM193N, quarterly. Gold anchor data for 1933–1983 from the Board of Governors of the Federal Reserve System, 101st Annual Report

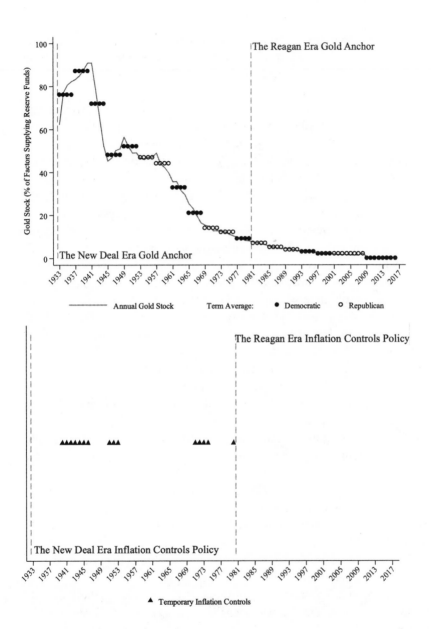

The Reagan Era Gold Anchor

The New Deal Era Gold Anchor

Annual Gold Stock   Term Average: ● Democratic   ○ Republican

The Reagan Era Inflation Controls Policy

The New Deal Era Inflation Controls Policy

▲ Temporary Inflation Controls

(2014), 296–297. Data for 1984–2016 from 105th Annual Report (2018), 298. Temporary inflation controls data from Hugh Rockoff, *Drastic Measures: A History of Wage and Price Controls in the United States* (New York: Cambridge University Press, 1984) and Allan H. Meltzer, *A History of the Federal Reserve, Volume 2, Book 2, 1970–1986* (Chicago: University of Chicago Press, 2009), 1049–1056. Data accessed in 2017 and 2018.

average size of the rate changes remained relatively great after increasing during the 1970s. (2.2) The average level of the discount rate declined during the Bush administration, the use of the discount rate remained relatively great, and the average size of the rate changes remained relatively great. (2.3) The average level of the discount rate generally decreased during the Clinton administration and beyond, the use of the discount rate remained relatively great on average, and the average size of the rate changes generally remained relatively great.

The third key component is the gold anchor, measured as the percentage of gold comprising the Fed's balance sheet, which is calculated here as securities held outright plus the gold stock. Providing a historical overview of this component, the CRS explains, "The current U.S. monetary system is based on the use of paper money that is backed only by the 'full faith and credit' of the federal government. . . . This has not always been the case. Over most of its history the U.S. has been on some type of metallic standard," which anchored monetary policy by controlling the amount of paper currency that could be issued. Specifically, in 1879, a "true gold standard emerged" that ended with the Great Depression in 1933. What emerged in 1934 was a "quasi-gold standard" that allowed gold convertibility of dollars only for international transactions, not domestic transactions, and therefore the "gold value of the dollar was largely meaningless." The quasi-gold standard then ended in the 1970s, and the "gold stock has not played any important role" since.[29]

The New Deal–era parameters: (3.1) After the abandonment of the true gold standard in 1933, a new quasi-gold standard became only a nominal anchor for monetary policy during the Roosevelt administration. Accordingly, after averaging 92 percent during the 1920s, the gold stock component of the Fed's balance sheet decreased to an average of 78 percent. (3.2) As the gold stock component of the Fed's balance sheet decreased to an average of 50 percent, the quasi-gold standard remained only a nominal anchor for monetary policy during the Truman administration. (3.3) As the gold stock component of the Fed's balance sheet continued to decrease, the quasi-gold standard remained only a nominal anchor for monetary policy during the Eisenhower administration and beyond.

The Reagan-era parameters: (3.1) After the abandonment of the quasi-gold standard during the 1970s, monetary policy remained entirely unanchored by gold during the Reagan administration. (3.2) Monetary policy remained entirely unanchored by gold during the Bush administration. (3.3) Monetary policy remained entirely unanchored by gold during the Clinton administration and beyond.

The fourth key component is temporary inflation controls, measured as the use of short-term, economy-wide wage, price, and/or credit controls to manage inflation. Providing the rationale for using short-term controls, a scholarly history of the subject explains, "Decreasing the rate of growth of the money supply" is "the conservative approach to monetary policy," whereas

> in the right circumstances temporary controls can make a positive contribution to the fight against inflation. This possibility exists because of the role of expectations in the inflationary process. Suppose that after a long period of expansionary monetary policy, with prices rising at ten percent per year, a new policy of slow monetary growth is adopted. Inflation would not stop instantaneously. Instead, because decision makers still expect inflation, they would continue to raise prices. Labor unions would seek contracts containing wage increases to cover the inflation they expect, and businessmen would raise their prices spurred by the fear of rising costs. . . . The result, in the short run, would probably be a severe recession. . . . [In such a situation], temporary wage and price controls could have a therapeutic effect.[30]

The New Deal–era parameters: (4.1) Temporary inflation controls were used on occasion during the Roosevelt administration, which limited the role of monetary policy. (4.2) Temporary inflation controls were used on occasion during the Truman administration, which limited the role of monetary policy. (4.3) Temporary inflation controls were used on occasion during the Eisenhower administration and beyond, which limited the role of monetary policy.

The Reagan-era parameters: (4.1) After the use of wage and price controls during the 1970s and credit controls in 1980, temporary inflation controls were not used during the Reagan administration, which strengthened the role of monetary policy. (4.2) Temporary inflation controls were not used during the Bush administration, which strengthened the role of monetary policy. (4.3) Temporary inflation controls were not used during the Clinton administration and beyond, which strengthened the role of monetary policy.

Putting together the individual components in this section—and building upon the analysis in the preceding sections—the quantitative overview provides evidence that Franklin Roosevelt and Harry Truman worked to create and secure, respectively, both the centralized New Deal–era apparatus in response to the Great Depression (and, in some cases, the Second World War) and the New Deal–era monetary policy parameters. In particular, Roosevelt and Truman worked to create and secure a *"managed currency" that generally operated as a secondary economic stabilization instrument in support of promoting "maximum employment."* The evidence here for the "managed currency" component includes the abandonment of the true gold standard and continuation of only a nominal quasi-gold standard anchor. The evidence here for the "generally operated as a secondary economic stabilization instrument" component includes the relatively infrequent, small discount rate adjustments on average and the occasional use of temporary inflation controls. The evidence here for the generally operated "in support of promoting 'maximum employment'" component includes the positive and continuously increasing average growth rate of the money supply, and—as discussed in the first section—the Employment Act and the fact that on occasion the inflation rate surpassed the unemployment rate as the government worked to lower the latter.

The quantitative overview also provides evidence that Ronald Reagan and George H. W. Bush worked to create and secure, respectively, both the decentralized Reagan-era apparatus in response to the Great Inflation and the Reagan-era monetary policy parameters. In particular, Reagan and Bush worked to create and secure a *"fine-tuned" monetary policy that generally operated as the primary economic stabilization instrument in support of promoting "price stability."* The evidence here for the "'fine-tuned' monetary policy that generally operated as the primary economic stabilization instrument" component includes the relatively frequent and large discount rate adjustments on average, the absence of even a nominal gold standard anchor, and the absence of temporary inflation controls. The evidence here for the generally operated "in support of promoting 'price stability'" component includes the initial decrease and then steadiness in the average growth rate of the money supply, the overall decline in the average discount rate, and—as discussed in the first section—the Full Employment and Balanced Growth Act and the fact that the average annual inflation rate has not exceeded the average annual unemployment rate since 1981.

To further demonstrate the differences between the New Deal–era approach and the Reagan-era approach to monetary policy, especially in managing the economy, figure 3.9 shows a key economic growth variable: the real (inflation-adjusted) growth in gross domestic product (GDP), which is the leading measure of the US economy's size. This analysis provides evidence that in primarily promoting "maximum employment," the New Deal–era public-finance apparatus and policy parameters worked to create and maintain a relatively fast-growing economy. Economic growth averaged 4.6 percent a year throughout the New Deal era (1933–1980), which included an average of 6.1 percent a year during the Roosevelt and Truman administrations (1933–1952) and 3.5 percent a year from the Eisenhower administration through the Carter administration (1953–1980).

This analysis also provides evidence that in primarily promoting "price stability," the Reagan-era public-finance apparatus and policy parameters worked to create and maintain a relatively slow-growing economy. Economic growth averaged 2.7 percent a year throughout the Reagan era (1981–2016, the last year

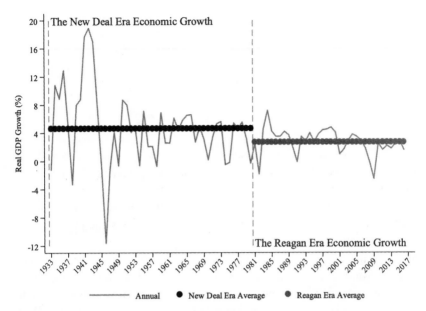

Figure 3.9   Historical Variation in Economic Growth
Source: US Bureau of Economic Analysis, gross domestic product, percent change from preceding period, annual, chained 2012 dollars. Data accessed in 2020.

of the analysis here), which included an average of 3.1 percent a year during the Reagan and Bush administrations (1981–1992) and 2.6 percent a year from the Clinton administration through the Obama administration (1993–2016). This means that the average economic growth rate during the New Deal era substantially exceeded that during the Reagan era for each comparison group.

Similar to the earlier qualifier for fiscal policy and economic inequality, monetary policy is obviously not the only thing that affects economic growth, but it is one of the most important public-policy instruments. As the CRS explains, "An examination of U.S. economic history will show that money- and credit-induced demand expansions can have a positive effect on U.S. GDP growth and total employment." Fiscal policy also affects economic growth. For example, the CRS adds that an "expansionary fiscal policy is generally used to boost GDP growth and economic indicators that tend to move with GDP, such as employment and individual incomes."[31]

Altogether, the earlier analysis of income and wealth inequality and the above analysis of economic growth provides evidence that in response to the Great Depression, the New Deal–era public-finance apparatus and policy parameters supported the creation and continuation of a relatively fast-growing economy with a relatively equitable distribution of income and wealth, whereas in response to the Great Inflation, the Reagan-era public-finance apparatus and policy parameters supported the creation and continuation of a relatively slow-growing economy with a relatively inequitable distribution of income and wealth.

CONCLUSION

As noted in the opening, this quantitative overview of historical variation in public-finance policymaking serves two primary purposes. First, it provides an initial test of the theory of historical variation in presidential control by showing that public-finance administration and policy are closely connected and change in relation to variation in public-finance problems and prioritization. Second, it provides an extensive empirical foundation for the case studies that follow. In particular, this quantitative overview provides evidence that Franklin Roosevelt and Ronald Reagan oversaw the most complete restructuring of public-finance administration and policy in response to the two most exceptionally severe and highly prioritized problems, the Great Depression and the Great Inflation, respectively. To further understand this process and the impact on subsequent presidents, the remaining parts of the book trace in detail the variation in presidential control from one incumbent to the next, beginning with the collapse of the policy domain during the Great Depression.

Part III
Historical Variation in Presidential Control during the New Deal Era

As the first case study component of the multimethod analysis, this part of the book initially traces the creation of the New Era apparatus and its collapse while assisting Herbert Hoover during the Great Depression. It then traces the variation in presidential control for the first three incumbents of the New Deal era: Franklin Roosevelt, Harry Truman, and Dwight Eisenhower. To be clear, the case studies here do not provide a comprehensive history of public-finance policymaking, which would require an examination of the key role of Congress, interest groups, and more. Rather, the primary objective is to show that presidential control over administration is a foundational component of public-finance policymaking and operates as a historical variable.

4. Collapse: The Failing New Era Apparatus Limits Hoover's Control

The quantitative overview provided evidence that in the domain of public finance, Herbert Hoover governed with the support of the decentralized New Era apparatus due largely to a combination of party continuity and the initial limited severity and prioritization of the Great Depression, which only began to weaken the average restrictions on presidential control and only began to strengthen the average incentive to maximize control, especially when he first assumed office and set the course for his administration. This chapter initially traces the creation of the decentralized New Era apparatus and then traces the process of the established, gradually failing New Era apparatus and its principals in limiting Hoover's control.

THE CREATION OF THE NEW ERA APPARATUS

Looking back on the 1920s and early 1930s, Herbert Hoover remarked, "Our reconstruction from the [First World War] had proceeded with such steady success, and the other impulses to progress were so very great that, with . . . growing optimism, they gave birth to a foolish idea called the 'New Economic Era.' That notion spread over the whole country. We were assured that we were in a new period where the old laws of economics no longer applied."[1] The administrative apparatus for this "new economic era," or what I label here the New Era apparatus, included three primary institutions: the Treasury Department, the Federal Reserve System, and the Bureau of the Budget.

First, an act passed in 1789 created the Treasury Department in order to maintain responsibility for all matters of public finance. In particular, the act instructed the Treasury secretary both "to digest and prepare plans for the improvement and management of the revenue and the support of the public credit" and "to perform all such services relative to the finances as . . . directed to perform."[2] Also notable, in practice the Treasury supported balancing the budget. As Treasury Secretary Andrew Mellon—one of the longest serving Treasury secretaries in history—explained, "Two guiding principles have dominated the financial policy of the government. One is the balancing of the budget, and the other is the payment of the public debt."[3]

Second, the Federal Reserve Act of 1913 created the Federal Reserve System in order "to furnish an elastic currency." The act also directed the new institution to operate under the guidelines of the real-bills doctrine in the short term, which would complement the gold standard, the source of currency elasticity in the long term. As the act put it, Federal Reserve Banks were to "discount notes, drafts, and bills of exchange arising out of actual commercial transactions"—or real bills—rather than "notes, drafts, or bills covering merely investments or issued or drawn for the purpose of carrying or trading in stocks, bonds, or other investment securities."[4] In practice, the real-bills doctrine meant that the Fed would increase or decrease the money supply in the short-term—or on a seasonal basis—in response to an increase or decrease respectively in commercial activity, thereby limiting discretion in monetary policymaking and in turn the potential for inflation.[5]

To carry out this self-regulating, procyclical monetary policy and to placate both the opponents and proponents of a central bank, the Federal Reserve Act divided authority between the Federal Reserve Board in Washington and twelve Federal Reserve Banks across the country. The Board consisted of two ex officio members—the secretary of the Treasury and the comptroller of the currency—and five Senate-confirmed members whom the president appointed to serve ten-year terms on a rotating basis but whom he had no power to remove. The president also appointed one member from the latter group to serve as governor.

In contrast to the politically appointed Board in Washington, the nine-member board of directors for each district's Reserve Bank consisted of three members "chosen by and . . . representative of the stock-holding banks," three members "actively engaged in their district in commerce, agriculture, or some other industrial pursuit" and also chosen by the stock-holding banks, and three members "designated by the Federal Reserve Board."[6] Each Reserve Bank's board of directors then appointed its own governor. Further complicating the matter, the act declared that the Board was authorized to exercise "general supervision" over the Reserve Banks without clarifying the parameters of that supervisory role.[7]

Third, the Budget and Accounting Act of 1921 created the Bureau of the Budget within the Treasury Department, it directed the new institution to act "with a view of securing greater economy," and it authorized the president to appoint, without Senate confirmation, a director and an assistant director.[8] The act also directed "every department and establishment" both to "furnish to the Bureau such information as the Bureau may from time to time require" and to "designate an official thereof as budget officer."[9] With unprecedented access to all existing institutions and a designated official serving as a direct link to each one, the BOB was designed to become the principal depository of information for the executive branch as a whole.[10]

In addition to the creation of the BOB, the Budget and Accounting Act expanded the responsibilities of the president. In particular, it directed the president to "transmit to Congress on the first day of each regular session" his "estimates of expenditures and appropriations necessary . . . for the support of the Government for the ensuing fiscal year."[11] In other words, rather than continue to allow each executive agency to act independently, the act created a coordinated process that made the president responsible for the oversight of all spending proposals to Congress. At the same time, the act increased the president's authority over taxation by directing him to "make recommendations to Congress for new taxes, loans, or other appropriate action" if "the estimated receipts . . . are less than the estimated expenditures for the ensuing fiscal year contained in the Budget."[12]

Although these three public-finance institutions were created separately, each one affected the others in practice. Specifically, once the Fed assumed primary responsibility for monetary policy, the Treasury's jurisdiction narrowed. However, the boundaries remained imprecise, as the Treasury secretary maintained a position on the Board. Moreover, once the BOB assumed primary responsibility for spending, the Treasury's jurisdiction narrowed further, leaving it primarily responsible for taxation. However, here too the boundaries remained imprecise, as the BOB operated within the Treasury Department, meaning that the Treasury secretary had the potential to undercut the budget director. For example, Charles Dawes, the founding budget director, acknowledged, "A small or jealous" Treasury secretary could "make the Budget Director's life miserable and his work largely ineffectual. The Budget bureau really should not be a Treasury bureau, since it operates directly under the President."[13]

Adding to the situation, although the Fed and the BOB were primarily created in response to the Panic of 1907 and the First World War, respectively, the operations of both institutions changed as new issues arose. Notably, the international gold standard was suspended in 1914 following the outbreak of war in Europe, meaning that the intended long-term guideline for monetary policy was not even in place for the first full year of the Fed's existence. The Fed also began to deviate from the real-bills doctrine—its intended short-term guideline—due to the combination of an evolving understanding of monetary policy throughout the 1920s and the unclear lines of authority between the Reserve Banks and the Board. In particular, the Board was more inclined to support the real-bills doctrine, whereas the Reserve Banks tended to support a more active monetary policy through the increasing use of open-market operations.[14]

A significant operational change also occurred with the BOB. As noted, the statutory guideline was to act "with a view of securing greater economy," and as Budget Director Charles Dawes explained, it was essential for the new institution to "work in such close and harmonious relations with the Cabinet heads, with authority and custom so firmly established . . . that the Cabinet demagogues of the future may be discouraged . . . in challenging the system."[15] To secure that end, Dawes issued Budget Circular 49 in 1921, which required that every agency or departmental proposal for legislation "[creating] a charge upon the public treasury" be submitted to the BOB for review. The BOB then determined which proposals were "in accord with the financial program of the President" and only those proposals were forwarded to Congress.[16] As initially designed, legislative clearance had a narrow scope—pertaining only to the cost of proposals rather than substance—but its significance was sweeping in forcing all department and agency heads to accept the placement of the BOB between them and the president.[17]

Altogether, the decentralized New Era apparatus was in place by the middle of the 1920s. In general, the Treasury Department, oriented in practice toward balancing the budget, and the Bureau of the Budget, operating within the Treasury and oriented in practice and statute toward "securing greater economy," would assist the president in proposing an annual budget and directing fiscal policy more generally. At the same time, the independent Federal Reserve Board and the Federal Reserve Banks—working under the guidelines of the gold standard and, to varying degrees, the real-bills doctrine—would share control over monetary policy.

Moving forward, this meant that each president's control in the domain of public finance was a contingency that would turn in large part on the alignment of his preferences and the policy parameters that the New Era apparatus and its principals structured.

THE FAILING NEW ERA APPARATUS LIMITS HOOVER'S CONTROL

As his opening move in the domain of public finance, Herbert Hoover retained the existing principals that his fellow Republican predecessors—Warren Harding and Calvin Coolidge—had appointed. Once Hoover appointed his own principals for the top three positions, he only selected individuals with significant experience in either the Harding administration, the Coolidge administration, or both. Specifically, at the Treasury Department, Andrew Mellon, a Harding appointee from 1921, remained in office until the start of 1932; and his successor, Ogden Mills, had served as the undersecretary of the Treasury since the Coolidge administration. At the Fed, Governor Roy Young, a Coolidge appointee from 1927, remained in office until the second half of 1930, when he then became governor of the Reserve Bank in Boston, a telling sign of the diffusion of power within the Fed at the time; and his successor, Eugene Meyer, had served as director of the War Finance Corporation under both Harding and Coolidge. At the Bureau of the Budget, Director Herbert Lord, a Harding appointee from 1922, remained in office through the first half of 1929; and his successor, James Roop, had served as the first assistant director of the BOB under Harding.

At the time, Hoover's use of the appointment power was understandable, as these were the individuals who had overseen a strong economy for much of the preceding decade—or in Hoover's words, the birth of the "New Economic Era"—and there was little reason for the president to question the established approach to public finance, especially when he first assumed office and set the course for his administration. As Hoover explained in his inaugural address, "We have reached a higher degree of comfort . . . than ever existed before in the history of the world" and the "devotion to and concern for our institutions are deep and sincere."[18] Equally revealing, when the stock market showed the first signs of instability in early October 1929, Hoover publicly embraced the experienced Treasury secretary in announcing that he had "asked Mr. Andrew Mellon to remain in his cabinet for the next three and a half years, or for the balance of the administration."[19]

In hindsight, it became clear that Hoover's use of the appointment power was problematic. In his memoirs Hoover acknowledged, "Each President must have his own major policy-making officials sympathetic with his ideas, irrespective of the appointments of his predecessors."[20] Undoubtedly, Hoover first came to this critical realization based on the troubled relationship with his Treasury secretary.

Like Treasury Secretary Mellon, Hoover had worked as a department head under both Harding and Coolidge. Yet, unlike Mellon, Hoover was a progressive Republican and his appointment as commerce secretary eight years earlier had been tied to the appointment of the Treasury secretary in an attempt to appease the progressive and conservative wings of the party, respectively.[21] In other words, the two men held starkly different views on the role of government, with Mellon routinely emphasizing its limits and Hoover often expanding its reach, even if only through coordinating voluntary efforts. In particular, whereas Hoover had organized and chaired the President's Conference on Unemployment in 1921 and had supported the final report recommending the use of public-works spending to reduce unemployment, Mellon had played no part in the conference and rejected the very idea that properly planned spending on public works should or could smooth fluctuations in unemployment and business activity.[22]

After Hoover became president, the ideological division deepened. Notably, when the stock market collapsed in October 1929—which essentially launched the Great Depression and followed Hoover's public pledge to retain his experienced Treasury secretary—Mellon remained unsupportive, bluntly telling the president, "[The speculators] deserved it."[23] Further underscoring the significant opposition from within his own administration, Hoover later complained that Mellon headed the "'leave it alone liquidationists' . . . who felt that government must keep its hands off and let the slump liquidate itself."[24]

In stark contrast the president moved quickly to implement the economic-stabilization plan that he had helped to develop as commerce secretary. Focusing first on the federal government, he asked all department heads to expedite spending on public works, and he recommended that Congress make additional appropriations for the same purpose and also pass a tax cut that would add to "the capital available for general business."[25] Turning to the states, he informed the governors that it would "be helpful if road, street, public building and other construction of this type could be speeded up . . . to [increase] employment."[26] Lastly, he secured from the leading industrialists an agreement to maintain existing wages.

While Hoover took the lead in directing the primary stabilization measures on the fiscal front, the independent Federal Reserve System maintained responsibility for directing the primary stabilization measures on the monetary front—namely, keeping interest rates low and credit flowing. At first, the New York Reserve Bank acted aggressively, both in lowering the discount rate from 6 percent to 5 percent and then in implementing a program of open market purchases of securities to expand the money supply. It also continued to lower the discount rate over the next nineteen months, eventually settling at 1.5 percent. However, the combination of the real-bills doctrine and the division of power between the Board and the Reserve Banks restricted the scale of additional open-market purchases. In particular, the Fed's short-term guideline for monetary policy called for a passive policy at this point because the economic downturn was considered a natural correction to the expansionary policies of the New York Reserve Bank in 1927. As a result, when the New York Reserve Bank proposed a new program of open-market purchases in the middle of 1930, several Reserve Bank governors and Board members opposed the measure. The New York Reserve Bank itself then opposed making additional purchases three months later when Board members proposed doing so.[27]

Although a dispute existed over the correct course of action, the back-and-forth between supporting and opposing additional open-market purchases was not an issue of whether the Fed should implement an "easy"—or expansionary—monetary policy because this was already believed to be the case due to the low level of the discount rate. Rather, the issue was whether additional purchases were necessary to make the existing policy even easier. A major problem, however, was that the Fed's indicators failed to distinguish between real and nominal interest rates. Specifically, while the discount rate had declined by 4.5 percentage points since the stock market crash, prices had fallen by 11.6 percent, meaning that the real cost of borrowing had increased by more than 7 percentage points.[28]

Adding to the situation, the president had no legal authority or precedent for intervening, a constraint that he was well aware of because his predecessor had rejected his own proposal to pressure the Fed to change course during the "credit inflation" of the mid-1920s. Recalling that decision, Hoover explained, "I urged President Coolidge, as I had done eighteen months before, to send for [Fed Governor] Crissinger and express alarm at the situation. Mr. Coolidge, a strict legalist, again insisted that the Reserve Board had been created by the Congress entirely independent of the Executive and that he could not interfere."[29]

At the same time, Hoover played a limited role in revising the tariff, one of the primary sources of federal revenue. In April 1929, several months before the start of the Great Depression, Hoover called for a special session of Congress to address "farm relief and limited changes in the tariff," and he warned, "In determining changes in our tariff we must not fail to take into account the broad interests of the country as a whole. . . . It is obviously unwise protection which sacrifices a greater amount of employment in exports to gain a less amount of employment from imports."[30] However, Congress ignored the president and proceeded to raise tariff rates significantly. Making clear Hoover's limited role, much like that of his predecessors in the congressional logrolling process of tariff making, the White House announced in October that the "President has declined to interfere or express any opinion on the details of rates . . . as it is obvious that . . . he could not pretend to have the necessary information in respect to many thousands of commodities which such determination requires."[31]

In June 1930—nearly a year after Hoover's call to address the matter—Congress passed the Smoot-Hawley Tariff Act, meaning that the Republican-controlled government ultimately increased tariff rates following the start of the Great Depression. This move spurred retaliatory tariff rate increases from other countries and contributed to a collapse of world trade that deepened the economic downturn. To be sure, at Hoover's insistence, the new tariff act included a "flexible tariff" provision designed to strengthen the role of the president in making revisions based on findings of the independent Tariff Commission—in Hoover's words, "a progressive advance" that "gives great hope of taking the tariff away from politics, lobbying, and logrolling." Yet, in practice, this provision had little impact and came at a high cost. As the president conceded in his memoirs, "I may say here that raising the tariff from its sleep was a political liability despite the virtues of its reform."[32]

* * *

Although Hoover worked to manage the Great Depression in late 1929 and throughout 1930 by employing a number of fiscal-stabilization measures, the domain of public finance collapsed over the next two years. Most notably, as the unemployment rate soared to nearly 16 percent in 1931, the wage rate agreement fell apart; the limited leverage of the federal government over state government, local government, and private-sector spending became apparent; and the fear of crowding out those entities from financial markets undercut support for increased spending by the federal government itself.[33] Worse still, Britain shook the international financial system when it abandoned the gold standard in September. As Hoover explained, "With the Bank of England's collapse," it was evident "that bold action must be taken if panic were not to extend to the United States."[34]

Two significant steps followed. First, the New York Reserve Bank quickly raised the discount rate a full 2 percentage points. While this move aimed to strengthen the country's ability to maintain the gold standard, the higher cost of borrowing weakened the already depressed economy. Second, the president put forward a proposal in December to, as he put it, strictly "balance the budget by drastic decreases and postponements of ordinary expenditures, and increased taxation," which was necessary, he added, "to reestablish confidence and . . . restore the flow of credit which is the very basis of our economic life."[35] This complete change in course revealed a key constraint at play. Rather than operate on separate tracks, with the independent Fed overseeing monetary policy and the president overseeing fiscal policy, the Fed's restrictive monetary policy and the commitment to the gold standard were now driving the agenda for the domain of public finance as a whole, thereby significantly limiting the president's control in even the one area in which it was supposed to be substantial.[36]

The shackling of fiscal policy became even more apparent over the next six months. Once the president, charged with "[making] recommendations to Congress for new taxes," proposed a tax increase in late 1931 and then employed the BOB to use its system of financial clearance to reduce departmental appropriations, no other political authority was willing to take responsibility for blocking the new course even though the economy had contracted by more than 6 percent over the last year. As a result, the president signed into law the Revenue Act of 1932—the largest peacetime tax increase in history at that point—during the most severe economic downturn of the twentieth century in order to support the nation's currency. As Hoover explained, "While many of the taxes are not as I desired, the bill will effect the great purpose of assurance to the country and the world of the determination of the American people to maintain . . . their currency on a sound basis."[37] Further underscoring the perceived necessity of this move, Hoover later noted, "To balance the budget," which was critical to preventing a further increase in interest rates, "we were compelled to ask for an increase . . . in taxes."[38]

At the same time that monetary policy was setting the course for fiscal policy, the president attempted to deal with the growing number of bank failures, which the Fed had all but ignored despite being created in large part to act as a lender of last resort. Adding to the problem, as Treasury secretary, Mellon was the ex officio chair of the Federal Reserve Board. Yet, rather than use the resources of either the Treasury or the Fed to help resolve the banking crisis, the Treasury secretary remained unsupportive. As Hoover explained, "The real trouble with [Secretary Mellon] was that he insisted that this was just an ordinary boom-slump and would not take the . . . situation seriously." In fact, Hoover added, "[Mellon] held that even a panic was not altogether a bad thing."[39]

With the established public-finance apparatus and its principals offering no real support, Hoover necessarily turned elsewhere, initially organizing the National Credit Corporation, a voluntary banking organization that put together a $500 million pool of credit to rescue troubled banks. Once that voluntary effort quickly failed, Hoover took two major steps: he proposed the creation of the Reconstruction Finance Corporation, a governmental organization authorized to make loans to a variety of financial institutions; and he backed the passage of the Glass-Steagall Act of 1932, an amendment to the Federal Reserve Act that allowed government securities to operate as collateral for notes. Although both measures marked the start of a fundamental departure from the operations and ideas embodied in the original Federal Reserve Act, each largely proved ineffective during the Hoover administration.

First, in addition to major statutory restrictions meant to ensure that the RFC would not undercut private lenders, which in turn undercut its own lending, the new institution further decentralized responsibility for the banking system. In particular, Fed officials maintained that the RFC, not the Fed, was responsible for subsequent bank failures despite the RFC's insufficient and inferior resources. Further complicating the matter, the governor of the Federal

Reserve Board, Eugene Meyer, simultaneously served as chair of the RFC, even though the new institution had been established largely because of older institution's failure to resolve the ongoing crisis. With the same individual in charge and major statutory constraints in place, the RFC, like the Fed, failed to stem the banking crisis or reverse the economic downturn more generally.[40]

The relationship between Hoover and Meyer deteriorated during this period as well, due in large part to Meyer's handling of monetary policy and his opposition to expanding the RFC's operations into welfare, relief, and public-works spending, a proposal that the president supported. Making clear this divide—and adding to the list of unsupportive public-finance principals—Hoover later remarked that the dual Fed governor–RFC chair was "obstructive and disloyal."[41]

A similar problem undercut the effectiveness of the second measure. In allowing government securities to operate as collateral, the Glass-Steagall Act of 1932 marked a significant departure from the real-bills doctrine in favor of a more discretionary and expansionary monetary policy. As Hoover explained, this law "so increases the already large available resources of the Federal Reserve Banks as to enable them beyond question to meet any conceivable demands that might be made on them." However, there was no major accompanying change in the Fed's principals, most of whom still adhered to the old monetary doctrine of limiting collateral to commercial paper. Accordingly, the Fed simply used the newly relaxed collateral requirement to carry out a program of open-market purchases from late February through mid-August 1932, a month after the congressional session ended. Once Congress went on leave, removing the threat of further inflationary action, the program ended, and the Fed showed no interest in moving forward with a new one.[42] Further underscoring his lack of control over monetary policy, and making clear his desire to chart a different course, Hoover complained, "I am afraid I cannot run the Federal Reserve Banks, much as . . . I might like to have it that way."[43]

Finally, with the president struggling to control the established public-finance apparatus and its principals, with the unemployment rate above 23 percent, and with the economy having contracted by nearly 13 percent that year, Franklin Roosevelt won the presidential election in late 1932, triggering, as Hoover put it, "a great fear that currency tinkering would be undertaken by the new Administration."[44] Adding to the problem, the New York Reserve Bank began a program of open-market sales in January 1933, which further restricted the money supply and worked together with election-induced uncertainty to generate a full-blown panic. Roosevelt then refused to accept any responsibility until his inauguration in March, and neither the Reserve Banks nor the Board could agree on a system-wide response.[45]

The Fed's inaction became increasingly evident during Hoover's final weeks in office. On February 22, Hoover wrote to the Board, "I should like to be advised . . . as to whether the Board considers the situation is one that has reached a public danger" such that new "measures should be undertaken at this juncture and especially what, if any, further authority should be obtained." Three days later, the Board responded, "At the moment [we do] not desire to make any specific proposals for additional measures or authority but [we] will continue to give all aspects of the situation its most careful consideration."[46]

Equally revealing, Hoover turned to the Board on March 2 to address the use of an old war power. "I understand that the Board is meeting this evening to consider recommending to me the use of the emergency powers under Section 5 of the Enemy Trading Act," the president wrote. "I shall be glad to have the advice."[47] Yet, once again, the Board refused to offer any support.

At the same time, the principals serving directly under the president largely mirrored and reinforced the Fed's inaction. As Hoover explained, "I had consulted our legal advisors as to the use of a certain unrepealed war power over bank withdrawals and foreign exchange. Most of them were in doubt on the ground that the lack of repeal was probably an oversight by the Congress," and the Treasury secretary "held that no certain power existed."[48]

Attempting to make sense of this increasingly severe and increasingly prioritized problem, Hoover himself later laid much of the blame on the established public-finance apparatus and its principals. In particular, the president concluded that the Fed was "a weak reed for the nation to lean on in time of trouble." It "was the primary agency of the government in matters of banking and currency" and was therefore "in a position to take some leadership." But, Hoover added, "The majority of the Board seemed paralyzed."[49]

* * *

The case study analysis here shows that the established, gradually failing New Era apparatus and its principals allowed Hoover to strengthen his control to a degree but, for the most part, limited his control. First, in heading the "leave it alone liquidationists" and in maintaining "that even a panic was not altogether a bad thing," the Treasury Department and its conservative secretary limited Hoover's control. Second, in ignoring the president's call in 1929 to make only "limited changes in the tariff," an issue that he could not address in detail himself because he lacked "the necessary information," and then in "compell[ing]" the president in 1931 to propose a tax increase and a spending cut in support of the currency despite his own strong belief early on that the opposite course would help to bolster the economy, Congress's control over the tariff making process and the New Era apparatus's subordination of fiscal policy to monetary policy both further limited Hoover's control. Third, in overseeing monetary policy despite the president's desire to "run the Federal Reserve Banks" and his frustration that "the Board seemed paralyzed," the independent Federal Reserve System and its "obstructive and disloyal" governor limited Hoover's control further still.

5. Innovation: Roosevelt Strengthens His Control in Restructuring the Policy Domain

The quantitative overview provided evidence that in the domain of public finance, Franklin Roosevelt oversaw the creation of both the centralized New Deal–era apparatus and the New Deal–era policy parameters due largely to the full impact of the Great Depression, an exceptionally severe and highly prioritized problem that weakened the average restrictions on presidential control and strengthened the average incentive to maximize control. This chapter traces the process of Roosevelt strengthening his control in restructuring the policy domain during the Great Depression, and it also traces the major developments in the policy domain during the Second World War.

ROOSEVELT STRENGTHENS HIS CONTROL IN RESTRUCTURING THE SUBDOMAIN OF MONETARY POLICY

In contrast to his predecessor, Franklin Roosevelt worked to seize control of the appointment power before he even assumed office. As Raymond Moley, a top advisor, explained, "The offer of appointment as Secretary of the Treasury to Senator Carter Glass was virtually imposed upon Roosevelt because of Glass's proven capacity and the great respect for him which prevailed in Congress, in the Democratic Party, and in the financial community."[1] This was far from an inconsequential imposition. As the chair of the House Committee on Banking and Currency in 1913, Glass had overseen the legislation creating the Federal Reserve System, and he continued to support the real-bills doctrine and the decentralized administrative arrangement. The influential senator also had two requirements prior to accepting a position in the new administration: he wanted to know the president-elect's position on inflation and he sought the assurance of having, as Moley put it, a "completely free hand to name his own subordinates in the Treasury."[2]

Where stability in public finance and party continuity had undercut Hoover's control in setting up his administration four years earlier, ensuring Andrew Mellon's continuation as Treasury secretary, instability and a party transition considerably strengthened Roosevelt's ability to maneuver from the start. "So far as inflation goes," the president-elect instructed Moley to tell Glass, "you can say that we're not going to throw ideas out of the window simply because they're labeled inflation. If you feel that the old boy doesn't want to go along, don't press him."[3] In response, the senator turned down the position of Treasury secretary.

After the negotiation with Glass, Roosevelt took Moley's advice and offered the position to William Woodin, the president of the American Car and Foundry Company. As Moley explained, Woodin's "absolute personal loyalty to Roosevelt" was one of "his essential qualifications for the job."[4] Indeed, with the supportive Treasury secretary–designate in place, the president-elect immediately expanded his options moving forward. This was apparent when, the night before his inauguration, Roosevelt informed Glass that he planned to close all the banks in order to stem the ongoing panic. "You will have no authority to do that," Glass protested, "no authority to issue any such proclamation." However, Roosevelt insisted that his own advisers believed "precisely the opposite" based on the same World War I–era law that the Federal Reserve Board and Hoover's advisers had considered and rejected.[5]

Once in office Roosevelt followed through on his plan, issuing a proclamation in early March that closed all the banks and prohibited the export, hoarding, and earmarking of gold or silver under the authority of the Trading with the Enemy Act. Congress also then acted by quickly passing the Emergency Banking Act. Among its many provisions, the law approved all the orders that the president and the Treasury secretary had issued, expanded the president's authority to regulate monetary transactions during any "period of national emergency," and established a process to examine and reopen healthy banks.[6] Underscoring the administration's rapid success on this front and the critical role of the new, responsive Treasury secretary, Moley remarked, "Capitalism was saved in eight days, and no other single factor in its salvation was half so important as the imagination and sturdiness and common sense of Will Woodin."[7]

Although the Roosevelt administration had resolved the banking panic in short order, the status of the gold standard—specifically, whether the earlier suspension was temporary or permanent—remained unclear, and efforts to clarify the issue sharply divided the administration. As Roosevelt explained, "It is simply inevitable that we must inflate and though my banker friends may be horrified, I still am seeking an inflation which will not wholly be based on additional government debt."[8] Working toward that end, the president announced to several top advisers in April that the country was now officially "off the gold standard," meaning that the Treasury would no longer issue export licenses. Roosevelt also made it known that he planned to support the Thomas Amendment to the Agricultural Adjustment Act, which contained three key provisions: it granted the president the authority to issue up to $3 billion in US notes if "an economic emergency" or other factors "[require] an expansion of credit" and the actions of "the several Federal Reserve Banks and the Federal Reserve Board . . . prove to be inadequate"; it granted the president the authority to reduce the gold content of the dollar by as much as 50 percent; and it granted the president authority to establish bimetallism.[9]

The extraordinary grant of authority over monetary policy was a clear repudiation of not only the Fed's independence but also the accepted principles of "sound finance," which dictated adherence to the self-regulating gold standard and a balanced budget. Accordingly, all "hell broke loose in the room" following the announcement, Moley recalled. In fact, several advisers—namely, Budget Director Lewis Douglas; James Warburg, a New York banker; and Herbert Feis, an economic adviser in the State Department—"were so horrified," Moley added, "that they began to scold Roosevelt as though he were a perverse and particularly backward schoolboy."[10]

Notwithstanding the president's decision and the grant of statutory authority, the status of the gold standard remained unsettled through the first half of 1933. Most notably, after fiercely attacking the president's position only a few months earlier, Warburg and Feis began to work with Oliver M. W. Sprague, an adviser in the Treasury Department, to develop a program for the upcoming World Economic Conference, which Hoover had organized the previous year in the hope of adopting a currency stabilization agreement. The central issue was whether international or domestic stability would take priority. Revealing the public-finance principals' continued prioritization of the former, Feis noted that the "first plan of stabilization put up to the President was far-reaching in character and would have required renunciation of *his* monetary policy."[11]

While the president's delegation worked toward securing an international stabilization agreement, the president himself moved to undercut that effort in order to promote domestic stability. In a surprise message to the conference, Roosevelt made his own position clear, explaining, "The world will not be lulled by the specious fallacy of achieving . . . an artificial stability in foreign exchange. . . . The sound internal economic system of a Nation is a greater factor in its well-being than the price of its currency in changing terms of the currencies of other Nations." For this reason, he added, the "old-fetishes of so-called international bankers are being replaced by efforts to plan national currencies."[12] Underscoring the impact of the president's message, the *New York Times* reported, "No international gathering has ever met a harder blow than that dealt by President Roosevelt to the World Economic Conference today."[13]

After preventing Glass's appointment in February, suspending the gold standard in March, deciding to maintain the suspension in April, and rejecting an international stabilization agreement in July—all of which required the president's personal attention—Roosevelt still struggled to develop and implement a new monetary policy in opposition to the formal public-finance principals. Centered in the Treasury and the Reserve Bank of New York, and headed by Sprague, Warburg, and Undersecretary of the Treasury Dean Acheson—Woodin was seriously ill at the time and no longer involved in day-to-day affairs—this group held fast, recommending the "establishment of an improved gold standard" and "international cooperation."[14] At the same time, Roosevelt continued to make clear his opposition, remarking, "I do not like or approve the report of the special monetary group. They have failed to take into consideration the United States, and look at things, I fear, from the point of view of New York and banking."[15]

Although the public-finance principals remained unsupportive, that opposition increasingly strengthened a group of informal advisers. Headed by George F. Warren and Irvin Fisher—professors of economics at Cornell and Yale, respectively—and operating under the political guidance of Henry Morgenthau, Jr., the head of the new Farm Credit Administration, this group proposed a considerably different approach, one in line with the president's instruction for a recommendation on how to obtain the objective of an increase in commodity prices and "that objective only."[16] In particular, they recommended that a rise in prices was best accomplished "by reducing the gold content of the dollar," and that move was itself best accomplished, Warren explained, by purchasing gold in the open market at increasingly higher prices each week. Tired of "the same old suggestions" from Sprague and the other formal principals, the president aligned himself with Warren and Fisher in late October.[17]

Once the new Farm Credit Administration and the informal economic advisers working through that institution prevailed over the Treasury and the Fed in developing a plan for creating, in Roosevelt's words, a "managed currency," the president turned his attention to the matter of implementation. Confirming the difficulty of this step, Roosevelt complained that getting the Treasury to act was "like punching your fist into a pillow."[18] The problem was that Dean Acheson, the now-acting secretary of the Treasury, questioned the legality of the gold purchase program and aimed to delay its enactment, if not block it entirely. As Acheson explained,

> The battle was on. I said that the time for argument was not over; it had only just begun, for the plan had not been subjected to any real examination. Furthermore, I was the official who under the plan would have to authorize the payment of government funds without, as I believed, legal authority. If any ex-

isted, someone could surely point it out. If they could not, I would not violate the law.[19]

In response to the Treasury's continued opposition, the president turned elsewhere for support once again, explaining to several advisers, "I have a method of my own to break the law."[20] Where Hoover had supported the creation of the Reconstruction Finance Corporation in an effort to support the banking system, Roosevelt now used that institution to dismantle the old gold standard. Each weekday morning for more than two months, the president met with Morgenthau, Warren, and Jesse Jones, the new chair of the RFC, in order to set the price at which the repurposed institution would buy gold that day. Further revealing the novelty of the entire process, Morgenthau noted in his diary, "If anybody ever knew how we really set the gold price through a combination of lucky numbers, etc., I think they would be frightened."[21]

Although the gold purchase program lasted only a few months, it had a considerable impact on public-finance administration in two key ways. First, it triggered major changes in personnel. Sprague criticized the program and resigned; Warburg, who had resigned earlier, primarily due to the president's handling of the World Economic Conference, also attacked the policy of "experimentation"; and Roosevelt fired Acheson due to his obstructionism.[22] Underscoring the importance of these departures, the president remarked, "I have had the shackles on my hands for months now and I feel for the first time as though I [have] thrown them off."[23]

With the top position now open, Roosevelt appointed Morgenthau to head the Treasury. As a personal friend with no experience in the government besides his brief tenure at the FCA, Morgenthau was more supportive of unconventional policies and procedures; he would make the Treasury's resources more accessible to the president, even when he personally disagreed with a policy; and he would play a key role in the appointment of new principals to head the Fed and the Bureau of the Budget, all of which would further strengthen the president's control.

Second, the gold purchase program had a considerable impact on the public-finance apparatus. Once the price of gold reached $35 per ounce in January, up from $20.67 a few months earlier, Roosevelt ended the program, signed the Gold Reserve Act of 1934, and issued a proclamation setting the gold value of the dollar at 59 percent of its former value. In addition to placing the country on a new quasi-gold standard—a gold standard for transactions between the United States and foreign governments but an irredeemable paper standard for domestic transactions—the Gold Reserve Act transferred $2 billion of the profit from the devaluation of the dollar to a new Exchange Stabilization Fund.[24]

In another clear attack on the role of the Fed, the Exchange Stabilization Fund operated, in the words of its founding statute, "under the exclusive control of the Secretary of the Treasury, with the approval of the president, whose decisions shall be final and not be subject to review by any other officer of the United States."[25] Along with the authority granted under the Thomas Amendment, Roosevelt and Morgenthau now had $5 billion at their disposal—more than twice the amount of the Fed's balance sheet—to conduct open-market operations if and when necessary. Accordingly, the president and the Treasury secretary, not the Fed, controlled monetary policy. As the Treasury secretary later explained, the Fed has "very little power to enforce their will. . . . Our power has been the Stabilization Fund plus many other funds that I have at my disposal and this power has kept the open-market committee in line and afraid."[26]

* * *

Following the gold purchase program, Roosevelt and his principals took the lead in restructuring the Federal Reserve System. This process began with the appointment of Marriner Eccles to head the Fed based on the recommendation of the new Treasury secretary. As an outspoken advocate of deficit spending and, like the Treasury secretary, a newcomer to the federal government, the new Fed governor provided support for unorthodox policies and increased governmental activism. Before his appointment Eccles explained, "I believe, contrary to the opinion of most people" that the government "must so regulate through its power of taxation" and "through its power over the control of money and credit . . . the economic structure as to give men who are able, worthy, and willing to work, the opportunity to work, and to guarantee them sustenance."[27]

Once in office, Eccles worked alongside Lauchlin Currie—another Morgenthau recruit then serving in the Treasury's "Freshman Brain Trust"—to compose a memo for the president on "desirable changes" to the Fed. Addressing one of the key causes of the Great Depression—namely, the failure of a procyclical monetary policy under the real-bills doctrine—Eccles and Currie explained,

> Experience shows that without conscious control, the supply of money tends to expand when the rate of spending increases and tends to contract when the rate of spending declines. Thus, during the depression the supply of money instead of expanding to moderate the effect of decreased rates of spending, contracted, and so intensified the depression. . . . If the monetary mechanism is to be used as an instrument for the promotion of business stability conscious control and management are essential.[28]

Furthermore, to ensure "conscious control"—or a countercyclical monetary policy—moving forward, the two advisers recommended transforming the Fed into a "real central bank," and Roosevelt responded that he supported these "necessary" changes even though it would require "a knock-down and drag-out fight to get [them] through" the legislature.[29]

With the president fully on board, the new Fed governor oversaw the drafting and passage of the landmark Banking Act of 1935. Among its many provisions, the law weakened the statutory support for the real-bills doctrine by instructing the Fed to operate not only "with a view to accommodating commerce and business" but also with regard to "the general credit situation of the country." Moreover, to implement this new governing objective—and further diminishing the real-bills doctrine—the law empowered the Board to prescribe as broadly as it desired the types of assets eligible to secure loans, liberalizing and making permanent the emergency powers first issued under the Glass-Steagall Act of 1932.

Along with restructuring the orientation and composition of monetary policy, the law restructured the organization of the Federal Reserve System. In particular, the Banking Act of 1933 had established the Federal Open Market Committee to direct monetary policy, and the Banking Act of 1935 then shifted control over the FOMC from the Reserve Banks to the Board by changing the membership of the FOMC from the twelve Reserve Bank governors and no Board members to all seven Board members and only five Reserve Bank governors.[30]

Notwithstanding the law's sweeping changes—especially in consolidating control over monetary policy in the new Board-dominated FOMC, thereby creating a "real central bank" in statute for the first time—the president and the Treasury secretary largely retained control in practice due to three key factors. First, the law strengthened the Board's independence, but it also granted Roosevelt the one-time power of appointing an entirely new Board. The president used this opportunity to select five new members while retaining M. S. Szymczak and Eccles, two of his earlier appointees.[31] Second, by strengthening the Board, the law strengthened the power of its top official—now titled chair—but the Roosevelt-appointed chair maintained a narrow conception of independence, defining it as simply "the opportunity" for the central bank "to express its views in connection with the determination of policy."[32] This was due in large part to Eccles's belief that rising economic inequality had caused the Great Depression, which meant that fiscal policy, not monetary policy, was the most important economic-stabilization instrument. Third, the president and the Treasury secretary still maintained the powers from the Thomas Amendment and the Exchange Stabilization Fund, allowing them to circumvent the newly strengthened Fed if it failed to act or to offset any undesired policies if and when it did act.

Roosevelt's continued control over monetary policymaking following the Banking Act of 1935 was evident when Eccles sought the president's approval for the Fed's first major action—raising the reserve requirement in 1936. As the responsive Fed chair later revealed, "I called at the White House and presented this issue to Roosevelt. . . . Under the Banking Act of 1935 the Board could change the required reserve without his approval. Yet I felt the country would hold him responsible."[33]

Further underscoring the restructuring of the subdomain of monetary policy following its collapse during the Hoover administration, Herbert Hoover later remarked, "The march toward 'managed currency' came quickly . . . following Roosevelt's inauguration," and in the process, Roosevelt acquired "legal authority over money as absolute as that of Tiberius Caesar or Henry VIII, Stalin or Hitler. It consummated the dreams and promises of every American tinkerer with the currency since the foundation of the Republic."[34]

* * *

The case study analysis here shows that Roosevelt significantly strengthened his control in the subdomain of monetary policy in working to create the New Deal–era apparatus and policy parameters. First, in working with the support of unconventional principals to create a "managed currency," a process that required the president to "break the law" in bypassing the Fed and the Treasury, both of which were largely staffed with conventional principals that had been "the shackles on [his] hands for months," Roosevelt strengthened his control. Second, in working with the support of unconventional principals to restructure the Fed, and then in maintaining a veto power over the restructured central bank due to the support of both the new Treasury secretary, who used the Exchange Stabilization Fund to "[keep] the open-market committee in line and afraid," and the new Fed chair, who "felt the country would hold [the president] responsible" for its actions, Roosevelt further strengthened his control. Third, in overseeing the restructuring of the subdomain of monetary policy, Roosevelt took a key step in unshackling the subdomain of fiscal policy, which, as will be clear in the next section, would even further strengthen his control.

ROOSEVELT STRENGTHENS HIS CONTROL IN RESTRUCTURING THE SUBDOMAIN OF FISCAL POLICY

Along with restructuring the subdomain of monetary policy, Franklin Roosevelt worked to restructure the subdomain of fiscal policy. This process began with the Bureau of the Budget, which was designed to "secur[e] greater economy" regardless of the preferences of the president.[35] In accordance with the BOB's statutory government objective, Roosevelt appointed Lewis Douglas, a Democratic congressman, to head the institution, and the new budget director then quickly took the lead in pushing through Congress the Economy Act, which granted the president sweeping authority to reduce government spending.[36] Underscoring the important role of the BOB and its new director, Harry Hopkins and a small group of advisers remarked to Marriner Eccles in late 1933, "We are all for your [deficit spending] thesis. But how are you going to get around Lew Douglas over in the Bureau of the Budget . . . holding Roosevelt fast to a budget-balancing policy?"[37]

Similar to bypassing acting Treasury Secretary Dean Acheson and other public-finance principals in creating a "managed currency," the president himself ultimately circumvented Douglas in the process of creating a new fiscal policy. The first move occurred in late March 1933. Without consulting the budget director, Roosevelt announced that he expected to end the current fiscal year with a balanced budget for "ordinary expenditures." Yet, contrary to established practice, the ordinary budget proposal now excluded the funds for debt retirement, public works, and other "extraordinary and emergency expenditures."[38]

Following this initial step, which Douglas derided as a move that "fools no one," the battle between the president and the budget director intensified. In April 1933, when Roosevelt took the country off the gold standard, Douglas criticized the move, declaring, "This is the end of western civilization." In July, when Roosevelt rejected the currency stabilization agreement, Douglas condemned the decision, telling the president, "The only way to prevent [Hitler] from achieving supreme power is by offering an alternative revival of world trade" and "you sir, have destroyed all hope of that." In October, when Roosevelt decided to implement the gold purchase program, Douglas denounced the policy, describing it in an untendered letter of resignation as "so dishonest and so immoral and so unethical that it is beyond my comprehension that you could even contemplate taking it." In November, when Roosevelt fired the acting Treasury secretary, Douglas criticized the change in personnel, commenting that the "Administration lost real ability in Acheson . . . and has acquired stupidity and Hebraic arrogance and conceit in Morgenthau."

The next year the battle continued. In January, when Roosevelt officially devalued the dollar, Douglas attacked the policy, remarking that devaluation "had been a crime since the dawn of history" and "they used to hang kings for it." Moreover, when Roosevelt failed to keep spending down, Douglas made a detailed record of his opposition. As Roosevelt explained, "After I fired Dean Acheson . . . Lew Douglas set out to make a written record. He makes a written record of everything. If things go wrong he wants to be in a position so he can show that on such and such a date he advised the President not to do thus and so." Worse still, in August, when Roosevelt made a personal plea that Douglas hold off on resigning in opposition to the administration's policies, at least until after the midterm election, the departing budget director refused.[39]

In response to this fierce and increasingly disloyal opposition, Roosevelt once again turned to Henry Morgenthau, Jr., his loyal Treasury secretary. Underscoring the seriousness of the situation, the president remarked that Douglas's resignation "means the loss of the Congressional elections." Roosevelt then instructed Morgenthau that he had "until midnight to [find] a new Director of the Budget."[40]

Based on Morgenthau's recommendation, Roosevelt appointed Daniel Bell as acting budget director the following day. The new appointee was the commissioner of accounts and deposits in the Treasury at the time, and he remained a civil servant in order to maintain his pension, meaning that Bell served simultaneously as an assistant to the Treasury secretary and as acting budget director. Because the dual civil servant and acting director had no outside political support or independent standing—unlike Douglas—he was less likely to resign in opposition to any new policy or procedure. This was evident when Roosevelt manipulated the budget proposal the following year and Bell described the process as "faking" the budget but made no threat to resign. Equally revealing, after Bell's appointment, which effectively removed the BOB as an administrative constraint, Morgenthau observed, "You could tell that [Roosevelt] had a great weight off his shoulders."[41]

In addition to strengthening his control over the three primary administrative institutions in the domain of public finance through the use of novel appointments—Treasury Secretary Morgenthau, Fed Chair Eccles, and Acting Budget Director Bell—Roosevelt worked to restructure the parameters of fiscal policy in three key steps, all of which, as the president put it, built "on the ruins of the past a new structure designed better to meet the present problems."[42]

First, Roosevelt worked to restructure tariff policy. As he explained to Congress in March 1934, "world trade has declined with startling rapidity," and it was therefore essential to grant the president unilateral authority to establish trade agreements with foreign countries and modify existing tariff rates. Such legislation, he added, was "part of an emergency program necessitated by the economic crisis through which we are passing."[43] In response, Congress passed the Reciprocal Trade Agreements Act in June and—at only two pages in length, compared to the 170-page Smoot-Hawley Tariff Act of 1930—the ambiguous law revolutionized the tariff-making process in transferring sweeping power to the executive branch.[44]

In particular, Roosevelt used his new statutory power to grant the State Department, not the Treasury, control over the interdepartmental Committee on Trade Agreements created to oversee the implementation of the RTAA. This promoted an institutional bias toward expanding trade and lowering rates independent of any impact on revenue. Accordingly, after functioning as the primary revenue source during the eighteenth and nineteenth centuries, revenue from tariffs fell to less than 1 percent by the end of the Roosevelt administration, effectively removing the tariff as a key component of fiscal policy moving forward.[45] Furthermore, in reducing rates through foreign trade agreements, rather than the old process of a unilateral tariff reduction, implementation of the RTAA made it more difficult for future administrations to reverse course. As Secretary of State Cordell Hull put it, once the program began, it "gain[ed] momentum."[46]

Second, Roosevelt worked to create a sweeping welfare system in 1934 when he called for Congress to consider a plan that would "provide at once security against several of the great disturbing factors in life—especially those which relate to unemployment and old age."[47] In response, Congress passed the Social Security Act the following year, establishing, as Roosevelt put it, "a structure intended to lessen the force of possible future depressions."[48]

In particular, the landmark law provided for the payment of benefits to the unemployed and retired, and it mandated the collection of a new combined employer-employee payroll tax, starting at 2 percent in 1937 and increasing 1 percentage point every three years until reaching 6 percent in 1949. Although the Committee on Economic Security—which Roosevelt had created to develop the proposal—had ignored his instruction that "the funds necessary to provide this insurance should be raised by [payroll] contribution rather than by an increase in general taxation," Treasury Secretary Morgenthau had worked quickly to create a revised proposal in line with the president's preference.[49] Moreover, like the RTAA, implementation of the Social Security Act—which ultimately passed in the president's preferred form—all but ensured that future administrations could not dismantle the new program. As Roosevelt explained, "We put those payroll contributions there so as to give the contributors a legal, moral, and political right to collect their pensions and their unemployment benefits. With those taxes in there, no damn politician can ever scrap my social security program."[50]

Third, Roosevelt worked to restructure tax policy in 1935. Specifically, with his loyal Treasury secretary overseeing the creation of the proposal based on an intensive study of the tax system, with the new Fed chair publicly declaring that "our problem now is one of distribution of income" and "the most effective way of achieving a better balance is through income taxes," and with no independent budget director standing in the way, Roosevelt moved forward with a sweeping progressive-tax proposal in June. As the president explained, "The transmission from generation to generation of vast fortunes by will, inheritance, or gift is not consistent with the ideals and sentiments of the American people," for "vast personal incomes come not only through the effort . . . of those who receive them, but also because of the opportunities for advantage which Government itself contributes" and therefore government must "restrict such incomes by very high taxes."[51]

Less than three months later, Roosevelt signed the Revenue Act of 1935. Among its many provisions, the landmark law imposed a graduated corporate income tax, with a top rate of 15 percent; it increased the top estate tax rate to 70 percent; and it increased the top individual income tax rate to 79 percent, the highest in history at that point.[52] Although the income level at which the top statutory income tax rate went into effect was high at $5 million, the combination of the unprecedented 79 percent top tax rate during a period of peace and the emphasis on redistribution rather than revenue helped to shift the tax debate moving forward—meaning that, like the RTAA and the Social Security Act, the Revenue Act of 1935 made it difficult for future administrations to change course. Underscoring the substantial shift in the tax debate at the time, Moley explained, "The 'soak-the-rich' and corporate-surplus proposals represented a complete departure from the principles of taxation for revenue and reform *in* taxation. They signalized the adoption of a policy of reform *through* taxation."[53]

* * *

Following the initial restructuring of the subdomain of fiscal policy during his first term, Roosevelt proposed a balanced budget for the first time at the start of his second term in 1937, a move intended to fulfill a campaign pledge from the 1932 and 1936 elections. Additionally, with unemployment at 14 percent, down from a high of nearly 25 percent, and with production finally at pre–Great Depression levels, the president felt confident in highlighting the "end of the depression" in his annual message that year.[54] Yet, seven months later, another recession was underway—the second most severe downturn of the twentieth century—and it continued for nearly a year.[55]

Like the Great Depression proper of 1929–1933, which generated the restructuring of monetary policy and the initial restructuring of fiscal policy, the Recession of 1937–1938—part of the more broadly defined Great Depression—generated the further restructuring of fiscal policy. However, the groundwork had begun several years earlier when Morgenthau assembled, as Lauchlin Currie put it, "the best young brains he could find in the fields of monetary theory, public finance, and banking legislation" and then "[gave] them absolutely free rein" to "see what they could come up with." This group became known as the Treasury's "Freshman Brain Trust," of which Currie, a Harvard-trained economist, was a member. Similar to Eccles, Currie had no experience in government at the time and was, in his own words, "the most outspoken academic critic of Federal Reserve policy."[56]

Following Eccles's appointment as Fed governor, Currie also moved to the Fed, where he served as assistant director of the Division of Research and Statistics and—building upon his work in developing a countercyclical monetary policy—began to make the case for a countercyclical fiscal policy. In 1934 he analyzed the idea of "business confidence" and concluded that an increase in government spending, not a balanced budget, would make it profitable for businesses to expand their operations.[57] He then provided the first detailed estimates of the "pump priming deficit" necessary to restore "full employment."[58] In 1935 he created the "net federal contribution" statistical series, providing for the first time a monthly measure of the difference between income-decreasing taxes and income-increasing spending.[59] In 1936 his influence increased even more due to a new working relationship with the head of the Democratic National Committee, Leon Henderson. As Currie explained, "Henceforth, what I had to say and write influenced to a greater or lesser extent not only Eccles, but also the whole inner New Deal group."[60] Last but not least, in late 1936, roughly half a year before the start of the first major economic downturn since the Great Depression, the influential economist proved prescient, warning of a likely recession within the next twelve months.[61]

Although the Treasury secretary and nearly everyone else within the administration recommended a balanced budget to restore business confidence once the recession began in August 1937, Eccles and a small group of advisers relied upon the intellectual guidance of Currie to push for increased spending. Three months later the tide of influence began to shift when Currie made his most important contribution yet with the "Causes of the Recession" memo, the contents of which he presented directly to the president.[62] While Roosevelt contemplated his next step, Currie continued to revise, as Eccles put it, the "now famous memorandum" that was shared throughout the government and became the principal document in the struggle within the administration to establish a new spending program.[63]

In particular, a revised draft of the memo explained, "From 1934 to 1936, the largest single factor in the steady recovery movement was the excess of Federal activity-creating expenditures over activity-decreasing receipts." Therefore, the primary cause of the recession, the memo added, was "the drastic decline" in net spending beginning in late 1936 and continuing through 1937 due to a combination of the end of the veterans' bonus payments and the start of the new tax for Social Security. In other words, rather than discredit the theory of deficit spending, as the balanced-budget supporters contended, Currie effectively argued that his new data and the current situation showed "the soundness of the case for a compensatory fiscal policy in a severe depression."[64]

With the economy continuing to decline, with the loyal Treasury secretary on vacation, with no independent budget director to stand in the way, with the novel Fed chair and a small group of other advisers recommending increased spending based on Currie's work, and with no threat of a restrictive monetary policy offsetting an expansionary fiscal policy due to the earlier restructuring of the former subdomain, the president decided to abandon the balanced-budget approach in early April 1938.[65] Further revealing the novelty of the policymaking process that led to this decision, Morgenthau remarked to Roosevelt on his return from vacation, "Nobody in the Treasury has had time to study this [spending] program and we have not been consulted as to whether it can or cannot be financed" or "whether it will achieve the results you desire." Morgenthau then added, "You are asking your general, in charge of finances, to carry out a program when he had nothing to do with the planning."[66] But, in contrast to the opposition from Lewis Douglas and others—and further underscoring the full extent of the Treasury secretary's loyalty—Morgenthau quickly accepted the president's decision, clearing the way for the new economic-recovery program to move forward.

Two weeks later Roosevelt presented a $5 billion program to Congress that fundamentally restructured the government's approach to fiscal policy and managing the economy. Where Hoover had recommended raising taxes and cutting spending in late 1931 in order to support the nation's currency, Roosevelt now recommended increased spending in order to restore "the purchasing power of the Nation." Moreover, where the independent Fed had implemented a restrictive monetary policy and Hoover had complained of his inability to "run the Federal Reserve Banks," Roosevelt now acted unilaterally in implementing an expansionary monetary policy. As the president explained, "The Administration proposes immediately to make additional bank resources available for the credit needs of the country. This can be done without legislation. It will be done through the de-sterilization of approximately [$1.4 billion] of Treasury gold."[67]

In addition to overseeing the creation of both a countercyclical—or "compensatory"—fiscal policy as the primary economic-stabilization instrument and a countercyclical monetary policy as a secondary economic-stabilization instrument, Roosevelt oversaw the further restructuring of the public-finance apparatus. This occurred in several steps. First, in 1938 he established the Fiscal and Monetary Advisory Committee, which included the Treasury secretary, the Fed chair, and the budget director. If the government was to succeed in stabilizing the economy moving forward, coordination was essential, particularly in ensuring that fiscal policy and monetary policy did not work at cross-purposes. As Roosevelt explained, this committee "will study the whole range of a great many problems that relate to fiscal and monetary policies" as well as the "conditions essential to avoiding the peaks and valleys of booms and depressions."[68]

The next year Roosevelt took another major step, signing into law the Reorganization Act of 1939. This was necessary, he explained, to remedy the "plain fact . . . that the present organization and equipment of the Executive Branch . . . defeat the Constitutional intent that there be a single responsible Chief Executive."[69] Among its many provisions, the law authorized the president to hire six administrative assistants, and Roosevelt used the opportunity to appoint Currie to one of the new positions, making him the first professional economist to serve on the White House staff. This appointment was critical not only in securing support for a countercyclical fiscal and monetary policy for the remainder of the Roosevelt administration but also in setting a precedent for subsequent incumbents. As Currie explained,

> Now that the great battle has been fought and decided in favor of those who maintained that it is the proper role and responsibility of the State to insure that the economic machine functions more or less at full capacity—to my mind, the greatest and most enduring contribution of the New Deal—economists will be able to play a more important technical role in assisting the State to discharge this responsibility adequately.[70]

The law also authorized the president to implement "reorganization plans," and Roosevelt used this power to establish the Executive Office of the President, explaining that one of the major functions of the institutions operating under this new umbrella organization would be to "inform the President of the general trend of economic conditions and to recommend measures leading to their improvement of stabilization."[71]

Building on the latter development, Roosevelt transferred the Bureau of the Budget from the Treasury to new EOP, another critical step. As the institution responsible for the management of the public credit, the Treasury was oriented in favor of a balanced budget, the policy that the president had just abandoned. Independence from the older institution was therefore necessary to ensure that the BOB would continue to support a countercyclical fiscal policy moving forward. To further secure that objective, Roosevelt appointed Harold Smith, an expert in public administration, as the new budget director, making him the first nonacting director since 1934. Like Morgenthau and Eccles, Smith had never before served in the federal government, meaning that he had little-to-no attachment to old policies and procedures.[72]

With real independence from the Treasury for the first time, with a new director in place, and with the president supporting the entire effort, the BOB changed in three key ways. First, it created the Fiscal Division in 1940. The function of this division, Smith explained, was "[to compile] overall financial and budgetary information and [to study] the consequences of various aspects of the budgetary program upon the country's economic structure."[73]

Second, the BOB expanded the legislative clearance process. Although legislative clearance began during the 1920s in order to organize the president's financial program despite explicit authorization under the Budget and Accounting Act, that step was more or less in accordance with the intentions of the law. Roosevelt went considerably further, however, creating an entire system of policy clearance to oversee the New Deal legislative program. This process began in 1935 when Budget Circular 336 directed the BOB and the National Emergency Council to review all reports on proposed legislation in order to determine their relation to the "financial program of the president" and the "policy program of the president," respectively. Then, in 1937—and following the dissolution of the NEC—Budget Circular 344 removed that distinction in requiring the BOB to review all proposed legislation in order to determine its relation to the "program of the president."[74] Finally, in 1940, and operating as a counterpart to the new Fiscal Division, the BOB created the Legislative Reference Division. Its purpose, Smith explained, was "[to test] legislative proposals on a basis broader than the interests of any one Federal agency and [to give] committees of Congress the point of view of the Administration."[75]

Third, in line with the expansion of its operations and the thirteen-fold increase in its staff, the institutional orientation of the BOB shifted from an explicit charge of "securing greater economy" to, for the time being, an implicit charge of maintaining economic stability and "full employment." This was evident in the starkly contrasting views of the budget directors. Whereas Douglas had believed that spending and "excessive debt contributed to the causes of the depression" and that "the various acts of the Administration" more generally were "the reasons why business cannot proceed to perform its normal function," Smith now reasoned that "economic objectives"—especially "higher standards of living, and full employment"—"must be considered in shaping expenditure programs and revenue plans."[76]

The rise of the BOB's influence also became apparent during this period, especially in the growing frustration of the Treasury secretary. Whereas Charles

Dawes had acknowledged that the Treasury secretary, if he so desired, could "make the Budget Director's life miserable and his work largely ineffectual," Treasury Secretary Morgenthau now complained to Roosevelt that the budget director was "like a termite undermining the foundation of the Treasury. . . . I have heard him before a committee publicly say that he wanted to have the taxing authority of the budget as well as the expenditure [authority]. . . . He is constantly undermining [the Treasury]."[77]

Further underscoring the restructuring of the subdomain of fiscal policy during the Roosevelt administration, the president himself explained in 1940, "In the early thirties . . . fiscal policy was exceedingly simple in theory and extraordinarily disastrous in practice. It consisted in trying to keep expenditures as low as possible in the face of shrinking national income" and "persistence in this attempt came near to bankrupting both our people and our Government." Regarding the change in course in 1938, the president added, "If the recession were not to feed on itself and become another depression, the buying power of the people . . . had to be maintained. To this end, . . . I recommended a further use of Government credit" and the "soundness of this . . . fiscal policy" was "strikingly demonstrated."[78]

* * *

The case study analysis here shows that Roosevelt significantly strengthened his control in the subdomain of fiscal policy in working to create the New Deal–era apparatus and policy parameters. First, in circumventing the initial budget director, who strongly opposed the president's actions and "[made] a written record" of the things "he advised the President not to do," and in appointing a civil servant as acting director, which took "a great weight off [the president's] shoulders," Roosevelt strengthened his control. Second, in working with the support of unconventional principals to develop and implement a countercyclical fiscal policy that replaced an approach that was "simple in theory and extraordinarily disastrous in practice" and that required the Treasury secretary "to carry out a program when he had nothing to do with the planning," Roosevelt further strengthened his control. Third, in establishing the Fiscal and Monetary Advisory Committee, in overseeing the restructuring of the Bureau of the Budget, and in appointing a professional economist to the White House staff, all of which replaced the old "organization and equipment of the Executive Branch" that "defeat[ed] the Constitutional intent that there be a single responsible Chief Executive" with a new apparatus that coordinated the "program of the president" and examined its effect on economic stability, particularly with regard to "full employment," Roosevelt strengthened his control further still.

BUILDING ON THE PREWAR DEVELOPMENTS IN THE DOMAIN OF PUBLIC FINANCE

Following the restructuring of the domain of public finance in response to the Great Depression, the Second World War generated several major developments that largely built on those that the Great Depression had initiated. As Budget Director Harold Smith put it, "In many ways the war has intensified trends that were already evident."[79]

This process was first apparent in the subdomain of monetary policy. One of the prevailing beliefs to come out of the Great Depression was that monetary policy was relatively ineffective—or, more specifically, its effect was asymmetric, meaning it could stop an economic expansion but it could not end a contraction. As Fed Chair Marriner Eccles explained in 1935, "One cannot push on a string. We are in the depths of a depression and . . . there is very little, if anything, that the [Federal Reserve System] can do toward bringing about recovery."[80] In line with this belief, the Fed essentially stopped using open-market operations and the discount rate after 1933—the New York Reserve Bank lowered the discount rate from 2 percent in 1933 to 1.5 percent in 1934, then to 1 percent in 1937, the level at which it would remain for more than a decade. Further revealing the Fed's diminished role, its 1938 annual report explained, "The Federal Reserve System's power to influence credit conditions as an aid to greater economic stability arises largely out of its ability to regulate the volume of member bank reserves. . . . Under existing conditions the Treasury's powers to influence member bank reserves outweigh those possessed by the Federal Reserve System."[81]

The trend continued during the Second World War. Rather than rely on the Fed to control inflation, Roosevelt issued an executive order in April 1941 that established the Office of Price Administration and Civilian Supply. Created, he declared, "by virtue of the authority vested in me by the Constitution and [various] statutes," the new agency placed roughly 50 percent of the nation's wholesale prices under controls in fewer than ten months.[82] The next year the Emergency Price Control Act provided statutory support for the earlier unilateral move, and the Stabilization Act added wage controls, expanding the overall scope of the effort and authorizing the president to "[make] adjustments with respect to prices, wages, and salaries, to the extent that he finds necessary to aid in the effective prosecution of the war or to correct gross inequities."[83]

Adding to this development, the Fed relinquished its remaining limited control over monetary policy when it announced in April 1942 that it would purchase all ninety-day treasury bills on offer at a fixed rate of 0.375 percent in order to assist the Treasury in financing the war.[84] In practice, this meant that the Fed would increase the money supply to the level necessary to keep the price of government securities fixed, rather than maintain discretionary power to alter the money supply in order to manage inflation, unemployment, or some other objective. Underscoring the significance of this move, Eccles explained, "By the fall of 1943 my work in Washington had largely settled down to a routine administrative job. The pattern of war finance had been firmly established by the Treasury; the Federal Reserve merely executed Treasury decisions."[85]

In contrast to further diminishing the role of monetary policy and the independence of the Fed, the war further strengthened the role of fiscal policy. Most importantly, the unemployment rate was still high at nearly 10 percent in 1941 due to several factors: it had started at the exceptionally high level of nearly 25 percent in 1933; after declining for four straight years, it had climbed back to 19 percent during the Recession of 1937–1938, essentially reversing the progress made since 1935; and although Roosevelt had supported intentional deficit spending after early 1938, at no point since then had the deficit exceeded 5 percent of GDP. In other words, the government had not implemented a sufficient level of deficit spending to lower the unemployment rate to its pre–Great Depression level.

The war finally resolved this shortcoming. As the deficit jumped from 4 percent of GDP in 1941 to 14 percent in 1942, the unemployment rate fell from 10 percent to 5 percent; then, as the deficit soared to 30 percent in 1943, the unemployment rate sank to 2 percent, all of which made the effectiveness of a sufficient countercyclical fiscal policy even more apparent. As the president explained in 1945, "Huge war expenditures have brought full employment."[86]

Along with strengthening the overall role of fiscal policy as the primary economic-stabilization instrument, particularly in promoting "full employment," the war strengthened the role of taxation. The major development in fiscal policy to come out of the Great Depression was that of deficit *spending*. The aim early on had been to achieve certain effects quickly—namely, the employment of those on relief—and therefore Roosevelt had supported only limited, directly targeted deficit spending during his first term. Once he accepted in 1938 that jobs might also be provided as the indirect consequence of a demand-stimulating fiscal policy more generally, he continued to propose only increased spending for at least two reasons—a tax cut was viewed as providing benefits primarily for the wealthy, and it took too long to implement relative to a spending program because the tax on income from the current year was not paid until the following year.

Legislation passed during the war removed both concerns. First, the Revenue Act of 1942 broadened the tax base from 13 million to 50 million people. Second, the Current Tax Payment Act of 1943 required employers to withhold income taxes from every paycheck. Together, this meant that a change in tax rates now had the potential to affect the income left in the hands of millions of taxpayers across a wide range of income levels and in a timely manner. Along with the increasing realization that it was the *deficit*, not the spending, that mattered, taxation became a major instrument in stabilizing the economy moving forward.[87]

Legislation passed during the war also continued to make the tax system more progressive. The Reciprocal Trade Agreements Act, which diminished the fiscal-policy role of regressive tariffs, was extended in 1943 and 1945, following similar extensions in 1937 and 1940, and several revenue acts—the Revenue Act of 1940, the Second Revenue Act of 1940, the Revenue Act of 1941, the Revenue Act of 1942, and the Individual Income Tax Act of 1944—worked together to raise the top individual income tax rate to 94 percent, the top corporate income tax rate to 40 percent, and the estate tax rate to 77 percent.[88]

Finally, Roosevelt built upon prewar efforts to promote "full employment" when he unveiled a "second Bill of Rights" in 1944 that included the "right to adequate protection from the economic fears of old age, sickness, accident, and unemployment," and he "ask[ed] the Congress to explore the means for implementing this economic bill of rights" after the war.[89]

* * *

The case study analysis of fiscal policymaking and monetary policymaking in this chapter shows that the centralized New Deal–era apparatus and the New Deal–era policy parameters were all largely in place by the end of the Roosevelt administration. They were then secured during the Truman administration.

6. Stabilization: Truman Relinquishes His Control in Securing the Policy Domain

The quantitative overview provided evidence that in the domain of public finance, Harry Truman oversaw the securing of both the centralized New Deal–era apparatus and the New Deal–era policy parameters due largely to party continuity and a decreasingly severe and decreasingly prioritized problem, all of which began to strengthen the average restrictions on presidential control and began to weaken the average incentive to maximize control. This chapter traces the process of Truman relinquishing much of his control to Franklin Roosevelt in working to secure the newly restructured policy domain.

TRUMAN RELINQUISHES HIS CONTROL IN SECURING THE SUBDOMAIN OF FISCAL POLICY

In 1946 Harry Truman signed the Employment Act, a landmark law that he had played almost no part in initiating. In May 1945—less than a month after he assumed office and with the Second World War still underway—a reporter asked the new president about his "attitude toward the full employment bill of Senator [James] Murray." Truman responded, "I am not familiar with Senator Murray's full employment bill, but I am for full employment, and shall do everything in my power to create full employment as soon as hostilities end."[1] Even more notable, Truman highlighted the importance of the Employment Act after overseeing its implementation, explaining in his memoirs, "Occasionally, as we pore through the pages of history, we are struck by the fact that some incident, little noted at the time, profoundly affects the whole subsequent course of events. I venture the prediction that history, someday, will so record the enactment of the Employment Act of 1946."[2]

In line with the president's prediction, the Employment Act aimed to "[affect] the whole subsequent course of events" in two key ways. First—and building upon Franklin Roosevelt's call in 1944 to ensure "adequate protection from the economic fears of . . . unemployment"—the law established a universal governing objective that made it "the continuing policy and responsibility of the

113

Federal Government to use all practicable means . . . to promote maximum employment."[3] This meant that all of the existing administrative institutions comprising the public-finance apparatus—the Treasury Department, the Federal Reserve, and the Bureau of the Budget—now had to balance their individual governing objectives with the new universal governing objective.

Second, the Employment Act created the Council of Economic Advisers, which was to operate with no other governing objective except that of promoting "maximum employment." This new institution—situated within the relatively new Executive Office of the President—was to "be composed of three members . . . each of whom shall be a person who, as a result of his training, experience, and attainments, is exceptionally qualified . . . to formulate and recommend national economic policy to promote employment."[4]

In addition to the unprecedented statutory qualification for the individual members of the CEA, the scope of the new institution's jurisdiction was unprecedented. Whereas the Fed addressed monetary policy, and the Treasury and the BOB primarily addressed individual components of fiscal policy—taxation and spending, respectively—the Employment Act charged the CEA with "formulat[ing] and recommend[ing] national economic policy."[5] This meant that the new institution's jurisdiction overlapped with all three of the other public-finance institutions, as national economic policy incorporates both fiscal policy and monetary policy. Moreover, because the CEA had a single governing objective, whereas the other institutions had at least two—their individual governing objective and the new universal governing objective—the Employment Act all but ensured that the CEA's "exceptionally qualified" members would battle with the other public-finance principals, particularly the Treasury secretary, the head of the dominant pre–New Deal–era public-finance institution. As CEA Chair Leon Keyserling later explained, "The matters on which the Secretary of the Treasury and I disagreed were matters of the President's overall economic policy or the parts that [were] related to the whole" and "[Truman] felt that I was in a better position to give him advice."[6]

Further promoting the new universal governing objective, the Employment Act directed the president—with the support of the CEA—to "transmit to the Congress within sixty days after the beginning of each regular session" an economic report that addresses future "levels of employment." It also directed the president to put forward "a program for carrying out the policy declared in [the act]."[7]

Although the Employment Act passed during the Truman administration, it largely secured developments set into motion during the Roosevelt administration. As Edwin Nourse, the founding chair of the CEA explained, "The Employment Act of 1946 should be seen in the perspective of earlier developments . . . toward formulating national economic policies that would make for stabilization. So viewed, it may properly be regarded as the capstone of such an arch of earlier and partial building stones."[8] In particular, when the Employment Act went into effect in 1946, Harold Smith, a Roosevelt appointee, still headed the BOB and already supported the idea of using the budget to promote "full employment." Likewise, Marriner Eccles, a Roosevelt appointee, still headed the Fed, and as early as 1935, he had supported revising the Fed's mandate to address employment. As Eccles explained, "What I asked for in 1935 was a preview of what ultimately became the declaration of national policy that Congress in the Employment Act of 1946 set down for the government."[9]

Similar to the governing objective under the Employment Act, the CEA was created during the Truman administration, but it largely secured developments set into motion during the Roosevelt administration. In 1938 Roosevelt had created the Fiscal and Monetary Advisory Committee; in 1939 he had appointed Lauchlin Currie as the first professional economist to serve on the White House staff; and in 1940 he had overseen the creation of the BOB's Fiscal Division. The new CEA essentially integrated all those developments. Making clear the important connection between the BOB's Fiscal Division and the CEA, Nourse explained in his memoirs,

> [Gerhard Colm, one of the top experts in the Fiscal Division], in consultation with Director Webb of the Bureau of the Budget, decided that, since the Employment Act assigned intensive study and policy recommendations in the area of national income and fiscal policy definitely to the Council, it was logical for Mr. Colm to transfer to the new agency. This he did early in October, thus becoming one of the charter members of our group of top specialists, bringing to our explorations the momentum of several years of work already done by the Bureau of the Budget.[10]

Also revealing, the BOB eliminated the Fiscal Division shortly after the creation of the CEA, and Gerhard Colm further confirmed that the Employment Act and CEA "formalized responsibilities that were already recognized as governmental and presidential duties."[11]

* * *

While the Employment Act secured the universal governing objective of promoting "maximum employment" and centered the formulating and recommending of "national economic policy" in the new, stand-alone Council of Economic Advisers, the Bureau of the Budget began to expand its legislative clearance operations. The Roosevelt administration had initiated legislative proposals in a piecemeal fashion, and the president had then relied upon the newly expanded legislative clearance process to ensure that those proposals were more or less in accord with his "program" before they moved forward to Congress.[12] Underscoring the orientation and limited scope of the process, Roger Jones, the chief of the Legislative Reference Division, explained, "The work . . . had been very largely negative. . . . [T]here had been almost no part played by the Bureau in the development of the President's legislative program."[13]

This changed over the course of the Truman administration. In 1946—shortly before the passage of the Employment Act—the president combined the annual Budget Message and the State of the Union Address into a single report, wherein he proposed his basic legislative program to Congress. Similar to the consolidation of the budget process under the Budget and Accounting Act, this move was a recognition of the fact that it had become necessary to consolidate the president's legislative program, which had expanded substantially during the New Deal and was therefore now intimately connected to the budget. As Truman explained, "A quarter century ago the Congress decided that it could no longer consider the financial programs of the various departments on a piecemeal basis. Instead it has called on the President to present a comprehensive Executive Budget." Truman then added, "At the same time, it is clear that the budgetary program and the general program of the Government are actually inseparable."[14]

The passage of the Employment Act later that year strengthened Truman's initial step. As noted, the new law required the president to submit to Congress an annual economic report and a "program" to promote "maximum employment."[15] However, the CEA did not have the administrative capacity to execute that responsibility on its own; it was also simply not practical to develop a new "program" to promote "maximum employment" independent of the recently integrated "budgetary program" and "general program of the Government." Therefore, moving forward, the White House, the BOB, and the CEA worked together in compiling information for the State of the Union Address, the Budget Message, and the Economic Report in order to coordinate the president's overall annual program.[16]

As the first step in securing this new, multi-institutional process, Truman sent out a letter in 1947 directing the head of each agency to submit by November 1 "such material as you would propose for inclusion in the 1948 State of the Union Message or the Economic Report of the President" and also all such information on "legislation of concern to [the agency] which you anticipate may be considered by the Congress."[17] Then, along with specialists from the CEA and the other divisions of the BOB, the Legislative Reference Division took the lead in organizing this requested material into a single document that highlighted the major problems in each policy domain and the proposed solutions.[18]

The following year the Truman administration repeated the entire process and expanded the request for information on each department's "proposed legislative program."[19] The result was the creation of the "Fair Deal" program. Underscoring its scope, the *New York Times* reported, "In the State of the Union message—and in the President's Economic Report . . . sent to Congress two days later—[President Truman] spelled out the 'fair deal.' . . . He demanded new legislation in the fields of social welfare, social security, education, medical care, economic controls, civil rights—even a hint of possible Government ownership of certain means of production."[20]

Although the expansion of legislative clearance occurred during the Truman administration, it largely secured developments set into motion during the Roosevelt administration. Most notably, it helped to establish the Fair Deal as the more orderly successor to the haphazard New Deal, and it helped to ensure that the White House staff, the BOB, and the CEA would continue to work together in developing an annual program.[21] Highlighting the role of the Truman administration in securing the more informal operations of the Roosevelt administration, Budget Director Frank Pace explained, "[Truman] believed that one of his great contributions was his capacity to institutionalize what had been . . . essentially a personal function up to that time."[22]

In the process of securing the New Deal–era apparatus, Truman also helped to secure several key New Deal–era fiscal policies. He proposed and signed bills in 1948, 1949, and 1951 that extended the Reciprocal Trade Agreements Act. This worked together with the creation of an international trade agreement to secure the new president-dominated, non-revenue-based tariff system.[23] Truman also proposed and signed bills in 1950 and 1952 that "doubled insurance benefits and brought 10 million more persons under old age and survivors insurance," thereby significantly expanding Social Security, the foundational component of the growing welfare system.[24] Further underscoring the role of the Truman administration in securing and expanding New Deal–era policies more generally, CEA Chair Leon Keyserling explained, "The Fair Deal was an extension of the New Deal" and "all of the Democratic programs since, really, have not been so much innovating as [an] extension of the boundaries of existing New Deal programs."[25]

* * *

In addition to overseeing the creation of the Council of Economic Advisers, the expansion of the Bureau of the Budget's legislative clearance operations, and the passage of several bills that secured and expanded key New Deal–era fiscal policies, Truman supported the CEA's rise as an influential institution through the appointment of its "exceptionally qualified" second chair, which in turn had significant policy consequences during the Korean War.

Following the passage of the Employment Act, Truman first appointed Edwin Nourse, a former president of the American Economic Association, to the new position of CEA chair and he appointed Leon Keyserling, a lawyer and economist, to the new position of vice chair. Although the president exercised the power of appointment in law, Senator Robert Wagner essentially controlled its use in practice in the case of the vice chair. As Nourse confirmed, "Keyserling was named in response to Senator Wagner's wishes."[26] After Nourse resigned in 1949, Truman relied upon the simple shortcut of elevating the number two principal—Wagner's original appointee and an experienced New Dealer—to the top position. Making clear the extent of the new CEA chair's experience in government during the New Deal era, Keyserling later explained, "Long before there was a Council, I was very, very much a part of . . . the Roosevelt administration. . . . I had been in the Executive branch, I had been in the congressional branch, so I was very much a part of things for almost two decades, from March 1933 forward."[27]

The significance of Keyserling's appointment becomes even clearer when considered in relation to the budget director, the head of the institution that worked most closely with the CEA. Initially, Truman retained Roosevelt's budget director, Harold Smith. Once Smith resigned in 1946 due to failing health, Truman appointed James Webb, the executive assistant to the undersecretary of the Treasury. Then when Webb—who, like his predecessor, had studied public administration and supported the expansion of legislative clearance—resigned in 1949, Truman returned to the simple shortcut of elevating the number two principal by appointing Frank Pace, a self-described "fiscal conservative."[28] However, now the appointment of Keyserling—an "ultra liberal" in the words of the Treasury secretary—came into play, as Pace resigned the following year due to ideological differences with the CEA chair.[29] Confirming the divide between the two principals, Pace explained, "I . . . told Mr. Truman that I felt that he should have someone else as Director of the Budget because basically I didn't agree with the economic philosophy of Leon Keyserling."[30]

Rather than appoint a new CEA chair, Truman demonstrated his commitment to securing the New Deal–era apparatus and policy parameters by replacing the budget director, even though that principal's views on public finance were more closely aligned with his own. Pace—the self-described "fiscal conservative"—explained, "Truman was socially a liberal, but fiscally a conservative. He was really a joy for a Budget Director to work with."[31] Moreover, in replacing Pace, Truman once again relied upon the simple shortcut of elevating the number two principal, Fred Lawton, the assistant director and a nonpolitical careerist.[32]

To be clear, the incompatibility between a "liberal" CEA chair and a "conservative" BOB director was due to the role of the CEA in setting the parameters of the budget as part of its statutory charge to "formulate and recommend national economic policy." As Keyserling explained,

> A full year in advance the Budget Bureau would ask us for a complete portrayal of likely economic developments and broad outlines of what size budget was compatible with these prospective developments and with our targets for the economy. . . . That involved continuous relations over the course of the year between our people and the Budget Bureau people. In that way our economic responsibilities and projections and goals and prospects entered into the making of the budget itself.[33]

Finally, with the new public-finance principals in place, Truman oversaw two critical fiscal-policy decisions: a substantial increase in national defense spending, which helped to boost the economy; and a substantial increase in taxation, which was necessary to fund the increase in spending and helped to secure the progressive tax system.

In the years after the Second World War, Truman supported lower defense spending. In 1948 he explained, "In the long run, . . . I hope" to spend "between $5 and $7 billion" a year. "We are spending [$14.4 billion for fiscal year 1949]. We can't keep that up."[34] This was the basic budgetary setting in April 1950 when the National Security Council issued Report 68, which called for the "rapid build-up of political, economic, and military strength in the free world" to win the Cold War.[35] Although the report initially contained no specific cost estimates, it essentially proposed—with the support of the CEA—a three-fold increase in defense spending in order to contain the rising threat of the Soviet Union. Underscoring the influential role of the new CEA chair, Charles Murphy, special counsel to the president, later explained,

> One of the things that was discussed a great deal in the NSC senior staff group was the capacity of the economy to support a larger defense effort. From time to time we would turn to [Keyserling] and ask, "How much can the country afford to spend on defense?" And [Keyserling] would say, "I don't know exactly, but you have not reached the limit yet." And this, it seemed to me, was enormously important.[36]

While the NSC continued to work out the details of the new strategy, the start of the Korean War in June 1950 and the pledge of military support two days later—a step that the president took only after the planning for NSC-68 was underway—resulted in Truman approving a revised draft of the report that projected defense spending of more than $40 billion annually through fiscal year 1955.[37] In other words, two years after announcing that it was not sustainable to spend $14 billion a year on defense—and based in large part on the "enormously important" advice of his CEA chair, who argued that even a much higher level of defense spending was feasible over a sustained period—the president now proposed spending nearly three times the amount that he had initially criticized. The president also made it clear that this was not simply a one-off request, explaining to Congress, "We must be prepared to endure a long period of tension."[38]

Truman himself later revealed a key source of the "enormously important" role of the public-finance principals, especially that of the "exceptionally qualified" CEA chair, in structuring the fiscal-policymaking process. As the president explained in memoirs, "The federal budget is one of the most talked-about activities of government and one of the least understood," as it is now "so enormous in volume and so complex in scope that [it] has become difficult to grasp except for those who work on it from day to day." Indeed, "it cannot be expected that a President can personally do more than take part in the final stages of preparing the budget and then concern himself with only the major items."[39]

Second, and related to the first development, the government covered the cost of the Korean War—and the Cold War more generally—by raising taxes rather than by running enormous deficits as it had during the Second World War. Providing the rationale for this approach in an influential report submitted to the president in 1950, Keyserling explained, "The prospect that the defense effort will be prolonged makes it particularly important to cover the cost through taxes. Borrowing has its place in the financing of a short, intensive effort; but it is dangerous for a long drawn-out effort."[40]

In line with the CEA chair's recommendation, and with substantial support from the CEA more generally, the president proposed and signed into law three major tax acts during the Korean War: the Revenue Act of 1950, which increased the top individual income tax rate from 82 percent to 91 percent and increased the top corporate income tax rate from 38 percent to 45 percent; the Excess Profits Tax Act of 1950, which increased the top corporate income tax rate to 47 percent; and the Revenue Act of 1951, which increased the top individual income tax rate to 92 percent and the top corporate income tax rate to 52 percent.[41] Confirming the influential role of the CEA, Keyserling later explained, "We, broadly speaking, developed the tax program for the President, in consultation with the Treasury to be sure, but we really developed that."[42] The president himself also confirmed that a key objective was to make the tax system more progressive, explaining to Congress, "Over the years, we have made important progress in building a good tax system. However, much remains to be done," especially in "improv[ing] the distribution of the tax load to make it conform better with tax paying ability."[43]

Working together, the increase in defense spending and the Korean War revenue acts significantly increased the size of the budget, and the increase in spending significantly boosted the economy. The economy grew by 8.7 percent in 1950 and 8.0 percent in 1951, levels not surpassed since then, and the unemployment rate fell from 5.4 percent to 2.5 percent, the lowest level since the end of the Second World War. Further confirming the significance of this progrowth "national economic policy" and his role in "formulat[ing] and recommend[ing]" it, Keyserling later remarked, "I think the greatest single decision made, both in its immediate importance and its long-range importance was the decision to go for a program of very large economic expansion." He added, "My initiation and participation in that was about as large as that of any one individual could be in influencing policy."[44]

The influence of the CEA chair is more apparent still when compared to that of the Treasury secretary, the dominant public-finance principal before the New Deal. Notably, Treasury Secretary John Snyder had opposed the expansionary economic policy at the start of the Korean War after also opposing the Fair Deal—as the president put it—in "the frankest and most explicit terms," both of which explain why Snyder later conceded, "My greatest problem" as Treasury secretary "was largely generated by the economic advisers" and "largely with one man—Keyserling."[45] For his part, the CEA chair later remarked, "I got along with [Snyder] very well, really because as to the Fair Deal program, and as to the early Korean war program, the President . . . was won over to our side and there wasn't any point in carrying on the battle."[46]

Further underscoring Truman's commitment to securing his predecessor's work, Truman himself explained in his memoirs, "In my senatorial experience I had followed the leadership of and the political and economic program of Franklin Roosevelt," and as president, "my objective was to carry out . . . the economic bill of rights which had been formulated by President Roosevelt."[47]

* * *

The case study analysis here shows that Truman relinquished much of his control to Roosevelt in the subdomain of fiscal policy in working to secure the New Deal–era apparatus and policy parameters. First, in supporting the Employment Act, which established the universal governing objective of promoting "maximum employment" and created the Council of Economic Advisers, both of which largely secured developments set into motion during the Roosevelt administration and thereby fulfilled the president's pledge "to carry out . . . the economic bill of rights . . . formulated by President Roosevelt," Truman relinquished much of his control to his predecessor. Second, in expanding and securing the Bureau of the Budget's legislative clearance operations, which helped "to institutionalize what had been . . . essentially a personal function up to that time," and in developing the Fair Deal legislative program, which was largely "an extension of the New Deal," Truman further relinquished much of his control to his predecessor. Third, in overseeing the implementation of NSC-68, which secured the growing and structurally balanced budget that generally operated as the primary economic stabilization instrument, and in overseeing the Korean War tax program, which secured the progressive tax system, both of which were directed in large part by the CEA chair, an "ultra liberal" New Deal economist who had been "very much a part of . . . the Roosevelt administration," Truman relinquished even more of his control to his predecessor.

TRUMAN RELINQUISHES HIS CONTROL IN SECURING THE SUBDOMAIN OF MONETARY POLICY

In 1945 Harry Truman signed the Bretton Woods Agreement Act, granting the United States membership in the International Monetary Fund, an arrangement that the Roosevelt administration had taken the lead in developing and that secured a key goal of the "march toward 'managed currency.'" Rather than adjust domestic policy to support international policy—as had occurred during the Hoover administration—the new system established fixed but adjustable exchange rates that allowed international policy to adjust in support of domestic policy, meaning the Bretton Woods Agreement Act strengthened the government's ability to implement the new universal governing objective under the Employment Act passed the following year.[48]

The Bretton Woods Act also made it more difficult for subsequent incumbents to control monetary policy. In particular, the law directed the Treasury secretary to use $1.8 billion from the Exchange Stabilization Fund to pay for the US subscription to the IMF. This decreased the available resources under the ESF from its original total of $2 billion in 1934, the equivalent of 75 percent of the Fed's balance sheet, to $299 million in 1947, the equivalent of 1 percent of the Fed's balance sheet.[49] Coupled with two important but little noted developments during the Second World War—the expiration of the Thomas amendment's authorization to devalue the dollar and the repeal of the authorization to issue additional US notes—the president and the Treasury secretary no longer had the power to act unilaterally or to offset undesirable policies.[50]

Although these developments weakened presidential control over monetary policy, two other factors worked to limit the role and independence of the Fed in practice immediately after the Second World War: the use of wage and price controls and the continuation of the interest rate peg.

Like his predecessor, Truman supported the use of wage and price controls to check inflation rather than depend solely upon monetary policy under the management of the independent central bank. This occurred in a series of steps that involved, as the president put it, "stabilizing the economy during the reconversion period."[51] In 1946 Truman announced that it was necessary for the Democratic-controlled Congress "to renew the [wage and price control legislation] as soon as possible."[52] In 1947 he called on the new Republican-controlled Congress "to extend once more the Second War Powers Act" because "a few controls . . . under [that law] would be needed" to check double-digit inflation.[53] And in 1948 he continued the battle with the Republican-controlled Congress, later explaining, "In accepting the nomination for President . . . I strongly criticized this Eightieth Congress for . . . its failure to provide stand-by controls."[54]

In addition to wage and price controls, the Fed remained subservient to the Treasury due to the interest rate peg. Reinforcing that development, monetary policy remained subservient to fiscal policy more generally, due to the perceived failure of the former in responding to the Great Depression. Making clear the relatively weak role of the Fed and monetary policy at the time, Fed Chair Marriner Eccles later revealed, "I told [President Truman]" after he assumed office "that my term as Chairman had nearly three years to run, but this need not deter him from designating someone of his own choice; he could at any time indicate to me that he desired my resignation."[55]

Unlike Roosevelt, who had appointed his own Fed chair, Truman initially retained his predecessor's appointee. However, as the president and the Treasury secretary continued to support the interest rate peg—and as inflation increased from 2 percent in 1945 to 8 percent in 1946, and then to 14 percent in 1947—the Fed chair began to oppose the administration's policies more forcefully. Addressing the reason for the growing divide and rising inflation, Eccles explained, "The difficulties that arose between the Treasury and the Federal Reserve were not due to a clash of personalities. They were due to a conflict of responsibilities" that "[arose] after the war over the continuance of the cheap-money policy of the wartime period of heavy deficit financing."[56]

In response to Eccles's growing opposition, Truman finally appointed Thomas McCabe—the Board chair of the Reserve Bank in Philadelphia and a friend of the Treasury secretary—to head the Fed in 1948. This move was designed to resolve the Treasury–Fed divide in a manner acceptable to the Truman administration, meaning an outcome that favored the Treasury's preferred "continuance of the cheap-money policy." Further making clear that, like Roosevelt, he intended to limit the independence of the central bank, Truman remarked during a meeting with the heads of the Federal Reserve Banks shortly thereafter, "Now gentlemen, you represent the greatest financial institution in the history of the world, except the Treasury of the United States."[57]

* * *

As in his first term, Truman worked to limit the role and independence of the Fed following his reelection in 1948. This was evident when Congress once again granted the president sweeping authority to implement wage and price controls due to the start of the Korean War. Highlighting both the relatively limited role of the Fed in managing the economy at the time through the use of monetary policy and the expanded role of the president, the Defense Production Act of 1950 declared that, "to prevent inflation and preserve the value of the currency . . . the President may issue regulations and orders establishing . . . ceilings on the price . . . of any material or service" and he may also "issue regulations and orders stabilizing wages, salaries, and other compensation."[58]

In addition to spurring the implementation of wage and price controls due to fears of another spike in inflation, the start of the Korean War intensified the battle between the Treasury and the Fed. Once in office, Thomas McCabe, the new Fed chair soon took a position similar to that of his predecessor because the dispute between the Fed and the Treasury was—as Eccles explained—a "conflict of responsibilities," not a conflict of personalities or a matter of loyalty.[59] In another attempt to resolve the dispute on the administration's terms, Truman invited the entire Federal Open Market Committee to meet with him at the White House in January 1951—the first and only meeting of its kind, and one designed to publicly pressure all the key players, not simply the Board and its chair. Like the earlier move it proved ineffective. As Truman later revealed, "I was given assurance at this meeting that the [Fed] would support the Treasury's plans," and "I was taken by surprise when subsequently they failed to support the program."[60]

Recognizing that he could not simply pressure the Fed publicly, and without his predecessor's powers to act unilaterally, Truman appointed an interagency group headed by Charles Wilson, the director of the Office of Defense Mobilization, to resolve the ongoing dispute. However, the Treasury and the Fed both opposed the idea of an outsider imposing a solution, and therefore Treasury Secretary John Snyder authorized William McChesney Martin, Jr., the assistant secretary of the Treasury, to negotiate directly with the Fed. This move undercut the president's directive and finally generated an agreement.[61] In March 1951 the Treasury and the Fed released a joint statement that they had "reached full accord with respect to debt-management and monetary policies to be pursued in furthering their common purpose to assure the successful financing of the government's requirements and, at the same time, to minimize monetization of the public debt."[62] In other words, the Treasury–Federal Reserve Accord established that the Fed would be allowed to oversee—within undefined limits—the newly established "managed currency" for the first time since it had pledged in 1942 to keep the interest rate on treasury bills fixed.

Although the Fed had secured an agreement with the Treasury, Truman still aimed to limit the central bank's undefined independence. Acting quickly—and in line with Eccles's admission that "[the president] could at any time indicate . . . that he desired [the Fed chair's] resignation"—Truman accepted McCabe's resignation the following week, explaining that the latter's "services were no longer satisfactory."[63] In effect, the president fired the Fed chair through sustained pressure that forced the latter to offer his resignation; Truman then used this opening to appoint William McChesney Martin, Jr., the individual who had negotiated the accord on the Treasury side. Yet, once in office, the new chair, like his predecessors, supported the Fed's independence.[64]

Despite the failed effort to appoint a Fed chair who would support the position of the president and the Treasury, the Truman administration continued to limit the Fed's independence due to three key developments, all of which operated in addition to Truman's power to "at any time indicate . . . that he desired [the Fed chair's] resignation."

First, the Employment Act established a universal governing objective. Therefore, even though the Fed had acquired greater independence from the Treasury after the accord, the central bank still had to operate with a view of promoting "maximum employment."[65]

Second, the Employment Act directed the president to develop a "program" to promote "maximum employment," which required policy coordination. As Leon Keyserling explained, there were "consultations between the Council and the [Bureau of the] Budget, between the Council and the [Treasury]" and "between the Council and the Federal Reserve. They were all in effective, high-geared operation."[66] With this arrangement in place, the CEA then worked to undermine the Fed's independence in the process of "formulat[ing] and recommend[ing] national economic policy." Making clear the CEA's inclination to limit the Fed's independence, Leon Keyserling later explained, "Monetary policy isn't any more important than tax policy. . . . It is an anachronism . . . to claim that the money power of the nation should be 'independent' in the central bank."[67]

Third, the implementation of NSC-68 increased the portion of the budget devoted to national defense from 31 percent in 1948 to 68 percent in 1952, meaning that if the Fed stopped assisting the Treasury in maintaining a stable market for government securities, it threatened to undermine national security first and foremost, an inconceivable option that further reinforced the subordination of monetary policy to fiscal policy. As Truman warned, "If people lose confidence in Government securities all we hope to gain from our military mobilization, and war if need be, might be jeopardized."[68]

Finally, and further underscoring its limited independence in practice due largely to these key New Deal–era policymaking constraints, the new Fed chair himself acknowledged that following the Treasury–Federal Reserve accord, the central bank now only has "independence within the government, not independence of the government."[69]

Also notable, Truman explained in his memoirs, "These problems of discount rates and bond issues are not matters that are likely to make the headlines . . . yet on their settlement can depend the financial soundness of the government and the prosperity of countless individuals." Then, making clear both his commitment in general to securing his predecessor's policies and his commitment in particular to securing his predecessor's moves to keep control over monetary policy in Washington rather than in the regional Reserve Banks, Truman added, "I pledged myself to carry out the war and peace policies of Franklin Roosevelt," and "my approach to all these financial questions always was that it was my duty to keep the financial capital of the United States in Washington. This is where it belongs—but to keep it there is not always an easy task."[70]

* * *

The case study analysis here shows that Truman relinquished much of his control to Roosevelt in the subdomain of monetary policy in working to secure the New Deal–era apparatus and policy parameters. First, in supporting the Bretton Woods Agreement Act, which secured developments set into motion during the Roosevelt administration and thereby fulfilled the president's pledge "to carry out the war and peace policies of Franklin Roosevelt," Truman relinquished much of his control to his predecessor. Second, in supporting the continued use of wage and price controls, in essentially firing the Fed chair, in supporting the Employment Act, in supporting fiscal- and monetary-policy coordination, and in supporting the prioritization of the Treasury's debt management, all of which worked to limit the Fed's independence even after the accord and thereby further fulfilled the president's pledge both "to carry out the war and peace policies of Franklin Roosevelt" and "to keep the financial capital of the United States in Washington," Truman further relinquished much of his control to his predecessor.

Altogether, the case study analysis of fiscal policymaking and monetary policymaking in this chapter shows that the centralized New Deal–era apparatus and the New Deal–era policy parameters were both firmly in place by the end of the Truman administration.

The New Deal–Era Apparatus: In general, the weakened Treasury Department, directed in statute to promote "maximum employment" but oriented in practice toward balancing the budget, and the strengthened Council of Economic Advisers and Bureau of the Budget, both directed in statute to promote "maximum employment" and the latter institution restricted in practice due to direct coordination with the former institution, would all assist the president in proposing an annual budget and broader "program" that together would operate as the primary economic-stabilization instrument. At the same time, the weakened Federal Reserve—legally independent and oriented toward checking inflation but restricted in statute and practice due to the "maximum employment" directive, policy coordination, and debt management operations—would generally maintain a supportive role in managing monetary policy, which would operate as a secondary economic-stabilization instrument.

The New Deal–Era Policy Parameters: In structuring the policymaking process, the New Deal–era apparatus and its principals would play a key role in supporting the New Deal–era policy parameters. In particular, the established policy parameters now had the support of not only distinct political coalitions and a status quo–biased constitutional system but also an established public-finance apparatus and its principals committed to maintaining stability following the end of the Great Depression. On the fiscal front, the established New Deal–era policies included a growing and structurally balanced budget that generally operated as the primary economic-stabilization instrument; a highly progressive tax system; and an unrestricted general spending system and growing Social Security spending. On the monetary front, the established New Deal–era policy included a "managed currency" that generally operated as a secondary economic-stabilization instrument in support of promoting "maximum employment."

Moving forward, this meant that each president's control in the domain of public finance was a contingency that would turn in large part on the alignment of his preferences and the policy parameters that the New Deal–era apparatus and its principals structured.

7. Constraint: The New Deal–Era Apparatus Limits Eisenhower's Control

The quantitative overview provided evidence that in the domain of public finance, the centralized New Deal–era apparatus and the New Deal–era policy parameters both remained in place throughout Dwight Eisenhower's presidency and beyond due largely to the absence of an exceptionally severe and highly prioritized problem, which strengthened the average restrictions on presidential control and weakened the average incentive to maximize control. This chapter traces the process of the established, relatively stable New Deal–era apparatus and its principals in supporting the established New Deal–era policy parameters and limiting Eisenhower's control.

THE NEW DEAL–ERA APPARATUS LIMITS EISENHOWER'S CONTROL IN THE SUBDOMAIN OF FISCAL POLICY

Dwight Eisenhower assumed office in 1953 with unified party control of the government and a strong desire to change the course in the subdomain of fiscal policy that Franklin Roosevelt had initiated in response to the Great Depression. In his memoirs Eisenhower explained, "I was determined, if humanly possible, to carry on the fight to conduct a revolution which would reverse the trend of the budgets of the past twenty years." Going further, Eisenhower wrote, "With the chance for new policies and ideas to come into the federal government after twenty years of another political philosophy, I wanted to make it clear that we would not be simply a continuation of the New Deal and Fair Deal, in purpose or execution."[1]

Despite this strong desire to change the established course, the New Deal–era apparatus and its principals failed to provide the new president with an actual plan "to conduct a revolution." Moreover, the president himself had no such plan. As Eisenhower confessed in his diary,

> Today I give my first "state of the union." . . . I feel it a mistake for a new administration to be talking so soon after inauguration. . . . Time for study, exploration, and analysis is necessary. But, the Republicans have been so long out of

power they want, and probably need, a pronouncement from their president as a starting point. This I shall try to give. I hope, and pray, that it does not contain blunders that we will later regret.[2]

Without sufficient "time for study, exploration, and analysis," Eisenhower immediately struggled to chart a new course. This was evident in January 1953 when Daniel Reed, the Republican chair of the House Ways and Means Committee, introduced a bill to move up the expiration date for the income tax rate increase under the Revenue Act of 1951 so that it would coincide with the expiration date of the excess-profits tax increase under the Excess Profits Act of 1950. Considering that Eisenhower had campaigned on cutting taxes, the proposal was certainly understandable. But it was also expected to cost the government roughly $2 billion in revenue at a time when there was already a projected budget deficit. The new president therefore opposed his own party's first major legislative proposal. As Eisenhower later noted, "I was emphatic in my opposition." Making clear the reason, he added, "I could not accept the argument that early 1953 was the time to begin reducing taxes. My promise to cut taxes had been predicated on a simultaneous balancing of the budget."[3]

Four months later, and relying primarily on the assistance of Treasury Secretary George Humphrey—the former head of a steel manufacturing company, and a traditional, balanced-budget, small-government conservative—Eisenhower presented his own tax proposal. Most notably, it recommended that Congress extend for six months the excess-profits tax increase and rescind the reduction of corporate and excise taxes scheduled for April 1954.[4] Not surprisingly, the president's proposal—essentially the complete opposite of Reed's proposal—triggered a major split within the Republican Party. As Eisenhower explained, "A prolonged debate ensued. I used every possible reason, argument, and device, and every kind of personal and indirect contact to bring Chairman Reed to my way of thinking. . . . When I could not make him see reason I informed him that we would fight the matter."[5] Ultimately Reed surrendered due to the combined support of the Treasury secretary and the Republican leadership in Congress; the House and Senate then passed the administration's proposed tax extension, and Eisenhower labeled the entire episode a "success."[6]

Although the president had prevailed in this initial showdown with Congress, the limits of his "success" were readily apparent. Rather than select from a set of desirable policy alternatives that would produce a balanced budget, Eisenhower supported the extension of taxes that he philosophically opposed. In his diary the president confessed, "Our excise taxes are onerous, heavy, and, in many cases, not only unjust but positively stupid."[7] The Treasury secretary then revealed the reason for the tax extension, explaining, "Our inheritance of obligations both immediate and planned is staggering. . . . Accumulations of twenty years cannot be removed in ninety days."[8]

Adding to the situation, the president reversed course less than five months later in order to stabilize the economy. Making clear his concern at the time, Eisenhower explained, "For more than twenty years economic depression had been the skeleton in the Republican closet. . . . In many minds the suspicion lurked that this problem might once again prove to be the party's undoing. To dispel this fear," the administration "had to pass through a trial of fire."[9]

The "trial" began in September 1953, when Arthur Burns, the new chair of the Council of Economic Advisers, warned the president of an impending economic contraction. In line with the requirement that members be "exceptionally qualified," Burns had a PhD in economics from Columbia University, he had served as the director of the National Bureau of Economic Research, and he was an expert on business cycles—the first chair whose specialty was the CEA's primary activity. Based on his training, he was not someone who would have been appointed to a top public-finance position in the Eisenhower administration had the Roosevelt administration not established the precedent of appointing a professional economist to the White House staff and—building on that development—had the Employment Act not created the CEA. Underscoring the novelty of Burns's appointment, Sherman Adams, the president's chief of staff, later noted,

> When I took my first look at Burns, on the day he came to my office before I was to take him in to meet the President, I had a sinking sensation. If somebody had asked me to describe the mental image I had of the type of New Deal official we were in the process of moving out of Washington, this was it. . . . I wondered if we would both be thrown out of Eisenhower's office.[10]

Similar to Adams's hesitation with regard to Burns, the president remained highly skeptical of the CEA. Burns later explained, "Eisenhower was by no means certain that he wanted a CEA. In fact, he was inclined not to continue it."[11]

Although Burns was the "type of New Deal official" that the new administration was "in the process of moving out of Washington," and although Eisenhower would not have created the CEA and was even "inclined not to continue it," the new president ultimately retained this key component of the New Deal–era apparatus largely based on the recommendation of Burns and the fear that the mismanagement of another economic downturn "might once again prove to be the party's undoing." As the individual charged with "formulat[ing] and recommend[ing] national economic policy," Burns then took the lead in putting together the administration's "program" to promote "maximum employment" once the Recession of 1953–1954 began. In particular, the CEA chair recommended that the Eisenhower administration support credit easing operations, develop a plan for increased spending, and support the tax cuts that it had fought to block in the spring.[12] The first proposal confirmed the CEA's involvement in monetary policy, which effectively weakened the restructured Federal Reserve's independence under the first Republican administration of the New Deal era; and the last two measures set the stage for a showdown with the Treasury secretary, who had worked to prevent the tax cuts in the first place and strongly opposed the idea of a countercyclical fiscal policy. As Humphrey later explained, making clear his own starkly different views on public finance, "I will contest a tax cut out of deficits as long as I am able. . . . I don't believe in this idea that you can cut taxes out of deficits, and then build up from that."[13]

Notwithstanding both the Treasury secretary's opposition to budget deficits and the president's willingness to fight the Republican-controlled Congress several months earlier in an effort to balance the budget, the two men quickly acquiesced to the expert in this situation. Eisenhower informed Burns, "Arthur, you are my chief of staff in handling the recession. You are to report every week . . . on where we are going and what we ought to be doing."[14] Likewise, Humphrey conceded, "We must not let this happen; you must tell us what to do."[15] Equally revealing, Burns himself later explained that Eisenhower "had no special background . . . in the economic area. . . . To help him I would have to teach him."[16]

With the CEA chair in charge, the Treasury secretary announced in late September that the Eisenhower administration would not oppose the tax cuts scheduled to go into effect at the start of 1954. Confirming his influential role in this decision, Burns explained, "Humphrey was reluctant to make a categorical statement and wanted to leave the way open for continuing the taxes if it later proved necessary or desirable, but I persuaded him to come out with solid reassurance to the business community that the cuts would go through as scheduled."[17] The release of the economic report required by the Employment Act in January further strengthened the CEA chair's control over the public-finance agenda, which helped to ensure that the Eisenhower administration accepted the New Deal–era approach to managing the economy. As the president explained, the economic report "set forth our determination to move swiftly with preventive action to arrest the downturn before it might become more severe; to avoid a doctrinaire position; to do everything possible to stimulate consumers to spend more money and businessmen to create more jobs."[18]

Finally, in March Eisenhower signed into law a bill that cut excise taxes, the largest direct fiscal action taken in response to the recession. Although the president and the Treasury secretary both strongly opposed the measure, the CEA chair successfully persuaded the president to sign it for "countercyclical reasons."[19] Later that month Eisenhower announced that all told, the administration's actions amounted to a $7.4 billion tax cut. Demonstrating his new, though brief acceptance of the New Deal–era approach to fiscal policy, the president added, "We have every reason to believe that it will be a stimulating factor in our economy."[20]

Remarkably, there was no mention of a balanced budget, the president's preferred policy. During his second term Eisenhower made his own preference exceptionally clear, explaining to his advisers,

> If we do not pay as we go . . . we will have no recourse than to do what we desperately do not want to do: to desert liberty as we understand it. . . . If I have to show an unbalanced budget, if I have to show a trend of upward spending— then I am defeated. . . . We must remember: frugality, economy, simplicity with efficiency, I cannot tell you how deeply I believe this.[21]

The president's chief of staff also later revealed that "[Eisenhower] once told the Cabinet that if he was able to do nothing as President except balance the budget he would feel that his time in the White House had been well spent."[22] Nevertheless, in 1953 and 1954—the only period of unified party control of the government during the Eisenhower administration—the CEA chair successfully directed the new president to support the promotion of "maximum employment" rather than "fight to conduct a revolution which would reverse the trend of the budgets of the past twenty years." As Burns put it, successfully managing the economy "involved certain sacrifices of other values."[23]

* * *

While the Council of Economic Advisers took the lead in managing the economy, the Bureau of the Budget took the lead in developing the president's annual "program" more generally, which complemented the economic-recovery program. This process began when Eisenhower, in his own words, sent Joseph Dodge for "indoctrination" into the operations of the federal government immediately after the election.[24] In particular, the Truman administration granted the budget director–designate complete access to the BOB during the final two months, meaning that he discussed budgetary matters with the staff and sat in on meetings to learn how and why certain decisions were made. Ultimately, Dodge—a banker and former financial adviser to the US military during and after the Second World War—was so impressed with the restructured institution's operations and staff that he decided not to make any major changes. In fact, after the transition, he appointed Frederick Lawton, Truman's final budget director, as a special assistant, and he retained Roger Jones, the chief of the Legislative Reference Division.[25]

With the "indoctrinated" budget director in place and relying upon the experienced staff that had been hired and trained during the Roosevelt and Truman administrations, the positively oriented legislative clearance process moved forward in 1953. In January Dodge and the BOB staff provided a briefing to each incoming cabinet member on his department's legislative program as compiled during the last year of the Truman administration. This weakened the opposition to several programs and emphasized the importance of continuity more generally within the new Eisenhower administration, which—as the president himself conceded—had little "time for study, exploration, and analysis." Underscoring the significance of this step, Jones explained,

> It was [President] Truman's view that we should try to persuade Dodge, as the incoming Budget Director, that we should participate in and arrange for extensive briefings about the budget and the legislative programs with the incoming Cabinet officers; the very first time this had ever been done. It was done with outstanding success. I participated in it and used very extensively the materials which I had prepared because President Truman had told us to prepare them.[26]

That summer the positively oriented legislative clearance process continued when the BOB sent out its annual call for budget estimates. Identical in language to that of the Truman administration, the call included instructions for each agency to provide information on "all items of legislation . . . which the agency contemplates proposing during the ensuing twelve months." The BOB staff also briefed the new president on his predecessor's practice. This led Eisenhower, like Truman, to send an identical letter to each cabinet member requesting substantive ideas appropriate for the "formulation of a carefully planned, specific legislative program."

By mid-September, hundreds of proposals had flown into the BOB, a significant portion of which resembled measures from the New Deal and the Fair Deal, which was hardly surprising considering the earlier information sessions and the continuity in key personnel and procedures. In October more than three hundred major proposals were then sent to the White House, and in November and December the president's staff spent a significant portion of its time reviewing the proposals. At the same time, as the chief of the Legislative Reference Division, Jones assisted in educating the new White House staff on the pros and cons of each measure.[27]

Finally, in January 1954, Eisenhower became the first Republican president to submit a comprehensive legislative program to Congress. Notably, the Eisenhower administration had not put forward its own comprehensive program during the first year, nor had it submitted its own budget. As Eisenhower explained, "When my administration began, in January 1953, it . . . undertook the work of modifying and revising the documents and programs earlier sent to the Congress by the Truman administration" because "our own opportunities at that time for making the necessary studies and analyses . . . were limited." The president then added that, in 1954 "my administration had the entire responsibility for the content of the State of the Union message, the Budget message, and the Economic Report, the three major messages sent annually," and based on that responsibility, "I made 232 specific requests for legislation."[28]

Remarkably, the 1954 program largely followed the established course despite Eisenhower's strong desire that his administration "not be simply a continuation of the New Deal and Fair Deal." In particular, the program included a bill to extend unemployment insurance, a bill to extend Social Security coverage to approximately ten million people, a bill to increase Social Security benefits, and a bill to extend the Reciprocal Trade Agreements Act.[29] Underscoring the continuity in policy across the New Deal, the Fair Deal, and the first Republican program of the era, the *New York Times* reported, "In its broad objectives, the program outlined by the President made no large departures from the policies of his two Democratic predecessors."[30]

The basic continuity in policy under Eisenhower was due in no small part to the continuity in administration that the BOB provided as well as the president's inexperience and prioritization of other issues. Confirming that he never again proposed such a large program, Eisenhower later wrote, "These requests constituted the most massive and comprehensive set of recommendations of my entire eight years."[31] Moreover, Jones confirmed the president's prioritization of other issues, explaining, "Eisenhower himself was not initially terribly interested in the legislative process," and it was only "as the administration wore on" that he got more involved.[32]

The next year the key role that the New Deal–era apparatus and its principals had played in structuring the fiscal-policymaking process during the critical period of unified party control of the government became even more apparent when the Treasury secretary—whose views most closely matched those of the president—denounced the economic report that Burns had written and that highlighted many of the policies the CEA and the BOB had promoted throughout 1953 and 1954. In particular, Humphrey complained that the report was "socialistic," and he demanded that it be "scrapped."[33] This view essentially matched Eisenhower's own assessment that under his two Democratic predecessors, who had also governed with the support of the New Deal–era apparatus, the "cloud of an unwanted socialism seemed to be, at least faintly, appearing on the economic horizon."[34] Moreover, in a continuation of the division between the Treasury secretary and the Lauchlin Currie–led group during the second term of the Roosevelt administration and the division between the Treasury secretary and the CEA chair during the Truman administration, Humphrey went even further, directly attacking Burns himself. "You're giving the President advice on taxation" and "trespassing on my function," he complained. "Now the fact that you are doing it is bad enough; the fact that your advice differs sharply from mine makes things worse. This is an intolerable condition."[35]

Continuing to make clear his own strong view, Eisenhower explained to Burns during the second term, "I realize that to be conservative . . . and flatly to say so . . . can well get me tagged as an unsympathetic, reactionary fossil. But my honest conviction is that the greatest service we can . . . do for our country is to oppose wild-eyed schemes of every kind."[36] No doubt, the "232 specific requests for legislation" in 1954—which, as the president himself acknowledged, was "the most massive and comprehensive set of recommendations of my entire eight years"—included many "wild-eyed schemes of every kind" that Eisenhower later regretted.

* * *

Following the Democratic takeover of Congress in 1955, the New Deal–era apparatus and its principals continued to limit Eisenhower's control. The most prominent example of this process first occurred in 1957. After Percival Brundage—a former deputy director promoted to head the Bureau of the Budget—reviewed the fiscal-year 1958 budget proposal with the president, Eisenhower complained, "I've never felt so helpless."[37] Indeed, rather than "cut Federal spending to something like $60 billion within four years," as Eisenhower had pledged during the 1952 campaign, his administration's budget proposal, as the *New York Times* reported, "projected record high spending in a wide range of categories," all of which totaled nearly $72 billion.[38]

Although Eisenhower had substantial legal control over the centralized New Deal–era apparatus and a strong desire "to conduct a revolution which would reverse the trend of the budgets of the past twenty years," the election and foreign affairs had occupied his attention while the BOB and the CEA had put together the budget proposal. At this point he simply did not have enough time to cut his administration's own proposal before presenting it to Congress. In an effort to remedy this misstep, the Treasury secretary recommended releasing a statement encouraging the Democratic-controlled Congress "to make actual and substantial reductions" in the budget proposal; further underscoring the similarity in their views on public finance, Eisenhower concurred.[39] As the president later explained, "George and I had discussed the problem of high governmental expenditures time and again." Then, confirming his role with regard to the proposed statement in particular, the president added, "I . . . personally edited [it]."[40]

In addition to the unusual public request for the opposition party–controlled Congress to significantly revise the president's official budget proposal—a move that confirmed Eisenhower's limited control in proposing the budget in the first place—the Treasury secretary caused a major stir following the release of the prepared statement when he announced that maintaining the existing course of spending and taxing would eventually generate "a depression that will curl your hair."[41] This statement forced the president to distance himself from his Treasury secretary, whom he had put forward in an effort to distance himself from the initial BOB- and CEA-produced budget.

Worse still, total spending for the fiscal-year 1958 budget ultimately closed at $72 billion, essentially the same amount as the initial BOB- and CEA-produced budget proposal and nearly $3 billion above total revenue, meaning that the president had failed to balance the budget once again. Underscoring the impact of Eisenhower's continued inability to balance the budget or even put forward his preferred proposal, Arthur Larson, special assistant to the president, explained, "If I were to select the point at which . . . the Eisenhower administration began to turn from moderate progressivism to conservatism, it would be about [April] 1957. . . . To me, the most telling symptom of the change was the increasing obsession of President Eisenhower with the budget."[42]

This "turn from moderate progressivism to conservatism" included two key moves during the president's second term: the rejection of a tax cut in 1958 and the balancing of the fiscal-year 1960 budget, both of which provide even more evidence that the New Deal–era apparatus and its principals significantly limited Eisenhower's control in supporting the opposite course during the first term. Providing still more evidence of their key role in structuring the fiscal-policymaking process, the New Deal–era apparatus and its principals took the lead in reversing both moves once Eisenhower left office.

In 1958 Arthur Burns, who had resigned as CEA chair but remained an outside adviser, and Raymond Saulnier, the new CEA chair, both recommended that the president support a tax cut to stimulate the economy in response to the Recession of 1957–1958. As Eisenhower explained, "The weeks rolled by and several of my leading economic advisers came to the conclusion that, as in 1954, the administration should urge the Congress to cut taxes."[43] But unlike 1954, and notwithstanding the more dire economic situation—unemployment peaked at 7.5 percent in 1958 compared to 6.1 percent in 1954—the more experienced president successfully pushed back this time, informing Burns, "I have not yet been convinced" that a tax cut is a "necessity."[44] Further underscoring the divide between the CEA and the first Republican president of the New Deal era, the president articulated his own view of the administration's ideological orientation, writing in his diary, "We are basically conservative. . . . We believe in a private enterprise rather than a 'government' campaign to provide the main strength of recovery forces."[45] This stood in stark contrast to the "socialistic," Burns-authored economic report of 1955, which, in praising the Eisenhower administration's sweeping response in 1953 and 1954, declared, "The Government has taken many steps, both legislative and administrative, to put into effect policies that augment the expansionary powers of our economy."[46]

Although Eisenhower ultimately succeeded in preventing a tax cut in 1958, he left the New Deal–era apparatus in place, and once his second term ended in 1961, the CEA simply took the lead in convincing another new president to pass a tax cut to boost the economy, much as it had done in 1954. In fact, during the Kennedy administration, CEA Chair Walter Heller first worked to prevent a tax *increase*. As Heller explained, the CEA "persuaded [the president] to cancel the idea of a tax increase to finance the Berlin expenditures" in 1961. Regarding the president's shift to support for a tax cut in 1962, Heller added, "I believe it was in considerable part the [CEA's] persuasions. . . . Though politics was always a factor, I don't think it's unfair to say that we really had Kennedy pretty much on board with modern economics by [that point]."[47] Further highlighting the continuity in the recommendations of the CEA across Democratic and Republican administrations in general and the divide between Eisenhower and his former CEA chair in particular, the *New York Times* reported in 1963, "Dr. Arthur F. Burns, former chairman of the Council of Economic Advisers, endorsed today [in his testimony before the Joint Economic Committee of Congress] the income tax cut as proposed by President Kennedy."[48]

Following the development of the tax cut proposal during the Kennedy administration, Lyndon Johnson signed the measure into law in 1964, and the next year the new president made clear its primary rationale, explaining, "[T]he success of the 1964 tax cut . . . proves that taxes do much more than raise revenue to finance Government—they also affect the health and strength of the Nation's economy."[49] In particular, the CEA determined in 1962 that the "full employment target for stabilization policy" was a 4 percent unemployment rate, and it then worked to secure that policy, which explains in large part both the decline in the unemployment rate from an average of 5.6 percent in 1962 to 4 percent in December 1965 and the continuation of a 4 percent or lower unemployment rate for the rest of the decade.[50]

The other major move during Eisenhower's second term played out much the same way as the blocked tax cut in 1958 and its reversal during the 1960s. In 1959 Eisenhower moved to balance the last full budget of his presidency following the previous year's budget that, even without a tax cut, had produced a

$12.9 billion deficit, the largest peacetime deficit in history at the time. This led the president to further focus his attention on a key policymaking constraint at play throughout his tenure—the failure of the New Deal–era apparatus and its principals to develop proposals in line with his preferences. As Eisenhower explained to his cabinet, "We must not compromise $600 million proposals for $200 million proposals and feel that we have accomplished something, when we did not believe in the proposals in the first place."[51]

To address this key constraint and balance his final budget, Eisenhower took several important steps. First, to ensure that the president—not the CEA and BOB—maintained the first-mover advantage in the process, Eisenhower announced publicly a month before formally presenting the budget that it would be balanced at $77 billion. Second, in putting together the overall target for the proposal, Eisenhower ignored the recommendation of several principals, including the CEA chair, who was concerned with the damaging effects of such a large swing in the budget. Third, to hold the level of spending as steady as possible, Eisenhower succeeded in shrinking the administration's legislative program, recommending to Congress that it was time to "take a breather and check up on things."[52]

When the fiscal-year 1960 budget ended with a surplus, Eisenhower achieved his greatest fiscal-policy victory. As the New York Times reported, "Regardless of whether the 1960 surplus turns out to be $500 million or $600 million, it will remain a major accomplishment for those who recall the skepticism that greeted President Eisenhower when he set a balanced budget as the basic objective of fiscal policy a year and a half ago."[53]

Although Eisenhower succeeded in balancing his last full budget by seizing control from the BOB and CEA and "tak[ing] a breather" on the legislative program, he left the New Deal–era apparatus in place. Once his second term ended, the BOB and CEA therefore simply assisted subsequent presidents in developing a sweeping legislative program and an unbalanced budget at the start of their tenure, much as they had done during the Eisenhower administration. Theodore Sorensen, special counsel to the president, confirmed the significant role of the BOB in developing John Kennedy's "New Frontier" program—which included "277 separate requests" in 1961, closely matching in size Eisenhower's "232 specific requests" in 1954. As Sorensen explained,

In November and December [1960], with the help of the Budget Bureau staff . . . a master check list of all possible legislative, budgetary and administrative issues for Presidential action was prepared. This list was then refined and reduced to manageable proportions in a conference with our new Budget Director and his hold-over Deputy Director; and on December 21 a list of over

250 items . . . was reviewed in a rugged all-day and late-night session with the President-elect in Palm Beach. . . .

On the basis of that December 21 conference, a detailed letter of questions and requests was sent to each prospective member of the Cabinet, assignments were meted out for the drafting of detailed proposals and documents, new budget estimates were prepared . . . and a Kennedy Presidential program took definite shape. . . . Clearly it made it possible for the new President to take the legislative initiative immediately. In almost every critical area of public policy . . . comprehensive Presidential messages and some 277 separate requests would be sent to the Congress in Kennedy's first hundred days.[54]

Likewise, Lyndon Johnson confirmed the significant role of the CEA in launching the "War on Poverty," a major component of the "Great Society" program during the Johnson administration. As the president explained,

Walter Heller, [the] chairman of the Council of Economic Advisers, . . . came to see me at 7:40 in the evening [on the first full day of my presidency]. . . .

[He] told me that in November he had asked the departments and agencies of the federal government for ideas that could be used in developing a program to alleviate poverty. He said that he had discussed the subject with John Kennedy three days before his assassination. At that time, Heller told me, President Kennedy had approved his going ahead with plans for a program but had given no guidance as to the specific content. Now Heller had come to ask me an urgent message: Did I want the Council of Economic Advisers to develop a program to attack poverty? . . .

The poverty program Heller described was my kind of undertaking. "I'm interested," I responded. "I'm sympathetic. Go ahead. Give it the highest priority. Push ahead full tilt."[55]

Altogether, the CEA-initiated Kennedy–Johnson tax cut and the increase in spending due to the BOB and CEA-supported New Frontier and Great Society programs contributed to a growing budget that remained unbalanced for eight straight years, thereby reversing Eisenhower's effort in 1960 to limit spending and bring the budget into strict balance moving forward. To be clear, the budget remained structurally balanced throughout this period because the annual deficit remained smaller than the level of economic growth on average, meaning the debt continued to decline in relation to the size of the economy, which strengthened the government's long-term financial position. But Eisenhower strongly opposed anything other than a strictly balanced budget each year, which was the pre–New Deal–era standard. Further making clear his position, the former president took the unusual step of publicly attacking his successor's policies. As

Eisenhower explained in 1963—a month after his former CEA chair publicly endorsed the opposite position—"I start by stating my conviction that if the Government is to accept deliberately a massive deficit, and then simultaneously embark upon lavish new spending and a huge new tax cut, the nation is headed for trouble. If we do this we will convict ourselves of fiscal recklessness."[56]

* * *

The case study analysis here shows that the established, relatively stable New Deal–era apparatus and its principals significantly limited Eisenhower's control in the subdomain of fiscal policy. First, in directing the administration to cut taxes at the expense of "other values" in 1954 despite the president's desire "to conduct a revolution which would reverse the trend of the budgets of the past twenty years," the CEA and its chair, who resembled the "type of New Deal official we were in the process of moving out of Washington," limited Eisenhower's control during the critical period of unified party control of the government. Second, in directing a sweeping legislative program largely along established lines in 1954 despite the president's desire that his administration "not be simply a continuation of the New Deal and Fair Deal," the BOB and its "indoctrinated" director further limited Eisenhower's control during the critical period of unified party control of the government. Third, by frequently developing unbalanced budgets and other proposals that the president "did not believe in . . . in the first place" and that made him feel "helpless," the CEA and BOB limited Eisenhower's control further still. Fourth, in working to develop the Kennedy–Johnson tax cut and the New Frontier and Great Society programs, all of which promoted "fiscal recklessness" in reversing the two major achievements of Eisenhower's second term, the CEA and BOB limited even the long-term impact of Eisenhower's limited control.

THE NEW DEAL–ERA APPARATUS LIMITS EISENHOWER'S CONTROL IN THE SUBDOMAIN OF MONETARY POLICY

Similar to the subdomain of fiscal policy, Dwight Eisenhower assumed office in 1953 with unified party control of the government and a strong desire to change the course of monetary policy that Franklin Roosevelt had initiated in response to the Great Depression. In his memoirs Eisenhower explained, "I wanted to see a tax reduction. But I wanted even more to stop the deterioration of the currency."[57] Eisenhower also confirmed that "it was my intention to redeem the pledges of the [1952 Republican Party] platform," which called for the restoration of both the "dollar on a fully-convertible gold basis" and the "Federal

Reserve System exercising its functions in the money and credit system without pressure for political purposes from the Treasury or the White House."[58]

Despite this strong desire to change the established course, the New Deal–era apparatus and its principals failed to provide the new president with an actual plan to ensure both the restoration of the "dollar on a fully-convertible gold basis" and the "Federal Reserve System exercising its functions . . . without pressure . . . from the Treasury or the White House." The president himself also had no such plan. In his first annual message—which excluded the issue of returning to the pre–New Deal–era gold standard—Eisenhower proposed no major changes in the operations of the public-finance apparatus and instead simply announced, "Past differences in policy between the Treasury and the Federal Reserve Board have helped to encourage inflation. Henceforth, I expect that their single purpose shall be . . . to stabilize the economy and encourage the free play of our people's genius for individual initiative."[59]

The absence of a plan was further evident in the limited use of the appointment power. Although Fed Chair William McChesney Martin, Jr., offered to resign in 1953 in order to avoid becoming, in his words, "a persona non grata" to the new administration—a telling example of the Fed's weak independence at the time—Gabriel Hauge, special assistant to the president for economic affairs, advised Eisenhower not to make any change in personnel.[60] As Hauge explained, "At the Federal Reserve Board, things are in pretty good shape under [Martin], an example of the right kind of Democrat" who "understands the Treasury–Federal Reserve relationship."[61]

In contrast to the gold standard and the Treasury–Fed relationship, wage and price controls received considerable attention. As the president explained in his first annual message,

> The great economic strength of our democracy has developed in an atmosphere of freedom. The character of our people resists artificial and arbitrary controls of any kind. . . . Our whole system . . . is based upon the assumption that, normally, we should combat wide fluctuations in our price structure by relying largely on the effective use of sound fiscal and monetary policy, and upon the natural workings of economic law.[62]

Further making clear his own view, Eisenhower removed the existing wage and price controls and later explained, "In 1951 Winston Churchill based his comeback campaign—victoriously—on the slogan 'Set the People Free.' In February 1953, with the sweeping away of economic controls, we had begun to do just that in the United States."[63]

Notwithstanding these initial steps—expecting the Treasury and the Fed to act now with a "single purpose," retaining the "right kind of Democrat" as Fed

chair, and removing wage and price controls in order to "set the people free"—
Eisenhower failed to oversee the restoration of both the "dollar on a fully-
convertible gold basis" and the "Federal Reserve System exercising its functions . . . without pressure . . . from the Treasury or the White House," which in
turn contributed to a failure "to stop the deterioration of the currency," the president's primary objective. In addition to not providing a comprehensive plan to
change the established course, the New Deal–era apparatus and its principals
contributed to this development in three key ways during the critical period of
unified party control of the government.

First, the Treasury's debt management limited the Fed's independence and
ability "to stop the deterioration of the currency." This began when the Fed
approved an increase in the discount rate in January 1953, a move intended
to showcase its independence following the Treasury–Federal Reserve accord.
In April Martin then announced that the Fed "no longer needs to inject periodically into credit markets large amounts of reserve funds [by purchasing
Treasury securities], which are difficult to withdraw before they have resulted
in undesirable credit developments."[64] That same day, the Treasury launched a
program to extend the maturity structure of the national debt, and due largely
to the Fed chair's announcement that the central bank would no longer support
Treasury securities as it had in the past, the offering began to fail.

This left the Fed with two basic options: either let the Treasury possibly fail
in the financing of the debt or help the Treasury by reversing the earlier tightening of monetary policy, which would undermine the Fed's independence.
In line with its subordinate position since the Roosevelt administration, the
Fed took the latter course.[65] Underscoring the significance of this move and
the limits of the Fed's independence more generally at the time, the *New York
Times* reported, "The Federal Reserve System has just set the stage for what is
probably the most irksome task the nation's central banking system has ever
undertaken. The job is to expand further the money supply of an inflated and
booming economy so that the Treasury can readily borrow money."[66]

Second, the Employment Act's universal governing objective limited the
Fed's independence and ability "to stop the deterioration of the currency."
Rather than maintain a passive, procyclical monetary policy, as it would have
done under the real-bills doctrine, the Fed implemented a policy of "active
ease" in response to the Recession of 1953–1954 in order to promote "maximum
employment" and "avoid deflationary tendencies."[67] Putting the New Deal–era
countercyclical monetary policy—or "managed currency"—in his own words,
Martin explained, "Our purpose is to lean against the winds of deflation or
inflation, whichever way they are blowing."[68]

This countercyclical monetary policy presented several difficulties. The Fed had little experience in determining which way the "wind" was blowing at any given time as well as determining how hard it should "lean." Moreover, unlike the Council of Economic Advisers, the Fed was not headed by an "exceptionally qualified" economist trained to make these complicated decisions. As Martin later confessed, "Here I am, the new chairman of the Fed and I'm doing my best—I'm not the brightest fellow in the world but I'm working hard on this—and I haven't the faintest idea of how you figure the money supply. Yet everybody thinks I have it at my fingertips."[69]

Third, policy coordination limited the Fed's independence and ability "to stop the deterioration of the currency." After Eisenhower appointed Arthur Burns as the "chief of staff in handling the recession," the CEA chair worked to undermine the Fed's independence by pushing for it to "lean" even harder against the "winds of deflation" than it would have done otherwise. In 1954 Eisenhower noted in his diary, "I talked to the secretary of the treasury in order to develop real pressure on the Federal Reserve Board for loosening credit still further. This is a project strongly supported by Dr. Burns, who believes that bankers have always acted 'too late and with too little' in the face of approaching recession."[70]

* * *

Following the Recession of 1953–1954 and the Democratic takeover of Congress in 1955, Eisenhower continued to fail to oversee the restoration of both the "dollar on a fully-convertible gold basis" and the "Federal Reserve System exercising its functions . . . without pressure . . . from the Treasury or the White House," which in turn continued to contribute to a failure "to stop the deterioration of the currency."

The Treasury's debt management continued to limit the Fed's independence and ability "to stop the deterioration of the currency." This was evident when the Fed increased the discount rate by 0.25 percentage points in April 1955, a restrictive move that was necessary, as Martin put it, to show that the Fed was not "operating on a perpetually easy-money philosophy."[71] The Fed then continued to tighten monetary policy for several months, eventually increasing the discount rate by 0.75 percentage points. In November, however, the Treasury once again sought the Fed's support in managing the debt, which forced the central bank to reverse course. Underscoring the significance of this move, Martin warned, "We should make it clear that this is an exception. . . . It would be very unwise for the Treasury to think that any time it gets into trouble on an issue the Federal Reserve will bail it out."[72]

Despite the Fed chair's concern, the central bank never established an alternative to what became known as the "even keel" policy, even as the frequency of this constraint increased considerably over the course of the Eisenhower administration. For example, in 1959 the Fed maintained an even keel for eleven periods, compared to two periods in 1955. This increase was due in large part to the growing budget deficit. Also, because each even-keel period lasted for three weeks on average, the Fed had no control over monetary policy for more than half the year in 1959.[73] Further confirming the importance of this key constraint, Martin complained that "the time intervals during which the Federal Reserve System could appropriately take policy action have been relatively few in number and relatively limited in duration."[74]

Adding to the situation, the Treasury refused to change its approach to managing the debt in order to assist the Fed. In 1959 the Treasury secretary informed Congress, "Under existing techniques, the primary constraint on [the] administration of monetary policy arises from the relative frequency of Treasury debt operations and the necessity for the Federal Reserve to maintain an even keel during financing periods." In response to the question of whether the Treasury should develop new procedures—namely, the auctioning of government securities—to remove this "primary constraint," the Treasury secretary simply dismissed the idea, explaining, incorrectly in this case, "Adoption of the auction technique would, in itself, do nothing to change this situation. . . . The Treasury believes that the present practice . . . results in an effective distribution of new issues at a minimum cost to the taxpayer."[75]

Second, policy coordination continued to limit the Fed's independence and ability "to stop the deterioration of the currency." Most notably, the Fed implemented an easy monetary policy to counteract the Recession of 1957–1958, a course of action that the CEA strongly pushed. Raymond Saulnier, the CEA chair, wrote to Martin in April 1957, "My feeling is that [monetary policy] is unnecessarily tight and that bank reserves should not be allowed to remain at the current [negative] level."[76] Like Burns, Saulnier worked to gain the president's support to increase pressure on the Fed. As Saulnier explained, Eisenhower finally "asked me to call Bill Martin and to say . . . that in view of what we were doing through budget expenditures to help promote economic recovery, he thought the Fed ought to put its shoulder to the wheel and do something dramatic."[77] However, unlike the Recession of 1953–1954, and due largely to the Fed's inability to lean equally against the winds of deflation and inflation during the earlier recession and recovery periods, inflation now continued to climb even as the economy contracted and the unemployment rate increased. Addressing this new, rising problem—and no doubt regretting his own earlier CEA-recommended role in pressuring the Fed—Eisenhower concluded that "creeping" inflation had now become an "insidious danger" to the country.[78]

Third, the Employment Act's universal governing objective continued to limit the Fed's independence and ability "to stop the deterioration of the currency." In 1959, due to the rise of "creeping" inflation, Eisenhower recommended for the first time that Congress "amend the Employment Act of 1946 to make it clear that [the] Government intends to use all appropriate means to protect the buying power of the dollar."[79] This was a direct acknowledgment that the statutory governing objective of promoting "maximum employment" was a significant constraint in the battle against inflation. Because the proposal came so late in his presidency—and most importantly, after losing unified party control of the government—it now had no chance of passing.

Finally, although the three primary New Deal–era policymaking constraints established during the Roosevelt and Truman administrations largely contributed to the rise of "creeping" inflation—or the failure "to stop the deterioration of the currency"—the practical and statutory limits of the appointment power during the Eisenhower administration also contributed to this process. Most importantly, in 1956 Eisenhower appointed his predecessor's Fed chair to a new four-year term as chair and to a full fourteen-year term on the Federal Reserve Board, thereby granting Martin the opportunity to remain in his position until 1970, which ultimately occurred. Eisenhower also only appointed four new members to the seven-member Board due to their rotating fourteen-year terms, and his second appointee served for less than three months, meaning the president's appointees never constituted a majority of the Board, much less a majority of the twelve-member Federal Open Market Committee, which made the most important decisions concerning monetary policy.[80]

This low turnover in the members of the Board and the continuity in the Fed chair were due in no small part to a combination of the relative economic stability at the time, especially during the first term, and the president's limited understanding and limited prioritization of monetary policy early on. It was not until late 1957, his fifth year in office, that Eisenhower asked his Treasury secretary to write a memo that explained the basics of monetary policy, meaning, like fiscal policy, it was essential for the president's principals to—in Burn's words— "teach" him about the subject because he "had no special background . . . in the economic area."[81]

Finally, with the Treasury secretary supporting the "present practice" of the government's debt management, with the CEA chair using policy coordination to limit the Fed's independence in the process of "formulat[ing] and recommend[ing] national economic policy," with the "maximum employment" mandate under the Employment Act still in place, and with substantial continuity in personnel at the Fed, especially in the top position, the president was left to rely on the exceptionally limited approach of increasing public awareness to the new problem of "creeping" inflation during his final years in office. As Eisenhower later put it, "There was, in the end, only one way to win: to alert the country to the dangers of cheap money."[82]

* * *

In addition to Eisenhower's failure to oversee both the restoration of the "dollar on a fully-convertible gold basis" and the "Federal Reserve System exercising its functions . . . without pressure . . . from the Treasury or the White House" during his own time in office, which in turn contributed to the rise of "creeping inflation"—or a failure "to stop the deterioration of the currency"—the New Deal–era apparatus and its principals continued to structure the monetary-policymaking process under subsequent presidents. This contributed to the further "deterioration of the currency," the further dismantling of the qua-si-gold standard, and the return of wage and price controls, which reversed Eisenhower's move in 1953 to "set the people free."

First, the Treasury's debt management continued to limit the Fed's independence and ability "to stop the deterioration of the currency." Due largely to rising budget deficits, the average number of even-keel periods each year increased from two in 1955 to seven during the Kennedy and Johnson administrations.[83] Underscoring the continued significance of this constraint, the president of the Federal Reserve Bank in St. Louis complained during a meeting of the FOMC in 1967 that the even-keel policy was a "pernicious doctrine. . . . When the Federal budget was excessively stimulative and . . . running deficits, instead of getting the needed complementary monetary restraint, monetary actions were also excessively stimulative."[84]

Second, policy coordination and the Employment Act's universal governing objective to promote "maximum employment" continued to work together to limit the Fed's independence and ability "to stop the deterioration of the currency." For example, after visiting with the Fed chair in order to "assess whether he would be cooperative or obstructionist," CEA Chair Walter Heller informed President-elect Kennedy that Martin "foresees successful coordination of policy" and "went out of his way to be cooperative."[85] Similarly—and further revealing the divide between Eisenhower and his former CEA chair—Arthur Burns, who became a top adviser to Richard Nixon, moved to check the independence of the central bank at the start of the Nixon administration. "Eisenhower liked to talk about the independence of the Federal Reserve," Burns explained. "They begin to believe it. Let's not make that mistake and talk about the independence of the Fed again."[86]

This New Deal–era combination of the Treasury's debt management, policy coordination, and the Employment Act's universal governing objective continued to significantly limit the Fed's independence and ability to check inflation, which increased from an average of 2 percent a year during the second term of the Eisenhower administration to nearly 3 percent a year during the Johnson administration and then to nearly 5 percent a year during the first term of the Nixon administration. The rise in inflation in turn contributed to the further dismantling of the quasi-gold standard. In 1965 Lyndon Johnson oversaw the removal of the gold requirement against Federal Reserve deposits; in 1968 he oversaw the removal of the remaining 25 percent gold requirement against Federal Reserve notes, thereby severing the last gold provisions under the Federal Reserve Act; and in 1971 Richard Nixon closed the gold window, meaning the government would no longer exchange gold for dollars at the request of foreign central banks—one of the last steps in a long process that had increasingly diminished the role of gold as even a nominal anchor for monetary policy.[87]

In an effort to check inflation while monetary policy remained expansionary, the public-finance principals supported the use of wage and price controls, which Eisenhower had removed nearly two decades earlier and which Nixon reluctantly implemented in 1971. Like Eisenhower, who had removed the controls to "set the people free," Nixon complained that "mandatory wage and price controls crush economic and personal freedom."[88]

Further highlighting the government's failure "to stop the deterioration of the currency" and the continued key role of Arthur Burns, who became the next Fed chair, Martin—whom Eisenhower had appointed to a full fourteen-year term in 1956—remarked upon his retirement from the Fed in 1970, "I wish I could turn the bank over to Arthur Burns as I would have liked. But we are in very deep trouble. We are in the wildest inflation since the Civil War." Then, making clear the role of the New Deal–era apparatus and its principals in enabling this development, Martin confessed, "I've failed."[89]

* * *

The case study analysis here shows that the established, relatively stable New Deal–era apparatus and its principals significantly limited Eisenhower's control in the subdomain of monetary policy. First, in failing to provide Eisenhower with an actual plan early on to oversee the restoration of the "dollar on a fully-convertible gold basis" and the "Federal Reserve System exercising its functions . . . without pressure . . . from the Treasury or the White House," both of which contributed to "the deterioration of the currency," the New Deal–era apparatus and its principals limited Eisenhower's control, especially during the critical period of unified party control of the government. Second, in attempting to "lean against the winds of deflation or inflation"—or maintain a "managed currency"—rather than operate under the guidelines of the real-bills doctrine and the pre–New Deal–era gold standard, in promoting "maximum employ-ment" through policy coordination, and in prioritizing the management of the debt rather than operating with a "single purpose" in order "to stop the deteri-oration of the currency," the Fed, the CEA, and the Treasury all further limited Eisenhower's control. Third, in continuing to attempt to "lean against the winds of deflation or inflation," in continuing to promote "maximum employment" through policy coordination, and in continuing to prioritize the management of the debt under subsequent incumbents, all of which contributed to the fur-ther "deterioration of the currency," the further dismantling of the quasi-gold standard, and the return of wage and price controls that Eisenhower had re-moved to "set the people free," the Fed, the CEA, and the Treasury limited even the long-term impact of Eisenhower's limited control.

Altogether, the case study analysis of fiscal policymaking and monetary policymaking in this chapter shows that the established, relatively stable New Deal–era apparatus and its principals reinforced the established New Deal–era policy parameters during the Eisenhower administration and beyond in the process of significantly limiting the president's control. Further underscoring the president's limited impact in the domain of public finance, Eisenhower him-self explained in 1965, "If the nation should turn decisively . . . toward sound fiscal procedures in government" and "methods calculated to prevent further erosion in the value of our currency, then the future would hold encomiums for my administration as the first great break with the political philosophy of the decades beginning in 1933." But, Eisenhower added, if "the federal government should intensify its practice of the theories of recent Democratic administra-tions"—as ultimately occurred—then "our time in office would be represented as only a slight impediment to the trend begun in 1933 under the New Deal."[90]

Part IV
Historical Variation in Presidential Control during the Reagan Era

As the second case study component of the multimethod analysis, this part of the book initially traces the collapse of the New Deal–era apparatus while assisting Richard Nixon, Gerald Ford, and Jimmy Carter during the Great Inflation. It then traces the variation in presidential control for the first three incumbents of the Reagan era: Ronald Reagan, George H. W. Bush, and Bill Clinton. Like part III, the case studies here do not provide a comprehensive history of public-finance policymaking. Rather, the primary objective is to show that presidential control over administration is a foundational component of public-finance policymaking and operates as a historical variable. Another major, related objective is to demonstrate that although the same sequence of presidential control follows the collapse of the policy domain, control over administration for the first three presidents of the Reagan era is diminished relative to each president's counterpart during the New Deal era due to the shift from a centralized to a decentralized public-finance apparatus.

8. Collapse: The Failing New Deal-Era Apparatus Limits Carter's Control

The quantitative overview provided evidence that in the domain of public-finance, Richard Nixon, Gerald Ford, and Jimmy Carter governed with the support of the relatively centralized New Deal–era apparatus due largely to the initial limited severity and limited prioritization of the Great Inflation, which only began to weaken the average restrictions on presidential control and only began to strengthen the average incentive to maximize control. In particular, the quantitative overview provided evidence of the following: First, the Great Inflation was not exceptionally severe and highly prioritized when Nixon assumed office and set the course for his administration. Second, although the severity and prioritization of the Great Inflation had increased by the time that Ford assumed office, party continuity and the unusual transition following Nixon's resignation limited the new president's control. Third, the severity of the Great Inflation temporarily decreased by the time that Carter assumed office but then significantly increased over the course of his administration. This chapter initially traces the preliminary collapse of the New Deal apparatus during the Nixon and Ford administrations and then traces the process of the gradually failing New Deal-era apparatus and its principals in limiting Carter's control.

THE PRELIMINARY COLLAPSE OF THE NEW DEAL-ERA APPARATUS

Richard Nixon largely accepted the New Deal–era approach to public-finance policymaking during his first term. While submitting a budget with a planned deficit of $12 billion in 1971, Nixon declared, "It will be a full employment budget, a budget designed to be in balance if the economy were operating at its peak potential. By spending as if we were at full employment, we will help to bring about full employment."[1] Highlighting a key source of this continuity, Herbert Stein, the chair of the Council of Economic Advisers, explained, "[Nixon's] economists, especially the CEA, considered themselves far apart from their liberal Democratic predecessors, but in fact they were only at the other edge of a rather narrow spectrum that was mainstream economics."[2]

At the start of his second term, Nixon began to reject the New Deal–era approach, turning instead to what the CEA chair labeled as the "old-time religion" of strictly balancing the budget in an effort to stop rising inflation.[3] In 1973 Nixon explained, "When inflationary pressure is strong" and "when confidence in our management of fiscal affairs is low . . . we cannot afford to live by that minimum standard" of balancing the budget at full employment. Rather, "we must take as our goal the more ambitious one of balancing the actual budget."[4] This change in course occurred at a time when the average annual inflation rate was higher than at any point in two decades. Moreover, because the inflation rate was not offset by an exceptionally low unemployment rate, the public-finance problem index climbed to double digits, marking the start of the thirteen-year-long run of the Great Inflation.[5]

Based on the belief that rising government spending was contributing to rising inflation, Nixon not only stressed the importance of bringing the budget into actual balance but also impounded appropriated funds to an unprecedented degree in an effort to do so. Most notably, in 1973 Nixon refused to spend almost $20 billion that Congress had appropriated, up from an average of $11 billion per year during his first term and three times the annual average that Dwight Eisenhower, John Kennedy, and Lyndon Johnson had impounded.[6] In response to Nixon's growing use of the impoundment power, Congress passed the Congressional Budget and Impoundment Control Act of 1974.[7] Among its many provisions, the law established new procedures that formalized the impoundment process and diminished the ability of the president to act unilaterally.

At the same time, in an effort to strengthen the budget powers of Congress more generally, the law created the Congressional Budget Office, designed to operate as the congressional counterpart to the Bureau of the Budget and the Council of Economic Advisers. Like the BOB, the principal depository of information for the executive branch as a whole, the law instructed the CBO "to secure information, data, estimates, and statistics directly from the various departments, agencies, and establishments of the executive branch of Government."[8] Moreover, like the CEA, charged with "formulat[ing] and recommend[ing] national economic policy," the law directed the CBO to submit an annual report that contains "a discussion of national budget priorities" and that addresses how changes in the budget will "affect balanced growth."[9] Unlike the BOB and CEA, both of which were headed by presidential appointees, the law mandated that the CBO director "be appointed by the Speaker of the House . . . and the President pro tempore of the Senate . . . without regard to political affiliation."[10]

Further strengthening the role of Congress, the Congressional Budget and Impoundment Control Act added a new congressional-led budget process to the old executive-led process, and it expanded the time horizon of the budget. Under the former process the president submitted a one-year budget proposal and Congress worked on revising that proposal. Under the new process, the president submitted a budget proposal for the "ensuing fiscal year" as well as "projections for the four fiscal years immediately following."[11] At the same time, now relying on the assistance of the CBO and two new budget committees, Congress developed its own multiyear budget proposal, meaning that the executive branch no longer had a clear first-mover advantage or informational advantage relative to the legislative branch.

Adding to this development, Nixon implemented a reorganization plan in 1970 that transformed the BOB into the Office of Management and Budget. The objective was to strengthen the management arm of the BOB and shift matters of policy to a new Domestic Council. As Nixon put it, "The Domestic Council will be primarily concerned with what we do; the Office of Management and Budget will be primarily concerned with how we do it, and how well we do it."[12] In practice, however, the OMB essentially continued to address "what [the administration would] do."[13] Moreover, in 1973 Nixon placed new politically appointed program assistant directors between the budget director and the career staff in an effort to increase presidential control over the OMB. Then in 1974, in response to the president's unprecedented use of the impoundment power, Congress passed a law that made the budget director and the deputy director subject to Senate confirmation.[14] These changes contributed to the growing perception that the OMB had become a politicized institution and called into question the credibility of its work at the same time that the new CBO was beginning to provide its own nonpartisan analyses under the leadership of a director appointed "without regard to political affiliation."

Along with the developments in the budget-making process, the volatility in interest rates due to rising inflation led the Treasury to change its procedures for managing the debt. Specifically, with the average annual inflation rate above 5 percent for two years running for the first time since the 1940s, the Treasury finally moved to establish a system of auction sales in 1970 to finance the debt. This marked the beginning of the end of the even-keel policy, meaning that it was no longer necessary for the Fed to inject additional reserves or to halt its own operations in order to support the Treasury.[15]

Although the end of the even-keel policy removed one key constraint on the Fed's independence, the use of wage and price controls continued to operate as another major constraint. Underscoring the perceived failure of that approach, Nixon explained, "Three years after controls had completely ended, both unemployment and inflation hovered around 7 percent, and there was even nostalgia for the 'good old days' in 1971 when we had only 4 percent inflation and 6 percent unemployment."[16]

In addition to the use of wage and price controls, policy coordination and the statutory requirement to promote "maximum employment" continued to limit the Fed's independence. After letting the brakes off the money supply in 1972, Fed Chair Arthur Burns confirmed the central bank's reluctance to push too forcefully or quickly in implementing a tighter monetary policy, explaining in 1973, "Reduction in the rate of inflation would require an environment of tighter budgets and a relatively restrictive monetary policy, and it would take time. An attempt to deal with the problem quickly would probably not be successful and could do permanent damage to the economy."[17] Equally revealing, when the growth rate of the money supply suddenly declined two months later, Burns confirmed that the Fed now believed that it needed to move forcefully and quickly in implementing an easier policy. "If the System were to allow the period of very low or negative growth in the money stock to continue," he explained, "it would not only be damaging to its credibility; it would be failing to meet its responsibilities to the economy and to the nation."[18]

Finally, CEA Chair Herbert Stein confirmed that the domain of public finance was not restructured during the Nixon administration despite several notable developments in response to the initial rise of the Great Inflation. As Stein put it, "Nixon did not come into office to make a conservative revolution in economic policy. He had certain conventional leanings in that direction but did not feel strongly about it and it was not his main interest."[19] In particular, Nixon had other, more pressing problems to manage during his two terms. Concerning the first term—which preceded the Great Inflation—Stein explained, "The economy was not the main focus of attention at the time. . . . Attention was on the Vietnam War."[20] Concerning the second term—which coincided with the start of the Great Inflation—Stein added, "Watergate was absorbing the nation's attention to the exclusion of everything else. It is significant that in all of President Nixon's press conferences during 1973, there was not one question about the budget."[21]

* * *

Following Nixon's resignation in August 1974, the Great Inflation continued to drive the collapse of the New Deal–era apparatus under Gerald Ford. To start, the new president immediately labeled inflation—now in double digits—the top domestic priority. "If we take care of inflation and get our economy back on the road to a healthy future," Ford explained, "I think most of our other domestic . . . problems will be solved."[22] To manage the problem, Ford proposed a one-year tax increase of $5 billion on corporate and "upper-level" individual incomes, and he called on citizens to act as "volunteer inflation fighters."[23]

Although it was not known at the time of the proposal, the economy was in the midst of the longest and most severe economic downturn since the 1930s. This soon became evident as the unemployment rate climbed from less than 6 percent in August 1974 to more than 8 percent in January 1975, the highest level since the Second World War. As a result, Ford quickly changed course in proposing a $16 billion tax cut.[24] Addressing the new problem in managing the economy, the president explained, "Conventional economic theory held that when you had high inflation, unemployment was low. That may have been true in the past, but it wasn't true any longer. Inflation still was running at a double-digit pace" and "unemployment figures were worsening rapidly."[25] Equally revealing, the public-finance principals had no plan in place to address the new problem. "At the economic summit meeting in Washington six weeks earlier," Ford noted, "not one of the assembled experts warned me that unemployment would become an even more serious problem than inflation in just sixty days time."[26]

Along with the abrupt change in course in fiscal policy, the Fed continued to prioritize the promotion of "maximum employment" through an increasingly active monetary policy that changed course five times in a little over a year and a half. As the Fed chair explained, "Fear of immediate unemployment, rather than fear of current or eventual inflation, . . . dominate[d] economic policy-making" and "inevitably gave an inflationary twist to the economy."[27]

Adding to the situation, the "inflationary twist" induced by the New Deal–era apparatus generated the complete end of the quasi-gold standard, a process several decades in the making. Specifically, after taking several important steps—the abandonment of the gold standard for domestic transactions in 1933, the removal of the gold requirement against Federal Reserve deposits in 1965, the removal of the gold requirement against Federal Reserve notes in 1968, and the closing of the gold window in 1971—the government removed from statute the definition of the dollar in terms of gold in 1976, thereby marking the official end of the remaining limited gold standard.[28]

Finally, and making clear that the domain of public finance was not restructured during the brief Ford administration despite the increasing rise of the Great Inflation, Ford later explained, "If the reasons for the crisis were clear, the solutions were not. . . . Some people believe that all a President has to do to end inflation and unemployment is to flick a switch. The realities are that you can't do that. . . . You must have a sound economic plan—and the guts to stick with it."[29] Ford then revealed one of the key reasons he did not have a "sound economic plan," adding, "I took office with a set of unique disadvantages. Normally, Presidents have about seventy-five days of grace between their election and their inauguration. They use this 'shakedown' period to recruit the members of their Cabinet and staff and to decide their legislative priorities." Unlike other presidents, however, "I didn't have that luxury, and the lack of a normal transition time caused problems right away."[30]

* * *

Altogether, the centralized New Deal–era apparatus began to collapse during the second term of the Nixon administration and the two years of the Ford administration due to the initial rise of the Great Inflation, but no new apparatus replaced it. In particular, the Congressional Budget Act of 1974 created the Congressional Budget Office to rival both the Council of Economic Advisers and the Office of Management and Budget; it added a new congressional-led budget process to the old presidential-led process; and it extended the time frame of budgeting. No substantial multiyear budget passed during this period, however, and the role of the CBO and the operations of multibranch budgeting remained unclear in practice. Moreover, the Treasury's new approach to debt management eliminated a major constraint on the Fed, but the use of wage and price controls, policy coordination, and the statutory requirement to promote "maximum employment" all continued to limit the Fed's independence.

THE FAILING NEW DEAL–ERA APPARATUS LIMITS CARTER'S CONTROL

Jimmy Carter assumed office in January 1977 with unified party control of the government and put forward a legislative program that, based on the recommendation of Council of Economic Advisers Chair Charles Schultze, included a tax cut to boost the economy.[31] Confirming the influential role of the CEA chair in general, Carter explained, "Usually in the final stages, I turned to Charlie Schultze," who "would sit down with me in the Oval Office and . . . narrow down the most advantageous policies."[32] However, like Ford, the new president quickly reversed his initial course, in this case withdrawing the proposal for a tax cut due to rising inflation. Underscoring the lack of any meaningful first-mover advantage in the fiscal-policymaking process, Carter later conceded, "The obvious inconsistency in my policy during this rapid transition from stimulating the economy to an overall battle against inflation was to plague me for a long time."[33]

Another important change in course occurred the following year. After announcing that the "economy had not yet fully recovered from the [1973–1975] recession," Carter proposed a $25 billion tax cut, again based largely on the recommendation of the CEA.[34] As Schultze explained to the president, "Unless tax reductions are enacted . . . the growth of the economy will slow later in 1978 or in 1979" and "unemployment [will] begin to rise." The CEA chair then added that there is "no sign that inflation is heating up again, or is likely to do so over the next two years."[35] Three months later, following an upward revision in the inflation forecast, Carter changed course, recommending a smaller tax cut and postponing its effective date. Highlighting the reason for this move, the *New York Times* reported, "Key Administration officials acknowledged that today's announcement was the first broad gauge policy shift based on the . . . new assessment . . . that inflation had become the country's dominant economic problem."[36]

Along with the haphazard management of fiscal policy during the first two years of the Carter administration, the Fed struggled to manage monetary policy. Most notably, it remained uncertain as to whether it should even take the lead in tackling inflation. As Fed Chair Arthur Burns remarked during a meeting of the Federal Open Market Committee in 1977, "We need to consider the degree to which, if any, our monetary policy should contribute to unwinding the inflation from which our economy has been suffering since the mid-1960s." The issue "is peculiarly important for us . . . because no other branch of government . . . has anything approaching an articulate policy for bringing down the rate of inflation."[37]

Even if the Fed decided to take the lead in tackling inflation, policy coordination significantly limited its ability to do so. In 1977 the CEA chair wrote to Carter, "A weaker economy next year because of inadequate growth of money and credit will affect prices very little, and real output and employment a lot." Going further, Schultze proposed that the president put pressure on the Fed to support the fiscal program. "A tax cut can keep the pace of expansion from lagging," he explained, only "if money and credit are permitted to increase fast enough to keep the higher growth rate of the economy from pushing up interest rates."[38]

Despite the almost unprecedented growth rate of the money supply at the time, the influential CEA chair worked not only to limit the Fed's independence through policy coordination but also to ensure the appointment of a new chair. As Schultze advised the president, "While Arthur Burns is not completely inflexible in the short run, he is fundamentally unsympathetic towards giving joint priority to reducing unemployment and inflation. . . . We should not expect a Fed chairman to follow an administration policy line, but he should work closely with us."[39]

In line with that recommendation, Carter appointed William Miller to replace Burns at the Fed in early 1978. However, this push for greater cooperation and coordination quickly backfired. As Schultze took the lead organizing an unprecedented meeting with the entire Federal Reserve Board in order "to assess their views" and urge a more expansive monetary policy, average annual inflation increased to nearly 8 percent and would surpass 11 percent the following year.[40] By early 1979 even Schultze realized that monetary policy under the leadership of Miller had become too expansive, and therefore the CEA chair now pushed the Fed to change course. Making clear both the unusual nature of this move and the president's displeasure, Schultze later revealed, "I carried on a leaked campaign in the press . . . about how administration officials think the Fed ought to tighten up—normally it's the other way around—and we got a very nasty note from the President."[41]

* * *

As the economic situation continued to deteriorate in 1979, Carter decided to shake up his cabinet, including firing Treasury Secretary Michael Blumenthal. The president then appointed Fed Chair Miller to head the Treasury, and he appointed New York Reserve Bank President Paul Volcker to head the Fed. Confirming the lack of any comprehensive plan, Lyle Gramley, a member of the CEA, later explained, "In many respects, [Carter's] willingness to accept Paul Volcker as Federal Reserve chairman, which he did despite reservations expressed by the Council of Economic Advisers," was "because in part he felt that he just had to do something." Gramley then added, "I don't think [Carter] had any conception what this would mean, in terms of the course Volcker would take. Neither did anybody else, as far as that goes."[42]

Although the appointment of the new Fed chair in August 1979 was not part of any comprehensive plan for managing the economy, it proved highly consequential in building upon two earlier developments. First, in 1977, due to several consecutive years of high inflation, Carter signed the Federal Reserve Reform Act, which directed the Fed "to promote effectively the goals of maximum employment" and "stable prices," thereby making price stability—or low inflation—a statutory governing objective.[43] Second, in 1978 Carter signed the Full Employment and Balanced Growth Act, which altered the governing objective of the public-finance apparatus as a whole by replacing the old New Deal–era aim of promoting "maximum employment" with the new dual aim of promoting "full employment" and reasonable "price stability."[44] At the time, the Carter administration had largely viewed the Full Employment and Balanced Growth Act as securing the work of the CEA by statutorily defining "full employment" for the first time as an unemployment rate of 4 percent or below.[45]

Following the creation of the dual statutory governing objective for the public finance apparatus as a whole, the orientation of the new Volcker-led Fed shifted significantly. Rather than continue to accept that there was a tradeoff between inflation and unemployment, the Fed now maintained that low inflation would also produce low unemployment in the long run. For example, when a reporter asked Volcker how high an unemployment rate he was prepared to accept in order to tackle inflation, the Fed chair responded, "You know my basic philosophy is over time we have no choice but to deal with the inflationary situation because over time inflation and unemployment go together. . . . Isn't that the lesson of the 1970s?"[46]

To implement the new statutory governing objective, Volcker took the lead in changing the Fed's primary operating target from interest rates to the money supply. This new procedure was designed to change the Fed's behavior and send a clear signal that it was finally committed to tackling inflation. As Volcker explained, "Once the Federal Reserve put more emphasis on the money supply, not just by publicly announcing the target but by actually changing its operating techniques to increase the chances of actually hitting it, we would find it difficult to back off even if our decisions led to painfully high interest rates."[47]

Although Volcker succeeded in quickly implementing the new procedure, the initial results were discouraging. In particular, the Fed struggled to stay near its target for money growth; long-term interest rates behaved in an unexpected manner, creating pressure for a return to interest rate targeting; and other monetary innovations at the time created unforeseen problems.[48]

Adding to the situation—and based on a recommendation a year earlier from the influential CEA chair—Carter pressured the Fed in March 1980 to impose supplemental credit controls on borrowing as part of a larger anti-inflation program.[49] "The traditional tools used by the Federal Reserve to control money and credit expansion are a basic part of the fight against inflation," the president explained. "But in present circumstances, these tools need to be reinforced so that effective constraint can be achieved in ways that spread the burden reasonably and fairly."[50]

Similar to the use of wage and price controls during the Nixon administration, the supplemental credit controls proved problematic, contributing to a recession in early 1980. Even though it was the shortest downturn of the postwar period, lasting only six months, it was also one of the sharpest, forcing the Fed to abandon its new operating procedure and anti-inflation program more generally and reversing the gains of the prior six months.[51]

Making matters worse, the Carter administration struggled to develop a coherent fiscal policy that year. In January the president pursued a self-described "strategy of restraint" in proposing a budget with "a deficit of $15.8 billion, the lowest deficit in 7 years."[52] In March, following a jump in inflation, the president withdrew his first proposal and put forward a new one that eliminated the deficit entirely, explaining, "I will soon set forth a revised budget for fiscal year 1981" that "will be a balanced budget."[53] And in August—this time following a sharp jump in the unemployment rate—the president reversed course once again, recommending a new economic-recovery program of multiyear tax cuts and increased spending that would add $6 billion to a revised deficit now projected at $30 billion. Further highlighting the haphazard management of fiscal policy in 1980, the *New York Times* reported, "The Carter administration is making another change in its economic course. This, Mr. Carter's third economic plan in eight months, reverts to the notion that tax cuts and increased Government spending are useful in restoring economic health, a theory that he emphatically rejected five months ago."[54]

Shortly after the last change in course on the fiscal front, and less than two months before the presidential election of 1980, the Volcker-led Fed resumed its novel attack on inflation. Once more the president interfered, this time remarking that "the strictly monetary approach to the Fed's decision . . . is ill-advised."[55] Although the administration attempted to walk back the criticism, the damage was done. As the *New York Times* reported, with that comment, "the Fed found itself in the not-too-unusual position of being blasted from all sides."[56] Volcker also later acknowledged that without the full support of the president, it was "a mostly wasted year restoring credibility in the attack on inflation."[57]

Finally, with an inconsistent fiscal policy, with repeated presidential interference and an inconsistent monetary policy, and with simultaneous high inflation and high unemployment raising the problem—or "misery"—index above 20 percentage points for the first time since the Great Depression, Carter lost the election in a landslide. "If I had to do it over again," he conceded, "I'd put more emphasis on inflation."[58]

Further addressing the failure in managing the Great Inflation, Schultze later explained that "Carter, in his first two years was a fiscal conservative who . . . was going along with deliberately beefing up the deficit because he guessed he had to. He turned with more conviction to austerity during his last two . . . years, even though it was much messier." Then, confirming why the situation got "much messier," the CEA chair added, "We were always, in terms of an anti-inflationary program, six months to a year behind the game."[59] Equally notable, the Fed chair later placed the blame largely on the president's own principals. As Volcker put it, "Day after day, what I seemed to be seeing before my eyes was a president with basically conservative instincts finding his preliminary decisions challenged by advisers."[60]

* * *

The case study analysis here shows that the established, gradually failing New Deal–era apparatus and its principals allowed Carter to strengthen his control to a degree but, for the most part, limited his control. First, in directing an inconsistent fiscal policy that was "to plague [the president] for a long time," in routinely challenging the president's "preliminary decisions" and "conservative instincts," and in failing to provide a timely "anti-inflationary program," the CEA and its influential chair limited Carter's control. Second, in pushing for the appointment of a Fed chair who would "work closely with us" in implementing an easier monetary policy, and then in "carr[ying] on a leaked campaign in the press" that the newly appointed Fed chair "ought to tighten up"—all of which contributed to an inconsistent monetary policy and the appointment of another new Fed chair who implemented an unexpected, "ill-advised," "strictly monetary approach"—the CEA and the Fed further limited Carter's control.

9. Innovation: Reagan Strengthens His Control in Restructuring the Policy Domain

The quantitative overview provided evidence that in the domain of public finance, Ronald Reagan oversaw the creation of both the decentralized Reagan-era apparatus and the Reagan-era policy parameters due largely to the full impact of the Great Inflation, an exceptionally severe and highly prioritized problem, which weakened the average restrictions on presidential control and strengthened the average incentive to maximize control. This chapter traces the process of Reagan strengthening his control in restructuring the policy domain.

REAGAN STRENGTHENS HIS CONTROL IN RESTRUCTURING THE SUBDOMAIN OF FISCAL POLICY

In contrast to his recent predecessors, Ronald Reagan had a plan to change the established course in the domain of public finance more than a year before he assumed office. Written by Martin Anderson, the chief domestic-policy adviser, "Policy Memorandum No.1" began by identifying the problem in the policy domain. "By a wide margin," the memo explained, "the most important issue in the minds of voters today is inflation. If we add other economic related issues"—unemployment and high taxes—"it is clear that national economic policy is of critical importance." The memo then argued that it was necessary "to break free from the discredited economic beliefs of the past and to craft a realistic economic policy powerful enough to halt our slide into economic chaos."[1]

This new, "realistic economic policy" included several key proposals: To "speed up economic growth" and "provide more jobs," it was necessary to "reduce federal tax rates" and "index federal income tax brackets." To "control" federal spending—that is, not "cut federal spending from its current levels" but only "reduce the rate of increase"—it was necessary to "reduce and eliminate waste and extravagance" and "establish effective controls." "To ensure that [the budget] stays in balance"—assuming that the above steps were taken, thereby ensuring that the budget "move[d] rapidly toward balance"—it was necessary to "add a balanced-budget amendment to the Constitution." And to reduce "uncertainty"—one of the "fundamental causes of inflation . . . and high unemployment"—it was necessary both to promote "consistent" and "dependable" policies in general and to pass "a constitutional amendment to prohibit the imposition of wage and price controls" in particular.[2]

Altogether, the memo provided the first comprehensive plan for addressing the domain of public finance since its restructuring during the Roosevelt administration in response to the Great Depression. As Anderson put it, "[The memo] showed clearly . . . that economic policy is not tax policy alone, or spending control alone . . . or monetary policy. It showed that it is all . . . of these together, at the same time."[3]

Building on this initial plan, Reagan made increased defense spending one of his top priorities during the campaign in 1980. Together with the tax cut and the aim of moving toward a balanced budget, the new spending proposal made the economic forecast supporting the entire public-finance program even more critical. As Anderson explained, "Economic forecasts play a major role in determining economic policy, because they define the general limits. For example, if the forecasts show that future tax revenues will be greater than future spending and there is money left over . . . that money could be used to reduce tax rates."[4]

In addition to developing a comprehensive plan before assuming office, the new Reagan administration moved quickly to implement it, especially in the subdomain of fiscal policy. In a memo in late 1980, David Stockman, the incoming budget director, noted, "If bold policies are not swiftly, deftly, and courageously implemented in the first six months, Washington will quickly become engulfed in political disorder commensurate with the surrounding economic disarray," and the "opportunity for permanent conservative policy revision and political realignment could be thoroughly dissipated before the Reagan administration is even up to speed."[5]

In contrast to recent budget directors, the thirty-five-year-old Stockman was, in his own words, a "supply sider, dedicated to [the] cause of shrinking Big Government."[6] Prior to his appointment to the OMB, he had served two terms in the House, an experience that provided an education on the basics of budgeting more than an indoctrination of the New Deal–era approach to fiscal policymaking, which the Great Inflation had increasingly discredited. Making clear both the unraveling of old policies and procedures at the time and his limited knowledge, Stockman remarked, "Even the appearance of being an expert is self-validating. I didn't know much about budgets, but I knew more than the rest of them." He then added, "It was . . . a new era—the era of budget subtraction. For the first time since the New Deal, everyone was talking about cutting the budget instead of adding to it."[7]

Operating under the leadership of this young, highly conservative budget director, the Reagan administration moved forward quickly, beginning with the economic forecast, the foundation of the entire program. Despite the significance of this step, however, neither the chair of the Council of Economic Advisers nor the Treasury secretary performed their traditional roles. "The professional economist who heads the CEA is usually the one in charge of such forecasts," Stockman explained. "But by early January, no one had been appointed" and Treasury Secretary Don Regan "somehow got the idea that it was only [a] technical formality—something the OMB director needed in order to come up with his budget numbers."[8]

With this opening in place, the budget director proceeded to manipulate the economic forecast. As Stockman put it, "The forecasting sessions, which formerly had been crucibles of intellectual and ideological formulations, degenerated into sheer numbers manipulation." In particular, the OMB's forecast made it appear as though a rapidly growing economy would support the Reagan administration's sweeping program. However, the numbers had no grounding in reality. "Nearly $200 billion in phantom revenues tumbled into our budget computer in one fell swoop," Stockman confessed, meaning the "massive deficit inherent in the true supply-side fiscal equation was substantially covered up."[9]

Once the so-called "rosy scenario" economic forecast was in place, the next step was to put together the administration's budget. Like the economic forecast, the budget director proceeded to manipulate the proposal until it appeared workable. As Stockman explained,

> Bookkeeping invention thus began its wondrous works. We invented the "magic asterisk": If we couldn't find the savings in time—and we couldn't—we would issue an IOU. We would call it "Future savings to be identified."
>
> It was marvelously creative. A magic asterisk item would cost *negative* $30 billion . . . $40 billion . . . whatever it took to get to a balanced budget in 1984.[10]

Finally, to push through Congress the manipulated budget proposal built upon a manipulated economic forecast, the budget director relied upon, in his words, a "procedural innovation" that involved the budget reconciliation process, a little used rule under the Congressional Budget Act of 1974.[11] With the help of Senate Budget Chair Pete Domenici, Stockman pressed Congress to employ the budget reconciliation procedure at the start of the budgeting process rather than at the end, as originally intended. This allowed members of Congress to take just one vote upfront in support of the Reagan administration's budget, and it also ensured that the process could not be filibustered in the Senate, meaning the support of a simple majority was sufficient. Further underscoring the significance of this move, Stockman explained,

The normal procedure is to start with a budget resolution, which established the overall policy blueprint and the basic architecture of the entire fiscal plan. You debate and establish the economic assumptions, tax policy, defense policy, the deficit or surplus targets—everything which shapes the massive federal budget.

By contrast, our omnibus reconciliation bill shoved the fiscal blueprint aside and put the Senate to work laying some of the bricks first. The measure that would be brought to the Senate floor would say just one thing: Cut domestic spending by these precise amounts.[12]

In addition to the repurposed budget reconciliation process, the recent shift from single-year to multiyear budgeting strengthened the Reagan administration's ability to push its program through Congress. Confirming both the importance of this process and his limited understanding of it, Stockman conceded, "Our scorekeeping rules said we had cut . . . more than $140 billion over three years. The extent to which this victory was composed of promises and paper savings would only become apparent later. . . . No one understood this new, multi-year bookkeeping."[13]

The Reagan administration also attacked the relatively new Congressional Budget Office in order to undermine opposition to the OMB's manipulated numbers. In response to the release of the CBO's analysis in March, the president declared, "Their figures are phony."[14] At the same time, the budget director worked behind the scenes. "After countless meetings with Domenici," Stockman explained, "I had brow-beaten him into accepting most of Rosy Scenario's predictions instead of the [CBO] economic forecast, which would have brought our total 1984 deficit to $80 billion." Had the CBO's numbers been used, Stockman added, "that would have been the end of the Reagan Revolution right then and there."[15]

Taken together, these key moves—the development of a comprehensive program before 1981, the appointment of a relatively inexperienced, highly conservative budget director "dedicated to [the] cause of shrinking Big Government," the manipulation of the economic forecast, the manipulation of the budget proposal, the repurposing of the budget reconciliation process, the novelty of multiyear budgeting, and the attack on the relatively new CBO—considerably strengthened the ability of the Reagan administration to propose and quickly push through Congress what appeared to be an unprecedented cut in spending, which in turn considerably strengthened the prospects of passing a historic tax cut, the president's top priority.

* * *

As with the plan for the broader public-finance program, Reagan's proposed tax cut predated the start of his administration. In 1978 Representative Jack Kemp and Senator William Roth laid the foundation for a new fiscal policy when they proposed a bill that would cut income tax rates by 30 percent over three years. Like half of the old demand-side—or Keynesian—fiscal policy that focused on managing aggregate demand through the use of either government spending or taxation, the new supply-side fiscal policy stressed the importance of taxation. However, the two approaches differed considerably in their emphases and prescriptions. As Paul Craig Roberts—a member of Kemp's staff, and later assistant secretary of the Treasury for Reagan—explained, "Keynesian fiscal policy emphasizes average tax rates, because Keynesians believe that taxation affects the economy by changing disposable income and thereby aggregate demand. Supply-side economics stresses marginal tax rates, because supply-siders believe that taxation affects the economy by changing the incentives to work, save, invest, and take risks. This different perspective is the essence of the supply-side revolution in economic policy."[16]

Unlike the rise of the demand-side fiscal policy in response to the Great Depression, the "supply-side revolution" in fiscal policy in response to the Great Inflation began in Congress. This was due in part to the Congressional Budget Act of 1974, which created a Budget Committee in the House and Senate and provided Republicans with a venue to develop the supply-side approach as the Great Inflation was undercutting the foundation of the dominant demand-side approach. As Paul Craig Roberts—who also served as the first chief economist on the minority staff of the House Budget Committee—explained, "We were not merely arguing for tax cuts." Rather, we "were developing an alternative fiscal policy" and "the Budget Committee was the necessary forum. Without the Congressional Budget Act of 1974, there probably would not have been a Kemp-Roth bill."[17]

This "alternative fiscal policy" provided Republicans with a competitive program to rival the traditional spending program of Democrats. Before the supply-side revolution Republicans generally maintained the relatively negative position of balancing the budget—preferably by cutting spending and, if that failed, by preventing tax cuts. Moreover, even as Republicans slowly began to accept that orthodox economics justified deficits to manage the economy, the debate centered on the size and source of deficits, and on that ground demand-side fiscal policy prioritized spending over tax cuts due to "leakage." For example, $1 in government spending, it was argued, would stimulate the economy more than $1 in tax cuts because only some part of the tax cut would be spent and the other part would be saved. Therefore, to stimulate the economy by the same amount, a program based on tax cuts would have to increase the deficit more than a program based on spending, making tax cuts less efficient.

The rise of supply-side economics called into question the old line of thinking. As Roberts put it, "Once supply-side economics appeared on the scene the Democrats could no longer claim that government spending stimulated the economy more effectively than tax cuts. Tax cuts were now competitive."[18]

Supply-side economics also provided a credible theory to support what Reagan already believed. As the president explained,

> At the peak of my career at Warner Bros., I was in the ninety-four percent tax bracket; that meant that after a certain point, I received only six cents on each dollar I earned and the government got the rest. The IRS took such a big chunk of my earnings that after a while I began asking myself whether it was worth it to keep on taking work. Something was wrong with a system like that: When you have to give up such a large percentage of your income in taxes, incentive to work goes down. . . .
>
> The same principle that affected my thinking applied to people in all tax brackets: The more the government takes in taxes, the less incentive people have to work. . . . A few economists call this principle supply-side economics. I just call it common sense.[19]

With Reagan already in favor of a major tax cut in particular and the underlying theory of supply-side economics in general, he simply incorporated the Kemp-Roth bill as part of his own program during the Republican nomination process in 1980. Once in office, the new president and his principals then took several key steps to ensure the quick passage of the tax cut.

First—complementing the appointment of Stockman, the self-proclaimed "supply-sider" working in the OMB to make the tax cut appear affordable—Reagan appointed several supply-siders to the Treasury, the institution traditionally responsible for tax policy. In particular, Paul Craig Roberts, a former Kemp aide and the drafter of the original Kemp-Roth bill, was appointed assistant secretary of the Treasury for economic policy; Norman Ture, a former staff member of the Joint Economic Committee and director of tax studies at the National Bureau of Economic Research, was appointed undersecretary of the Treasury for tax and economic affairs; and Donald Regan, a Wall Street banker with no experience in government, was appointed to head the Treasury. In operation, the experienced supply-siders oversaw the details of the tax program, while the inexperienced Treasury secretary with no independent political standing ensured that the Treasury remained fully supportive. As the new Treasury secretary put it, "I didn't come to make tax policy. My job is to execute and sell what the President has already decided. So there's not much left to do except tie the ribbon on Kemp-Roth."[20]

Along with these key appointments and the concurrent budget process ensuring that the tax cut appeared affordable to members of Congress who were not supply-siders, Reagan prioritized the proposal and played a direct role in ensuring its passage. As Stockman observed, "Getting the tax cut passed was one of the few episodes involving domestic policy and legislative bargaining in which [the president] firmly called the shots."[21]

Most importantly, Reagan worked to reorder Republican orthodoxy by pushing ahead without waiting to see whether the administration's proposed cut in spending and economic projection would actually cover the cost of the proposed tax cut and balance the budget in 1984. The president addressed this issue with Congress in February 1981, explaining,

> Over the past decades we've talked of curtailing government spending so that we can then lower the tax burden. Sometimes we've even taken a run at doing that. But there were always those who told us that taxes couldn't be cut until spending was reduced. Well, you know, we can lecture our children about extravagance until we run out of voice and breath. Or we can cure their extravagance by simply reducing their allowance.
>
> It's time to recognize that we've come to a turning point. We're threatened with an economic calamity of tremendous proportions, and the old business-as-usual treatment can't save us. Together, we must chart a different course.[22]

The president then went on national television in July and made a direct appeal to the public to "contact your Senators and Congressmen. Tell them of your support for this bipartisan proposal."[23] This generated, in the words of the Democratic Speaker of the House, "a telephone blitz like this nation has never seen" that helped to push the tax bill through the Democratic-controlled House.[24] Underscoring the president's success during a period of divided party control of the government, the New York Times reported, "The key vote, 238 to 195, gave Mr. Reagan a third upset victory over the Democratic House majority on fiscal issues."[25]

Finally, in August 1981, due largely to these key developments—an "economic calamity of tremendous proportions"; the concurrent, manipulated budget process overseen by a "supply sider, dedicated to [the] cause of shrinking Big Government"; the president's public call to "chart a different course" by "reducing [the] allowance" of the spenders rather than wait "until spending was reduced"; and the president's public pressure on Congress—Reagan signed into law the Omnibus Budget Reconciliation Act (OBRA) and the Economic Recovery Tax Act (ERTA).

Among their many provisions, OBRA projected the single largest cut of nondefense spending spread across more than two hundred domestic programs, and even more importantly, ERTA phased in a 25 percent reduction in individual income tax rates over three years; reduced the top rate from 70 to 50 percent in the first year; indexed the tax brackets for inflation starting in 1985, essentially making the tax cut permanent by eliminating future increases in revenue automatically generated through bracket creep; and lowered the estate tax from 70 to 55 percent, all of which produced the largest tax cut of the modern period, reducing annual revenue by 4.15 percent of GDP during the fourth year of the law's enactment—the longest measure available for a comprehensive comparison. In contrast, the second largest tax cut of the modern period, the Revenue Act of 1945, had reduced annual revenue by only 2.7 percent of GDP, and no tax cut since the Korean War had reduced annual revenue by more than 1.6 percent of GDP.[26]

Together, OBRA and ERTA initiated the most substantial and durable shift in fiscal policy since the Roosevelt administration. After reaching all-time highs of 20.4 and 20.6 percent of GDP during fiscal years 1981 and 1982 respectively, the budget—measured as the average of spending and taxes—fell below 20 percent during fiscal year 1983, and it remained below 20 percent through the end of the Reagan administration. Moreover, although the president would sign into law several tax increases after 1981—the Tax Equity and Fiscal Responsibility Act of 1982, the Deficit Reduction Act of 1984, the Omnibus Budget Reconciliation Act of 1987, and more—the Economic Recovery Tax Act was so large that the Reagan administration still oversaw a total reduction in tax revenue equal to 2 percent of GDP. This was the most substantial tax reduction by any president since Franklin Roosevelt, and it drove the creation of a steady and structurally unbalanced budget that generally operated as a secondary economic-stabilization instrument.[27] Further underscoring the combined significance of OBRA and ERTA, Reagan declared when signing the two laws, "They represent a turnaround of almost a half a century of a course this country's been on and mark an end to the excessive growth in government bureaucracy, government spending, government taxing."[28]

* * *

Following the 1981 program, which, in relying primarily on the OMB and the Treasury, passed with the support of a temporary, relatively centralized public-finance apparatus, Reagan and his principals oversaw four key developments, all of which either further restructured the key parameters of fiscal policy, contributed to the creation of a decentralized public-finance apparatus that helped to secure the new fiscal-policy parameters moving forward, or both.

The first key development began during the second half of 1981. A few weeks after the passage of OBRA and ERTA, it became clear that the budget was on course to produce record deficits rather than move into balance by fiscal year 1984. Two dynamics largely accounted for this outcome: the Fed implemented a highly restrictive monetary policy that triggered a recession in 1981, meaning, rather than growing by the projected 4 percent, the economy actually contracted. At the same time, the cut in spending turned out to be smaller than originally planned, and the tax cut turned out to be larger.[29]

Based on the newly projected budget deficits and the politicized manner in which the 1981 program passed, fiscal policy became increasingly shackled, and control over it significantly shifted from the executive branch to the legislative branch. This was evident in 1982 when the Republican-controlled Senate Budget Committee unanimously declared the Reagan administration's new budget "dead on arrival," notwithstanding Stockman's attempt to repeat, in part, his earlier approach. "Since no one in the White House wanted to propose the first triple-digit budget deficit in history," Stockman confessed, "I out-and-out cooked the books, inventing $15 billion per year of utterly phony cuts."[30] This time, however, the CBO effectively checked the OMB, projecting the deficit more accurately at $132 billion. "That was our finest hour in some ways," CBO Director Alice Rivlin later explained, adding, "By then CBO's right" to check the OMB "was not questioned in the Congress."[31]

Later that same year, with the influential CBO alerting the government to "the risk of an unprecedented clash between monetary and fiscal policy" due to the 1981 program, Reagan signed into law the Tax Equity and Fiscal Responsibility Act (TEFRA), which rescinded a significant portion of the earlier tax cut. Notably, however, this tax increase was much smaller than the 1981 tax cut and left in place the income tax component, the core of the 1981 program.[32] Moreover, when Reagan signed TEFRA in September 1982, the country was in the midst of a severe recession—the economy shrank by nearly 2 percent that year, and unemployment exceeded 10 percent—meaning the government had raised taxes during a downturn for the first time since the Great Depression. Making clear the key role of the Fed in using its increased control over monetary policy to direct this change in fiscal policy—which effectively marked the transition from fiscal policy to monetary policy as the primary economic-stabilization instrument—Treasury Secretary Regan later explained, "[The Fed chair] had assured me that . . . he would ease money to bring interest rates down if he could see some movement by us on the deficits."[33]

In contrast to the rising influence of the CBO and the Fed, the influence of the Council of Economic Advisers, like that of the OMB, diminished significantly. After serving for only eighteen months—the shortest tenure of an incoming chair in the institution's history at that point—CEA Chair Murray Weidenbaum resigned, due to his opposition to the new fiscal policy. As Weidenbaum later put it, "Knowing that I would be expected to defend the President's budget when it was released . . . I decided during this period to quietly leave the administration."[34]

Over the next several years the same administrative dynamics continued. In particular, both the OMB and the CEA, the institutions traditionally responsible for overseeing the budget, believed that further spending cuts were not feasible and so continued to push for tax increases to reduce the run of historic peacetime deficits. This in turn continued to generate a divide within the Reagan administration that left the Treasury as the president's primary source of support and further diminished the influence of the other two institutions, especially the CEA. In 1984 Reagan noted in his diary, "We're really divided. Don Regan [and] I want to battle down to the wire for more spending cuts as an answer to the deficits. [Budget Director David] Stockman [and CEA Chair Martin] Feldstein . . . want a tax increase, I think they are wrong as [hell]."[35]

In response to this continued divide, the president's second CEA chair resigned in 1984. At this point Reagan considered eliminating the once influential institution, but that required legislative action; so the president simply left the top post unfilled for nearly a year, further diminishing its influence. Moreover, Feldstein's eventual replacement, Beryl Sprinkel, made no effort to restore the CEA's influence. As acting CEA Chair William Niskanen explained, "The major lasting effect of the Feldstein episode was the choice of a new chairman" who "was comfortable with a short leash."[36]

The second key development following the 1981 program was the passage of the Social Security Act Amendments of 1983. Despite the tax increase in 1982, the deficit continued to climb, reaching nearly 6 percent of GDP; in conjunction with the ongoing Great Inflation, this created a growing problem based on two earlier developments. First, the government had added Social Security to the unified budget during the 1960s due to its growing size, meaning any change affected not only the financial health of the welfare program but also the size of the budget deficit. Second, the government had indexed Social Security benefits to inflation during the 1970s, which began to make the welfare program insolvent when prices started to rise faster than wages during the Great Inflation. To address these issues, Reagan created the National Commission on Social Security Reform (NCSSR) in 1981, explaining that "inflation has created great uncertainty about our social security system."[37] Two years later, based on a proposal from the NCSSR, the president signed legislation that changed the trajectory of Social Security, especially in initiating the first significant reduction in benefits.

In particular, the law delayed the cost-of-living adjustment for six months and gradually increased the retirement age from 65 to 67; it gradually raised the total combined payroll tax rate to 15.3 percent; and it mandated the removal of the program from the unified budget.[38] Altogether, these adjustments left Social Security intact, but they marked the end of its nearly five-decade-long expansion and the start of a more "balanced" welfare system that would take into greater account the tax component of the program. As Reagan explained, "In this compromise we have struck the best possible balance between the taxes we pay and the benefits paid back. Any more in taxes would be an unfair burden. . . . Any less would threaten the commitment already made to this generation of retirees and to their children."[39]

The third key development following the 1981 program was the passage of two laws that further restructured the budget process. First, due still to the ongoing effects of the 1981 program, the deficit remained at 5 percent of GDP in 1985, spurring the passage of the Balanced Budget and Emergency Deficit Control Act—also known as the Gramm-Rudman-Hollings (GRH) Act. The new law established annual deficit caps to bring the budget into balance by fiscal year 1991; to enforce those deficit caps, the law created a process that required the directors of the OMB and the CBO to submit to the comptroller general of the General Accounting Office a sequestration report that included the following: an estimate of total taxes and spending; a determination of whether the projected deficit would exceed the statutory deficit limit; an estimate of economic growth; and if the deficit limit was exceeded, an estimate of the reductions in the applicable defense and nondefense programs necessary to eliminate the excess deficit. The comptroller general was then required to review the joint OMB-CBO report and, "with due regard for the data, assumptions, and methodologies used," issue his own report that included estimates similar to those required in the OMB-CBO report and explained any differences. This left the elected branches less than two months to pass legislation to reduce the deficit; if they failed to act, a budget sequester would go into effect, automatically cutting an equal amount of defense and nondefense spending in order to bring the deficit under the statutory limit.[40]

Both by statute and in practice, GRH significantly altered the fiscal-policymaking process. In relying on both budgeting institutions, it elevated the CBO to a position equal to that of the OMB; in excluding the CEA, it further diminished the standing of that once influential institution; in calling attention to the "data, assumptions, and methodologies used," it further diminished the ability of future administrations to employ the same budget measures that the Reagan administration had employed in 1981; and in establishing deficits limits, it further shackled fiscal policy, which in turn further strengthened the role of the Fed in managing the economy through the use of monetary policy. To be sure, although GRH was largely a congressional initiative, it was developed in response to the 1981 program, and Reagan succeeded in shaping its scope, thereby making considerable progress in "establish[ing] effective controls on federal spending," one of his primary objectives. As Budget Director Jim Miller—Stockman's successor—explained, "The congressional leadership prevailed on the overall Gramm-Rudman-Hollings sequester formula: half from defense and half from domestic programs. . . . But the president prevailed in keeping the formula based on spending, not taxes."[41]

In 1987 Reagan built upon GRH in signing the Balanced Budget and Emergency Deficit Control Reaffirmation Act, also known as Gramm-Rudman-Hollings II. A year earlier the Supreme Court had struck down the sequestration process included in GRH, ruling that the comptroller general, an official of the legislative branch, could not force the president to act. GRH II corrected this issue and made several other changes. In particular, it extended the statutory deficit caps to fiscal year 1993 and ensured that the sequestration process would be triggered based on the report of the OMB director. However, whereas GRH allowed the directors of both the OMB and the CBO to use their own economic and technical assumptions with the comptroller general averaging the difference in the estimates, GRH II required the OMB director to "[apply] the technical assumptions . . . and methodologies used in the report of the Director of [the] CBO," meaning that the new law elevated the CBO to a position greater than that of the OMB.[42] Further underscoring the new balance of institutional influence, Budget Director Miller remarked, "The objective was to make the OMB director perform a bookkeeping function, with no true authority."[43] In contrast, CBO Director Rudolph Penner—Rivlin's successor—later remarked that during "the Reagan era . . . CBO acquired a lot of credibility."[44]

The fourth key development following the 1981 program was the passage of the Tax Reform Act of 1986. This process began several years earlier and gained traction in 1985 when Reagan informed Congress that he had "asked Treasury [Secretary Regan] to develop a plan to simplify the tax code" and, in response, the "Treasury Department has produced an excellent reform plan, whose principles will guide the final proposal."[45] Further highlighting the key role of the Treasury Department and its head, Secretary Regan noted, "I urged a major push for tax simplification" even though the other principals "were less enthusiastic about the proposal . . . and spoke again about the necessity of new taxes to reduce the deficit."[46] Moreover, the OMB director confirmed the Treasury secretary's responsiveness to the president, explaining, "Regan operated on the 'echo' principle. Whatever the President insisted on, he would try to get—without regard to price." It was an "inversion of the normal role of the Secretary of the Treasury."[47]

The next year Reagan signed the Tax Reform Act of 1986, which further restructured the tax system and was based in large part on the Treasury's initial proposal developed under the oversight of the highly responsive secretary. Among its many provisions, the deficit-neutral law lowered the top individual income tax rate from 50 to 28 percent; it decreased the number of brackets from fourteen to two; it reduced the top corporate tax rate from 46 to 34 percent; and it reduced or eliminated more than seventy tax expenditures, mainly those benefiting business and investors.[48] Further making clear the significance of this landmark law and his support for it, Reagan declared, "With the tax cuts of 1981 and the Tax Reform Act of 1986, I'd accomplished a lot of what I'd come to Washington to do."[49]

Finally, the president proclaimed that his new policies, especially the supply-side tax system, had played a key role in ending the Great Inflation. As Reagan put it,

> A number of things that happened during my watch as president gave me great satisfaction, but I'm probably proudest about the economy. . . . The [1981] tax cut, followed by the Tax Reform Act of 1986, touched off a surge of growth in America that brought down inflation, brought down interest rates, brought down unemployment, and created a cascade of additional tax revenue for government. . . . We got government out of the way and began the process of giving the economy back to the people."[50]

* * *

The case study analysis here shows that Reagan significantly strengthened his control in the subdomain of fiscal policy in working to create the Reagan-era apparatus and policy parameters. First, in appointing a budget director who was a "supply sider, dedicated to [the] cause of shrinking Big Government," and who manipulated the economic forecast, manipulated the budget proposal, repurposed the budget reconciliation process, and attacked the CBO all in order to take advantage of the "opportunity for permanent conservative policy revision," Reagan strengthened his control. Second, in appointing a Treasury secretary who worked "to execute and sell what the President . . . already decided" in the case of the 1981 tax cut and then worked with the president "to develop a plan to simplify the tax code" in the case of the 1986 tax reform, all of which was an "inversion of the normal role of the Secretary of the Treasury" and contributed to the creation of an "alternative fiscal policy," Reagan further strengthened his control. Third, in weakening the CEA and to a lesser extent the OMB, in creating a more "balanced" Social Security system, in overseeing the rise of the CBO and the creation of deficit caps, which operated as "effective controls on federal spending," and in overseeing the end of the Great Inflation by getting the "government out of the way"—all of which either further restructured the key parameters of fiscal policy, contributed to the creation of a decentralized public-finance apparatus that helped to secure the new fiscal-policy parameters moving forward, or both—Reagan strengthened his control further still.

REAGAN STRENGTHENS HIS CONTROL IN RESTRUCTURING THE SUBDOMAIN OF MONETARY POLICY

Along with restructuring the subdomain of fiscal policy, Ronald Reagan worked to restructure the subdomain of monetary policy. This process also began with "Policy Memorandum No. 1," which recommended the implementation of a "consistent" and "dependable" monetary policy and the passage of "a constitutional amendment to prohibit the imposition of wage and price controls," meaning that, unlike the Carter administration, the incoming Reagan administration supported the Fed's new, preferred course under the leadership of its new chair, Paul Volcker.[51]

This shift in support for the Fed was further evident when Reagan presented his initial public-finance program to Congress in February 1981. As the president explained, "The final aspect of our plan requires a national monetary policy which does not allow money growth to increase consistently faster than the growth of goods and services. In order to curb inflation we need to slow the growth in our money supply." The president then added, "We fully recognize the independence of the Federal Reserve System and will do nothing to interfere with or undermine that independence."[52] Also notable, Budget Director David Stockman confirmed that, like taxation, monetary policy was one of the issues that Reagan personally prioritized and understood. As Stockman put it, "This was one thing that the President knows in detail. . . . The money supply 'zoomed' in every election year—'flooding the economy with money'" and "after the election, the Fed 'pulled the string' and the economy went into recession."[53]

Developments in economic theory also supported the president and the Fed's new, preferred course for monetary policy. In particular, Milton Friedman, a professor of economics at the University of Chicago and one of Reagan's personal advisers on the subject, had promoted the idea of "monetarism" as an alternative to the dominant Eccles-Currie—or Keynesian—approach to monetary policy. This theory was most prominently developed in three parts in a speech to the American Economic Association in 1967. First, Friedman addressed the old view of monetary policy as a relatively ineffective, or asymmetric, stabilization instrument, explaining that the Great Depression had generated the belief that "monetary policy was a string. You could pull on it to stop inflation but you could not push on it to halt a recession"; this widely accepted view "in the economics profession meant that for some two decades monetary policy was believed by all but a few reactionary souls to have been rendered obsolete by new economic knowledge." Second, Friedman addressed the new, increasingly important role of monetary policy relative to fiscal policy, explaining that "the revival of belief in the potency of monetary policy was strengthened . . . by increasing disillusionment with fiscal policy, not so much with its potential to affect aggregate demand as with the practical and political feasibility of so using it." Third, Friedman addressed the new monetarist approach to policymaking, recommending that "the monetary authority . . . [adopt] publicly the policy of achieving a steady rate of growth in a specified monetary total. . . . By setting itself a steady course and keeping to it, the monetary authority could make a major contribution to promoting economic stability."[54]

With the incoming president supportive of the central bank's independence in general and the shift to monetarism in particular, the Volcker-led Fed moved to tackle inflation in a way that it had not since its restructuring during the Great Depression. As the Fed chair explained to the other members of the Federal Open Market Committee in December 1980, "We have . . . taken the position . . . that we are going to do something about inflation maybe not regardless of the state of economic activity but certainly more than we did before. . . . It is a very important distinction."[55]

Similar to the initial shift in targeting the money supply during the Carter administration, the Fed allowed interest rates to soar during the start of the Reagan administration in an effort to bring down inflation. Unlike its earlier moves, however, the Fed now held firm. In particular, it allowed the interest rate on interbank borrowing in June 1981 to increase to an all-time high of 19 percent despite the economy contracting at an annual rate of nearly 3 percent at the time. Then, despite the official start of the Recession of 1981–1982 in July, the Fed maintained its tight policy, and the Reagan administration provided support. Beryl Sprinkel—the undersecretary of the Treasury for monetary affairs and a former student of Friedman—explained in a memo in November, "It is important that concern about the recession not lead to quick-fix attempts to reverse the economic slowdown, such as a rapid reacceleration of money growth."[56] The president himself also provided support by allowing the Fed to operate without interference. "Unlike some of his predecessors," Volcker later explained, "[Reagan] had a strong visceral aversion to inflation and an instinct that . . . it wasn't a good idea to tamper with the independence of the Federal Reserve."[57]

The result of the Fed's shift to monetarism this time was striking. By maintaining a tight monetary policy through an economic downturn and a substantial rise in the unemployment rate—which climbed above 8 percent in 1981—the Fed quickly strengthened its credibility as an inflation fighter. As Fed Vice Chair Frederick Schultz put it at a meeting of the FOMC in December 1981, "The credibility of the Federal Reserve is much higher than it has ever been before."[58] The Fed then used its new credibility to promote the idea that inflation was a more fundamental problem than unemployment. "The rapid rise of prices clearly is the single greatest barrier to the achievement of balanced economic growth, high employment . . . and sustained prosperity," Volcker explained in his testimony to Congress.[59]

The next year, the Fed's monetarism-based process of disinflation continued. Importantly, even as unemployment climbed past 9 percent and the economy contracted at an annual rate of more than 6 percent during the first quarter, the Fed maintained a highly restrictive monetary policy. At the same time, the increasingly influential Fed chair continued to publicly reject the old New Deal–era approach. In his testimony to Congress, Volcker explained, "More inflation has been accompanied not by less, but by more unemployment and lower growth. We have not 'traded off' one for the other." He then added that "inflation itself is the greater threat to economic stability."[60]

After maintaining the monetarism-based process of disinflation for more than a year and a half, the Fed finally began to ease its policy in July 1982, due to a combination of factors. Most importantly, unemployment was nearly 10 percent at this point, the financial system was beginning to falter due to the economic contraction, and the Fed's credibility as an inflation fighter had become more firmly established.

Related to this shift in monetary policy, the Senate passed its version of the Tax Equity and Fiscal Responsibility Act (TEFRA) the same month, all but ensuring the passage of the law in September, as the House had passed its own version of the bill the previous December. To be sure, there was no formal agreement, but it was apparent that the elected branches had passed a substantial tax increase in the midst of both a midterm election year and a severe recession in order to reduce the deficit and thereby support the Fed's move to an easier monetary policy. The budget director confirmed that the Fed chair "was telling everyone, 'If you give us some relief on the deficits, it will take the pressure off.'"[61] Reagan also endorsed the arrangement, remarking in August, "If we do not get spending cuts and reduce the deficit, this downward trend on interest rates could be reversed. While I am reluctant to raise taxes, the price is not excessive to get the deficit down and to ensure the continuation of economic recovery."[62]

TEFRA essentially marked the transition from fiscal policy to monetary policy as the primary economic-stabilization instrument. In practice, this meant that rather than use fiscal policy to produce a desired economic outcome directly, fiscal policy would now often operate in support of monetary policy in order to generate that outcome—in this case, rather than cut taxes during a recession in order to boost the depressed economy, the government raised taxes in order to allow the Fed to take the lead in managing the economy through the use of an easier monetary policy at its discretion. Several factors contributed to this development, including the new perspective on the importance of monetary policy, and the slower, more restricted policymaking process for fiscal policy relative to monetary policy.[63] Addressing this transition, Volcker explained, "If all the difficulties growing out of inflation were going to be dealt with at all, it would have to be through monetary policy" because "fiscal policy is notoriously inflexible; as an operating matter, week to week, month to month, quarter to quarter, it is likely to be monetary policy that counts among the instruments available to government."[64]

After the easing of monetary policy and transition in economic-stabilization instruments, the Fed abandoned its primary targeting of the money supply. Although the new monetarism-based approach had considerably strengthened the Fed's ability to bring down inflation—which fell from an annual average of nearly 14 percent in 1980 to 10 percent in 1981 and then to 6 percent in 1982—it had also proven difficult to implement. This was due in part to changes in the definition of the various categories of money following the unfortunately timed Depository Institutions Deregulation and Monetary Control Act of 1980 and in part to changes in the velocity of money—the frequency at which money turns over in the economy.[65] Most importantly, the monetarism-based approach called for the further tightening of the money supply during the second half of 1982, but the Fed now believed that doing so might trigger an economic collapse. In October Volcker explained, "Following a mechanical operation . . . and driving the economy into the ground isn't exactly my version of how to maintain credibility over time."[66] Moreover, unlike the intentional public initiation of the monetarism-based approach, the Fed ended the experiment rather discreetly, treating it like a technical adjustment. As the *New York Times* reported, " [Volcker] announced a technical but important change in how the Federal Reserve would monitor the nation's money supply to help prevent an unwarranted rise in interest rates. . . . 'In the circumstances,' Mr. Volcker said, 'I do not believe that in actual implementation of monetary policy, we have any alternative but to attach much less than usual weight to movements in M-1, over the period immediately ahead.'"[67]

Although the Fed moved away from primarily targeting the money supply, it had no clear alternative target in place during the second half of 1982. This was evident during the first meeting of the FOMC the next year. As Volcker noted, "The Committee is on two horses. . . . One is targeting and one is flex-ibility." He then added, "We can look at a lot of things in addition to interest rates, which I think is probably what we're doing."[68]

With a lack of clear operating guidelines, the Fed essentially maintained a steady course throughout 1983. However, in early 1984, it applied the brakes to the growing economy in order to further secure its hard-won credibility as an inflation fighter. As Volcker explained in April, "We haven't passed the test of maintaining control over inflation during a period of prosperity."[69] This shift to a restrictive monetary policy occurred while the unemployment rate was still above 7 percent for the fourth year running, and the president provided politi-cal cover by refusing, as the *New York Times* reported, "to endorse criticism of the Federal Reserve Board" that other officials had expressed.[70]

The tightening of monetary policy in 1984 ultimately occurred too late to impact Reagan's sweeping reelection in November—the economy still grew by more than 7 percent that year—but this move demonstrated the Fed's continued commitment to check inflation, now during not only "a period of prosperity" but also a presidential election.

That same year—more than five decades after Roosevelt first abandoned the gold standard, the original anchor of the monetary system—it was clear that there was still no consensus at the Fed on operating guidelines. As Volcker remarked at the FOMC meeting in December, "I wonder whether we'd be kid-ding ourselves by making" any "automatic rule . . . that would inhibit making discretionary changes."[71]

Without a consensus on an interest rate or money supply operating guide-line, the newly independent Fed simply employed, as the chair put it, the "fine tuning" of monetary policy to manage the economy, an approach that proved successful in lowering the public finance problem—or "misery"—index to single digits by 1986.[72] This effectively marked the end of the Great Inflation and primarily consisted of restoring "price stability" rather than "full employ-ment"—average annual inflation fell below 2 percent in 1986 after peaking at nearly 14 percent in 1980, whereas unemployment fell to just below 7 percent in 1986 after peaking at nearly 11 percent in 1982. The Fed's restructuring of mone-tary policy to prioritize price stability was part of, in Volcker's words, a "renais-sance of central banking" that occurred during the Reagan administration. "I realize that there is great wisdom in the old adage that what you think depends upon where you sit," Volcker explained. "Nonetheless, I am convinced there is objective reality in my impression that central banks are in exceptionally good repute these days."[73]

Although the Fed chair deserved substantial credit for the "renaissance of central banking" during the Reagan administration, the president played an equally important role. As Volcker explained, "An effective central bank must be a strong central bank, with substantial autonomy in its operations and with insulation from partisan and passing political pressures."[74] This became increasingly apparent after the "mostly wasted year restoring credibility in the attack on inflation" under Carter, meaning that without Reagan the Fed would not have had the necessary "insulation from partisan and passing political pressures" that allowed the process of disinflation to take hold. In particular, Reagan, unlike Carter, never proposed temporary inflation controls that interfered with the Fed's management of monetary policy, and he never publicly criticized the central bank's decisions. Volcker himself later confirmed, "There's no doubt there were times . . . when the president, preparing for press conferences or otherwise, was urged by his staff to take on the Fed. He never did so publicly."[75] Likewise, Volcker's successor, Alan Greenspan, observed, "Reagan gave Volcker the political cover he needed; no matter how much people complained, the president made it his practice never to criticize the Fed."[76]

* * *

In addition to overseeing the shackling of fiscal policy, opposing temporary inflation controls, and providing political cover, all of which allowed for the creation of a "fine-tuned" monetary policy that generally operated as the primary economic-stabilization instrument in support of promoting "price stability"—or low inflation—Reagan helped to secure the new monetary policy by appointing an entirely new Federal Reserve Board, the first president to do so since Franklin Roosevelt and due in large part to the Reagan administration's increased prioritization of the issue. In 1982 Reagan appointed Preston Martin; in 1984 he appointed Martha Seger; and in 1986 he appointed Wayne Angell, Manuel Johnson, and Robert Heller, thereby creating a Reagan-appointed majority on the seven-member board. Then in 1987 he appointed Edward Kelley, Jr., and Alan Greenspan, who replaced Volcker as chair. And in 1988 he appointed John LaWare, thereby creating a Reagan-appointed majority on the twelve-member Federal Open Market Committee.[77] Underscoring the importance of this development, the *New York Times* reported in 1988 that LaWare's confirmation "would mean all seven governors would be Reagan appointees," which "is especially significant because of the immense power that the Fed's chairman, Alan Greenspan, and his fellow governors wield over the economy. Since Congress is preoccupied with the national elections and the major spending and tax decisions for the fiscal year 1989 have been made, the Fed stands, in effect, alone in trying to manage the economy and steer it clear of inflation and a recession."[78]

The appointment of Volcker's successor was especially important in securing the new Reagan-era monetary policy. Prior to the selection of Arthur Burns in 1970, no Fed chair had had a professional background in economics. William McChesney Martin, Jr.—Burns's predecessor and the longest-serving chair of the New Deal era—had little understanding of economic theory and had actively prevented his staff from making and using economic forecasts. William Miller, Burns's successor, also had no background in economics and had quickly failed in managing the Fed. In contrast, Volcker had a B.A. in economics from Princeton, an M.A. in political economy from Harvard, and had worked on a doctoral dissertation at the London School of Economics. Similarly, Greenspan—who would become the longest-serving chair of the Reagan era—had a PhD in economics from New York University. During the Reagan era, then, the CEA no longer operated as the sole depository of "exceptionally qualified" economists "formulat[ing] and recommend[ing] national economic policy."

Further underscoring the restructuring of the subdomain of monetary policy during the Reagan administration, the president himself explained during the swearing-in ceremony of Greenspan, "The economic expansion is now just 2 months short of becoming the longest peacetime economic expansion in American history. For some 5 years now, inflation has stayed well below the rates of the late 1970's, with interest rates coming down sharply as well. We've seen a burst of new business formations, a virtual riot of new technologies, and the creation of over 13-1/2 million new jobs."[79] Reagan then added, "I want to express my gratitude to Paul Volcker for the part he played in these accomplishments. And I want to restate my confidence in Alan Greenspan to carry these accomplishments still further, all the while maintaining the Fed's traditional independence."[80]

* * *

The case study analysis here shows that Reagan significantly strengthened his control in the subdomain of monetary policy in working to create the Reagan-era apparatus and policy parameters. First, in overseeing the shackling of fiscal policy, in pledging from the start to "fully recognize the independence of the [Fed] and . . . do nothing to interfere with or undermine that independence," in opposing temporary inflation controls, and in providing the Fed "insulation from partisan and passing political pressures" through several key episodes— an economic downturn, a midterm election year, a "period of prosperity," and a presidential election year—all of which allowed the Fed "to curb inflation," one of the president's primary objectives, Reagan strengthened his control. Second, in appointing an entirely new Federal Reserve Board for the first time since its restructuring during the Roosevelt administration—which helped to restore "the Fed's traditional independence" and the ability of its new chair "to carry these accomplishments still further"—Reagan further strengthened his control.

Altogether, the case study analysis of fiscal policymaking and monetary policymaking in this chapter shows that the decentralized Reagan–era apparatus and the Reagan–era policy parameters were all largely in place by the end of the Reagan administration. They were then secured during the Bush administration.

10. Stabilization: Bush Relinquishes His Control in Securing the Policy Domain

The quantitative overview provided evidence that in the domain of public finance, George H. W. Bush oversaw the securing of both the decentralized Reagan-era apparatus and the Reagan-era policy parameters due largely to party continuity and a decreasingly severe and decreasingly prioritized problem, all of which began to strengthen the average restrictions on presidential control and began to weaken the average incentive to maximize control. This chapter traces the process of Bush relinquishing much of his control to Ronald Reagan in working to secure the newly restructured policy domain.

BUSH RELINQUISHES HIS CONTROL IN SECURING THE SUBDOMAIN OF FISCAL POLICY

In contrast to his predecessor, George Bush largely relied upon public-finance principals with experience in the previous administration. Addressing this issue, John Sununu, the president's chief of staff, explained,

> There are two kinds of transitions: one is a transition between the two political parties, and the other occurs when the same party as the sitting president has won. Surprisingly, it is harder when the transition is within the same political party, which was the situation we had to deal with late in the fall of 1988. It was especially difficult because many of the Reagan appointees wanted to stay on.[1]

In particular, Bush retained Ronald Reagan's final Treasury secretary, Nicholas Brady; he appointed Richard Darman, who had served in a number of important posts during the Reagan administration, to the position of budget director; and he appointed Michael Boskin, a professor of economics at Stanford University and the only top principal without government experience, to serve as chair of the Council of Economic Advisers. But, in line with the institution's significant decline during the Reagan administration, the CEA chair remained—as Darman put it—"irrelevant" to the policymaking process throughout the Bush administration.[2] Supporting this account, Boskin himself later noted that the "CEA Chairman . . . is a very weak position. . . . There have been CEA Chairmen that have been quite influential" but the importance of the position has diminished due in large part to "the change in the budget act and the change in responsibilities for budgeting and the proliferation of economists throughout the government."[3]

Additionally, Alan Greenspan remained chair of the Federal Reserve, the position Ronald Reagan had appointed him to in 1987, and congressional leaders selected Robert Reischauer, an academic economist, to serve as director of the Congressional Budget Office. Underscoring the importance of this relatively new post, which operated entirely independent of the president's appointment power, the *New York Times* reported that the CBO director was "one of the most influential staff positions in Congress. . . . Mr. Reischauer will be [that body's] chief economist and play a central role in providing budget analyses and economic projections."[4]

As confirmed in part by both the principals and the mix of existing positions, there was substantial continuity in public-finance administration moving from the Reagan administration to the Bush administration. Reinforcing this continuity—and in further contrast to his predecessor—the incoming president had no plan in place to manage the subdomain of fiscal policy. To be sure, as a candidate, Bush had called for a "flexible freeze" to check government spending, but that was hardly a plan.[5] The incoming budget director therefore took the lead in writing up a basic blueprint less than two months before the start of the Bush administration. As Darman put it, "Slowly but surely, I did what the campaign policy staff had evidently been unable to do in any detailed and systematic way. I forced the group to focus on the hard budget realities."[6]

The incoming budget director began by addressing the new statutory deficit caps. "Even with the optimistic Reagan economic forecast," he noted, "total spending growth had to be limited to 2.8 percent in order to meet the Gramm-Rudman target."[7] Moreover, rather than try to move "swiftly, deftly, and courageously" from the start, as Reagan's budget director had advised in late 1980, Bush's budget director made it clear that moving first was now a *disadvantage*. As Darman explained, "It's exactly because the budget is this hard that the Democrats are demanding (and will continue to demand) that President-elect Bush go first—that he submit his own plan."[8]

In an effort to circumvent this first-mover disadvantage, one of Darman's initial actions as budget director-elect was to examine the possibility of "skipping the ordinary budget process" and instead "[initiating] bipartisan leadership meetings [with Congress]." That approach, he reasoned, "would avoid our budget being declared 'dead on arrival'" and "would override the congressional budget process, which was contentious and unproductive." After talking with the Democratic leaders in Congress, however, it was evident, Darman added, that "they were determined to force [the president] to embarrass himself, and insisted that we must submit our budget before any negotiations could begin."[9]

At the same time that the incoming Bush administration struggled to develop a workable plan—and, if possible, avoid moving first—the Fed moved to influence fiscal policy through the threat of a restrictive monetary policy. As Darman later confirmed, Greenspan "made it clear he wanted a major deficit reduction package. His polite implication was that he would not allow higher money supply growth or higher real economic growth without our first achieving a legislative solution to the deficit problem."[10]

Adding to the situation, the president had boxed himself in during the campaign. Making clear his commitment to his predecessor's policies, Bush had declared during the Republican National Convention, "My opponent won't rule out raising taxes but I will, and the Congress will push me to raise taxes, and I'll say no, and they'll push, and I'll say no, and they'll push again, and I'll say to them, 'Read my lips: no new taxes.'"[11]

With no clear plan in place and several major constraints at play—the statutory deficit caps, the "contentious and unproductive" congressional budget process, the Fed's use of monetary policy to influence fiscal policy, and the "no new taxes" pledge—Bush decided to delay the hard decisions on the budget. "The President-elect seemed strongly inclined toward a not-in the-first-year formulation," Darman explained, and after the election "he met alone for lunch with his old friend from the Ways and Means Committee, Chairman Dan Rostenkowski," who agreed to "avoid embarrassing the new President on taxes for one year—but for only one year."[12] This "not-in-the-first-year formulation" resulted in Darman developing, as he put it, a "moderately credible" one-year budget proposal that Bush presented to Congress in early 1989.[13]

By mid-April—and following a nine-week "budget summit"—there was a basic deal in place for, in Darman's words, a "modest" deficit reduction program that would "at least meet the Gramm-Rudman target (as estimated by both OMB and the Congressional Budget Office)."[14] The budget agreement was designed to reduce the deficit by $28 billion, split evenly between spending cuts and revenue increases. The majority of the revenue increases consisted of tax compliance reforms, higher user fees for government services, and the sale of government assets, none of which technically violated the "no new taxes" pledge.[15] However, there was still $5 billion that needed to be raised, and rather than request a tax increase, Bush pushed for a capital gains tax cut, taking the supply-side view that it would increase revenue—a view that he had publicly criticized eight years earlier. Highlighting this shift, the *New York Times* reported, "Despite Mr. Bush's present enthusiasm for supply-side tax cuts, he once ridiculed [Ronald] Reagan on the subject," labeling the idea "voodoo econom-ics."[16] Although the amount was small, the debate over the capital gains tax cut delayed the budget agreement and triggered a $16 billion sequester in October in order to comply with the statutory deficit caps.

Finally, Bush signed the Omnibus Budget Reconciliation Act of 1989 in December following an agreement to replace the capital gains tax cut with an increase in revenue from other sources that still maintained the "no new taxes" pledge, and the budget sequester remained in place until February 1990 in order to produce an equivalent reduction in spending.[17] Making clear his support, the president explained, "We find ourselves having to use the fail-safe deficit reduc-tion measure that the law requires: across-the-board spending cuts, known as sequester," which is "a necessary discipline."[18] Also notable, Bush announced to Congress that year, "Many Presidents have come to this Chamber in times of great crisis: war and depression, loss of national spirit. And 8 years ago, I sat in that very chair as President Reagan spoke of punishing inflation and devastat-ingly high interest rates and people out of work—American confidence on the wane." Then, addressing his own situation and further making clear his support for securing his predecessor's work, Bush added, "Our challenge is different. We're fortunate—a much changed landscape lies before us. . . . So, I don't pro-pose to reverse direction. We're headed the right way, but we cannot rest."[19]

* * *

Along with supporting the supply-side tax system and the statutorily restricted general spending system during his first year, Bush continued to work to secure the Reagan-era apparatus and fiscal-policy parameters when he presented his new multiyear budget to Congress in January 1990. Addressing the important role of the statutory deficit caps in structuring the process, the president de-clared that his proposal "meets the deficit target of $64 billion for [fiscal year] 1991 established by the Gramm-Rudman-Hollings law" and "balance[s] the budget by 1993 as required by that law."[20] Yet, as the initial steps of this highly restricted policymaking process unfolded, "each new release of economic statis-tics," Darman noted, "made it clear that the earlier tightening by the Greenspan Fed was slowing the economy" and undercutting the prospect of balancing the budget.[21]

Adding to the situation, the CBO reported in March that "the [fiscal year] 1991 budget deficit under the President's policy proposals would be $131 billion, almost $70 billion higher than the Administration's estimate."[22] Underscoring the institution's standing at the time—and in contrast to the OMB director, who later later confessed, "I felt like the director of nothing"[23]—CBO Director Reischauer explained that the CBO is "one of the great success stories of American government. . . . This hasn't been recognized enough, but it's an important institution" that was "greatly enhanced by the fact that . . . the Reagan administration . . . for political or ideological reasons, doctored the evidence, so to speak."[24]

Further adding to the complex budget-making process, Congress moved ahead with its own proposal in 1990. As Darman explained, "Rosty had given the President his one-year reprieve on taxes and was now ready to make a big move. He was unilaterally going to put a serious deficit reduction plan forward."[25]

In response to these developments, the Bush administration dropped its original proposal and focused on negotiating with Congress in order to create a plan acceptable to the two elected branches as well as the Fed. Further making clear the influential role of the central bank, Darman acknowledged that the goal was to produce a deficit reduction plan "capable of earning the Federal Reserve's respect and cooperation."[26] Moreover, with the deficit continuing to increase—it would eventually reach 4.4 percent of GDP, the highest level since 1986—the Bush administration concluded that it was necessary to reconsider the budget-making process under the Gramm-Rudman-Hollings laws. However, due to the previous year's contentious budget negotiations, the Democratic-controlled Congress was reluctant to take part without reassurance that a tax increase was at least on the table. Bush therefore agreed in May to begin negotiations with "no preconditions" this time, a move that, as the budget director put it, "undid the in-your-face absolutism of read-my-lips without necessarily agreeing to increased taxes."[27]

Complicating the process further still, the Fed soon stepped up its pressure. "While the vaunted 'negotiators' were sitting around the table in evidently unproductive chatter," Darman explained, "interest rates had headed up," and Greenspan was "insisting on a budget agreement before he would provide even a modest cushion of monetary relaxation."[28] This impelled Bush to explicitly abandon the "no new taxes" pledge in late June. Then in July the CBO revised the projected budget deficit for fiscal year 1991 from $161 billion to more than $230 billion.[29] And in August Iraq invaded Kuwait, leading the president to inform Congress the following month that it was essential to pass a deficit reduction package in order to "avoid the ax of sequester—deep across-the-board cuts that would threaten our military capacity and risk substantial domestic disruption."[30]

All of these factors severely weakened the president's bargaining position. As Darman explained, "With the growing deficit, it became evident that the potential sequester was too large to be manageable. This was especially obvious in the case of the Department of Defense, which was readying itself for a possible war."[31] The president's own priorities also shifted due to the war. "'Read my lips' was rhetorical overkill," Bush conceded. "When push came to shove and our troops were moving oversees, we needed a fully functioning government. I simply had to hammer out a compromise to keep the government open."[32]

Spurred by the impending war in Iraq and the size of the looming sequester, the budget negotiations produced a deal in late September that the Bush administration had ensured would strengthen the statutorily restricted spending system and not weaken the supply-side tax system. As the president explained in an address to the nation,

> It's the toughest deficit reduction package ever, with new enforcement rules to make sure that what we fix now stays fixed. . . . This agreement will also raise revenue. I'm not, and I know you're not, a fan of tax increases. But if there have to be tax measures, they should allow the economy to grow, they should not turn us back to higher income tax rates. . . . Our bipartisan agreement meets these tests.[33]

Despite both components—the inclusion of "new enforcement rules" on the spending front and the meeting of key "tests" on the tax front—a group of Republicans in the House worked to undercut the proposal, leading to a government shutdown in October and strengthening the influence of the Democrats in shaping the final agreement, particularly on the tax front. As Darman explained, "The President was forced to renegotiate with the Democratically-controlled Congress from a weakened position" due to the Republican defection, and therefore "a small increase in the top income tax rate . . . was substituted for most of the gasoline tax increase."[34]

Although a heated political battle between the president and various factions in Congress decided the final makeup of the deficit reduction program, the Fed chair—along with the impending war in Iraq and the size of the looming sequester—had played a key role not only in spurring the creation of the program but also in ensuring its passage. Greenspan later noted, "In a congressional hearing in October when the budget was finally up for approval, I pronounced the plan 'credible'—which might sound like faint praise, but it was enough to make the stock market jump, as traders bet that the Fed would instantly cut interest rates."[35] Supporting the Fed chair's account of his influential role, the headline in the *New York Times* the following day announced, "Greenspan Calls Budget Proposal a 'Credible' Plan."[36]

Finally, in November Bush signed the Omnibus Budget Reconciliation Act of 1990, a five-year, $500 billion deficit-reduction program and the most important fiscal-policy legislation of his presidency.[37] To be sure, the law proved politically damaging in violating the "no new taxes" pledge, but it helped to secure the restructured subdomain of fiscal policy in at least four key ways.

First, OBRA helped to secure the supply-side tax system. In particular, it raised the top income tax rate, but only from 28 to 31 percent, well below the New Deal–era average of more than 80 percent. The law also left the top corporate income tax rate at 34 percent and the estate tax rate at 55 percent, both of which were well below their New Deal–era averages.

Second, OBRA helped to secure the statutorily restricted spending system. In particular, the law established discretionary spending caps and pay-as-as-you-go procedures—referred to as PAYGO—that required that all new direct spending and revenue legislation be deficit neutral or deficit reducing. Unlike the restrictions under the Gramm-Rudman-Hollings Acts that targeted the size of the deficit, which is highly sensitive to economic conditions, the provisions under the Budget Enforcement Act—Title XIII of OBRA—targeted the level of spending, which Congress controls directly. Moreover, like GRH, the BEA established a sequestration process that would automatically cut spending rather than raise taxes to offset any net increase in the deficit.

Further securing the statutorily restricted spending system, the BEA incorporated the Senate's "Byrd rule" into the Congressional Budget Act of 1974. Established in 1985, the same year as the original Gramm-Rudman-Hollings Act and working toward the same end, the Byrd rule limited the ability of the Senate to incorporate "extraneous matter"—legislation that is merely incidental to the budget or that would increase the deficit beyond the current budget window—into the reconciliation process as a means of circumventing the filibuster.

Third, OBRA helped to secure the more "balanced" welfare system in leaving Social Security essentially untouched following the 1983 amendments. Most notably, after increasing from less than 1 percent of GDP in 1940 to just under 5 percent in 1983, Social Security spending remained under 5 percent of GDP throughout the Bush administration. And after increasing from 2 percent in 1937 to 15.3 percent under the 1983 amendments, the combined payroll tax rate remained unchanged.

Fourth, OBRA helped to secure the shackling of fiscal policy and its role as a secondary economic-stabilization instrument due in large part to the combination of the supply-side tax system, the statutorily restricted general spending system, and the end of the growth in Social Security spending. In particular, the budget—measured as the average of total spending and taxes—remained below 20 percent of GDP throughout the Bush administration, securing the ceiling that the Reagan administration had established following a five-decade-long expansion. Moreover, from July 1990 through March 1991, a recession was underway, the first since 1982. But rather than use fiscal policy to stimulate the economy directly, OBRA—like the Tax Equity and Fiscal Responsibility Act of 1982—lowered the deficit in order to support the Fed in managing the economy through the use of monetary policy.

Following the passage of OBRA, Bush took two additional steps to secure the restructured subdomain. In 1991 he battled with Congress over the passage of a $6 billion unemployment package, even as the unemployment rate hit 7 percent.[38] Then in 1992 he fought to protect the new statutory checks on spending, even as the unemployment rate climbed near 8 percent and the election approached. Further demonstrating his opposition to increased spending, Bush declared in August, "Beginning tonight, I will enforce the spending freeze on my own. If Congress sends me a bill spending more than I asked for in my budget, I will veto it fast."[39] Bush also declared that the 1990 tax increase was a "bad call," explaining, "It was a mistake to go along with the Democratic tax increase, and I admit it. . . . When the new Congress convenes next January, I will propose to further reduce taxes across the board."[40]

Although Bush ultimately lost the election and so was unable to "further reduce taxes," the pledge was significant in reaffirming his commitment to completing Reagan's work nearly four years into his own presidency. Making that commitment even clearer, Bush declared during the 1992 campaign that "my agenda keeps faith with the crusade we called the Reagan revolution."[41]

* * *

The case study analysis here shows that Bush relinquished much of his control to Reagan in the subdomain of fiscal policy in working to secure the Reagan-era apparatus and policy parameters. First, in proposing a capital gains tax cut as part of the Omnibus Budget Reconciliation Act of 1989 despite his previous criticism of "voodoo economics," and in implementing the budget sequester as "a necessary discipline" on the spending side, both of which supported the president's pledge that "I don't propose to reverse direction," Bush relinquished much of his control to Reagan. Second, in proposing and passing the Omnibus Budget Reconciliation Act of 1990 that worked to secure several key fiscal-policy components—the supply-side tax system, the statutorily restricted general spending system that strengthened the influence of the CBO, the more "balanced" welfare system, and the shackling of fiscal policy more generally that strengthened the influence of the Fed—all of which supported the president's pledge that his "agenda keeps faith with . . . the Reagan revolution," Bush further relinquished much of his control to Reagan. Third, in continuing to oppose increased spending after 1990, and in apologizing for the 1990 tax increase and pledging not to repeat that "mistake" moving forward, all of which supported the president's pledge to continue the "Reagan revolution," Bush relinquished much of his control to Reagan further still.

BUSH RELINQUISHES HIS CONTROL IN SECURING THE SUBDOMAIN OF MONETARY POLICY

Along with securing the restructured subdomain of fiscal policy, George Bush worked to secure the restructured subdomain of monetary policy. This process began in early 1989 when Bush publicly embraced Alan Greenspan, the Fed chair whom Ronald Reagan had appointed. Although it was technically outside the central bank's jurisdiction, Bush requested that the Fed commit, if necessary, to propping up the troubled savings-and-loan industry, and he also requested that the Fed chair personally attend the announcement of the administration's program in February.[42] The new president then made it clear during the press conference that he was delegating responsibility to the more experienced Fed chair and Treasury secretary, both of whom his predecessor had appointed. When questioned on the proposed program, Bush remarked, "I again would ask you to ask the specifics of the Treasury burden to the Chairman of the Federal Reserve [Alan Greenspan] or the Secretary of the Treasury [Nicholas Brady]. Ask how they see that."[43]

In addition to providing support for the savings-and-loan proposal and serving as a public prop at the start of the Bush administration, Greenspan moved to consolidate his control over monetary policy, especially the federal funds rate—the rate at which banks lend reserve balances to other banks. Unlike the discount rate—the rate at which Federal Reserve Banks directly lend to member banks—the federal funds rate is managed through the Federal Open Market Committee's use of open-market operations and it became the primary interest rate target over the course of the 1980s. Laying the groundwork for this process during the final years of the Reagan administration, Greenspan explained to the other members of the FOMC in 1988, "We have to find the mechanism by which we are perceived to be in a general consensus. The reason I say that is that it's fairly obvious that the [Reagan] Administration is beginning to wind down. There are elections coming up and we are turning out to be the only people who are minding the store." He then added, "The one thing I would particularly like . . . is to find a way . . . in which we can speak with a single voice."[44] To carry out this objective, Greenspan proposed that the FOMC grant him the authority to unilaterally adjust the federal funds rate—or, in technical terms, issue an "asymmetric directive"[45]—between the eight regularly scheduled meetings each year, and the twelve members of the FOMC, dominated by

Reagan appointees, unanimously agreed. Underscoring the significance of this development, the president of the Reserve Bank in Philadelphia remarked, "My congratulations to you, Mr. Chairman. You have performed a miracle."[46]

Following the start of the Bush administration in 1989, Greenspan continued to consolidate his control over monetary policy. First, after increasing the federal funds rate several times during the early part of the year in order to check an uptick in inflation, the Fed chair changed course, lowering the targeted rate unilaterally in June and again in July.[47] The objective of this "fine-tuned" monetary policy was to slow the economy without triggering a recession. As one member put it, the FOMC is "committed to bringing inflation down but we also don't want to have a recession; we're committed to a soft landing."[48]

Notwithstanding the Fed's effort, a recession began in July 1990, and in August Iraq invaded Kuwait, increasing the possibility of a larger war and higher energy costs. Faced now with a depressed economy and the possibility of higher inflation—during a year in which inflation averaged more than 5 percent, the highest level in nearly a decade—Greenspan rejected the growing demand for an easier monetary policy. At the meeting of the FOMC in August, he explained, "It is crucial that there be some stable anchor in the economic system. It's clearly not going to be on the budget side; it has to be the central bank." In another plea for unity, he added, "I'm not asking anyone to go against his or her particular view of where you would like policy to be, but if you can find your way clear, this is the type of meeting in which it would be helpful if we had a very substantial consensus."[49] Once again, Greenspan won the vote unanimously, ensuring that the Fed continued to prioritize the threat of inflation, even with a recession underway.

At the next meeting of the FOMC—and after testifying before Congress that the proposed deficit reduction program was "credible"—Greenspan went further in consolidating his control when he recommended lowering interest rates if and when the proposed budget program passed. For some members of the FOMC, this proposal went too far. Board Governor Wayne Angell complained, "Monetary policy does its job best when it looks at the price level. And this is not a monetary event in terms of its cause and it is not a good precedent to have a linkup with fiscal policy. It really is the worst form of fine tuning."[50] Despite the growing opposition within the FOMC, Greenspan prevailed and lowered the federal funds rate by 0.25 percentage points two days after Congress passed the Omnibus Budget Reconciliation Act of 1990.[51]

The following year, the Fed chair moved even more forcefully to cut interest rates and expand his unilateral powers in the process. In January he unilaterally lowered the federal funds rate by 0.25 percentage points, explaining to the members of the FOMC that this action was permitted "under the asymmetric directive."[52] Then in February he unilaterally lowered the rate by 0.5 percentage points, leading some members of the FOMC to question the lack of consultation. During the subsequent conference call the president of the Reserve Bank in St. Louis remarked, "I don't know whether you would consider this a technical point or not, but on the decision to [cut] the funds rate: Should that be an action taken by the FOMC?" Greenspan stood firm, however, responding that "as I understand it, this does not require FOMC action."[53]

Due to the growing concern over the unilateral rate changes—and based on the findings of a task force charged with determining the legal extent of the Fed chair's powers—Greenspan proposed a process of "enhanced consultation" at the next meeting of the FOMC. "If possible," he explained, "this would include advance notice to Committee members of the action contemplated and an opportunity for thorough discussion of the alternatives." However, some members of the FOMC now questioned the proposed solution. The president of the Reserve Bank in Cleveland remarked, "I'm not sure what 'enhanced consultation' means." He then added, "The authority for monetary policy actions . . . is with the FOMC. . . . And that seems somewhat inconsistent with what you're suggesting."[54] Once again Greenspan stood firm and offered only the faint possibility of addressing the limitations of his powers at a later date, responding that "we'll look back after a while and see whether or not we're doing it right."[55]

Implicitly acknowledging the importance of this on-the-job training during the Bush administration due to his initial inexperience, Greenspan explained in his memoirs,

> The Fed had always been a black box to me. Having watched [Arthur Burns] struggle, I did not feel equipped to do the job; setting interest rates for an entire economy seemed to involve so much more than I knew. . . . I'd scrutinized the economy every working day for decades and had visited the Fed scores of times. Nevertheless, when I was appointed chairman, I knew I'd have a lot to learn.[56]

Equally important, Bush continued to provide support while Greenspan consolidated his control over monetary policy. During his third year in office, the president remarked publicly, "The Fed is an independent, sometimes very independent organization over there, and [Greenspan's] got to lead that important enterprise the way he sees fit."[57]

* * *

In addition to providing an initial hands-off window for Greenspan to learn how "to lead [the Fed] the way he sees fit," Bush extended the tenure of this key

Reagan appointee. Making clear the Fed chair's standing by this point, in nom-
inating him for another term, the president explained, "The respect that Alan
Greenspan has around the world and in this country, particularly in financial
marketplaces, is unparalleled."[58] Moreover, the *New York Times* reported, "The
nation's large budget deficit prevents the President or Congress from using tax
and spending policies to influence the economy, and that leaves Mr. Greenspan
far and away the most important economic policy maker in the Government."[59]

The same week that Greenspan was nominated to a new term, he confirmed
that the Fed had continued to prioritize the "price stability" mandate throughout his tenure. As he explained to Congress, "At this stage, we are well on the
path of actually achieving the type of goals which we've set out to achieve: a
solid recovery with the unemployment rate moving down to its lowest sustain-
able, long-term rate, with growth at or close to its maximum long-term sustain-
able pace," and "with inflation wholly under control."[60]

The next year, due in large part to the continued prioritization of the "price
stability" mandate, unemployment became a growing concern, reaching nearly
8 percent in the months before the 1992 election, whereas average inflation declined to 3 percent. In response Bush publicly called for the Fed to act more
aggressively, explaining, "I'd like to see another lowering of interest rates. . . . I
can understand people worrying about inflation. But I don't think that's the big
problem."[61] However, by this point, the Fed's independence had grown too secure
under its chair—who was "lead[ing] that important enterprise the way he sees
fit"—for the president's remark, a rare break from the Reagan-initiated hands-
off approach, to have an impact. At a subsequent meeting of the FOMC, Board
Governor Lawrence Lindsey—Bush's own appointee—stated in response to the
president's remark, "We'd clearly establish credibility if we stood tall. . . . [P]er-
haps we could even raise rates and . . . really show our independence."[62]

That same year the Democratic-controlled Senate finally approved the Fed
chair's appointment to a new term after failing to act on the matter the year
before. This locked Greenspan in for another four years as Fed chair and also
provided him his own full fourteen-year term on the Board, meaning that the
Reagan-appointed Fed chair now had the potential to remain in that position
until 2006, nearly two decades after Reagan left office.[63] For the sitting president
facing reelection as unemployment climbed to nearly 8 percent, Greenspan's
confirmation and his use of monetary policy to bring "inflation wholly under
control" provided little immediate comfort. "I think that if interest rates had
been lowered more dramatically that I would have been reelected president,"
Bush later complained. "I reappointed [Greenspan] and he disappointed me."[64]
However, the president also believed that he had no real choice but to maintain
continuity in this key policy domain. As he made clear during the 1988 cam-

paign, "This election is really a question. Who can you most trust to continue the Reagan revolution? Who can you rely on to build on what we've done?"[65]

* * *

The case study analysis here shows that Bush relinquished much of his control to Reagan in the subdomain of monetary policy in working to secure the Reagan-era apparatus and policy parameters. First, in immediately and publicly embracing the Reagan-appointed Fed chair and in providing an initial hands-off window for that principal to learn "to lead [the Fed] the way he [saw] fit," all of which worked to bring "inflation wholly under control" and supported the president's pledge to "continue the Reagan revolution," Bush relinquished much of his control to Reagan. Second, in reappointing the Reagan-appointed Fed chair to a new four-year term as chair and a full fourteen-year term as a member of the Board, all of which further supported the president's pledge to "continue the Reagan revolution," Bush further relinquished much of his control to Reagan.

Altogether, the case study analysis of fiscal policymaking and monetary policymaking in this chapter shows that the decentralized Reagan-era apparatus and the Reagan-era policy parameters were both firmly in place by the end of the Bush administration.

The Reagan-Era Apparatus: In general, the weakened executive-branch institutions would assist the president in proposing a multiyear budget that would not only compete with the multiyear budget proposal of Congress but also be subject to the economic assumptions and scoring of the strengthened, nonpartisan Congressional Budget Office. At the same time, the strengthened Fed—directed in statute to promote "full employment" and reasonable "price stability" but oriented in practice toward prioritizing the latter—would generally maintain the lead role in managing the economy through the use of monetary policy. The Fed would also often use its control over monetary policy to influence the direction of fiscal policy.

The Reagan-Era Policy Parameters: In structuring the policymaking process, the Reagan-era apparatus and its principals would play a key role in supporting the Reagan-era policy parameters. In particular, the established policy parameters now had the support of not only distinct political coalitions and a constitutional system biased toward the status quo but also an established public-finance apparatus and principals committed to maintaining stability following the end of the Great Inflation. On the fiscal front the established Reagan-era policies included a steady and structurally unbalanced budget that generally operated as a secondary economic-stabilization instrument; a supply-side (or less progressive) tax system; and a restricted general spending system and steady Social Security spending. On the monetary front the established Reagan-era approach included a "fine-tuned" monetary policy that generally operated as the primary economic-stabilization instrument in support of promoting "price stability."

Moving forward, this meant that each president's control in the domain of public finance was a contingency that would turn in large part on the alignment of his preferences and the policy parameters that the established Reagan-era apparatus and its principals structured.

11. Constraint: The Reagan-Era Apparatus Limits Clinton's Control

The quantitative overview provided evidence that in the domain of public finance, the decentralized Reagan-era apparatus and the Reagan-era policy parameters both remained in place throughout Bill Clinton's presidency and beyond, due largely to the absence of an exceptionally severe and highly prioritized problem, which strengthened the average restrictions on presidential control and weakened the average incentive to maximize control. This chapter traces the process of the established, relatively stable Reagan-era apparatus and its principals in supporting the established Reagan-era policy parameters and limiting Clinton's control.

THE REAGAN-ERA APPARATUS LIMITS CLINTON'S CONTROL IN THE SUBDOMAIN OF FISCAL POLICY

Bill Clinton assumed office in 1993 with unified party control of the government and a strong desire to change the course in the subdomain of fiscal policy that Ronald Reagan had initiated in response to the Great Inflation. The Democratic Party platform declared, "The last 12 years have been a nightmare of Republican irresponsibility and neglect" and "we call for a revolution in government.... The Revolution of 1992 is about restoring America's economic greatness" and making "a radical change in the way government operates."[1] Likewise, Clinton himself declared, "The most important distinction in this campaign is that I represent real hope for change.... It's time to change."[2] In particular, Clinton pledged that "middle-class taxpayers will have a ... significant reduction in their income tax rate" and that "our strategy [will put] people first by investing more than $50 billion each year over the next four years to put America back to work."[3]

Despite this strong desire to change the established course, the Reagan-era apparatus and its principals significantly limited Clinton's control. To begin with, as president-elect Clinton appointed Robert Reich—a liberal professor of government at Harvard University and a friend of more than two decades—to head the transition's public-finance policy team. This decision was hardly a surprise as Reich's writings had largely formed the basis of the campaign's blueprint

197

for the policy domain. It was surprising, however, that Clinton then selected a team of experienced, conservative public-finance principals to oversee the now highly complex policymaking process. In particular, Clinton appointed Lloyd Bentsen, a member of the Senate since 1971 and chair of the Finance Committee, to the position of Treasury secretary, and he appointed Leon Panetta, a member of the House since 1977 and chair of the Budget Committee, to the position of budget director. "I hired people like Leon Panetta for their technical expertise on the budget," Clinton explained.[4]

The president-elect also appointed Laura Tyson, a professor of economics at the University of California, Berkeley, to serve as chair of the Council of Economic Advisers, and he appointed Robert Rubin, the co-chair of Goldman Sachs, to serve as director of the new National Economic Council. Alan Greenspan remained chair of the Federal Reserve, the position that George Bush had appointed him to in 1992, and Robert Reischauer remained director of the Congressional Budget Office, which operated entirely independent of the president's appointment power. After heading the transition team, Robert Reich had considered the top post at both the CEA and the NEC but ultimately decided to serve as secretary of labor.[5]

As confirmed in part by both the principals and the mix of existing positions, there was substantial continuity in public-finance administration moving from the Reagan and Bush administrations to the Clinton administration. However, the incoming president made one notable adjustment. Based on Reich's recommendation—and relying on an executive order—Clinton established the National Economic Council. Located within the Executive Office of the President, the new institution was charged with "coordinat[ing] the economic policy-making process." As Rubin later put it, the director's job was "to serve as an honest broker, summarizing everyone's positions and always presenting all sides of an issue fairly."[6]

Although the NEC was a notable development, its creation largely confirmed and accelerated the CEA's substantial decline, which had begun during the Reagan administration. As Alan Blinder, a member of the CEA during the Clinton administration, explained, "We viewed [the NEC] as a mortal threat" that "would staff up with a bunch of economists who would then start doing the work of the CEA."[7]

With the public-finance team in place, the first official meeting occurred on January 7—two weeks before the inauguration—and the experienced principals took control from the start. Rubin, the inexperienced NEC director later explained, "We were supposed to be developing an economic plan—but I had no idea what a presidential economic plan was or how to assemble it. I consulted Leon Panetta, who said we had to present the President-elect with a budget, which sounded right. So Leon drew up budget options."[8] However, rather than focus on Clinton's campaign promises—the middle-class tax cut and investment spending—the experienced principals used this meeting to make the budget deficit the dominant issue.

In particular, the principals whom Clinton had appointed "for their technical expertise on the budget" proposed that the new president support a deficit reduction program in order to bring down long-term interest rates, a move that, if all went according to plan, would eventually more than offset the short-term economic contraction due to the initial spending cut and tax increase. Like the Tax Equity and Fiscal Responsibility Act of 1982 and the Omnibus Budget Reconciliation Act of 1990, the experienced principals proposed to use fiscal policy as a secondary economic-stabilization instrument. This was the same proposal that the experienced, highly influential Fed chair—who played a key role in initiating the 1990 deficit reduction program—had informally presented to Clinton a month earlier. As Greenspan later explained,

> Short-term interest rates were rock-bottom low. . . . But long-term interest rates were still stubbornly high. They were acting as a brake on economic activity by driving up the costs of home mortgages and bond issuance. They reflected an expectation of ongoing inflation for which investors had come to require an extra margin of interest to offset the added uncertainty and risk.
>
> Improve investors' expectations, I told Clinton, and long-term rates could fall, galvanizing the demand for new homes and the appliances, furnishings, and the gamut of consumer items associated with home ownership. Stock values, too, would rise, as bonds became less attractive and investors shifted into equities. Businesses would expand, creating jobs. All told the latter part of the 1990s could look awfully good. . . . The path to a beneficent future, I told the president-elect, was lowering the long-term trajectory of federal budget deficits.[9]

When the president-elect now heard the same proposal from the principals he had just appointed, he remarked in a state of near disbelief, "You mean to tell me that the success of the program and my reelection hinges on the Federal Reserve and a bunch of fucking bond traders?" Then when Vice President–elect Al Gore suggested that the boldness of this proposal was reminiscent of the New Deal, Clinton responded that it directly contradicted his campaign promises. "Roosevelt was trying to help people," the president-elect complained. "Here we help the bond market, and we hurt the people who voted us in."[10]

Despite Clinton's reluctance, his principals suggested that he had essentially no choice in the matter. Panetta explained that the Fed or Congress "will come up with some other way to basically take the presidency away," either through higher interest rates, a balanced budget amendment, or legislation similar to

Gramm-Rudman-Hollings, and "so you can't afford not to confront this issue."[11] Yet, for the president-elect's political advisers—most of whom had been part of the campaign—signing on to this policy was itself the equivalent of allowing some other entity "to basically take the presidency away." As Stan Greenberg, Clinton's pollster, remarked afterwards, "The presidency has been hijacked."[12]

With the budget plan still not settled, Bentsen and Rubin arranged for Greenspan to meet with Clinton at the White House in late January. Continuing to make his position clear, the experienced Fed chair informed the new president that under its current trajectory the deficit would increase greatly after 1996 and interest on the debt would skyrocket, which would create considerable instability and possibly "lead to a financial crisis." The discussion no doubt had its intended effect. "As we finished," Greenspan recalled, "Clinton, unsurprisingly, looked grim."[13]

Following the meeting with the Fed chair, Rubin submitted a memo to the president that laid out the options for the 1997 deficit reduction target. "Greenspan believes that a major deficit reduction [above $130 billion] will lead to interest changes more than offsetting the demand effect," the memo explained. "He therefore believes that the probabilities of the program hurting the economy are low."[14] Underscoring the significance of this recommendation, the Fed chair later revealed, "I advised Bentsen on how deeply I thought the deficit would have to be cut" and that figure "made its way to the president and had a powerful effect."[15]

Notwithstanding the consensus among the experienced principals for a $140 billion deficit reduction target based on Greenspan's recommendation, Clinton still remained reluctant to abandon or severely cut back on his campaign promises. "If I do too little investment" spending, he complained, "then some other candidate won the election, not me." He also worried about replacing the middle-class tax cut with a program that would raise taxes, remarking, "These are the people who got screwed in the 8os. And it's a heck of a thing for me to propose this."[16]

In addition to the president's own uneasiness about the deficit reduction program, Laura Tyson—the chair of the weakened CEA and the appointee whose institutional orientation most highly prioritized the promotion of "maximum employment"—was the only top principal to question the near obsession with hitting the $140 billion target. Unaware that the number came directly from the Fed chair, she explained to the president, "I can't prove to you that there is anything magical about . . . $140 billion. There is a point where the bond market will take your program seriously. I don't know where that point is. Maybe it's at $135 billion or $140 billion or wherever."[17] However, the budget director and NEC director effectively pushed back, and the Treasury secretary went even further to ensure that the deficit reduction program hit the $140 billion target, recommending that the president drop his $3 billion proposal to "end welfare as we know it," another major campaign promise.[18]

With no set of alternative programs from which to choose—and no doubt keeping in mind the Fed chair's earlier warning of a "financial crisis"—Clinton finally signed off on the Greenspan-initiated plan. Further confirming the Fed chair's influence at the time, Secretary of Labor Reich wrote in his diary,

> Greenspan haunts every budget meeting, though his name never comes up directly. Instead, it's always our "credibility" with Wall Street. It is repeatedly said that we must reduce the deficit because Wall Street needs to be reassured, calmed, convinced of our wise intentions. . . .
>
> Time will tell who's right. But in the short term . . . Greenspan can prove his own theory correct because only he has the power to raise or lower short-term interest rates. . . . Greenspan has the most important grip in town: [Clinton's] balls, in the palm of his hand.[19]

With the deficit reduction plan now in place, the president presented it in two stages. On February 15 he broke the news that his program would not incorporate many of his campaign promises. As the *New York Times* reported, "Mr. Clinton delivered a message that was a far cry from the tax relief and other programs he promised in last year's Presidential campaign."[20] The president then presented the program to Congress on February 17, and at the recommendation of his public-finance principals—a number of whom had substantial experience in the legislative branch—he pledged to "[use] the independent numbers of the Congressional Budget Office" in order to demonstrate the seriousness of his commitment to deficit reduction. "I [am doing] this," he explained, "so that no one [can] say I was estimating my way out of this difficulty."[21]

Similar to his predecessor's initial public embrace of the Fed chair, Clinton invited Greenspan to sit next to the first lady during the speech in order to give the impression that the Fed supported the program. Then, in testifying before Congress that same week, Greenspan announced that the program was both "serious" and "credible," which—as in 1990—resulted in the *New York Times* reporting in its headline the following day: "Clinton's Program Gets Endorsement of Fed's Chairman."[22]

After abandoning the campaign promise of a middle-class tax cut in order to reduce the deficit, the fiscal-policymaking process took a turn for the worse in March when the House passed a budget resolution that followed the president's proposal in general but provided less than $1 billion in investment spending for the first year, less than $6 billion for the second year, and only a relatively small increase for the later years, all of which was well below the "more than $50 billion each year for the next four years" in investment spending that the president had proposed during the campaign. It was also significantly below even the reduced amount that the president had proposed as part of the deficit reduction program in February. This was due in large part to a new report from the CBO—the institution whose numbers the president had just promised to use "so that no one [can] say I was estimating my way out of this difficulty." The CBO had estimated that Clinton's proposal exceeded the discretionary spending caps established under the Omnibus Budget Reconciliation Act of 1990, and the House had therefore cut the proposed investment spending to remain under the caps.[23]

When Clinton learned what happened, he flew into a rage, calling into question the loyalty of his own principals, especially the highly experienced ones. As Reich noted in his diary,

> [Clinton] explodes. "Why didn't anyone tell me about the spending caps? We spent week after week going over every little budget item, and no one said a word about caps!" His face turns beet-red, and he hollers. "Why didn't they tell me?" Presumably he's referring to Panetta and [deputy director of OMB] Rivlin, who were, until they joined the White House, chairman of the House Budget Committee and director of the Congressional Budget Office respectively. If anyone knew about subtleties of the budget law, they did. If anyone knew that the House was unlikely to raise the caps, they did. Maybe he's also referring to Bentsen, who, as chairman of the Senate Finance Committee, surely was as aware of the existence of the spending caps and the difficulty of raising them in the Senate. . . .
>
> [Clinton] stalks around the room, fuming. "We're doing everything Wall Street wants! Everything Wall Street doesn't want gets slashed!" He takes another few steps. "We're losing our soul!" He talks to no one in particular, but I can't help imagining he's yelling at Alan Greenspan. "I can't do what I came here to do."[24]

Following the meeting, and further revealing the importance of the investment spending, the president refused to drop the issue. In the middle of a subsequent discussion on health care, Clinton complained, "Where are all the Democrats? I hope you're all aware we're all Eisenhower Republicans. We're Eisenhower Republicans here, and we are fighting the Reagan Republicans. We stand for lower deficits and free trade and the bond market. Isn't that great." Clinton then added, "I don't have a goddamn Democratic budget until 1996. None of the investments, none of the things I campaigned on. . . . We've gutted our investment program by turning the government over to [CBO Director] Reischauer!"[25]

By May, the president had grown so frustrated with his principals, particularly Bentsen and Panetta, that he began to refer to them privately as "incre-mentalists" and "Wall Street" advisers who did not share his sweeping vision for "change." Hillary Clinton agreed, remarking, "These guys are going to derail you. You didn't get elected to do Wall Street economics."[26]

Finally, in August, despite both the call to set the country on a "new course" and the advantage of unified party control of the government, the president signed the Omnibus Budget Reconciliation Act of 1993, the most important fiscal-policy legislation of his eight years in office and remarkably similar to the Omnibus Budget Reconciliation Act of 1990. As the *New York Times* reported, "It is hard to escape the parallels between this budget measure and the one Mr. Bush signed three years ago. Like that agreement, the new measure would lower the deficit from what it would otherwise be by nearly $500 billion over five years." The *Times* then addressed what was missing from the legislation: "Clinton advocated in his election campaign for new roads and bridges, commu-nications and information networks and environmental technology [that] are nowhere to be found. If the nation is on a new course, it is hardly perceptible."[27]

Among its many features the law cut discretionary and mandatory spend-ing, and it extended the existing discretionary spending caps and PAYGO rules. It also increased the top individual income tax rate from 31 to 39.6 percent and the top corporate tax rate from 34 to 35 percent, both of which remained signif-icantly below the rates that Reagan had inherited in 1981.[28] Relatedly, the me-dium- to long-term revenue effect of the law (a revenue increase of 0.83 percent of GDP in year four) was five times smaller in absolute value terms than that of the Economic Recovery Tax Act of 1981 (a revenue reduction of 4.15 percent of GDP in year four), meaning that Reagan had been far more successful than Clinton in setting the country on a new course in the subdomain of fiscal pol-icy.[29] Acknowledging his own disappointment with the law, Clinton remarked to several advisers, "I know this thing is a turkey."[30]

* * *

Following the passage of the deficit reduction program, Clinton presented his plan for health care reform in September 1993. "After decades of false starts," he announced, "we must make this our most urgent priority, giving every Amer-ican health security, health care that can never be taken away, health care that is always there."[31]

Although health care was a top priority during the first year, a Reagan-era constraint had already blocked the president's preferred course. Rather than incorporate health care reform into the deficit reduction program and then use the reconciliation process to bypass the filibuster in the Senate—which Clinton had wanted to do—the health care proposal had to be presented separately after the budget because it was deemed an "extraneous matter" under the Byrd rule. Making clear the significance of this constraint, Clinton later conceded that "I probably made a mistake in not . . . going for a multiyear strategy" at that point rather than attempt to push health care reform through before the midterm election.[32]

In addition to the Reagan-era constraint's effect on the timing of the health care proposal and the way in which it would proceed through Congress, the Reagan-era apparatus and its principals significantly affected the effectiveness of the president's framing of the proposal. A highly influential CBO report in 1994 presented two key findings, both of which were especially damaging.

First, the president had pledged that his health care proposal would reduce the deficit; he had then gone to great lengths to ensure that the CBO would support that claim. CBO Director Reischauer explained, "[W]e met with [Clinton administration officials] a number of times . . . and they were very forthcoming in sharing their methodology and their data with us. They were desperate to get us to come up with a number like theirs."[33] However, the CBO concluded that the legislation would make the deficit "increase by more than $70 billion."[34]

Second, the health care proposal was designed to create a system of regional and corporate alliances that would oversee individual health care plans and manage some of the funding. The Clinton administration had determined that those transactions should be excluded from the federal budget. However, here too, the CBO disagreed in concluding that the health alliances "would operate primarily as agents of the federal government" and therefore "should be included in the federal government's accounts."[35]

Despite the fact that much of the CBO report supported the Clinton administration's proposal—particularly in agreeing that it would eventually slow the growth of health care spending—the contrary findings on the deficit and the transactions of the alliances provided substantial ammunition for its critics to defeat the proposal, which ultimately occurred. While testifying to Congress, CBO Director Reischauer remarked, "I have considerable foreboding that the information contained in my statement and the CBO report might be used in destructive rather than constructive ways—that is, it might be used to undercut a serious discussion of health reform alternatives or to gain some short-term partisan political advantage."[36] Likewise, Newt Gingrich, soon to be the speaker of the House, accurately predicted after the release of the report, "With this analysis, the Clinton plan is . . . dead."[37]

* * *

Following the Fed-directed deficit reduction program and the CBO-derailed health care proposal, the Reagan-era apparatus and its principals continued to limit the president's control. In December 1994—roughly a month after the midterm election that put Republicans in control of both the House and the Senate for the first time since the Eisenhower administration—Clinton proposed a tax cut in an effort to return to his original campaign promise and distance himself from the earlier deficit reduction program. As the *New York Times* reported, "For the first two years of his Presidency, Bill Clinton insisted that reducing the Federal budget deficit was his highest calling. Tonight, he reversed course."[38]

Although the president aimed to change course following the disastrous midterm election, the Republican-controlled Congress used its expanded powers from the Congressional Budget Act to control the agenda. In particular, the House and Senate both passed resolutions in May that projected a balanced budget in seven years. Making clear the significance of this move, Speaker of the House Newt Gingrich declared, "The budget is the transformational document for this system. When you've changed the budget, you've really changed government, and until you change the budget, you've just talked about changing government."[39]

While Congress moved toward balancing the budget, the president acknowledged the insignificance of his own earlier move, complaining to his advisers, "I can't just sit here passively and not play a role in this debate. I have to get into the argument. But until I have a plan, I can't join the debate."[40] Even more revealing, in response to a comment that "Republicans have dominated [the] political debate in this country since they took over Congress in January," Clinton felt the need to declare, "The president is relevant."[41] Then, in an effort to become relevant, he reversed course once again, putting forward a proposal in June to balance the budget in ten years based on the OMB's scoring. Further underscoring the president's diminished role and the inconsistency of his proposals, the *New York Times* reported, "For the first time tonight, as he sought to regain ground lost to the Republicans in Congress, Mr. Clinton unequivocally embraced the goal of balancing the budget by a fixed date," an approach he had "explicitly abandoned just four months ago when he presented a budget that produced rising deficits into the future."[42]

After setting the terms of the debate during the first half of 1995, the Republican-controlled Congress further limited the president's control by using its expanded budgeting powers to push for both its preferred timeline in balancing the budget and its preferred scoring. In early 1996, following two government shutdowns that the Republican-controlled Congress initiated to create pressure to reduce spending, the president acquiesced in putting forward a proposal that would balance the budget in 2002 based on the CBO's scoring.[43]

Finally, in 1997 Clinton signed the Balanced Budget Act and the Taxpayer

Relief Act, which built upon the earlier negotiations with Congress and were designed to reduce the deficit by $200 billion and balance the budget by 2002.[44] Acknowledging the success of the Republican-controlled Congress in securing its preferred terms, the New York Times reported that "over the next five years" the deal "would balance the Federal budget" and "is analyzed according to Congressional Budget Office methods, a point that Republicans had insisted on and the Administration only reluctantly accepted, preferring the more liberal assumptions of the White House Office of Management and Budget."[45]

Following the two-year battle to project a balanced budget in 2002, the budget actually generated a surplus in 1998 due in large part to an increase in economic growth—or in Greenspan's terms, because the Clinton administration had taken the Fed-directed "path to a beneficent future" that included lower interest rates and removed a substantial "brake on economic activity." The budget then continued to generate a surplus through the rest of the Clinton administration and the president embraced this as his major legacy, explaining in his farewell address that "America must maintain our record of fiscal responsibility. Through our last four budgets we've turned record deficits to record surpluses, and we've been able to pay down $600 billion of our national debt—on track to be debt-free by the end of the decade for the first time since 1835."[46]

Although Clinton oversaw a substantial development in the subdomain of fiscal policy, it was one that the decentralized Reagan-era apparatus and its principals had largely imposed upon him. Specifically, the Fed chair had used his control over monetary policy to take the lead in developing the major deficit reduction program of the Clinton administration; then the Republican-controlled Congress had used its expanded budget-making powers and the CBO to maintain the path to a balanced budget by taking the lead in developing the second-largest deficit reduction program of the Clinton administration. Once Clinton left office, the Reagan-era apparatus and its principals also played a key role in reversing the "record of fiscal responsibility" that it had largely imposed upon the former president.

This process began in 2001 when the Reagan-era apparatus—especially the Fed and the CBO—provided George W. Bush considerable support in passing a tax cut.[47] First, the Fed and its Reagan-appointed chair publicly recommended a tax cut to address the new budget *surplus* problem, the opposite course from what Greenspan had directed in 1990 and 1993. By the end of the Clinton administration, the Fed had become increasingly concerned that rising budget surpluses would soon eliminate the national debt, a potentially severe problem because monetary policy is primarily conducted through the sale and purchase of the debt. As Greenspan explained,

Our primary lever of monetary policy was buying and selling treasury securities. . . . But as the debt was paid down, those securities would grow scarce. . . . For nearly a year, senior Fed economists . . . had been exploring the issue of what other assets we might buy and sell.

A result was a dense 380-page study. . . . [T]he bad news was that nothing could really match the treasuries market in size, liquidity, and freedom from risk. To conduct monetary policy, the report concluded, the Fed would have to learn to manage a complex portfolio of . . . other debt instruments. It was a daunting prospect.[48]

To avoid this problem, the influential Fed chair testified to Congress in January 2001 that a tax cut was not simply desirable but "required," a recommendation that, as Greenspan himself acknowledged, "proved to be politically explosive" and resulted in the *New York Times* headline: "In Policy Change, Greenspan Backs a Broad Tax Cut."[49]

Second, the CBO provided support for the Bush tax cut by revising its budget projection. In January 2001 the influential institution projected that budget surpluses will "rise in the future . . . accumulating to $5.6 trillion over the 2002–2011 period. That total is about $1 trillion higher than the cumulative surplus projected . . . in CBO's July 2000 report."[50] Underscoring the significance of this update, the *New York Times* reported, "The nation's most influential economic forecaster . . . [issued] a much more promising projection of the economy over the next decade than it had offered in the past. . . . Republicans saw it as the final piece of evidence that large tax cuts are in order."[51]

With the Fed and the CBO providing support for a "required" tax cut due to a "$1 trillion higher" budget surplus projection, Bush signed the Economic Growth and Tax Relief Reconciliation Act in May 2001. In its final form the surplus reduction program totaled $1.35 trillion over ten years, making it the largest tax cut since the first year of the Reagan administration. For comparison, the 2001 Bush program decreased tax revenues by 0.89 percent of GDP in year four, whereas the 1993 Clinton program increased tax revenues by 0.83 percent.[52] However, in order to use the reconciliation process to bypass a filibuster in the Senate and not violate the Byrd rule, the Bush tax cut could not extend beyond the ten-year budget window, meaning much of the program was temporary.

After 2001 Bush continued to push for tax cuts notwithstanding the shift from a budget surplus to a deficit, and the Fed chair now opposed these proposals due to the changed budget situation. Unlike earlier, however, he did not have the ability to use monetary policy to direct fiscal policy. In response to the threat of deflation, the Fed had lowered its primary short-term interest rate target from 6.5 percent at the end of 2000 to 1 percent in 2003, and it maintained that low rate through most of 2004. This new problem was in part a consequence of the Fed's prioritization of low inflation for more than two decades, which in turn temporarily disabled the central bank's ability to use—or even credibly threaten to use—a restrictive monetary policy to direct fiscal policy. Accordingly, the Bush administration passed tax cuts in 2002, 2003, and 2004, while the Fed primarily focused on the threat of deflation. Addressing the Fed's new focus at the time, Greenspan later explained,

> As officials whose entire careers had been devoted to fighting inflation, we found the experience of making such [interest rate] cuts decidedly strange. Yet, the economy was clearly in the grip of disinflation. . . . By 2003 . . . the economic funk and disinflation had gone on so long that the Fed had to consider a more exotic peril: a declining price level, deflation. This was the possibility that the U.S. economy might be entering a crippling spiral. . . . Deflation became the focus of increasing concern within the Fed."[53]

Greenspan added, "For the five years we overlapped, President Bush honored his commitment to the autonomy of the Fed. Of course, during most of that time we kept short-term interest rates extremely low," and "the president remained tolerant of, if not receptive to, my criticism of his fiscal policy."[54]

Altogether, the multiple tax cuts under Bush—along with the increase in spending due to two wars—fully reversed Clinton's "record of fiscal responsibility." Making clear his displeasure at the quick return of a structurally unbalanced budget, Clinton later lamented, "As the government abandoned balanced budgets in 2001 . . . the national debt, which had decreased from 49 percent to 33 percent of national income in the 1990s, soared back. . . . This is not the way I wanted the United States to start the twenty-first century."[55]

* * *

The case study analysis here shows that the established Reagan-era apparatus and its principals significantly limited Clinton's control in the subdomain of fiscal policy. First, in pushing forward a deficit reduction program in 1993 that the president complained would "hurt the people who voted us in" and meant that "I can't do what I came here to do," the Reagan-era apparatus and its principals limited Clinton's control during the critical period of unified party control of the government. Second, in separating and delaying the health care proposal in 1993, and then in publishing a prominent report in 1994 that "undercut a serious discussion of health reform" and ensured that "the Clinton plan [was] . . . dead," the Reagan-era apparatus and its principals further limited Clinton's control during the critical period of unified party control of the government. Third, in using the congressional budget-making apparatus to push forward a second deficit reduction program that was based on the preferred timeline and scoring of the Republican-controlled Congress and that the president changed course to support in order to become "relevant," the Reagan-era apparatus and its principals limited Clinton's control further still. Fourth, in supporting a "required" tax cut following a "$1 trillion higher" budget surplus projection, and then in failing to prevent additional tax cuts due to the new threat of deflation that temporarily disabled the Fed's ability to direct fiscal policy, all of which helped to reverse the "record of fiscal responsibility" that had largely been imposed upon the former president in the first place and was "not the way [he] wanted . . . to start the twenty-first century," the Reagan-era apparatus and its principals limited even the long-term impact of Clinton's limited control.

THE REAGAN-ERA APPARATUS LIMITS CLINTON'S CONTROL IN THE SUBDOMAIN OF MONETARY POLICY

Similar to the subdomain of fiscal policy, Bill Clinton assumed office in 1993 with unified party control of the government and a strong desire to change the course in the subdomain of monetary policy that Ronald Reagan had initiated in response to the Great Inflation. During the campaign Clinton declared, "We know economic growth will be the best jobs program we'll ever have." He then added, "The Republicans in Washington have compiled the worst economic record in fifty years: the slowest economic growth" and "slowest job growth . . . since the Great Depression." In sharp contrast, Clinton pledged to implement "the most dramatic economic growth program since the Second World War." Even more revealing, Clinton declared, "We cannot . . . create jobs and economic growth without a revolution in government," which requires "tak[ing] away power from the entrenched bureaucracies . . . that dominate Washington."[56]

Despite Clinton's strong desire to change the established course, the Reagan-era apparatus and its principals failed to provide the new president with an actual plan to implement "the most dramatic economic growth program since the Second World War." In his first annual address Clinton continued to make clear his own position, declaring, "Our immediate priority must be to create jobs, create jobs now."[57] In contrast, the experienced public-finance principals prioritized low inflation. Highlighting this divide and the lack of any substantial plan for changing course, Secretary of Labor Robert Reich noted in his diary,

[Treasury Secretary] Lloyd Bentsen argues that the administration should publicly state that the economy is approaching its "natural" rate of unemployment—the lowest rate achievable without igniting inflation. This, he reasons, will reassure Wall Street that we won't object if the Fed tightens the reins. . . . I'm flabbergasted. "How can we be near the natural rate of unemployment when eight and a half million people can't find jobs?" . . .

Out of concern that Lloyd's proposal will carry, I inject a political note. "Has anybody forgotten? . . . We're Democrats. Even if we are approaching the danger zone where low unemployment might trigger inflation, we should err on the side of more jobs, not higher bond prices. . . . So here's my proposal. The President should warn the Fed against any further increases in interest rates."

My idea is rejected out of hand.[58]

Worse still—and the reason that Reich's idea is immediately "rejected out of hand"—the public-finance principals had informed Clinton before he even assumed office that he would have to maintain the Reagan-initiated hands-off approach. As Alan Blinder, a top adviser, explained,

I . . . told [Clinton] back in Little Rock—he didn't like this—that in terms of economic policy he had just been elected to the second most powerful position in America. This was news to the Governor of Arkansas. He didn't like it because it was a hard job to get elected, and to think he was now second fiddle to Alan Greenspan didn't sit well. But . . . he listened to . . . myself and others who said, "Just hands off the Fed." . . . We were very disciplined that way, and so was Clinton . . . but he was really mad."[59]

In addition to the lack of support from the experienced public-finance principals, the inexperienced president himself had no plan to restructure the established Reagan-era apparatus and policy parameters in order to implement "the most dramatic economic growth program since the Second World War." As Clinton conceded, "The job is much tougher than I realized."[60]

With no plan in place for "a revolution in government" that would "take away power from the entrenched bureaucracies," Clinton quickly struggled to chart a different course. This was evident in the limited effectiveness of his first two Fed appointees in 1994—Alan Blinder, a member of the Council of Economic Advisers, and Janet Yellen, a professor of economics at the University of California, Berkeley. As the first Democratic appointees in fourteen years, it was widely believed that they would influence the Fed's management of monetary policy. The *New York Times* reported that Blinder and Yellen will "allow the President to start putting his stamp on an institution now run entirely by Republican appointees" because they are likely to place more emphasis "on increasing short-term economic growth rather than fighting inflation."[61]

Supporting the belief that the new Fed appointees would help to shift the central bank's priorities, Blinder had argued in his academic work on the Fed's dual mandate that "America has struck [the balance between inflation and unemployment] in the wrong place by exaggerating the perils of inflation and underestimating the virtues of low unemployment." In particular, Blinder rejected the idea that inflation was exceptionally costly to reverse once it took hold. "The myth that the inflationary demon, unless exorcised, will inevitably grow is exactly that—a myth," Blinder explained. "There is neither theoretical nor statistical support for the popular notion that inflation has a built-in tendency to accelerate."[62]

On learning of Blinder's nomination, Greenspan asked the outgoing vice chair, David Mullins, to review the writings of his successor. Mullins reported back, "Don't worry, it's not like [Blinder's] a Communist or anything. It's just in his early publications he's noticeably soft on inflation." For Greenspan, an avowed inflation hawk, this was more troubling. "I would have preferred he were a Communist," the Fed chair replied.[63]

In response to this potential threat to the Fed's established approach to managing monetary policy, Greenspan relied upon the agenda-setting powers of his position and the influence that he had acquired since the end of the Reagan administration to undercut the new Clinton appointees. This began when the experienced Fed chair proposed raising the federal funds rate by 0.75 percentage points in November 1994 as part of the continued tightening of monetary policy that he had initiated in February. It would be the largest rate change under the Greenspan-led Fed and would take effect while annual inflation was less than 3 percent and unemployment nearly 6 percent. Not surprisingly, Blinder opposed the move. Rather surprisingly, however, the new appointee declined to vote against it due to his respect for the Fed chair and the inclination of the governors to protect the central bank's hard-won independence. As Blinder explained to the other members of the Federal Open Market Committee before his vote,

> One thing we know about the hazards of fine-tuning is that we really can't do fine-tuning. That means that when we are close to target we should be very wary of oversteering. I think that with 3 percent inflation and the economy right about at capacity we are in an awfully good position, and so we should be extremely wary about oversteering. . . .
>
> I thought hard about whether I should dissent on this matter, and I did not decide until last night. I finally decided that I won't. . . . I think it is better to show a united Federal Reserve against the criticism that we are surely going to get for this move.[64]

Following this initial victory, Greenspan continued to dominate monetary policymaking during the Clinton administration. Most notably, after overseeing an increase in the federal funds rate from 3 percent to 6 percent during 1994 and early 1995 in order to slow the economy and ease inflationary pressure, Greenspan cut the rate by 0.25 percent in July 1995 to prevent a recession—or, in the Fed's terms, produce a "soft landing." Unlike the failed effort during the Bush administration, the Fed succeeded this time, leading Blinder to acknowledge that "Alan Greenspan has demonstrated that what we once called fine-tuning is indeed possible."[65]

The successful soft landing of 1995—which Greenspan labeled "one of the Fed's proudest accomplishments during my tenure"—undercut any remaining opposition to the chair's leadership.[66] Blinder resigned in 1996 and Yellen resigned in 1997, ending Clinton's most concerted effort to influence the Fed's management of monetary policy. Further confirming the limited influence of the president's initial appointees, Blinder himself later conceded, "Greenspan ran the show. If I had any influence, it was very peripheral." Blinder then added, "It's a bit like the Army, you salute the general. . . . This particular general has been on the job a long time" and "he's done a hell of a good job. . . . So how much argument is he going to get from the troops? He didn't get very much."[67] Moreover, Clinton remained frustrated with the Fed's management of monetary policy at the time and the limited influence of his appointees, but he maintained the Reagan-initiated "hands off the Fed" approach. As Greenspan later confirmed, "I did eventually hear that the president had been sore at me and the Fed for much of 1994, while we were hiking interest rates. . . . But he never challenged the Fed in public."[68]

After the much-hyped, but short-lived showdown with Blinder, Greenspan went even further in consolidating his control over the Fed. This was evident in 1996 when he played a key role in blocking the appointment of Felix Rohatyn. Greenspan's preemptive move was now possible not just because Republicans had gained control of the Senate following the midterm election but also because the key players in both the executive branch and the legislative branch increasingly consulted the Fed chair on appointments. As the *New York Times* reported, "Mr. Rohatyn's first problems were within the Administration itself: Several of Mr. Clinton's top economic advisers, including Secretary of the Treasury Robert E. Rubin, were reported to have reservations." The *Times* then revealed the underlying source of those "reservations," adding, "Mr. Greenspan's relationship with Mr. Rubin is said to be particularly good."[69]

Although the Fed chair worked behind the scenes to block the appointment, the president shared publicly his own considerable frustration with the outcome. "Wouldn't it be nice to have a debate" to see how fast the economy can grow without generating inflation, Clinton complained. "That's what I wanted to see done. And that's why I wanted to put Felix Rohatyn on the Federal Reserve. But the politics of Washington said, no, we insist on the conventional wisdom" and "we don't even think it's worth debating."[70]

Further underscoring the president's failure to implement a "revolution in government" that would "take away power from the entrenched bureaucracies," Clinton nominated the Reagan-appointed Fed chair to a third term in 1996. "Politics being what they are," Greenspan later explained, "I never thought Clinton would reappoint me. . . . He was a Democrat and no doubt he would want one of his own." But after the Fed's soft landing of the economy in 1995, Greenspan added, "my prospects had changed."[71] Supporting the Fed chair's account, the *New York Times* reported, "President Clinton today renominated Alan Greenspan . . . and filled two other vacancies with appointees considered unlikely to strongly dispute the chairman's slow growth strategy to control inflation," all of which indicates that the president has "backed away from using his appointees to press for a robust public debate on the pace of economic growth."[72]

* * *

In addition to limiting the effectiveness of the appointment power during Clinton's first term, the Reagan-appointed Fed chair oversaw the creation of an inflation target to guide the Fed's operations and thereby limit the effectiveness of the appointment power during Clinton's second term and beyond. Initially, Janet Yellen, Clinton's second appointee had successfully opposed this move. As Yellen explained at a meeting of the Federal Open Market Committee in 1995, "With the benefit of hindsight it seems to me that maybe the Fed should have accepted more unemployment and less inflation" during the 1970s. "But the extreme proposal—that we need . . . a pure inflation target—is to me draconian."[73] By the middle of 1996, however, inflation and unemployment were both relatively low for the third year running, a situation that lowered the perceived cost of establishing an inflation target. Further lowering that cost, a number of foreign central banks had already established inflation targets, and—fourteen years after the end of the monetarist experiment and nearly a decade into Greenspan's tenure—there was a growing desire within the Fed to establish a clearer long-term policy framework.[74]

In response to these developments, the Greenspan-led Fed established a 2 percent inflation target in 1996, meaning that the central bank would work toward keeping inflation at or below that level moving forward. Revealing the aim and significance of this move, Laurence Meyer, a new Clinton appointee, explained that the inflation target would "institutionalize" the Fed's "commitment to price stability, ensuring the continuation of a disciplined monetary policy after Greenspan."[75] Moreover, because the Federal Reserve Act of 1977 and the Full Employment and Balanced Growth Act of 1978 had established a dual mandate, the new inflation target required monetary policymakers to ignore a key part of existing law. As Greenspan explained, "[The Full Employment and Balanced Growth Act] says that we should have 3 percent adult unemployment. That is the law of the land." But, he added, "the fact that it is promulgated in a statute does not mean that it is achievable or that it is something that we assume is achievable." In order to prevent unwanted attention and opposition—and further underscoring the significance of this move, which stood in direct opposition to Clinton's prioritization of economic growth and job creation—Greenspan pressed the other members of the FOMC to keep the inflation target private. "If the 2 percent inflation figure gets out of this room," he warned, "it is going to create more problems for us than I think any of you might anticipate."[76]

* * *

In his final full year in office, Clinton nominated Greenspan to a fourth term, no doubt due to the state of the economy at the time. The Reagan-appointed Fed chair had overseen a decline in the unemployment rate from more than 7 percent in 1993 to 4 percent in 2000; he had also overseen economic growth of more than 4 percent a year throughout Clinton's second term. It was not "the most dramatic economic growth program since the Second World War," but the gains were impressive. As Greenspan put it, "In the late nineties, the economy was so strong that I used to get up in the morning, look in the mirror, and say to myself, 'Remember, this is temporary. This is not the way the world is supposed to work.'"[77] Most importantly, in reappointing Greenspan, Clinton had failed to "take away power from the entrenched bureaucrac[y]" in monetary policymaking. The result was that, once Clinton left office, the Reagan-era apparatus and its principals played a key role in overseeing the end of the "temporary" economic growth of the 1990s and the return of "the way the world is supposed to work."

The process of reversing the economic gains of the Clinton administration began with the Fed's management of the Recession of 2001 and its aftermath. As economic growth fell from an average of 3.9 percent a year during the Clinton administration to 2.2 percent a year during the George W. Bush administration, the Fed—which Clinton described as the most "important institution in our country" when it comes to managing economic growth—continued to prioritize "price stability" for two key reasons.[78] First, as Ben Bernanke, a Fed governor at the time, explained, "The Great Inflation of the 1970s had left a powerful impression on the minds of monetary policymakers."[79] Second, like Clinton, Bush maintained the Reagan-initiated "hands off the Fed" approach and nominated Greenspan to another term, thereby ensuring that the influential Reagan-appointed Fed chair remained in office until his full fourteen-year term on the Board ended in 2006.[80]

The process of reversing the economic gains of the Clinton administration continued with the Fed's management of the Great Recession of 2007–2009 and its aftermath. As economic growth fell to an average of 1.6 percent a year during the Obama administration, the Fed continued to prioritize "price stability" for the same two reasons. First, the Great Inflation-oriented monetary policymakers maintained control of the Fed and proceeded to make the 2 percent inflation target public in 2012. Revealing the aim of this move, Bernanke—who had replaced Greenspan as chair in 2006—explained that setting a public inflation target would "create an institutional commitment to continuing the Volcker and Greenspan policies."[81] Second, like Clinton and Bush, Obama maintained the Reagan-initiated "hands off the Fed" approach. Regarding his first meeting with the new president Bernanke remarked, "I was pleased that [Obama] made a point of emphasizing his support for the Federal Reserve's independence."[82]

Further underscoring the independent Fed's prioritization of "price stability" in managing the economy, personal consumption expenditure (PCE) inflation—the Fed's preferred measure for the public inflation target—fell from an average of 1.9 percent a year during the Clinton administration to 1.2 percent a year during the Obama administration, well below even the conservative 2 percent target. Addressing the growing belief that the prioritization of low inflation was restricting economic growth, the New York Times reported in late 2014,

> As the idea of a 2 percent [inflation] target has become the orthodoxy, a worrying possibility is becoming clear: What if it's wrong? What if it is one of the reasons that the global economy has been locked in five years of slow growth? Some economists are beginning to consider the possibility that 2 percent inflation at all times leaves central banks with too little flexibility to adequately fight a deep economic malaise.[83]

Overall, the Reagan-era apparatus and its principals oversaw economic growth that averaged 3.1 percent a year during the twelve years of the Reagan and Bush administrations; it increased to 3.9 percent a year during the Clinton administration; and it decreased to 1.9 percent a year during the sixteen years of the Bush and Obama administrations, meaning that the Greenspan-led Fed that Clinton left in place and the Bernanke-led Fed that operated under "an institutional commitment to continuing the Volcker and Greenspan policies" both oversaw significantly slower economic growth after the Clinton administration than the twelve years of Republican rule preceding it, a period that Clinton had criticized for generating the "worst economic record . . . since the Great Depression." Making clear his displeasure at the Reagan-era's "fine-tuned" monetary policy, which managed the economy primarily in support of "price stability," Clinton lamented after leaving office, "The debate changed in 1980" and the Reagan-era "policy failures have given us an anemic, increasingly unequal economy, with too few jobs."[84]

* * *

The case study analysis here shows that the established, relatively stable Reagan-era apparatus and its principals significantly limited Clinton's control in the subdomain of monetary policy. First, in failing to provide the president with an actual plan to "take away power from the entrenched bureaucracies" in order to implement "the most dramatic economic growth program since the Second World War," and in advising the president from the start to maintain the Reagan-initiated "hands off the Fed" approach, the Reagan-era apparatus and its principals limited Clinton's control, especially during the critical period of unified party control of the government. Second, in undercutting the effectiveness of the president's new appointees, which made him really "sore at [Greenspan] and the Fed," and then in undercutting the president's ability to appoint his most preferred candidate in the first place, demonstrating that the prioritization of "price stability" was not even "worth debating," the Reagan-era apparatus and its principals further limited Clinton's control. Third, in establishing a 2 percent inflation target that ignored what is "promulgated in [the] statute" directing the Fed's operations and that went against the president's prioritization of economic growth, the Reagan-era apparatus and its principals limited Clinton's control further still. Fourth, in continuing to prioritize "price stability" in managing the Recession of 2001 and the Great Recession of 2007–2009 due to both the "powerful impression" that the Great Inflation had left "on the minds of monetary policymakers" and the continuation by each president of the Reagan-initiated "hands off the Fed" approach, and then in announcing a public 2 percent inflation target that "create[d] an institutional commitment to continuing the Volcker and Greenspan policies," all of which contributed to "an anemic, increasingly unequal economy," the Reagan-era apparatus and its principals limited even the long-term impact of Clinton's limited control in the policy domain.

Altogether, the case study analysis of fiscal policymaking and monetary policymaking in this chapter shows that the Reagan-era apparatus and its principals reinforced the Reagan-era policy parameters during the Clinton administration and beyond in the process of significantly limiting the president's control. Further underscoring his limited impact in the domain of public finance, Clinton himself conceded in his memoirs, "I had underestimated how hard it would be to turn Washington around after twelve years on a very different course."[85]

Part V
Historical Variation in Presidential Control during the Great Recession and Beyond

As the third and final case study component of the multimethod analysis, this part of the book traces the variation in presidential control for two recent incumbents, Barack Obama and Donald Trump. The primary objective is to show that—unlike Roosevelt in response to the Great Depression and unlike Reagan in response to the Great Inflation—Obama failed increase his control in the domain of public finance in response to the Great Recession. The other major objective is to provide a preliminary examination of presidential control during the first two years of the Trump presidency.

12. The Reagan-Era Apparatus Limits Obama's Control in Managing the Great Recession

The quantitative overview provided evidence that in the domain of public finance, the decentralized Reagan-era apparatus and the Reagan-era policy parameters both largely remained in place throughout Barack Obama's presidency due to the diminished severity and diminished prioritization of the Great Recession relative to the Great Depression and the Great Inflation. In part this process mirrors both the New Deal–era apparatus and its principals in limiting Dwight Eisenhower's control and the Reagan-era apparatus and its principals in limiting Bill Clinton's control. Unlike Eisenhower and Clinton, however, Obama assumed office at a time when the policy domain had the potential to collapse. This case study analysis therefore shows that in order to avoid a repeat of the Great Depression—and importantly, having learned from that earlier episode—the Reagan-era apparatus and its principals initially limited Obama's control in promoting inadequate New Deal–era approaches to manage the policy domain. Moreover, once the emergency phase of the Great Recession passed, the Reagan-era apparatus and its principals limited Obama's control in promoting traditional Reagan-era approaches to manage the policy domain.

THE REAGAN-ERA APPARATUS LIMITS OBAMA'S CONTROL IN MANAGING A MIX OF APPROACHES IN THE SUBDOMAIN OF FISCAL POLICY

Barack Obama assumed office in 2009 with unified party control of the government and a strong desire to change the established course.[1] The 2008 Democratic Party platform declared, "We come together not only to replace [President Bush] and his party—and not only to offer policies that will undo the damage they have wrought. Today, we pledge" to start "renewing the American Dream for a new era—with the same new hope and new ideas that propelled Franklin Delano Roosevelt towards the New Deal."[2] Similarly, Obama himself declared during the campaign, "For eighteen long months, you have stood up, one by one, and said enough to the politics of the past. . . . You have shown what history teaches us—that at defining moments like this one, the change we need doesn't come from Washington. Change comes to Washington."[3]

Along with these calls to launch a "new era" and deliver "change" in general, there were calls to make substantial changes in the domain of public finance in particular. During the campaign Obama criticized the Bush administration for "eight years of failed economic policies, eight years of trickle-down, Wall Street–first, Main Street–last policies that have driven our economy into a ditch."[4] Once in office, Obama declared, "The state of the economy calls for action, bold and swift, and we will act not only to create new jobs but to lay a new foundation for growth."[5]

Despite these calls to change the established course, the Reagan-era apparatus and its principals significantly limited Obama's control. This process began when, as president-elect, Obama mostly selected a team of highly experienced public-finance principals to staff the new administration. He appointed Timothy Geithner, who had served in the Treasury Department during the Clinton administration and then as president of the Federal Reserve Bank in New York, to the position of Treasury secretary; he appointed Peter Orszag, who had served as an economic adviser to the president during the Clinton administration and as director of the Congressional Budget Office during the last two years of the Bush administration, to the position of budget director; he appointed Larry Summers, who had served as Treasury secretary during the Clinton administration, to the position of director of the National Economic Council; and he appointed Christina Romer, who had no previous experience in government, to the position of chair of the Council of Economic Advisers. Revealing the reason for most of these appointments, Obama explained, "When it came to assembling my economic team, I decided to favor experience. . . . I needed people who had managed crises before, people who could calm markets in the grip of panic."[6]

In addition to the incoming president's own appointments, Ben Bernanke remained the chair of the Federal Reserve, the position to which George W. Bush had appointed him in 2006, and congressional leaders selected Douglas Elmendorf, who had served over the past two decades in various posts in the Congressional Budget Office, the Fed, the Treasury, and the CEA, to the position of director of the CBO.

With this highly experienced public-finance team in place, the incoming Obama administration moved quickly to address the economic downturn. Importantly, however, the downturn was not nearly as severe as the Great Depression. For comparison, in 2008, the year Obama was elected, the unemployment rate reached 7.3 percent, and the economy declined by 0.1 percent; in 1932, the year Roosevelt was elected, unemployment reached 24 percent, and the economy declined by 12.9 percent. It was also not until a month after the 2008 election that the economy was even officially determined to be in a recession. As the *New York Times* reported on December 11, "The economy is formally in a recession, as the National Bureau of Economic Research and President Bush said last week. But the current crisis lacks a capital-letter name. . . . In the last week, 'Great Recession' has become a popular phrase."[7]

The following week—specifically, on December 15—the NEC director submitted to the president-elect a fifty-seven-page memo that "outline[d] four alternative [economic recovery plans] ranging in cost from $550 billion to $890 billion," all of which were estimated to keep the unemployment rate between 7 and 8 percent.[8] Initially, the memo included a $1.8 trillion plan from the CEA chair designed to eliminate the output gap entirely by "returning the economy to full employment."[9] But Summers had removed that option after deciding that it was impractical. As a compromise, Romer had developed a second plan totaling $1.2 trillion. Summers had removed that as well, explaining to the CEA chair that "$1.2 trillion is nonplanetary"—meaning that it would be dead on arrival in Congress. The final draft of the memo therefore included only the more limited plans ranging from $550 billion to $890 billion, leading the CEA chair to complain, "All of these stimulus options are set up to achieve eight percent unemployment. Since when is eight percent unemployment acceptable?"[10]

Worse still, after narrowing the alternatives from $550 billion to $890 billion primarily for political reasons, the NEC director made no mention of Congress in the memo, noting only that the selection of the final size of the program "was an economic judgment that would need to be combined with political judgments about what is feasible."[11] Summers also proceeded to dismiss larger alternatives on economic grounds—or more specifically on the belief of the more experienced public-finance principals that the bond market strategy employed during the Clinton administration applied to the present situation, at least in part. As Summers explained, "Notice that [none] of these packages returns the unemployment rate to its normal, pre-recession level. To accomplish a more significant reduction in the output gap would require stimulus of well over $1 trillion," but that "would likely not accomplish the goal because of the impact it would have on markets." Summers also made the political calculation that it is "easier to add down the road to insufficient fiscal stimulus than to subtract from excessive fiscal stimulus."[12]

Although the experienced NEC director had moved quickly to develop a set of economic-recovery plans to manage the Great Recession, this New Deal–era approach rested upon two flawed arguments. First, the argument that "stimulus of well over $1 trillion" would likely not be more effective "because of the impact it would have on markets" was based on the experience with the 1993 deficit reduction program that had generated economic growth during the second half of the Clinton administration through the lowering of interest rates. But that argument was much weaker in this case because interest rates were already exceptionally low. In November 2008 the Fed had launched a program to keep long-term interest rates low, and the thirty-year Treasury yield—one of the primary long-term interest rates—had already fallen below 3 percent, significantly lower than the 7 percent starting point during the Clinton administration. Then in December 2008, the same month that the stimulus plan was being developed, the Fed lowered the federal funds rate—its primary short-term interest rate target—to a range of 0 and 0.25 percent, the lowest level possible and significantly lower than the 3 percent starting point during the Clinton administration.[13]

As a scholar of the Great Depression and the only top incoming public-finance principal who had not served during the Clinton administration, Romer had pushed for a larger fiscal stimulus because she believed it would be more effective in this new low-interest rate environment. Similarly, Bernanke, who was also a leading scholar of the Great Depression, publicly supported a stimulus program, meaning, unlike the Clinton administration, the Obama administration was being directed by the Fed to increase the deficit, not decrease it. As the Fed chair explained, "With short-term interest rates already near zero, the economy certainly needed fiscal help—increased government spending, tax cuts to promote private spending, or both. I had said so . . . during the fall," which led the *Wall Street Journal* to editorialize "that I had effectively endorsed Obama for president. I wasn't endorsing a candidate, I was endorsing a program."[14]

Second, the argument that the Obama administration would be able to "add down the road to insufficient fiscal stimulus" simply had no grounding. David Obey, the chair of the Appropriations Committee in the House, warned several Obama administration officials, "You damn well better know how much you need to get this job done, and you damn well better err on the high side, because you won't be able to come back for a second kick at the can!"[15]

Adding to the situation, on the same day that the president-elect received the memo, he attended a six-hour meeting with his national-security team. Underscoring its importance and scope, Secretary of Defense Robert Gates explained that the meeting covered the ongoing wars in Iraq and Afghanistan and other "early action items," such as closing Guantanamo and signing executive orders on interrogation techniques and rendition, all of which confirmed for the incoming principals "the miserable shape U.S. national security and international relationships were in."[16] Even more notable, Obama himself later conceded, "Wars absorb so much energy on the part of any administration that even if people are doing an outstanding job, if they're in the middle of a war . . . that's taking up a huge amount of energy on the part of everybody. And that means that there are some things that get left undone."[17]

The next day—December 16—the president-elect held a meeting with his public-finance principals and top political advisers. Although Romer briefly made the case for a larger stimulus proposal, the discussion never really moved beyond the narrow alternatives that Summers had included in the memo the day before. As Romer put it, "The option of going well above $800 billion was . . . raised, but it was not discussed extensively."[18] Following the review of narrow alternatives, the experienced public-finance principals and Rahm Emanuel—the incoming chief of staff and another Clinton administration alumnus—quickly settled on a target of $775 billion.[19]

Strengthening the influence of the experienced public-finance principals, Obama appeared detached from the discussion, adding at one point, "There needs to be more inspiration here!"[20] This relatively hands-off approach was no doubt due to a combination of Obama's own limited knowledge and the wide range of complex issues on his plate. After the meeting one adviser remarked, "That's definitely the worst briefing any incoming president has gotten since FDR in 1932!" Obama responded—"only half-joking" by his own account—"that's not even my worst brief this week."[21] The president-elect added,

> I was spending much of my transition time in windowless rooms, getting the classified details on Iraq, Afghanistan, and multiple terrorist threats. Still, I remember leaving the meeting on the economy more energized than despondent. Some of my confidence was a matter of postelection adrenaline, I suppose—the untested, maybe delusional belief that I was up for the task at hand. I also felt good about the team I'd assembled; if anyone could come up with the answers we needed, I figured this group could.[22]

With the size of the stimulus program now settled upon, the incoming Obama administration quickly went to work in building support for it. The *New York Times* reported in early January, "Two weeks before assuming power, President-elect Barack Obama took his economic recovery package to Capitol Hill on Monday and worked to build a bipartisan coalition to endorse his plan of tax cuts and new spending with an urgent appeal 'to break the momentum of this recession.'"[23] The incoming administration also played a key role in developing the economic forecast. Romer and Jared Bernstein, the economic adviser to the vice president–elect, released a report in January explaining that if an economic-stimulus program "just slightly over the $775 billion currently under discussion" is implemented, the "unemployment rate in [the fourth quarter of 2010] is predicted to be approximately 7%, which is well below the approximately 8.8% that would result in the absence of a plan."[24]

Finally, on February 17—less than a month after assuming office—Obama signed the American Recovery and Reinvestment Act of 2009, which consisted of a roughly two-to-one mix of spending increases and tax cuts over two years, all of which totaled $787 billion, nearly the exact amount proposed.[25] On the one hand, this New Deal–era approach to managing the Great Recession was a considerable success. Most importantly, the president and his principals had accepted from the start that it was necessary to develop a countercyclical fiscal policy to prevent a second Great Depression. In moving so quickly, the program helped to bring about the official end of the Great Recession during the second half of 2009.[26] On the other hand, the Reagan-era apparatus and its principals had limited the president's control in two key ways.

First, in focusing on stabilizing the economy in the short term, the public-finance principals had failed to provide the president with a plan to restructure the subdomain of fiscal policy to the same degree that had occurred during the Roosevelt and Reagan administrations. For example, the medium- to long-term revenue effect of the Economic Recovery Tax Act of 1981 (a revenue reduction of 4.15 percent of GDP in year four) was more than 100 times greater in absolute value terms than that of the American Recovery and Reinvestment Act of 2009, which reduced revenue in years one, two, and three by 0.59 percent, 1.28 percent, and 0.26 percent of GDP respectively and then increased revenue in year four by 0.04 percent of GDP.[27]

Second, in narrowing the set of economic-recovery alternatives based on at least two flawed arguments, the public-finance principals had failed to keep the unemployment rate below even the conservative, public target of 8 percent. In fact when Obama signed the stimulus program in February, the unemployment rate was already 8.3 percent—which would not be known until the following month—and it would remain above 9 percent for the next thirty months. Acknowledging the inadequate size of the program as well as the quick breakdown of the "add down the road" argument, Treasury Secretary Geithner later conceded, "The Recovery Act had provided vital fiscal stimulus . . . but it wasn't big enough to fill the gaping hole the crisis had torn in U.S. output, or the brutal contraction in government spending at the state and local levels. We needed even more stimulus" but "there was no appetite for that on the Hill."[28] Geithner also noted that the Romer-Bernstein forecast gave "Republicans an enduring anti-stimulus talking point. . . . Economically their argument that stimulus was actually making things worse was ridiculous, but politically, it packed a punch. It was short and simple," and "[made] us look like an economic gang that couldn't shoot straight."[29]

After relying upon a team of highly experienced principals to "come up with the answers we needed," Obama himself later explained that at the start of his administration "nobody—not the public, not Congress, not the press, and (as I'd soon discover) not even the experts—really understood just how much worse things were about to get."[30]

* * *

While the public-finance principals oversaw the inadequate New Deal–era approach to managing the Great Recession, the president focused much of his own attention on health care reform, his top priority during the first year. Once again the Congressional Budget Office played a key role. Unlike Clinton's failed effort, however, Obama passed health care reform and used the CBO to his advantage, a process several years in the making.

In 2007 Peter Orszag, the newly appointed CBO director following the Democratic takeover, took the lead in lobbying Congress to expand the CBO's staff by nearly 10 percent in order to increase its work on health care. With the support of this staff expansion, the CBO issued two important reports in December 2008. The first report identified how the CBO would assess the budgetary treatment of various health care provisions, and the second report provided multiple options for health care reform and the costs associated for each, meaning that the two reports removed from the outset some of the major issues that had undercut Clinton's proposal.[31] In late 2008 Obama then selected Orszag to head the OMB in order to help develop and pass health care reform. Making clear the prioritization of this issue, the president-elect remarked to Orszag, "I'm definitely committed to health care reform for my first year."[32]

Once in office, Obama maintained that commitment notwithstanding the need to manage the Great Recession. Unlike Clinton, however, who had his principals draft a massive health care proposal that he submitted to Congress, the new president provided only key guidelines and allowed the relevant congressional committees to develop their own proposals. Most importantly, in July 2009 Obama "pledged that health insurance reform will not add to our deficit over the next decade."[33] Two months later he continued to push health care reform forward and repeated to Congress, "I will not sign a plan that adds one dime to our deficits, either now or in the future."[34]

Using its detailed knowledge of the CBO's scoring due to the 2008 reports, Congress proceeded to pass health care reform legislation that followed the president's key guidelines. In November 2009, the House passed a bill that the CBO estimated would reduce the deficit by nearly $140 billion over ten years; in December, the Senate passed a bill that the CBO estimated would reduce the deficit by nearly $120 billion; and in March 2010—following some procedural maneuvering in Congress—Obama signed the Affordable Care Act, which the CBO estimated would reduce the deficit by $140 billion.[35] Making clear the

CBO's role as an administrative resource rather than a constraint, Obama him-self stressed its scoring while pushing for health care reform. In late 2009 the president explained, "We keep on hearing these ads about how this is going to add to the deficit, the CBO has said that this is a deficit reduction, not a deficit increase. So all the scare tactics out there, all the ads that are out there, are sim-ply inaccurate."[36]

Among its many fiscal provisions the ACA increased spending—especially on Medicaid, the Children's Health Insurance Program, and subsidies for buy-ing private insurance. It also increased taxes—most importantly, it established a health insurance coverage mandate tax, excise taxes on health insurance pro-viders, an additional Medicare tax, and a net investment income tax.[37] To be sure, the ACA was the most sweeping health care legislation since the creation of Medicare and Medicaid in 1965, but its impact on fiscal policy was far less sweeping. For example, the medium- to long-term revenue effect of the Eco-nomic Recovery Tax Act of 1981 (a revenue reduction of 4.15 percent of GDP in year four) was nearly ten times greater in absolute value terms than that of the ACA, which increased revenue in year four by 0.43 percent of GDP.[38] In other words, relative to Roosevelt and Reagan, Obama simply never put forward a proposal to restructure the subdomain of fiscal policy, especially during the critical period of unified party control of the government.

* * *

Following the emergency phase of the Great Recession, and with the president prioritizing health care reform, the Reagan-era apparatus and its principals shifted from supporting an inadequate New Deal–era approach in the subdo-main of fiscal policy to supporting a Reagan-era approach, which continued to limit the president's control, especially his ability to "create new jobs" and "lay a new foundation for growth."

This process began in December 2009 when the experienced directors of the NEC and OMB submitted a memo to the president explaining that "unfa-vorable economic and technical re-estimates have worsened the deficit outlook by a total of $2.2 trillion" over the next decade and therefore it was essential to develop a plan to lower the deficit to "about 3 percent of [GDP] by 2015."[39] In line with this recommendation, Obama announced in his budget message in early 2010 that "our fiscal situation remains unacceptable," and he called for the creation of a "bipartisan fiscal commission charged with identifying additional policies to put our country on a fiscally sustainable path—balancing the Budget, excluding interest payments on the debt, by 2015."[40] Addressing this proposed change in course—at a time when unemployment stood at 9.8 percent—the

New York Times reported, "The president's shift from stimulus spending to deficit reduction in his new budget for the 2011 to 2020 fiscal years assumes that the economy will have fully recovered."[41]

In contrast to the NEC and OMB directors, the Fed chair opposed the move toward fiscal austerity, meaning, unlike the Clinton administration, the Obama administration still had little reason at the time to be concerned about the effect of a larger deficit on interest rates. As Bernanke explained, "Fiscal policy—at state, local and federal levels—was . . . blowing the wrong way" after 2009. "The federal deficit . . . was primarily a longer-run concern."[42]

After the passage of health care reform and the 2010 midterm election, which transferred control of the House to Republicans, the Reagan-era apparatus and its principals increased support for the Reagan-era approach to managing the subdomain of fiscal policy. To begin with, because the president had failed during the period of unified party control of the government to address the matter of the temporary Bush tax cuts from the early 2000s, the first of which were set to expire in 2011, he now agreed to extend them for two more years even though they included substantial benefits for the wealthiest Americans. As Obama conceded, "It was hard to justify that [top] 2 percent contributing significantly to economic growth. But we were in a political situation, having just gotten slaughtered in the House races . . . where we felt that what we did end up negotiating would give the best chance of continuing to grow the economy."[43]

This two-year extension cost roughly $900 billion, more than the initial economic recovery package, which indicates that Congress may have been willing to support a far larger fiscal program on the president's own terms in 2009 had he actually put one forward and pushed for it. Instead, the president was left to accept an extension of the previously criticized "trickle down" Bush tax cuts, a significant portion of which, by his own admission, were unlikely to "[contribute] significantly to economic growth." Further confirming his mishandling of the issue, Obama pledged not to repeat this misstep. "Let's protect the fragile economy," he remarked. "Come the next round when these things expire, I'm holding. Not happening again."[44]

Even more troubling, the Republican-controlled House intensified the move to lower the deficit that the Obama administration had initiated in early 2010. In part, this process was a repeat of the 1995 battle when the Republican-controlled Congress used its budget-making apparatus to shut down the government and pressure the Democratic president to put forward a balanced-budget proposal based on its preferred time frame and the CBO's scoring. Unlike 1995, however, Republicans now only controlled the House and worked to secure their preferred policy throughout the first half of 2011 by threatening to block any move to raise the debt ceiling, which would cause the government to default on its debt.

Based on a combination of his reelection concerns and a belief that a short-term extension would set a precedent for the Republican-controlled House to repeat this process, the president refused to accept any deal on the debt ceiling that did not extend beyond 2012. Underscoring the firmness of his position and the significance of this new threat, Obama informed his advisers, "I've decided that I am not going to take a short-term debt extension under any circumstances. I want you to understand, I am not going to do it.... This hurts the presidency."[45]

With Obama firmly opposed to any short-term extension, the debt ceiling negotiation centered on a longer-term deal that would reduce spending by an amount equal to the increase in the debt ceiling, possibly through the use of a trigger. This was necessary because neither side trusted the other, but the fact that the president was negotiating over the debt ceiling in the first place and that the negotiation focused on spending cuts rather than tax increases represented a major victory for Republicans. After a meeting at the White House, Speaker of the House John Boehner remarked to his aides, "I got 'em. I think if we give on the debt limit and go to a trigger—a policy trigger instead of a debt limit trigger—we'll get them on everything."[46]

The Obama administration itself then provided the policy trigger when Jack Lew, another Clinton administration veteran, who succeeded Orszag as budget director, recommended the use of budget sequestration.[47] This Reagan-era approach to managing fiscal policy was based on the Gramm-Rudman-Hollings Deficit Reduction Act of 1985, which Lew was familiar with, having worked for House Speaker Tip O'Neill during the 1980s. Essentially, the plan was to threaten Democrats and Republicans with unpalatable, across-the-board spending cuts—split evenly between defense and nondefense spending—in order to force a compromise on the budget and thereby resolve the debt ceiling standoff. Confirming the key role of the budget director, the *New York Times* reported that Lew "was the main proponent" for the proposal and that he "lifted language from [the] 1985 [Gramm-Rudman] law he helped negotiate."[48]

Finally, in August—with the unemployment rate still at 9 percent and the economy contracting slightly that quarter—Obama signed the Budget Control Act of 2011. Among its many provisions, the law extended the debt ceiling, established discretionary spending caps to reduce spending by more than $900 billion over ten years, and established the Joint Select Committee on Deficit Reduction, which was charged with developing a plan to reduce the deficit by another $1.2 trillion. Specifically, if the committee failed to put forward a plan the following year or if Congress failed to pass it, a budget sequestration process would go into effect, meaning that spending would be automatically cut by $1.2 trillion over ten years beginning in 2013.[49] Like the extension of the Bush tax cuts, this was not the outcome the president had desired. "Let's not do this again," he remarked. "We're not going to negotiate on the debt limit ever again."[50]

Making this undesired outcome even worse, the Joint Select Committee on Deficit Reduction failed to reach an agreement, and the combination of the impending budget sequester and the expiring Bush tax cuts threatened to trigger another economic downturn.[51] To prevent this impending "fiscal cliff," the Obama administration and House Republicans began to negotiate again after the 2012 election. This led to the passage of the American Taxpayer Relief Act, which made the Bush tax cuts permanent for families making less than $450,000 a year, restored the Clinton era rates for families making more than that amount, and delayed the start of the sequester for two months in an attempt to work out a deal.[52]

In contrast to the tax concession in 2010, Obama tried to sell this deal as a victory, declaring after its passage, "A central promise of my campaign for President was to change the Tax Code that was too skewed towards the wealthy at the expense of working middle-class Americans. Tonight, we've done that."[53] However, in simply restoring the top income tax rate to 39.6 percent—well below the 70 percent rate that Reagan had inherited—Obama failed to reverse the existing trajectory of income and wealth inequality in a substantial and durable way. The president himself essentially confirmed this when he explained nearly a year after signing the new tax law that "growing inequality" has become "the defining challenge of our time."[54]

Related to the limited changes in tax policy, the two-month delay for the budget sequester proved useless, largely because the sequester threatened only spending, not taxes. As the *New York Times* reported, "The bipartisan talking point has held that the $1.2 trillion in cuts over a decade . . . were intended to be so onerous to both sides that they would force Republicans and Democrats to unite around a bipartisan, comprehensive deficit package." However, "almost the opposite has proved true" because Republicans "made sure that failure to reach a bipartisan deal would not set off automatic tax increases, a decision that may have made the automatic cuts inevitable."[55]

To be sure, the Bipartisan Budget Acts of 2013 and 2015 would ease some of the spending restrictions in the short term.[56] Nevertheless, the Budget Control Act and its sequestration process proved effective in reducing government spending. After surpassing 23 percent of GDP from 2009 through 2011, government spending fell to 20.8 percent in 2013 and remained at that level in

2016. Relatedly, throughout the Obama administration, the overall budget—the average of spending and taxes—remained below the 20 percent of GDP ceiling established during the Reagan administration, further demonstrating the limited medium- to long-term fiscal impact of the president's signature legislation: the economic recovery program and health care reform.

Like the earlier missteps, Obama himself acknowledged that the sequester, which his own budget director had proposed, was a mistake. "It's just dumb," he remarked. "And it's going to hurt. It's going to hurt individual people and it's going to hurt the economy overall."[57]

* * *

The case study analysis here shows that the established Reagan-era apparatus and its principals significantly limited Obama's control in the subdomain of fiscal policy. First, in providing the president with a fiscal stimulus proposal that "wasn't big enough," in providing a forecast that made the new administration "look like an economic gang that couldn't shoot straight," and in failing to provide a comprehensive program for restructuring the subdomain of fiscal policy over the medium- to long-term to the same degree that had occurred during the Roosevelt and Reagan administrations, the Reagan-era apparatus and its principals limited Obama's control, especially during the critical period of unified party control of the government. Second, in failing to provide the president with a plan for either eliminating or extending the debt ceiling before the midterm election, and then in proposing the budget sequester as a policy trigger, all of which led to the passage of the Budget Control Act and the implementation of a budget sequester that was "just dumb" and that "hurt the economy," the Reagan-era apparatus and its principals further limited Obama's control.

THE REAGAN-ERA APPARATUS LIMITS OBAMA'S CONTROL IN MANAGING A MIX OF APPROACHES IN THE SUBDOMAIN OF MONETARY POLICY

Similar to the subdomain of fiscal policy, the Reagan-era apparatus and its principals significantly limited Obama's control in the subdomain of monetary policy. Here too, the process was underway before the new president assumed office. On December 16—the same day the incoming Obama administration developed its recovery proposal—the Fed cut its short-term interest rate target to zero and then shifted its focus to two new tools. The first tool was large-scale asset purchases that, in Fed Chair Ben Bernanke's words, "involve[d] buying hundreds of billions of dollars' worth of securities to hold on [the Fed's] balance sheet" in order to bring down long-term interest rates; the second tool was "open-mouth operations" that aimed "to convince the public and the markets that [the Fed] would keep short-term rates low for a long time."[58] Bernanke also later explained, "At the Federal Reserve, exempt from the wholesale personnel changes facing the . . . cabinet departments, we resolved to provide as much policy continuity as possible" after the election.[59]

Moving from the Bush administration to the Obama administration, the Fed's "policy continuity" became evident when it announced in March 2009 that it would purchase "up to an additional $750 billion of agency mortgage-backed securities," "up to $100 billion" of "agency debt," and "up to $300 billion of longer-term Treasury securities over the next six months" in order to "employ all available tools to promote economic recovery and to preserve price stability."[60] This program aimed at lowering long-term interest rates continued the enlargement of the Fed's balance sheet that began in 2008 and now became known as quantitative easing, or QE1. In employing its second tool—"open mouth operations," more popularly known as "forward guidance"—the Fed announced that it would maintain the range for its short-term interest rate target "at 0 to 1/4 percent . . . for an extended period."[61]

Although the Fed moved quickly to employ new policy tools, the overall approach, Bernanke explained, "drew heavily on classic prescriptions for fighting financial panics."[62] The Fed chair also made clear the reason for implementing this countercyclical monetary policy—or New Deal–era approach—explaining, "My colleagues and I were determined not to repeat the blunder the Federal Reserve had committed in the 1930s when it refused to deploy its monetary tools to avoid the sharp deflation that substantially worsened the Great Depression."[63]

Working alongside the Fed, the Treasury also provided substantial continuity. Timothy Geithner, who moved from president of the Federal Reserve Bank in New York to Treasury secretary, explained, "[Larry Summers's] mantra . . . was 'discontinuity,' the importance of distinguishing the Obama response from the pre-Obama response. Signaling a break with the past made sense politically, given . . . the yearning for change after the Bush years." But, Geithner added, "I didn't care much about discontinuity. . . . Our obligation was not to be different for the sake of being different, but to clean up the mess."[64]

Moving from the Bush administration to the Obama administration, the Treasury secretary's indifference to "discontinuity" became evident in the development of a two-step plan to stabilize the financial system that included a "valuation exercise"—later known as a "stress test"—and, if necessary, the injection of capital using funds from the Troubled Asset Relief Program, which was created during the final months of the Bush administration and provided the Treasury with $700 billion. As Geithner explained, "First, the Fed would design and execute a uniform test for the largest firms, analyzing the size of the losses each institution would face in a downturn comparable to the Great Depression." Second, once the Fed "determine[d] how much more of a capital buffer each bank would need to weather a catastrophic downturn," each would have "a chance to raise the funds privately. But if a bank failed to raise enough capital on its own, the Treasury would inject extra capital to fill the gap."[65]

In early May, less than four months into the start of the Obama administration, the results from the stress test were released, and the program quickly proved successful in stabilizing the financial system. However, this process undermined the new president, who had directed his public-finance principals to develop a proposal to restructure the financial system if necessary—a request that the Treasury secretary had ignored. In justifying this course of action, Geithner later explained that the debate within the administration "was resolved in the classic way, that plan beats no plan."[66] Then, addressing why "no one else had a plan" for restructuring the financial system, including the president, Geithner added, "[Obama] hadn't run for president to be a financial engineer. He relied on us to figure out what needed to be done, and he gave me a lot of deference on the substance. After all, he had a lot on his plate," including "waging wars in Iraq and Afghanistan."[67] For his part, and further revealing the general lack of responsiveness from the Treasury secretary, the president later confessed, "I was often pushing, hard, and the speed with which the bureaucracy could exercise my decision was slower than I wanted."[68]

The Treasury secretary's unwillingness to develop a plan for restructuring the financial system was only one example of a larger pattern of the public-finance principals limiting the president's control. As another example, David Axelrod, the president's chief strategist, recalled, "Over the Treasury Department's objections, I had included [in the president's speech] a line calling on Geithner to explore every avenue to block" bonuses at the American International Group (AIG), which had received taxpayer bailouts in 2008. But "[Geithner] and Summers had quietly lobbied against an amendment to the Recovery Act that would have significantly restricted the payment of bonuses at AIG and other firms receiving Troubled Asset Relief Program, or TARP, funds." Those efforts "flew in the face of the president's strong denunciation of the bonuses" and "made the president look like a phony, posturing to a receptive public while his operatives took the opposite tack out of view."[69]

By the end of 2009, the role of the public-finance principals in limiting the president's control had become so troubling that Pete Rouse, a senior adviser, addressed the matter in the first annual review of the Obama presidency. Highlighting four major findings, Rouse explained,

First, there is deep dissatisfaction within the economic team with what is perceived to be [Larry Summers's] imperious and heavy-handed direction of the economic policy process. Second, when the economic team does not like a decision by the President, they have on occasion worked to re-litigate the overall policy. Third, when the policy direction is firmly decided, there can be consideration/reconsideration of the details until the very last moments. Fourth, once a decision is made, implementation by the Department of the Treasury has at times been slow and uneven. These factors all adversely affect execution of the policy process.[70]

Further promoting policy continuity and further revealing the limits of the president's control during his first year, Obama appointed Bernanke to a second term as Fed chair in August 2009, a move that the experienced Treasury secretary, who was indifferent to "discontinuity," had recommended and that the Fed chair himself had strongly desired to support the institution's independence.[71]

Reinforcing that move, the new president adopted the Reagan-era approach to monetary policy in never publicly sharing his views on the subject during his first year, no doubt due to the "hands off the Fed" recommendation from the various Clinton administration alumni serving as public-finance principals. Going even further, Obama announced after reappointing the Fed chair, "We will continue to maintain a strong and independent Federal Reserve."[72]

* * *

While the Fed maintained the primary responsibility for managing the struggling economy through the use of monetary policy, the Obama administration took the lead on reforming the financial system. "I thought it made sense," Treasury Secretary Geithner explained, "to strike while the pain of the crisis was raw and the financial establishment was weak, rather than wait for memories to fade and the empire to strike back. I wanted to seize the first-mover advantage in setting the terms of the debate." However, Geithner also made clear the relatively limited scope of this effort, adding, "There are wars of necessity and wars of choice. Reform was a necessity. Reorganization felt like a choice that could mire the bill in the quicksand of interagency warfare; we wanted regulators focused on helping us fix the broken financial system, not fighting for their bureaucratic survival."[73]

Although the president's lead principal prioritized "reform" over "reorganization," there was one notable exception that built upon an earlier plan. As Geithner explained,

The one area where we did propose a massive reorganization was consumer protection. . . . Our team of reform architects drew inspiration from a 2007 article by Elizabeth Warren advocating that mortgages and other financial products should be regulated like toasters and other consumer products. . . . The case for a new institution to force change and signal a commitment to change was compelling to all of us. It felt like a just cause and a war of necessity.[74]

With the Treasury secretary providing support, Obama put forward a proposal in June 2009 that included the creation of a "powerful agency charged with . . . just one job: looking out for ordinary consumers."[75] Little more than a year later, the president signed the Dodd–Frank Wall Street Reform and Consumer Protection Act. Among its many provisions, the law, in the words of the Treasury secretary, "gave U.S. regulators the power to enforce their capital and liquidity rules more broadly across the financial system"; it "gave them new authorities to identify and monitor systemic risks"; and it created the Consumer Financial Protection Bureau, situated within the Federal Reserve System but designed to operate with considerable independence from the Federal Reserve Board.[76]

In particular, the law granted the president the power to appoint the director of the CFPB to a five-year term, and it made the director removable only for "inefficiency, neglect of duty, or malfeasance in office"; it granted the CFPB substantial supervisory, enforcement, and rulemaking authority over consumer financial products; and it directed the Fed to fund the CFPB through its own earnings, thereby eliminating the ability of Congress to weaken or dismantle the agency through the budget process.[77] Underscoring the significance of the new institution and his support for it, Obama explained, "The Consumer Financial Protection Bureau will be a watchdog for the American consumer, charged with enforcing the toughest financial protections in history," and "getting this agency off the ground will be an enormously important task, a task that can't wait."[78]

Dodd-Frank was the most sweeping financial-reform legislation passed in decades, but it was, in the Treasury secretary's words, "reform," not "reorganization." Further addressing its limitations, Geithner noted, "Our reforms largely left in place our stunningly fragmented regulatory structure. . . . This level of bureaucratic balkanization is better than what we had in 2007, but it is not good enough."[79] Although Dodd-Frank helped to stabilize the financial system and created a powerful new bureau within the Fed, the law did not alter the central bank's primary statutory governing objective, meaning that, unlike Roosevelt and Reagan, Obama failed to take the lead in restructuring the subdomain of monetary policy, especially during the critical period of unified party control of the government.

* * *

Following the emergency phase of the Great Recession, the Reagan-era apparatus and its principals continued to limit the president's control. The initial quantitative easing program ended in May 2010, and although the Fed had purchased more than $1 trillion in long-term securities since March 2009, its balance sheet had only increased from $1.9 trillion to $2.3 trillion due to the large number of securities that continued to mature at the same time.[80] Relatedly, the economy struggled to get going throughout 2010 while the Fed maintained primary responsibility for its management following the passage of the economic-recovery program. As Bernanke explained, "The economy was clearly losing momentum. . . . If growth did not pick up enough . . . the economy might tumble into a new recession. To me, with more fiscal help unlikely, it seemed clear that the economy needed more support from monetary policy"—which would not occur until after the 2010 midterm election.[81]

Reinforcing the Fed's inadequate response, the president remained quiet on the subject of monetary policy and failed to use the appointment power effectively. In addition to reappointing Bernanke as chair in 2009, Obama appointed Daniel Tarullo in early 2009 and Sarah Raskin and Janet Yellen in late 2010, but he left three of the seven seats on the Federal Reserve Board empty for most of his first two years, despite having unified party control of the government. Making clear the Obama administration's low prioritization of influencing monetary policy, Bernanke noted, "During the week between [Randy Krozner's] departure and [Dan Tarullo's] swearing-in, the Board would be left with only four members for the first time in its history."[82]

Following the 2010 midterm election, which transferred control of the House to Republicans, the Reagan-era apparatus and its principals shifted from supporting an inadequate New Deal–era approach in managing the subdomain of monetary policy to supporting a traditional Reagan-era approach, which further limited the president's control, especially his ability to "create new jobs" and "lay a new foundation for growth."

The process began in November 2010 when the Fed announced that it would "purchase a further $600 billion of longer-term Treasury securities by the end of the second quarter of 2011, a pace of about $75 billion per month." This was the second round of quantitative easing, or QE2. As part of its forward guidance, the Fed also announced that it would maintain the range for its short-term interest rate target "at 0 to 1/4 percent . . . for an extended period."[83] However, because the emergency phase of the Great Recession had passed and control of the House had changed, the opposition to the Fed's program was now much greater. As Bernanke explained, "The increasing hostility of Republicans to the

Fed and to me personally troubled me." He then added, "It seemed . . . that the crisis had helped to radicalize large parts of the Republican Party. . . . They saw inflation where it did not exist. . . . They denied that monetary or fiscal policy could support job growth" and "they advocated discredited monetary systems, like the gold standard."[84] At the same time, the president remained quiet on the subject of monetary policy in general and QE2 in particular.

Similar to QE1, QE2 ended at a set date even though the economy, in Bernanke's words, continued to fail "to reach escape velocity—to reach the point where growth was self-sustaining."[85] The Fed also finally moved to make its 2 percent inflation target public despite both slow economic growth and high unemployment. In a press release in January 2012, the Fed announced that the "inflation rate over the longer run is primarily determined by monetary policy" and "inflation at the rate of 2 percent . . . is most consistent over the longer run with the Federal Reserve's statutory mandate." Regarding its responsibility for managing unemployment, the press release added, "The maximum level of employment is largely determined by nonmonetary factors. . . . These factors may change over time and may not be directly measurable. Consequently, it would not be appropriate to specify a fixed goal for employment."[86]

This was a remarkable admission. Although the law mandated that the Fed promote both "full employment" and "price stability," the Fed had announced that it would continue to prioritize the latter, which, as Bernanke put it, "create[d] an institutional commitment to continuing the Volcker and Greenspan policies."[87] Making clear the practical consequences of this Reagan-era policy commitment, the *New York Times* reported that the Fed "expects to hit its inflation target over the next three years" but that it expects "to fall well short of its goals for unemployment."[88]

In addition to establishing a public inflation target, in late 2011 the Fed launched the Maturity Extension Program—better known as "Operation Twist." Unlike QE1 and QE2, Operation Twist was designed to lower long-term interest rates by changing the composition of the Fed's balance sheet rather than expand it.[89] Like QE1 and QE2, Operation Twist had a set end date—the middle of 2012—meaning that, four years after the start of the Great Recession, the Fed had still not made an open-ended commitment to keep its primary short-term interest rate low or to continue its purchases of long-term securities until the economy fully recovered. Underscoring the significance of this decision, Bernanke later conceded, "It would have been better to tie our policy plans more directly to conditions in the economy rather than setting a date."[90]

Once Operation Twist, like QE1 and QE2, failed to get the economy "to reach escape velocity," the Fed expanded its approach. In particular, the economy grew an annual rate of only 0.5 percent during the third quarter of 2012, and unemployment remained above 8 percent, which led the Fed to commit in September to "purchasing additional agency mortgage-backed securities at a pace of $40 billion per month."[91] This marked the start of the third round of quantitative easing, or QE3. Then in December the Fed announced that it would maintain the range for its short-term interest rate target "at 0 to 1/4 per-cent . . . at least as long as the unemployment rate remains above 6-1/2 percent" and as long as the inflation rate remains "no more than a half percentage point above the . . . 2 percent longer-run goal."[92] Put simply, the Fed finally made an open-ended commitment to keep its primary short-term interest rate low and to purchase long-term securities until the economy recovered. But even this commitment was based on an unemployment target well above the Fed's own conservative estimate of full employment. As Bernanke conceded, "We had estimated the unemployment rate consistent with full employment at about 5.5 percent"—not the 6.5 percent the Fed was now targeting—and after "three years of recovery, we were still far from that goal, and we weren't optimistic about the prospects for faster progress."[93]

Again the president remained quiet on the subject rather than publicly pressure the Fed, and he continued to use the appointment power ineffectively despite the advantage of his own party controlling the Senate. In order to fill the seven-member Federal Reserve Board for the first time since the start of the Great Recession, Obama nominated two governors in 2012—Jeremy Stein and Jerome Powell—but the new appointees, along with Betsy Duke, a remain-ing Bush appointee, failed to support an expansive monetary policy. Bernanke noted, "I was particularly concerned that I could lose the support of three Board members: Jeremy Stein, Jay Powell, and Betsy Duke." Bernanke then added, "[Powell] told me, we needed an 'off-ramp,'" meaning "if we concluded that [QE3] simply wasn't working, or if it was creating excessive risks, we would stop buying securities, even if we hadn't reached our goal of jump-starting the job market."[94]

The following year the Fed announced that it would begin to "reduce the pace of its asset purchases" even though unemployment stood at nearly 7 per-cent and the economy grew by less than 2 percent, meaning that the Fed was heading toward the Powell-recommended "off-ramp" from QE3 before it had reached its "goal of jump-starting the job market."[95] Rather than push back, Obama elevated Janet Yellen to the post of Fed chair in February 2014, and the new, highly experienced chair largely maintained the existing trajectory of monetary policy, no doubt due to her indoctrination while serving for several years on both the Greenspan-led Fed and the Bernanke-led Fed.[96]

The Yellen-led Fed not only wound down QE3 in 2014 but proceeded to raise the short-term interest rate target in December 2015, which contributed to a "localized recession" in 2016. A detailed account in the *New York Times* later explained, "When the Fed moved toward raising interest rates . . . in December 2015," it contributed to a "vicious circle of a stronger dollar, weaker emerging market growth and lower commodity prices" that "caused spending on certain types of capital goods to plummet." Therefore, although "the economy was in pretty good shape for people in large cities on the coasts, 2016 was rough for a lot of people in local economies heavily reliant on drilling, mining, farming or making the machines that support those industries." Put simply, "this was a localized recession—severe in certain places, but concentrated enough that it did not throw the overall United States economy into contraction."[97]

Further contributing to the overall poor economic recovery, the president remained quiet with regard to the end of QE3 in 2014, the start of rising interest rates in late 2015, and the localized recession in 2016, all of which stood in stark contrast to Roosevelt's role during the Great Depression. In his own research on the subject, Bernanke had stressed the importance of "Rooseveltian resolve" in ending the Great Depression, explaining, "Roosevelt's specific policy actions were . . . less important than his willingness to be aggressive and to experiment—in short, to do whatever was necessary to get the country moving again. Many of his policies did not work as intended, but in the end FDR deserves great credit for having the courage to abandon failed paradigms and to do what needed to be done."[98]

Obama himself also made clear the difference in his approach compared to that of Roosevelt, acknowledging in late 2015, a month before the Fed's shift to a restrictive monetary policy, "What I didn't fully appreciate, and nobody can appreciate until they're in the position, is how decentralized power is in this system." Going further, he explained, "I've got the Federal Reserve," one of many "federal agenc[ies] that technically is independent, so I can't tell them what to do" and "I'm hoping that they do the right thing."[99]

If the objective was to "create new jobs" and "lay a new foundation for growth," then simply hoping that the Fed would "do the right thing" in managing the economy proved far less effective than Roosevelt's effort to restructure "failed paradigms" and "do what needed to be done." In particular, economic growth averaged only 1.6 percent a year during the Obama administration—compared to 6.3 percent a year during the first two terms of the Roosevelt administration—and the unemployment rate (the percent of the labor force that is unemployed and looking for a job) decreased from 7.8 percent to 4.7 percent over the course of the Obama administration, but the labor force participation rate (the percent of the population that is working or actively looking for work) declined from 65.7 percent to 62.8 percent over the same period, meaning that the unemployment situation was worse than the unemployment rate suggested because a substantial proportion of the long-term unemployed had simply stopped looking for work. At the same time, and no doubt contributing to the unemployment problem and slow economic growth, inflation—the management of which the central bank had prioritized since the Reagan administration—stayed too low. Personal consumption expenditure (PCE) inflation, the Fed's preferred measure for the public inflation target, fell from an average of 4.4 percent a year during the Reagan administration, to 1.9 percent a year during the Clinton administration, and then to 1.2 percent a year during the Obama administration. "Inflation remained . . . below the Fed's 2 percent target," Bernanke later explained, and "as the world has learned, too little inflation is just as bad as too much inflation."[100]

Further contrasting his failed hands-off approach to Roosevelt's restructuring of "failed paradigms," Obama later confessed,

> FDR would never had made such mistakes. . . . FDR understood that to be effective, governance couldn't be so antiseptic that it set aside the basic stuff of politics: You had to sell your program, reward supporters, punch back against opponents, and amplify the facts that helped your cause while fudging the details that didn't. I found myself wondering whether we'd somehow turned virtue into a vice; whether, trapped in my own high-mindedness, I'd failed to tell the American people a story they could believe in.[101]

* * *

The case study analysis here shows that the established, relatively stable Reagan-era apparatus and its principals significantly limited Obama's control in the subdomain of monetary policy. First, in "provid[ing] as much policy continuity as possible," in downplaying "discontinuity," in "adversely affect[ing] execution of the policy process" by relitigating or often failing to implement decisions, in "ma[king] the president look like a phony," and in failing to provide a comprehensive program for restructuring the subdomain of monetary policy to the same degree that had occurred during the Roosevelt and Reagan administrations, the Reagan-era apparatus and its principals limited Obama's control, especially during the critical period of unified party control of the government. Second, in making public the 2 percent inflation target and relegating the "maximum level of employment" to something "largely determined by nonmonetary factors," in taking the "off-ramp" from quantitative easing before reaching the "goal of jump-starting the job market," and in raising the short-term interest rate before even reaching the conservative 2 percent inflation target, all of which undercut the president's ability to "create new jobs" and "lay a new foundation for growth," the Reagan-era apparatus and its principals further limited Obama's control.

Altogether, the case study analysis of fiscal policymaking and monetary policymaking in this chapter shows that the established Reagan-era apparatus and its principals reinforced the established Reagan-era policy parameters during the Obama administration in the process of significantly limiting the president's control. Further underscoring his limited impact in the domain of public finance, Obama himself later confessed, "I had engineered a return to pre-crisis normalcy" and "I wonder whether I should have been bolder in those early months, willing to exact more economic pain in the short term in pursuit of a permanently altered and more just economic order."[102]

13. A Preliminary Examination of Trump's Control

As demonstrated in the preceding chapters, the primary problem in the domain of public finance changes from time to time, and the management of one problem can contribute to the rise of a new problem. The initial exceptionally severe and highly prioritized problem in the policy domain during the modern period was the Great Depression, and the solution involved the government taking responsibility for maintaining economic stability in general and prioritizing the management of unemployment in particular. The second exceptionally severe and highly prioritized problem was the Great Inflation, which included simultaneous high unemployment and high inflation, due in large part to the government's work over several decades to trade off higher inflation for lower unemployment.

A similar process has been underway since the Great Inflation. The solutions for managing the Great Inflation involved on the fiscal front a steady and structurally unbalanced budget that generally operated as a secondary economic-stabilization instrument; a supply-side (or less progressive) tax system; and a restricted general spending system and steady Social Security spending. On the monetary front, the solution included a "fine-tuned" monetary policy that generally operated as the primary economic-stabilization instrument in support of promoting "price stability." These nearly four-decade-old solutions have in turn contributed to new problems: rising economic inequality and slowing economic growth.

Let's first consider rising economic inequality. The New Deal–era public finance apparatus and policy parameters worked to create and maintain a relatively equitable distribution of income and wealth, whereas the Reagan-era public-finance apparatus and policy parameters worked to create and maintain rising income and wealth inequality. As the Congressional Budget Office reported, "Income inequality was greater in 2016 than it was in 1979," the full time frame for the federal government's most prominent analysis of the income distribution.[1] Likewise, the Federal Reserve reported that the share of "wealth held by affluent families reached historically high levels" in 2016, whereas "the wealth share of the bottom 90 percent of families has been falling over most of the past 25 years," the full time frame for the federal government's most prominent analysis of the wealth distribution.[2]

The impact of rising economic inequality became especially apparent during the 2016 election—the first open presidential election following the Great Recession. Although the Great Recession was not an exceptionally severe and highly prioritized problem relative to the Great Depression and the Great Inflation, it played an important role both in contributing to rising economic inequality and in drawing attention to the problem, the latter of which played out on both political sides during the 2016 election. On the Democratic side, Bernie Sanders—who headed a populist insurgency and came close to winning the nomination—launched his campaign by declaring, "In America we now have more income and wealth inequality than . . . at any time since the 1920s. The issue of wealth and income inequality is the great moral issue of our time, it is the great economic issue of our time and it is the great political issue of our time."[3] Likewise, on the Republican side Donald Trump—who headed a populist insurgency and won the nomination as well as the general election—briefly pledged to break with nearly four decades of Republican orthodoxy. As he declared during the campaign, "The thing I'm going to do is make sure the middle class gets good tax breaks. Because they have been absolutely shunned. . . . For the wealthy, I think, frankly, it's going to go up. And you know what, it really should go up."[4] Trump also fully broke with Republican orthodoxy in repeatedly attacking existing "trade deals that strip us of our jobs and strip us of our wealth," and he pledged to address this source of economic inequality through the restructuring of trade policy. "I have a different vision for our workers," he declared, one that will generate "new wealth" and "improve the quality of life for all Americans."[5]

Now let's consider slowing economic growth. The New Deal–era public-finance apparatus and policy parameters worked to create and maintain a relatively fast-growing economy, whereas the Reagan-era public-finance apparatus and policy parameters worked to create and maintain a relatively slow-growing economy. Specifically, after interest rates peaked during the early 1980s due to rising inflation, the Fed took the lead in managing the economy through the use of a monetary policy that prioritized the promotion of "price stability" over "full employment." This quickly brought down inflation and more gradually brought down interest rates, which helped to generate average economic growth of more than 3 percent a year during the Reagan administration and just under 4 percent a year during the Clinton administration. This was the "path to a beneficent future" that two Fed chairs, Paul Volcker and Alan Greenspan, largely directed. Once the Fed succeeded in bringing down interest rates, however, its ability to continue to boost economic growth through the further lowering of interest rates was diminished, especially when managing each subsequent recession. As a result, economic growth slowed to an average of just above

2 percent a year during the George W. Bush administration, which began with a recession in 2001. Economic growth then slowed to an average of less than 2 percent a year during the Obama administration, which began with the Great Recession. Even worse, based on publicly available data at the time, the Obama administration became the first since the creation of the modern Fed not to achieve even a single year of 3 percent economic growth or higher.

The impact of this new problem became especially apparent during the 2016 presidential election. Here too, although the Great Recession was not an exceptionally severe and highly prioritized problem relative to the Great Depression and the Great Inflation, it played an important role both in contributing to slow economic growth and in drawing attention to the problem, the latter of which played out on both political sides during the 2016 election. On the Democratic side, Sanders attacked the independent central bank's management of the economy, explaining, "The recent decision by the Fed to raise interest rates is the latest example of the rigged economic system. . . . Raising interest rates now is a disaster for small business owners who need loans to hire more workers and Americans who need more jobs and higher wages." He added, "As a rule, the Fed should not raise interest rates until unemployment is lower than 4 percent. Raising rates must be done only as a last resort—not to fight phantom inflation."[6] On the Republican side, Trump implicitly pledged to radically alter the Fed's management of the economy when he declared during the campaign, "We're bringing GDP . . . up to 4 percent. And I actually think we can go higher than 4 percent. I think you can go to 5 percent or 6 percent."[7]

Altogether, the New Deal–era public-finance apparatus and policy parameters supported the creation and continuation of a relatively fast-growing economy with a relatively equitable distribution of income and wealth, whereas the Reagan-era public-finance apparatus and policy parameters supported the creation and continuation of a relatively slow-growing economy with a relatively inequitable distribution of income and wealth. These new problems in turn spurred the partial restructuring of the policy domain during the first two years of the Trump administration. Specifically, Trump's move to address economic inequality through a sweeping, unilateral tariff program initiated the partial restructuring of fiscal policymaking, and his move to address slow economic growth by abandoning the "hands-off the Fed" approach initiated the partial restructuring of monetary policymaking. At the same time, the relatively effective management of the standard problem indicators—unemployment and inflation—reinforced the established Reagan-era apparatus and policy parameters and limited the president's control. This mix of innovation and constraint suggests that Trump oversaw the initial collapse of the domain of public finance.

This chapter traces the process of the established, gradually failing Reagan-era apparatus and its principals in limiting Trump's control during his first two years in office.

THE LIMITS OF TRUMP'S CONTROL IN THE SUBDOMAIN OF FISCAL POLICY

Donald Trump assumed office in 2017 with unified party control of the government and what appeared to be a strong desire to change the established course. The Republican Party platform declared, "For the past 8 years America has been led in the wrong direction. . . . Americans have earned and deserve a strong and healthy economy." The platform added, "Republicans consider the establishment of a pro-growth tax code a moral imperative. . . . Getting our tax system right will be the most important factor in driving the entire economy back to prosperity."[8] Trump himself briefly broke with Republican orthodoxy on this issue, declaring during the campaign, "For the wealthy, I think, frankly, [the tax rate is] going to go up. And you know what, it really should go up."[9] However, at other times, Trump embraced Republican orthodoxy, declaring, "I have proposed the largest tax reduction of any candidate. . . . Middle-income Americans and businesses will experience profound relief, and taxes will be greatly simplified for everyone."[10]

In contrast to the back-and-forth on tax policy, Trump fully broke with Republican orthodoxy in repeatedly calling for the restructuring of trade policy as the primary remedy for rising economic inequality. In his acceptance speech at the Republican National Convention, Trump declared, "I have a different vision. . . . It begins with a new, fair trade policy that protects our jobs. . . . It's been a signature message of my campaign from day one, and it will be a signature feature of my presidency." This new approach, he added, will generate "new wealth" that "will improve the quality of life for all Americans."[11]

Despite these and other pledges to change the established course, the Reagan-era apparatus and its principals significantly limited Trump's control, especially during the critical period of unified party control of the government. This process began when, as a candidate, Trump moved to shut down his campaign's transition team, telling Chris Christie, the head of that team, "Chris, you and I are so smart that we can leave the victory party two hours early and do the transition ourselves."[12] After the election, due to the mistaken belief that he could personally manage the process, Trump fired the Christie-led transition team and threw out its work. Taken aback by the president-elect's limited knowledge of both the amount of effort required to staff the government effectively and the importance of this step, Trump's chief strategist remarked, "Holy fuck, this guy doesn't know anything."[13]

The consequences of a lack of meaningful transition planning became especially apparent in the president's ineffective use of the appointment power. After appointing Steve Mnuchin, the campaign's chief fundraiser, as Treasury secretary, Trump remarked, "I hired the wrong guy for Treasury secretary." After appointing Gary Cohn, head of Goldman Sachs, as director of the National Economic Council, Trump complained, "I made a huge mistake giving [that position] to you." And shortly after appointing Mick Mulvaney, one of the founding members of the House Freedom Caucus, as director of the Office of Management and Budget, Trump called for that group's members to be voted out of Congress, tweeting, "The Freedom Caucus will hurt the entire Republican agenda. . . . We must fight them . . . in 2018!"[14] Mulvaney himself also all but confirmed the limited role that Trump had played in his appointment, later revealing, "The first couple of times when I went to the White House, someone had to say, 'This is Mick Mulvaney, he's the budget director.'"[15]

The president's appointment power was no more effective for the other public-finance principals, and in most cases more restricted. Kevin Hassett, Trump's appointee as chair of the Council of Economic Advisers, was not confirmed until September 2017, nearly a year after the election. Janet Yellen remained chair of the Federal Reserve, the position to which Barack Obama had appointed her in 2014. And Keith Hall, who had been appointed by congressional leaders in 2015, remained director of the Congressional Budget Office.

With this group of public-finance principals providing support, Trump quickly struggled to maintain his campaign pledge to introduce several legislative proposals and "fight for their passage within the first 100 days" of his presidency. This included a proposal "to spur $1 trillion in infrastructure investment over ten years"; a proposal that "fully repeals Obamacare and replaces it"; and a proposal "designed to grow the economy 4% per year . . . through massive tax reduction and simplification" that primarily benefit the "middle class."[16]

First, the public-finance principals never provided during the first year—much less the first one hundred days—a detailed proposal "to spur $1 trillion in infrastructure investment." Instead, it took until early 2018 for the Trump administration to put forward an infrastructure proposal at all, and it was by no means detailed. As the *New York Times* reported,

> President Trump's long-awaited plan for overhauling the nation's crumbling infrastructure includes spending $200 billion in federal money over the next decade to spur an additional $1.3 trillion in spending from cities, states and private companies. . . .

The increased infrastructure spending would be offset by unspecified budget cuts. Officials would not detail where those cuts would come from, or how the proposal would effectively leverage at least $6.50 in additional infrastructure spending for every dollar spent by the federal government, a ratio many infrastructure experts consider far-fetched. The officials said Mr. Trump would leave it up to Congress—where there is little consensus about how to pay for such a plan—to figure out the details. . . .

Asking a polarized Congress to hash out a complex and contentious plan could complicate an already steep climb for a proposal that was a pillar of Mr. Trump's presidential campaign.[17]

The Trump administration also struggled to manage the budget more generally. In May 2017 Mick Mulvaney—the conservative budget director whom the new president did not initially know—took the lead in putting forward a proposal that would drastically cut government spending. Making clear the divide between the Trump administration's first budget proposal and the president's own populist campaign, the *New York Times* reported that the proposal "would most likely hurt some of the very voters in rural and economically distressed corners of the nation who catapulted Mr. Trump to the White House," and it "is reminiscent of the conservative House budget alternatives written by the Republican Study Committee, the group [Mulvaney] belonged to before defecting to form the even more conservative House Freedom Caucus." Like most presidential budgets after the first year of the Reagan administration, however, the Trump administration's proposal was ignored from the start. Underscoring its irrelevance, the *Times* added, "Presidential budgets, especially in times of divided government, are traditionally labeled dead on arrival. This one, with its deep domestic spending reductions, never even drew a breath, despite unified Republican control of Washington."[18]

The Republican-controlled Congress not only ignored the Trump administration's budget proposal but failed to pass a budget at all in 2017, leading to a government shutdown. This same dynamic—the ignored proposal and the failure to pass a budget—also played out during the second year of the Trump administration.[19] Further underscoring the irrelevance of the presidential budget proposal in general during the Reagan era—and demonstrating the irrelevance of the Trump administration's second proposal in particular—the *New York Times* reported, "While all presidential budgets are largely political exercises," Trump's newest budget "is widely anticipated to be the least relevant in decades."[20]

Second, the public-finance principals never provided during the first two years—much less the first one hundred days—a detailed proposal that "fully repeals Obamacare and replaces it." Highlighting the significance of this issue, Trump announced during the campaign, "Together we're going to deliver real change that once again puts Americans first. That begins with immediately repealing and replacing the disaster known as Obamacare . . . You're going to have such great health care, at a tiny fraction of the cost, and it's going to be so easy."[21] Once in office, however, revealing a complete lack of planning—in this case, for one of the most important political issues of the past decade—Trump confessed, "It's an unbelievably complex subject. Nobody knew that health care could be so complicated."[22]

The Congressional Budget Office then played a key role in undercutting the considerable effort of Congress to "repeal and replace" "Obamacare"—or the Affordable Care Act. In March 2017 the CBO undercut the House Republican plan in estimating that it would increase the number of uninsured by 24 million, and in June the CBO undercut the Senate Republican plan in estimating that it would increase the number of uninsured by 22 million.[23] Confirming the influential role of the CBO, Susan Collins, one of the key Senate Republicans, tweeted, "I want to work [with] . . . colleagues to fix the flaws in ACA," but the "CBO analysis shows [the] Senate bill won't do it. I will vote no."[24] Likewise, John McCain, another key Senate Republican, confirmed the influential role of the CBO when he refused to support any "repeal and replace" bill that had not been scored by that institution. As he explained in response to a failed last-ditch effort to quickly push through a bill before the reconciliation process deadline expired in September, "I cannot in good conscience vote for" this bill "without knowing how much it will cost, how it will affect insurance premiums, and how many people will be helped or hurt by it. Without a full CBO score, which won't be available by the end of the month, we won't have reliable answers to any of those questions."[25]

Third, the public-finance principals never provided a detailed tax proposal during the first one hundred days, and the proposal that Trump finally put forward in September 2017 was neither detailed nor aimed primarily at the "middle class." As the *New York Times* reported, "The president offered no measure of the plan's cost and scant detail about how working people would benefit from a proposal that has explicit and substantial rewards for wealthy people and corporations, including the elimination of taxes on large inheritances."[26]

Although the Republican Party believed that revising the tax system was "the most important factor in driving the entire economy back to prosperity," the new Republican president played an exceptionally limited role in developing and passing the 2017 tax bill, which was considered a political necessity following the failure to repeal and replace the ACA. Instead, the "Big Six"—the NEC director, the Treasury secretary, and four top congressional Republicans—

took the lead. Publicly praising Trump for staying out of the way, Speaker of the House Paul Ryan remarked, "[The president] just realized being more disciplined and letting the tax writers get this deal done was the best way to go."[27] When Trump then privately proposed breaking with Republican orthodoxy in raising the top personal income tax rate "to 44 percent if I can get the corporate rate to 15 percent"—a proposal more closely in line with his campaign pledge to increase tax rates on the wealthy, at least on the individual income tax side—the NEC director rejected the move. "You can't take the top rate up," he explained. "You just can't. You're a Republican. You will get absolutely destroyed if you take the top rate up."[28] After being relegated to the sidelines both publicly and privately, the president simply promised to sign whatever the Republican-controlled Congress passed. As Trump made clear in November, "America's tax code is a total dysfunctional mess. . . . But all that will change and it will change immediately if Congress sends a tax cut and reform bill. . . . If they send it to my desk . . . I promise you I will sign it. I promise. I will not veto that bill. There will be no veto."[29]

The next month Trump signed the Tax Cut and Jobs Act of 2017. Among its many provisions, the law temporarily lowered the top individual income tax rate from 39.6 to 37 percent and kept the core of the seven-bracket system in place; it permanently lowered the corporate income tax rate from 35 to 21 percent; it temporarily increased the estate tax exemption from $5.6 million to $11.2 million and kept the 40 percent tax rate in place; and it repealed the individual mandate under the Affordable Care Act but kept most of that law in place.[30] In an effort to promote the first and only substantial legislative achievement in 2017, the president declared, "This is the biggest tax and reform in the history of our country. This is bigger than, actually, President Reagan's many years ago."[31]

In truth, the 2017 "tax cuts and reform" bill was less than historic. For comparison, the major tax cut and tax reform acts of the Reagan administration—the 1981 tax cut and the 1986 tax reform—permanently lowered the top individual income tax rate from 70 to 28 percent and permanently reduced the total number of income tax brackets from fifteen to two; they permanently lowered the top corporate income tax rate from 46 to 34 percent; and they permanently lowered the top estate tax rate from 70 to 55 percent. Relatedly, the medium- to long-term revenue effect of the 1981 tax cut (a revenue reduction of 4.15 percent of GDP in year four) was more than four times greater than the 2017 tax cut, which was designed to produce a revenue reduction of 0.94 percent of GDP in year four.[32]

The 2017 tax bill also primarily benefited the wealthy. A prominent analysis estimated that in 2018 "taxpayers in the middle income quintile (those with income between about $49,000 and $86,000) would receive an average tax cut of about $900, or 1.6 percent of after-tax income," whereas "taxpayers in the 95th to 99th income percentiles (those with income between about $308,000 and $733,000) would benefit the most as a share of after-tax income, with an average tax cut of about $13,500 or 4.1 percent of after-tax income."[33] Rather than pass "massive tax reduction and simplification" that primarily benefits the "middle class" in order to combat economic inequality, the new tax bill would exacerbate economic inequality.

Taking into account the traditional areas of fiscal policymaking as a whole—the failed infrastructure proposal, the failed budget proposals, the failed effort to "repeal and replace" the ACA, and the passed tax cut that required "letting the tax writers get this deal done" and that ultimately benefited the wealthy over the "middle class"—the Reagan-era apparatus and its principals significantly limited Trump's control during the critical period of unified party control of the government. Further revealing both the new president's limited control and his surprise at the difficulties of governance, Trump himself confessed during his first year, "This is more work than in my previous life. I thought it would be easier."[34]

* * *

At the same time that the Reagan-era apparatus and its principals limited the president's control in the traditional areas of fiscal policymaking, Trump worked to expand his control over trade policy in implementing a sweeping, unilateral tariff program that increasingly became an important component of fiscal policy. Here too, however, the Reagan-era apparatus and its principals initially limited the president's control.

Before the Great Depression, the tariff—a tax on the import or export of goods—was the federal government's primary revenue source, making it a key component of fiscal policy and one that Congress largely dominated. That old tariff system collapsed when the Smoot-Hawley Tariff Act of 1930—the last general tariff legislation—set exceptionally high rates during the Great Depression, which led to retaliatory tariffs from other countries and deepened the economic downturn. In response, Franklin Roosevelt oversaw the passage and implementation of the Reciprocal Trade Agreements Act of 1934, which initiated the creation of a president-dominated, non-revenue–based tariff system. In particular, the RTAA delegated authority to the president to unilaterally negotiate and implement reciprocal trade agreements that reduced tariff rates within preset parameters. Roosevelt then delegated that authority to the State Department, which operated with an institutional bias toward expanding trade and lowering tariff rates independent of any impact on revenue. This removed the tariff—which generated less than 1 percent of federal revenue by the end of the Roosevelt administration—as a key component of fiscal policy.

Following the RTAA's initial separation of fiscal policy and trade policy, two key laws contributed to the further restructuring of the president-dominated, non-revenue–based tariff system. First, the Trade Expansion Act of 1962 delegated increased authority to the president to unilaterally negotiate and implement trade agreements that reduced tariff rates within new preset parameters; it granted the president authority to adjust imports if, based on the determination of the Department of Commerce, the continuation of the existing policy would "threaten to impair the national security"; and it granted the president authority to create the Office of Special Trade Representative within the Executive Office of the President. The latter development shifted control of trade policy to the STR—later renamed the United States Trade Representative—due to the belief that the State Department had been too focused on promoting diplomatic objectives over commercial interests in overseeing the RTAA. Second, the Trade Act of 1974 established a "fast track" process that expedited and restricted congressional voting on presidential proposals concerning non-tariff barrier agreements; it granted the president authority to impose temporary tariffs if the US International Trade Commission—an independent agency created in 1916—determined that the importation of certain goods was a "substantial cause or threat of serious injury" to a domestic industry; and it granted the USTR the authority to suspend trade agreements or impose import restrictions if a trading partner was "violating trade agreement commitments or engaging in discriminatory or unreasonable practices that burden or restrict U.S. commerce."[35]

This president-dominated—or relatively centralized—trade policy apparatus that Trump inherited in 2017 stood in stark contrast to the relatively decentralized public-finance apparatus. Even with substantial legal authority to act unilaterally, however, Trump initially struggled to develop and implement a tariff program to restructure trade policy. This was due in large part to the president's ineffective use of the appointment power. In particular, Trump appointed Peter Navarro, an academic economist with no previous experience in government, to serve as director of the National Trade Council, a new institution. He appointed Robert Lighthizer, who had served as a deputy US trade representative during the Reagan administration, to serve as USTR. And he appointed Wilbur Ross, a businessman with no previous experience in government, to serve as secretary of commerce.[36] All three appointees supported the president's desire to restructure trade policy. For example, nearly a decade earlier, Lighthizer had criticized "liberal elites" who "embrace unbridled free trade, even as it helps China become a superpower," and he had called for the return of the pre–New Deal, "overtly protectionist" Republican Party that had backed the "best traditions of American conservatism."[37]

In contrast to these appointments in support of restructuring trade policy, Trump made an on-the-spot decision in appointing Gary Cohn—a strong supporter of free trade—to serve as director of the National Economic Council. The president-elect also granted the new NEC director supervision over the entire economic-policymaking process, promising, "Of course, it'll be however you want it to run. We're going to do such great things." Making clear the lack of planning for this appointment, Reince Priebus, the incoming chief of staff, remarked to Trump afterward, "Shouldn't we talk about this? . . . Shouldn't we have a conversation before we offer a job like this?"[38]

Once in office, the NEC director worked with other free-trade supporters to undercut the primary trade-policy principals and the president's own strong desire to restructure the policy domain. In a memo during the first year, Navarro informed the president, "It is impossible to get a trade action to your desk for consideration in a timely manner" due to three key administrative obstacles. First, "any proposed executive action on trade that moves through the Staff Secretary process is highly vulnerable to dilution, delay or derailment." Second, the NEC director "has amassed a large power base in the West Wing" and is "fundamentally opposed to the Trump trade agenda." Third, "Treasury Secretary Mnuchin is part of Cohn's 'Wall Street Wing,' which has effectively blocked or delayed every proposed action on trade."[39] Trump himself also made clear the difficulty that he had encountered in gaining control over administration, complaining to advisers, "[This is] not what I've asked for the last six months. . . . I want tariffs. . . . I want someone to bring me some tariffs."[40] Going further, he yelled at another adviser, "What the fuck are you stalling for?"[41]

Reinforcing these obstructionist tactics in general, the NEC director worked from the start to weaken the new, protectionist-oriented National Trade Council, which Trump had created within the EOP to advise "on innovative strategies in trade negotiations."[42] Navarro, the founding director of the NTC, complained to the president, "Are you aware that under pressure from the Cohn faction, I was demoted on Day One from Assistant to Deputy, given zero staff on trade, went almost three weeks without an office and have had no direct access to the Oval Office?"[43] In mid 2017 John Kelly, the president's new chief of staff, also supported this obstructionist process in placing the new NTC—rebranded in April as the Office of Trade and Manufacturing Policy—under the oversight of the NEC.[44]

With "Cohn's 'Wall Street Wing'" having "effectively blocked or delayed every proposed action on trade" during the first year, it became clear that the restructuring of trade policy—which Trump had pledged to make "a signature feature of my presidency"—required, at minimum, the appointment of a new NEC director. This finally occurred in early 2018 due largely to the president's own prioritization of the issue. Revealing the reason for Cohn's departure and underscoring its significance, the *New York Times* reported, "[The NEC director's] decision to leave came as he seemed poised to lose an internal struggle over Mr. Trump's plan to impose large tariffs. . . . It leaves Mr. Trump surrounded primarily by advisers with strong protectionist views who advocate the types of aggressive trade measures, like tariffs, that Mr. Trump campaigned on but that Mr. Cohn fought inside the White House."[45] Trump himself also confirmed the significance of the NEC director's departure and his own initial ineffective use of the appointment power in remarking to Cohn, "Everyone wants your position. I made a huge mistake giving it to you."[46]

Finally, with substantial statutory authority to act unilaterally, with the responsive trade principals in place and supporting the return of the "overtly protectionist" Republican Party, and with the key obstructionist public-finance principal circumvented, Trump initiated the most sweeping, unilateral tariff program in support of restructuring trade policy since the creation of the president-dominated system. This unfolded in three key steps in 2018. First, in February Trump imposed a four-year, 30 percent tariff on certain solar products and a three-year, 50 percent tariff on washing machines. Second, in March Trump imposed an indefinite 10 percent tariff on aluminum imports from most countries and an indefinite 25 percent tariff on steel imports from most countries. Third, in July Trump launched a three-stage program of tariffs on goods from China: in stage one, he imposed an indefinite 25 percent tariff on 818 Chinese goods, effective in July; in stage two, he imposed an indefinite 25 percent tariff on 279 additional Chinese goods, effective in August; and in stage three, he imposed an initial 10 percent tariff on 5,745 additional Chinese goods, effective in September and the indefinite tariff then increased to 25 percent in early 2019. For context on the significance of these moves, the US tariff rate averaged only 3.4 percent in 2017.[47]

In working to restructure trade policy, the president's sweeping, unilateral tariff program not only substantially raised tariff rates and extended tariff coverage but also increased the tariff's role as a revenue source, thereby making it an increasingly important component of fiscal policy once again. In particular, tariff revenue increased from $19 billion during the first half of fiscal year 2018 to $36 billion during the first half of fiscal year 2019, a growth of 87 percent in one year.[48] Trump himself also repeatedly praised the use of tariffs as a new revenue source. In late 2018 he tweeted, "Billions of Dollars are pouring into the coffers of the U.S.A. because of the Tariffs being charged to China, and there is a long way to go. If companies don't want to pay Tariffs, build in the U.S.A. Otherwise, let's just make our Country richer than ever before!"[49]

Despite Trump's frequent claim that the tariffs were "being charged to China," tariffs on imported goods are actually domestic taxes and tend to be regressive, meaning that the president's tariff program operated as a tax increase that primarily harmed lower- and middle-income taxpayers, and it followed the 2017 tax cut that primarily benefited the wealthy. By most accounts the tariff program also hurt the US economy overall, meaning it failed to generate "new wealth" that would "improve the quality of life for all Americans." Even worse, the new tariffs threatened to more than offset the temporary tax cut for many Americans. As the *New York Times* reported,

> President Trump's tax cuts provided a temporary jolt to the United States economy by putting more money into taxpayers' pockets. The tariffs that Mr. Trump has grown so fond of may have the opposite effect.
>
> Two new analyses show that the tariffs Mr. Trump is using to punish China, Mexico, Europe and other governments would more than wipe out any gains from his $1.5 trillion tax cut for low- and middle-income earners, leaving them with less money to spend into a consumer-driven economy. Higher earners would fare only slightly better, with their tax gains significantly eroded but not entirely washed away.
>
> The potential for Mr. Trump's tariffs to nullify his signature tax cut shows how the president's trade war could undermine his biggest selling point going into his 2020 re-election campaign: a strong economy.[50]

Relatedly, the tariff program failed to generate widespread support. Gary Cohn, the former NEC director remarked publicly a year after leaving office, "The president needs a win" but "tariffs don't work. If anything, they hurt the economy."[51] Cohn's successor as NEC director, Larry Kudlow, then broke with the president's key claim—that the tariffs are "being charged to China"—admitting publicly that "both sides will suffer on this."[52]

* * *

The case study analysis here shows that Trump's move to address rising economic inequality through a sweeping, unilateral tariff program initiated the partial restructuring of fiscal policymaking, but for the most part the established, gradually failing Reagan-era apparatus and its principals limited Trump's control during his first two years in office. First, in never providing a detailed infrastructure proposal, in developing budget proposals that were some of "the least relevant in decades," in never providing a detailed proposal that "fully repeals Obamacare and replaces it," and in keeping the president on the sidelines in developing and passing the 2017 tax cut and instead "letting the tax writers get this deal done," the Reagan-era apparatus and its principals limited Trump's control during the critical period of unified party control of the government. Second, in overseeing the creation of the National Trade Council, in appointing responsive trade principals—the NTC director, the USTR, and the secretary of commerce—and in working to restructure trade policy through the use of a sweeping, unilateral tariff program, all of which helped to make the tariff an increasingly important component of fiscal policy once again and thereby initiated the partial restructuring of the policy domain, Trump strengthened his control. However, in employing an obstructionist process of "dilution, delay or derailment" during the first year that "effectively blocked or delayed every proposed action on trade" rather than working with the president to develop a more effective program and secure it in statute, all of which resulted in the implementation of a unilaterally reversible program that failed to generate "new wealth" and instead ensured that "both sides will suffer," the Reagan-era apparatus and its principals further limited Trump's control during the critical period of unified party control of the government.

THE LIMITS OF TRUMP'S CONTROL IN THE SUBDOMAIN OF MONETARY POLICY

As with the subdomain of fiscal policy, Donald Trump assumed office in 2017 with unified party control of the government and what appeared to be a strong desire to change the established course in the subdomain of monetary policy. The Republican Party platform declared, "Democrats tell us that we should accept the new normal of a slow-growing economy. The consequences are too dire to ever accept that: President Obama . . . will set a record of being the first modern president ever to leave office without a single calendar year of three percent economic growth."[53] Going further, Trump himself implicitly pledged to radically alter the Fed's management of the economy in declaring during the campaign, "We're bringing GDP . . . up to 4 percent. And I actually think we can go higher than 4 percent. I think you can go to 5 percent or 6 percent."[54]

Despite this pledge to change course, the Reagan-era apparatus and its principals significantly limited Trump's control, especially during the critical period of unified party control of the government. This process began when, as a candidate, Trump attacked the Federal Reserve for attempting to support the economy during the Obama administration. "They're keeping the [interest] rates down so that everything else doesn't go down," he complained. "We have a very false economy."[55] Trump then directly criticized Fed Chair Janet Yellen, remarking, "I think she should be ashamed of herself."[56] After the election, however, Trump immediately accepted the Reagan-era "hands off the Fed" approach, no doubt based on the recommendation of his public-finance principals. In fact, rather than attack the Fed chair, Trump commented during his first year that Yellen was "absolutely a spectacular person," who has served "with dedication and devotion."[57]

In shifting from publicly attacking the independent central bank to adopting the Reagan-era "hands off the Fed" approach, the new president immediately provided support for the established course of monetary policy. After raising short-term interest rates twice during the end of the Obama administration—once in 2015 and again in 2016—the Yellen-led Fed raised short-term interest rates three times during the first year of the Trump administration, and the president remained quiet on the subject each time.

Trump also selected governors during his first year who supported the established course of monetary policy and the Fed's prioritization of "price stability" more generally. He first appointed Randal Quarles, a former George W. Bush administration official who, as the New York Times reported, was "expected to favor raising interest rates." He then appointed Jerome—or Jay—Powell, an Obama-appointee already on the Fed, to serve as chair, beginning in February 2018.[58] The latter appointment was a partial innovation. On the one hand, declining to reappoint Janet Yellen broke with recent practice, and appointing a lawyer rather than an economist as her replacement broke with recent practice even further. On the other hand, Powell had served on the Fed since 2012, and he had pushed Fed Chair Ben Bernanke to take the "off-ramp" from quantitative easing before reaching the "goal of jump-starting the job market." Based on his record while serving on the Yellen-led Fed, it was widely believed that he would continue to increase interest rates and prioritize low inflation. As the Times reported in late 2017, Powell "is expected to stay the course on monetary policy."[59]

Further supporting the established course notwithstanding the president's partial innovation in appointing a lawyer, the new Fed chair himself quickly hired two highly experienced economists as his top advisers—Jon Faust, who had served as a senior adviser to both Ben Bernanke and Janet Yellen, and Antulio Bomfim, who had worked for more than a decade under Alan Greenspan.[60]

Taking into account all of these developments, Trump failed during his first year to restructure the Reagan-era public-finance apparatus, which contributed to his failure both to change the established course of monetary policy and—like Obama—to generate economic growth of even 3 percent, much less the pledged growth of 4 to 6 percent. In particular, the Yellen-led Fed continued to raise interest rates in 2017; with that restrictive monetary policy in effect, the economy grew by only 2.3 percent, the same average level per year as during

Obama's second term. Making clear the tension between the established course of monetary policy and the president's pledge to radically alter the government's management of economy, the *New York Times* reported, "[President] Trump and [the Fed] appear to be headed toward a collision, albeit in slow motion. Mr. Trump has said repeatedly that he is determined to stimulate faster growth while the central bank, for its part, is indicating that it will seek to restrain any acceleration in economic activity."[61]

* * *

In response to the failure to reach even 3 percent economic growth, Trump launched a public and—for the Reagan era—unprecedented attack on the Fed during his second year. At the same time, the public-finance principals downplayed that attack and continued to recommend the appointment of conventional Fed governors, undercutting the president's control.

Similar to the appointments of Powell and Quarles during his first year, Trump appointed Michelle Bowman and Richard Clarida during his second year, both of whom had served in the George W. Bush administration and were expected to support the established course of monetary policy. The *New York Times* reported, for example, that Clarida was "unlikely to radically pull the central bank away from its gradual approach to raising interest rates."[62] After the final interest rate increase in 2017, the *Times* also reported that Fed "officials still expect to raise rates three times next year."[63] But despite reports that the Fed would continue to raise interest rates in 2018 and that his own appointees—the new chair and three governors—would support that policy, the president appeared surprised when this actually happened. Revealing his limited understanding of monetary policy and his ineffective use of the appointment power, Trump later explained, "We have a Fed that keeps raising interest rates . . . and this was not what I thought we had."[64]

In stark contrast to his unintended support of the Fed through his ineffective use of the appointment power during his first two years, Trump abandoned the Reagan-era "hands off the Fed" approach during his second year. This occurred in three stages of increasing intensity in response to the Fed's continued—and from the president's perspective, unexpected and undesired—tightening of monetary policy.

First, the Powell-led Fed increased the short-term interest rate twice during the initial half of 2018—once in March and again in June. Confirming the continuity in policy, the new Fed chair announced after the interest rate increase in March, "This decision marks another step in the ongoing process of gradually scaling back monetary policy accommodation."[65] Most importantly, this was the Fed's first interest rate increase following the passage of the 2017 tax cut, meaning that the restrictive monetary policy was now working to offset the Trump administration's expansionary fiscal policy. In response, Trump publicly criticized the Fed for the first time as president, remarking in July, "I don't like all of this work that we're putting into the economy and then I see rates going up. I am not happy about it."[66]

Second, the Powell-led Fed increased the short-term interest rate in September. Confirming once again the continuity in policy, the Fed chair announced, "This action reflects the strength we see in the economy and is one more step in the process that we began almost three years ago of gradually returning interest rates to more normal levels." Powell also confirmed that while "fiscal policy is boosting the economy," the Fed's current "projections show gradual interest rate increases continuing . . . through 2020," meaning an increasingly restrictive monetary policy would continue to offset the Trump administration's expansionary fiscal policy.[67] In response, Trump went further in his public critique of the independent central bank, remarking the following month, "I think the Fed is making a mistake. They are so tight."[68]

Third, the Powell-led Fed raised the short-term interest rate in December. Addressing the reason for increasing the short-term interest rate four times in 2018 instead of three times as originally planned, the Fed chair explained that "the economy was somewhat more robust than expected, and this led to a slightly faster pace of policy normalization," meaning a more restrictive monetary policy was necessary to offset the "fiscal stimulus adopted near the start of the year [that] was larger and more front-end loaded than most had anticipated."[69] The Fed's restrictive monetary policy then contributed to a major downturn in the stock market, which experienced its worst year since the Great Recession.[70] In response, Trump began to discuss possibly firing the Fed chair, admitting privately that Powell's appointment was "one of the worst choices I've ever made," and complaining publicly that "the only problem our economy has is the Fed."[71]

While Trump abandoned the "hands of the Fed" approach in repeatedly attacking the central bank, the public-finance principals downplayed these attacks rather than work with the president to restructure the Fed in an effort to boost economic growth. After the first attack in response to the March and June interest rate increases, Treasury Secretary Mnuchin announced, "We as an administration absolutely support the independence of the Fed, and the president's made it clear that this is the Fed's decision."[72] After the attack in response to the September interest rate increase, NEC Director Kudlow explained, "[The president] knows the Fed is independent, and he respects that."[73] After the attack in response to the December interest rate increase, Budget Director Mick Mulvaney remarked that the president understands that he "doesn't have the ability" to fire the Fed chair and "tension between the president and an independent Fed is traditional as part of our system."[74]

The combination of the public-finance principals downplaying Trump's attacks and continuing to recommend the appointment of conventional Fed governors contributed to the president's failure both to change the established course of monetary policy and—like Obama—to generate economic growth of even 3 percent, much less the pledged growth of 4 to 6 percent. In particular, the Fed raised interest rates four times in 2018, and with that restrictive monetary policy in effect—and increasingly counteracting the expansionary fiscal policy—the economy grew by only 2.9 percent based on publicly available data at the time. Further underscoring the president's ineffective use of the appointment power to gain control over the Fed, the *New York Times* reported, "All four of the Fed governors [Trump] selected voted in favor of rate increases [in 2018], including Mr. Powell, Richard Clarida, Randal Quarles and Michelle Bowman."[75] Even more revealing, Trump himself complained after appointing four of the five sitting members, "We have people on the Fed that really weren't—they're not my people" and "they certainly didn't listen to me."[76]

* * *

The case study analysis here shows that Trump's move to address slow economic growth through the abandonment of the "hands off the Fed" approach initiated the partial restructuring of monetary policymaking, but for the most part the established, gradually failing Reagan-era apparatus and its principals limited Trump's control during his first two years in office. First, in recommending the appointment of conventional Fed governors that were "expected to favor raising interest rates," and in urging the president to maintain the "hands off the Fed" approach, all of which contributed to economic growth of only 2.3 percent in 2017 rather than "[bringing] GDP . . . up to 4 percent" and possibly "5 percent or 6 percent," the Reagan-era apparatus and its principals limited Trump's control during the critical period of unified party control of the government. Second, in breaking with the "hands off the Fed" approach during his second year, Trump moved to strengthen his control. In continuing to recommend the appointment of conventional Fed governors, however, and in downplaying the attack on the Fed rather than working with the president to develop and pass legislation to formally change the Fed's governing objective and/or weaken its independence, all of which contributed to economic growth of only 2.9 percent in 2018, the Reagan-era apparatus and its principals further limited Trump's control during the critical period of unified party control of the government.

Altogether, the case study analysis of fiscal policymaking and monetary policymaking in this chapter shows that Trump's move to address the new problems of rising economic inequality and slowing economic growth initiated the partial restructuring of the domain of public finance, but for the most part the established, gradually failing Reagan-era apparatus and its principals limited Trump's control. Further revealing the limits of Trump's control more generally, Steve Bannon, the president's chief strategist, declared in early 2017 that the Trump administration was in a battle for the "deconstruction of the administrative state." Later that year, however, Bannon acknowledged, "In the 48 hours after we won, there's a fundamental decision that was made. You might call it the original sin of the administration. We embraced the establishment. I mean, we totally embraced the establishment. . . . 'Cause ya had to staff a government."[77] Even more notable, when asked in 2019 what his "one do-over as president" would be if given the opportunity, Trump himself confessed, "Well, it would be personnel."[78]

14. Conclusion

The central argument of this book is that presidential control over administration is a foundational component of policymaking and operates as a historical variable. By "foundational component of policymaking," I mean that control over administration is often one of the first and most important requirements for the president to shift policy in a substantial and durable way, even in cases when the president has significant congressional support and popular support. By "operates as a historical variable," I mean that although the Constitution vests the executive power in a single president of the United States, control over the administrative apparatus for a given policy domain often varies significantly in practice from one president to the next.

The new historical approach developed here builds upon the contributions of the three leading approaches to studying the presidency and policymaking and also addresses some of their key limitations. The standard application of the unitary executive framework overlooks the fact that presidential control over administration often operates as a historical variable. The standard application of the principle-agent framework overlooks the fact that presidential control over administration often operates as a historical variable that incorporates the interaction of multiple administrative institutions. And the standard application of the political time framework overlooks the fact that presidential control over administration often operates as a historical variable within individual policy domains.

To explain the different configurations of presidential control over administration that recur throughout history and to test the theory, this book proceeded in five parts:

In Part I, chapter 2 presented a new theory of historical variation in presidential control. It explained why several key restrictions (time, knowledge, and the structure of government) and two key incentives (maintaining acceptable performance and implementing preferred policies) vary in response to the severity of the problem in the policy domain and the prioritization of that problem. These factors in turn largely determine whether the president accepts the established approach in managing the policy domain or works to restructure that approach. The theory also addressed two intermediary processes: overseeing the gradually failing approach or working to secure the newly established approach, the latter of which tends to incorporate an additional key restriction (party continuity) and an additional key incentive (implementing a predecessor's preferred policies). The chapter then reviewed the four configurations of presidential control that recur in succession: collapse, innovation, stabilization, and constraint.

In Part II, chapter 3 presented a quantitative overview of historical variation in public-finance problems, prioritization, administration, and policy. This provided an initial test of the theory of historical variation in presidential control by showing that public-finance administration and policy are closely connected and change in relation to historical variation in public-finance problems and prioritization. In particular, the quantitative overview provided support for the following three key findings:

First, in response to the Great Depression, an exceptionally severe and highly prioritized problem, Franklin Roosevelt oversaw the creation of both the centralized New Deal–era public-finance apparatus and the New Deal–era policy parameters. On the fiscal front, the established New Deal–era policies included a growing and structurally balanced budget that generally operated as the primary economic-stabilization instrument; a highly progressive tax system; and an unrestricted general spending system and growing Social Security spending. On the monetary front, the established New Deal–era policy included a "managed currency" that generally operated as a secondary economic-stabilization instrument in support of promoting "maximum employment." These fiscal and monetary policies in turn supported the creation and continuation of a relatively fast-growing economy with a relatively equitable distribution of income and wealth.

Second, in response to the Great Inflation, an exceptionally severe and highly prioritized problem, Ronald Reagan oversaw the creation of both the decentralized Reagan-era public-finance apparatus and the Reagan-era policy parameters. On the fiscal front, the established Reagan-era policies included a steady and structurally unbalanced budget that generally operated as a secondary economic-stabilization instrument; a supply-side (or less progressive) tax system; and a restricted general spending system and steady Social Security spending. On the monetary front, the established Reagan-era approach included a "fine-tuned" monetary policy that generally operated as the primary economic-stabilization instrument in support of promoting "price stability." These fiscal and monetary policies in turn supported the creation and continuation of a relatively slow-growing economy with a relatively inequitable distribution of income and wealth.

Third, relative to the Great Depression and the Great Inflation, the Great Recession was neither an exceptionally severe problem nor a highly prioritized problem for a sustained period, which prevented the restructuring of the policy domain.

Part III presented case studies that traced the historical variation in presidential control during the New Deal era. The analysis proceeded in four steps. Chapter 4 initially traced the creation of the decentralized New Era apparatus and then traced the process of the established, gradually failing New Era apparatus and its principals in limiting Herbert Hoover's control. Chapter 5 traced the process of Franklin Roosevelt strengthening his control in restructuring the policy domain in response to the Great Depression. Chapter 6 traced the process of Harry Truman relinquishing much of his control to Roosevelt in working to secure the newly restructured policy domain. Chapter 7 traced the process of the established, relatively stable New Deal–era apparatus and its principals in limiting Dwight Eisenhower's control.

Part IV presented case studies that traced the historical variation in presidential control during the Reagan era. The analysis proceeded in four steps. Chapter 8 initially traced the preliminary collapse of the New Deal–era apparatus under Richard Nixon and Gerald Ford and then traced the process of the gradually failing New Deal–era apparatus and its principals in limiting Jimmy Carter's control. Chapter 9 traced the process of Ronald Reagan strengthening his control in restructuring the policy domain in response to the Great Inflation. Chapter 10 traced the process of George H. W. Bush relinquishing much of his control to Reagan in working to secure the newly restructured policy domain. Chapter 11 traced the process of the established, relatively stable Reagan-era apparatus and its principals in limiting Bill Clinton's control.

Part V presented case studies that traced the historical variation in presidential control during the Great Recession and beyond. The analysis proceeded in two steps. Chapter 12 traced the process of the established Reagan-era apparatus and its principals in supporting a mix of inadequate New Deal–era approaches and traditional Reagan-era approaches, all of which limited Barack Obama's control in managing the Great Recession and its aftermath. Chapter 13 traced the process of the established, gradually failing Reagan-era apparatus and its principals in limiting Trump's control during his first two years in office.

FINAL THOUGHTS ON PRESIDENTIAL CONTROL

Based on the theory and empirical analysis provided in this book, there appear to be two probable courses of change in the domain of public finance moving forward: the eventual comprehensive restructuring of the policy domain or the periodic partial restructuring of the policy domain, both of which are likely to continue to generate historical variation in presidential control.

The first probable course of change follows the model of the New Deal era and the Reagan era. Specifically, in response to an exceptionally severe and highly prioritized problem, some president will eventually take the lead in restructuring the policy domain, which will likely generate substantial variation in presidential control from one incumbent to the next.

The two eras examined here include the same sequence of presidential control—collapse, innovation, stabilization, and constraint—suggesting that the next restructuring of the policy domain will unfold along the same or similar lines, though it provides no guarantee. A new problem—such as an unprecedented coronavirus pandemic–induced recession or some other unprecedented development—could affect public-finance policymaking in a way that generates a different method of presidential control, requiring a modified theory. An examination of presidential control in a different policy domain might also require a modified theory to address the unique features of that domain. The objective here was to show that presidential control over administration is a foundational component of public-finance policymaking and operates as a historical variable, not to identify one invariable sequence of presidential control in the domain of public finance or elsewhere.

Whether or not the next restructuring includes the same sequence of presidential control, one key development supports the first, comprehensive course of change moving forward: the Great Recession and its aftermath already initiated the process of weakening the established Reagan-era approach to public finance. This was evident in Donald Trump's move to address economic inequality through a sweeping, unilateral tariff program, and his move to address slow economic growth by abandoning the "hands-off the Fed" approach. This was further evident in response to the coronavirus pandemic–induced recession.

Although it is far too early to provide a comprehensive examination, it is worth noting that the coronavirus pandemic–induced recession was more severe than the Great Recession—unemployment peaked at 14.8 percent in 2020, compared to 10 percent in 2009; and the economy shrank by 3.5 percent in 2020, compared to 0.1 percent in 2008 and 2.5 percent in 2009. It is also worth noting that Donald Trump governed with divided party control of the government in 2020, and Joe Biden governed with unified party control of the government in 2021, the latter of which was certainly important, but the Democratic congressional majorities that year were considerably smaller than those that Barack Obama had in 2009. Notwithstanding the weaker congressional support, the combination of the more severe coronavirus pandemic–induced recession and the Great Recession's earlier weakening of the established approach generated a more substantial shift in public-finance policy.

On the monetary front, the Fed maintained its inflation target during the

Great Recession and its aftermath. In comparison, the Fed modified its inflation target in response to the coronavirus pandemic–induced recession. In August 2020, Trump's final full year in office, the Fed announced that it would now target "inflation that *averages* 2 percent over time," meaning that "following periods when inflation has been running persistently below 2 percent, appropriate monetary policy will likely aim to achieve inflation moderately above 2 percent for some time."[1] Underscoring the reason for and potential significance of this change, the *New York Times* reported,

> [Fed Chair Jerome] Powell's announcement codifies a critical change in how the central bank tries to achieve its twin goals of maximum employment and stable inflation—one that could inform how the Fed sets monetary policy in the wake of the pandemic-induced recession.
>
> The Fed had long raised rates as joblessness fell to avoid an economic overheating that might result in breakaway inflation—the boogeyman that has haunted monetary policy ever since price gains hit double-digit levels in the 1970s. But the Fed's updated framework recognizes that too low inflation is now the problem, rather than too high.[2]

On the fiscal front, Bush passed a $150 billion program in 2008 and Obama passed a $787 billion program in 2009, both in response to the Great Recession. In comparison, Trump passed a $2.2 trillion program in March 2020 and a $900 billion program in December 2020; Biden then passed a $1.9 trillion program in the first months of 2021, all in response to the coronavirus pandemic–induced recession. Even accounting for growth in the size of the economy since the Great Recession, the fiscal response to the coronavirus pandemic–induced recession was considerably larger. Beginning in 2021, it was also considerably more progressive. Addressing this shift in fiscal policy, the *New York Times* reported,

> The $1.9 trillion economic aid package President Biden signed into law last month includes a wide range of programs with the potential to help poor and middle-class Americans to supplement lost income and save money. . . . Forecasters predict that the government spending—even just what has been passed so far—will fuel what could be the fastest annual economic growth in a generation this year and next, as the country recovers and the economy reopens from the coronavirus pandemic. By jump-starting the economy from the bottom and middle, the response could make sure the pandemic rebound is more equitable than it would be without a proactive government response, analysts said.
>
> That is a big change from the wake of the 2007 to 2009 recession. Then, Congress and the White House passed an $800 billion stimulus bill, which many

researchers have concluded did not do enough to fill the hole the recession left in economic activity. Lawmakers instead relied on the Federal Reserve's cheap-money policies to coax the United States' economy back from the brink. What ensued was a halting recovery marked by climbing wealth inequality as workers struggled to find jobs while the stock market soared.[3]

It is too early for a detailed assessment of the key administrative dynamics at play. But one observation is especially notable. Unlike the Clinton and Obama administrations, Larry Summers—the director of the 2009 stimulus program—held no position in the Biden administration. From the sideline he then publicly criticized the new approach, calling it "the least responsible fiscal macroeconomic policy we've had for the last 40 years."[4] In contrast, President Biden explained that the considerable size and progressive orientation of the fiscal program was essential "to the economy we're building. . . . We want to get to something economists call 'full employment.' Instead of workers competing with each other for jobs that are scarce . . . we want the companies to compete to attract workers."[5]

It remains to be seen whether the coronavirus pandemic–induced recession will ultimately generate the comprehensive restructuring of the policy domain. What has been demonstrated, however, is that moves to restructure the policy domain increase as the established approach weakens, and that the severity and prioritization of the problem—the primary driver of presidential control—is often as or more important than the level of congressional support.

The second probable course of change moving forward in the domain of public finance follows the model of the Great Recession and its aftermath. Specifically, due to the relatively effective management of the primary leading problem indicators—unemployment and inflation—presidents will periodically take the lead in partially restructuring the policy domain in response to new, but less immediately severe and prioritized problems, such as rising economic inequality and slowing economic growth. This will likely produce variation in presidential control from one incumbent to the next within a more narrowed area of the policy domain. Barack Obama used the Congressional Budget Office to his advantage in passing the Affordable Care Act, for example, whereas the CBO significantly undercut efforts to "repeal and replace" the ACA during the Trump administration. To take another example, Donald Trump worked to restructure trade policy and in the process made it an increasingly important component of fiscal policy once again—at least during his second year—potentially limiting his successor's control in that area.

Two key developments support the second, narrower course of change moving forward. The first key development is the creation of a public-finance apparatus designed to promote economic stability, a process that began during the modern period with a focus on managing unemployment in response to the Great Depression and which expanded to include managing inflation in response to the Great Inflation. As demonstrated, one of the primary drivers of restructuring the domain of public finance has been an exceptionally severe problem, but the creation of a public-finance apparatus designed to promote economic stability works to limit the severity of any problem in the policy domain. This was especially evident when the public-finance apparatus and its principals acted quickly to prevent the Great Recession from becoming another Great Depression.

The second key development supporting the narrower course of change moving forward is the expansion of the government's responsibilities. As demonstrated, the other primary driver of restructuring the domain of public finance has been a highly prioritized problem, but the expansion of the government's responsibilities works to limit the prioritization of public-finance problems relative to problems in other domains. This was also especially evident during the Great Recession, when Barack Obama continued to focus on health care reform and foreign policy.

For a more comprehensive analysis, the expansion of the government's responsibilities is evident in the growing number of executive departments created since the founding. This currently includes the State Department (created in 1789); the Treasury Department (1789); the Defense Department (1947), which built upon the War Department (1789); the Justice Department (1870), which built upon the Office of Attorney General (1789); the Interior Department (1849); the Agriculture Department (1862); the Commerce Department (1913) and the Labor Department (1913), both of which built upon the Commerce and Labor Department (1903); the Health and Human Services Department (1979) and the Education Department (1979), both of which built upon the Health, Welfare, and Education Department (1953); the Housing and Urban Development Department (1965); the Transportation Department (1967); the Energy Department (1977); the Veterans Affairs Department (1989); and the Homeland Security Department (2002). ˙

The expansion of the government's responsibilities is further evident in the creation of more than sixty independent agencies and commissions that operate with varying degrees of independence and usually have overlapping jurisdictions with one or more of the executive departments. Some of the most notable independent agencies and commissions include the Federal Reserve System (created in 1913); the Federal Trade Commission (1914); the US International Trade Commission (1916); the Farm Credit Administration (1933); the Federal Deposit Insurance Corporation (1933); the Tennessee Valley Authority (1933);

the Export-Import Bank of the United States (1934); the Federal Communications Commission (1934); the Securities and Exchange Commission (1934); the National Labor Relations Board (1935); the Social Security Administration (1935); the Central Intelligence Agency (1947); the Small Business Administration (1953); the National Aeronautics and Space Administration (1958); the Federal Maritime Commission (1961); the US Agency for International Development (1961); the US Trade and Development Agency (1961); the National Transportation Safety Board (1967); the Environmental Protection Agency (1970); the Consumer Product Safety Commission (1972); the Federal Elections Commission (1974); the Commodity Futures Trading Commission (1975); the US Nuclear Regulatory Commission (1975); the Federal Energy Regulatory Commission (1977); the Office of Government Ethics (1978); the Office of Special Counsel (1979); the Federal Retirement Thrift Investment Board (1986); the Office of Director of National Intelligence (2005); and the Consumer Financial Protection Bureau (2011).[6]

Lastly, even a brief examination of the administrative institutions in other policy domains further supports the argument that presidential control over administration is a foundational component of policymaking and operates as a historical variable. Consider the domain of national defense, most recently restructured during the George W. Bush administration. In particular, the attack on September 11, 2001, was an exceptionally severe and highly prioritized problem that discredited the established approach to national-defense policymaking and generated the following changes: the Authorization for Use of Military Force in 2001 codified a new defense aim; the wars in Afghanistan and Iraq and the broader war on terrorism shifted the established policy parameters; and the new Department of Homeland Security and the Office of the Director of National Intelligence were incorporated into a restructured national-defense apparatus. Further underscoring the restructuring of the policy domain, Bush himself later explained, "My predecessors made their decisions in a different era."[7]

Equally important, Bush's successors were constrained by the restructuring of the policy domain in response to the new problem. Leon Panetta, who served in the Obama administration as director of the Central Intelligence Agency and then as secretary of defense, made clear that the established Bush-era apparatus and its principals significantly limited Obama's control early on in managing the war in Afghanistan. As Panetta explained, "The military, or at least some of the military's leading generals, were effectively boxing in their boss." Panetta added,

> To me, the debate over troop levels took too long and was too public, especially given that I believed it was destined to end pretty much where the military

wanted it to end. Obama was a new president, a Democrat without military experience. For him to defy his military advisers on a matter so central to the success of his foreign policy and so early in his presidency would have represented an almost impossible risk. [Secretary of Defense] Robert Gates might have resigned. Worse, the war might have soured, and Obama surely would have been blamed for losing the gains Bush had fought so hard to achieve.[8]

Obama himself also complained to his top military principals regarding the war in Afghanistan, "So let me get this straight, okay? You guys just presented me four options, two of which are not realistic" and two of which are basically the same. "So what's my option? You have essentially given me one option. You're not really giving me any options."[9]

A similar dynamic played out during the start of the Trump administration. Trump repeatedly criticized the war in Afghanistan during the 2016 campaign, remarking, "When will we stop wasting our money on rebuilding Afghanistan? We must rebuild our country first."[10] But after the election Trump initially accepted the existing approach to managing the war. As he conceded in his first national speech on the subject, "My original instinct was to pull out, and historically, I like following my instincts. But all my life, I've heard that decisions are much different when you sit behind the desk in the Oval Office."[11] The new president then revealed one of the key reasons why "decisions are much different" once in office, complaining to his national-defense principals, "I want to get out. And you're telling me the answer is to get deeper in. . . . You all are telling me that I have to do this."[12]

Together with the multimethod examination of public-finance policymaking, this brief examination of national-defense policymaking indicates that Obama and Trump were constrained by the Reagan-era apparatus in the domain of public finance and the Bush-era apparatus in the domain of national defense—the domain traditionally considered the most favorable to presidential control. This further supports the argument that presidential control over administration is a foundational component of policymaking and operates as a historical variable. These cases also suggest that it would be useful for future studies to focus more closely on this key historical variable in policymaking, which is too often overlooked in favor of other variables that are more easily measured but not necessarily more important.

APPENDIX: A STATISTICAL ANALYSIS OF PUBLIC-FINANCE ADMINISTRATION

To supplement the visual examination in chapter 3, this appendix provides a statistical analysis of public-finance administration in two parts.

Table A.1 shows the model fit for each possible post-Roosevelt restructuring of the public-finance apparatus as well as no subsequent restructuring. The results are based on the following linear equation:

$$A_t = b_0 + b_1 A_{t-1} + b_2 R_t + b_3 R_t A_{t-1} + e_t$$

where

t	indexes time by year;
A_t	is the level of centralization for the public-finance apparatus;
b_0	is an intercept;
A_{t-1}	is a lagged dependent variable;
R_t	is a restructuring dummy variable, coded as 0 for the years before a given president assumes office and 1 for the years after he leaves office;
$R_t A_{t-1}$	is an interaction term, measured as the product of the restructuring dummy variable and the lagged dependent variable; and
e_t	is an error term.

Table A.1. Public-Finance Apparatus Restructuring Test

	Adj. R-squared	Ranking
No Restructuring	0.852	12
Franklin Roosevelt	—	—
Harry Truman	0.886	7
Dwight Eisenhower	0.864	11
John Kennedy	0.880	9
Lyndon Johnson	0.887	6
Richard Nixon	0.891	4
Gerald Ford	0.901	2
Jimmy Carter	0.899	3
Ronald Reagan	0.908	1
George H. W. Bush	0.890	5
Bill Clinton	0.882	8
George W. Bush	0.871	10
Barack Obama	—	—

continued

Table A.1 *continued*
Sources: ProQuest Historical Newspapers database and ProQuest Newspapers database. Annual level of centralization is measured by multiplying each institution's centralization score (ranging from one to four) and its annual level of influence, then totaling the calculation for all six institutions. Data accessed in 2017.

In keeping with the finding from the visual examination, this statistical analysis shows that the model based on Ronald Reagan's overseeing of the second restructuring of the public-finance apparatus during the modern period is a better fit than the models for the other post-Roosevelt presidents as well as the model for no subsequent restructuring.

Building upon the preceding finding, Table A.2 shows the results for a more comprehensive statistical analysis of public-finance administration based on the following linear equation:

$$A_t = b_0 + b_1 A_{t-1} + b_2 RE_t + b_3 D_t + b_4 UG_t + b_5 UG_t D_t + b_6 VS_t + b_7 VS_t D_t + b_8 W_t + e$$

where

t indexes time by year;

A_t is the level of centralization for the public-finance apparatus;

b_0 is an intercept;

A_{t-1} is a lagged dependent variable;

RE_t is a Reagan-era dummy variable, coded as 0 for the years 1933 through 1980 and 1 for 1981 through 2016;

D_t is a presidential party dummy variable, coded as 0 for Republican presidents and 1 for Democratic presidents;

UG_t is a party control dummy variable, coded as 0 for divided party control of the elected branches and 1 for unified party control;

$UG_t D_t$ is an interaction term, allowing the effect of unified party control of government to vary by the party of the president;

VS_t is a vote share variable, measured as the percentage of the president's popular vote share in the last election;

$VS_t D_t$ is an interaction term, allowing the effect of vote share to vary by the party of the president;

W_t is a war dummy variable, coded as 0 for no war and 1 for war; and

e_t is an error term.

As discussed in chapter 1, quantitative studies on the presidency—particularly those employing a unitary executive framework—often emphasize the significance of congressional support and popular support. Accordingly, the supplemental statistical analysis here incorporates several conventional political variables as well as a war variable and two problem- and prioritization-based

Table A.2. Statistical Analysis of Historical Variation in Public-Finance Administration

	Administrative Apparatus: Level of Centralization							
	(1)	(2)	(3)	(4)	(5)	(6)	(7)	(8)
Admin. Apparatus$_{t-1}$					0.9***	0.9***	0.8***	0.8***
					(0.03)	(0.04)	(0.07)	(0.08)
Reagan Era			-0.5***	-0.5***			-0.1*	-0.1*
			(0.09)	(0.08)			(0.05)	(0.05)
Democratic President	-0.1	0.2		0.7		-0.6*		-0.4
	(0.13)	(0.98)		(0.76)		(0.26)		(0.26)
Unified Government		-0.3		-0.2*		0.01		-0.003
		(0.19)		(0.08)		(0.033)		(0.0298)
Unified Gov't * Dem.		0.7***		0.3*		0.03		0.03
		(0.22)		(0.13)		(0.048)		(0.049)
Vote Share		0.01		0.001		-0.005		-0.004
		(0.013)		(0.0074)		(0.0026)		(0.0024)
Vote Share * Dem.		-0.01		-0.02		0.01*		0.01
		(0.019)		(0.014)		(0.005)		(0.005)
War		0.1		0.1		-0.06*		-0.05
		(0.09)		(0.08)		(0.031)		(0.029)
Constant	3.0	2.5	3.2	3.2	0.2	0.5	0.6	0.9
	(0.10)	(0.69)	(0.06)	(0.40)	(0.09)	(0.15)	(0.22)	(0.28)
Observations	84	84	84	84	84	84	84	84
Adj. R-squared	-0.002	0.273	0.559	0.670	0.852	0.853	0.863	0.860

Newey-West standard errors in parentheses and two-tailed p-values: *$p<0.05$, **$p<0.01$, ***$p<0.001$.
Sources: Public-finance apparatus data from ProQuest Historical Newspapers database and ProQuest Newspapers database. Unified government data from US House of Representatives, "Party Divisions of the House of Representatives, 1789–Present," and US Senate, "Party Division in the Senate, 1789–Present." Vote share data from Lyn Ragsdale, *Vital Statistics on the Presidency,* 4th ed. (Washington, DC: CQ Press, 2014). War data for 1933–1999 from Congressional Research Service, "American War and Military Operations Causalities" (2015). Data for 2000–2016 from Iraq Coalition Casualty Count (iCasualties. org). The wars in Afghanistan and Iraq are coded as 1 for years with 500 or more combined causalities.

variables—specifically, a lagged dependent variable to account for stability in administration due to the absence of an exceptionally severe and highly prioritized problem on average, and a Reagan-era dummy variable to account for change due to an exceptionally severe and highly prioritized problem.

In keeping with the finding from the visual examination, this statistical analysis shows in four steps that public-finance problems and prioritization are closely related to public-finance administration. Model 1 shows that party control of the presidency is not statistically significant, meaning the public-finance apparatus has not varied on average based on whether the president was a Democrat or a Republican; and model 2 shows that this finding holds when controlling for several variables, including the president's congressional support and popular support. Model 3 shows that historical era is statistically significant, meaning the public-finance apparatus has varied on average based on whether the president assumed office following Roosevelt and the Great Depression or Reagan and the Great Inflation; and model 4 shows that this finding holds when controlling for several variables. Model 5 shows that the previous year's public-finance apparatus is statistically significant, meaning that the public-finance apparatus has been stable on average from one year to the next; model 6 shows that this finding is robust. Model 7 shows that historical era and the previous year's public-finance apparatus are both statistically significant, meaning that the public-finance apparatus has been stable on average from one year to the next within each era, but it has differed across eras; model 8 shows that this finding is robust.

NOTES

CHAPTER 1. INTRODUCTION

1. Arthur M. Schlesinger, Jr., *The Age of Roosevelt: The Coming of the New Deal* (Boston: Houghton Mifflin, 1959), 220, emphasis added.

2. Franklin Roosevelt, *F.D.R.: His Personal Letters, 1928–1945*, ed. Elliott Roosevelt (New York: Duell, Sloan & Pearce, 1950), 360–361.

3. Franklin Roosevelt, "Wireless to the London Conference," July 3, 1933, in American Presidency Project, https://www.presidency.ucsb.edu/.

4. Frederick T. Birchall, "London Gets Message," *New York Times*, July 4, 1933.

5. Dean Acheson, *Morning and Noon* (Boston: Houghton Mifflin, 1965), 187.

6. John M. Blum, *From the Morgenthau Diaries: Years of Crisis, 1928–1938* (Boston: Houghton Mifflin, 1959), 66.

7. Blum, *Years of Crisis*, 68.

8. Donald F. Kettl, *Leadership at the Fed* (New Haven: Yale University Press, 1986), 39.

9. Herbert Hoover, *The Memoirs of Herbert Hoover: The Great Depression, 1929–1941* (New York: Macmillan, 1952), 393, 395.

10. Marriner S. Eccles, *Beckoning Frontiers: Public and Personal Recollections*, ed. Hyman Sidney (New York: Alfred A. Knopf, 1951), 289.

11. Ron Suskind, *Confidence Men: Wall Street, Washington, and the Education of a President* (New York: Harper, 2011), 378.

12. Bill Simmons, "Obama and Bill Simmons: The GQ Interview," *GQ*, November 17, 2015.

13. Bob Woodward, *Fear: Trump in the White House* (New York: Simon & Schuster, 2018), 140.

14. Woodward, *Fear*, 59, 249; Binyamin Appelbaum, "Stock Market Rout Has Trump Fixated on Fed Chair Powell," *New York Times*, December 23, 2018.

15. Caitlin Oprysko, "Trump Accuses the Fed of Making a 'Big Mistake' with Its Interest Rate Hikes," *Politico*, June 10, 2019; Appelbaum, "Stock Market Rout"; Jeanna Smialek, "Trump's Feud with the Fed Is Escalating, and Has a Precedent," *New York Times*, June 24, 2019; Donald J. Trump, @realDonaldTrump, Twitter, December 24, 2018.

16. This section builds upon a critique of the unitary executive framework and a historical analysis presented in Patrick R. O'Brien, "A Theoretical Critique of the Unitary Executive Framework: Rethinking the First-Mover Advantage, Collective-Action Advantage, and Informational Advantage," *Presidential Studies Quarterly* 47 (2017): 169–185. For critiques of earlier research on the presidency, see Stephen J. Wayne, "An Introduction to Research on the Presidency," in *Studying the Presidency*, ed. George C. Edwards III and Stephen J. Wayne (Knoxville: University of Tennessee Press, 1983), 3–14; George C. Edwards III, John H. Kessel, and Bert A. Rockman, "Introduction," in *Researching the Presidency: Vital Questions, New Approaches* (Pittsburgh, PA: University of Pittsburgh Press, 1993), 3–19.

17. Richard E. Neustadt, *Presidential Power: The Politics of Leadership* (New York: John Wiley & Sons, 1960).

18. Terry M. Moe, "The Revolution in Presidential Studies," *Presidential Studies Quarterly* 39, no. 4 (2009): 701–724, quote on 703.

19. Moe, "Revolution," 704.

20. For studies that highlight the president's first-mover advantage, see Terry M. Moe and William G. Howell, "The Presidential Power of Unilateral Action," *Journal of Law, Economics, and Organization* 15 (1999): 132–179, especially 138; Kenneth R. Mayer, *With the Stroke of a Pen: Executive Orders and Presidential Power* (Princeton, NJ: Princeton University Press, 2001), 152; William G. Howell, *Power without Persuasion: The Politics of Direct Presidential Action* (Princeton, NJ: Princeton University Press, 2003), 27; David E. Lewis, *Presidents and the Politics of Agency Design: Political Insulation in the United States Government Bureaucracy, 1946–1997* (Stanford, CA: Stanford University Press, 2003), 73; Brandice Canes-Wrone, *Who Leads Whom? Presidents, Policy, and the Public* (Chicago: University of Chicago Press, 2006), 24; William G. Howell and Jon C. Pevehouse, *While Dangers Gather: Congressional Checks on Presidential War Powers* (Princeton, NJ: Princeton University Press, 2007), 7; Matthew N. Beckman, *Pushing the Agenda: Presidential Leadership in U.S. Lawmaking, 1953–2004* (New York: Cambridge University Press, 2010), 30; Mariah Zeisberg, *War Powers: The Politics of Constitutional Authority* (Princeton, NJ: Princeton University Press, 2013), 26; David E. Lewis and Terry M. Moe, "The Presidency and the Bureaucracy: The Levers of Presidential Control," in *The Presidency and the Political System*, ed. Michael Nelson, 10th ed. (Washington, DC: CQ Press, 2014), 374–405, especially 383–384.

21. For studies that highlight the president's collective-action advantage, see Moe and Howell, "The Presidential Power of Unilateral Action," 149; Mayer, *Stroke of a Pen*, 30, 37, 143, and 152; Howell, *Power without Persuasion*, 101–102; Lewis, *Presidents and the Politics of Agency Design*, 32 and 152; Howell and Pevehouse, *While Dangers Gather*, 8–9; Eric A. Posner and Adrian Vermeule, *The Executive Unbound: After the Madisonian Republic* (New York: Oxford University Press, 2010), 26–27; Lewis and Moe, "Presidency and Bureaucracy," 383.

22. For studies that highlight the president's informational advantage, see Moe and Howell, "Presidential Power," 138; Mayer, *Stroke of a Pen*, 220; Howell, *Power without Persuasion*, 101–102; Lewis, *Presidents and Politics*, 73; Canes-Wrone, *Who Leads Whom*, 32; Howell and Pevehouse, *While Dangers Gather*, 7; B. Dan Wood, *The Politics of Economic Leadership: The Causes and Consequences of Presidential Rhetoric* (Princeton, NJ: Princeton University Press, 2007), 15; Posner and Vermeule, *Executive Unbound*, 25–26; Jeffrey E. Cohen, *The President's Legislative Policy Agenda, 1789–2002* (New York: Cambridge University Press, 2012), 81–82; Zeisberg, *War Powers*, 26; Rebecca U. Thorpe, *The American Warfare State: The Domestic Politics of Military Spending* (Chicago: University of Chicago Press, 2014), 22 and 171.

23. Mayer, *Stroke of a Pen*, 152.

24. Lewis and Moe, "Presidency and Bureaucracy," 383.

25. Cohen, *President's Legislative Policy Agenda*, 81.

26. Howell, *Power without Persuasion*, 14–15 and 101.

27. Howell, 76–100, quote on 89.

28. Canes-Wrone, *Who Leads Whom*, 24 and 32.

29. Canes-Wrone, 51–81, quotes on 75–77.

30. On Jefferson and the Bank of the United States, see John T. Holdsworth, *The First Bank of the United States* (Washington, DC: Government Printing Office, 1910), 71–72; Raymond Walters, Jr., *Albert Gallatin: Jeffersonian Financier and Diplomat* (Pittsburgh, PA: University of Pittsburgh Press, 1969), 171–173.

31. Thomas Jefferson to George Washington, February 15, 1791, *The Works of Thomas Jefferson*, ed. Paul L. Ford (New York: G. P. Putnam's Sons, 1905).

32. Albert Gallatin to Thomas Jefferson, June 18, 1802, *The Writings of Albert Gallatin*, ed. Henry Adams (Philadelphia: J. B. Lippincott, 1879).

33. Thomas Jefferson to Albert Gallatin, October 7, 1802, *Works of Thomas Jefferson*.

34. Thomas Jefferson to Albert Gallatin, July 12, 1803, *Works of Thomas Jefferson*.

35. Thomas Jefferson to Albert Gallatin, December 13, 1803, *Works of Thomas Jefferson*.

36. Thomas Jefferson to P. S. Dupont de Nemours, January 18, 1802, *Works of Thomas Jefferson*, emphasis added.

37. On Jackson and the Bank of the United States, see Robert V. Remini, *Andrew Jackson: The Course of American Freedom, 1822–1832* (Baltimore, MD: Johns Hopkins University Press, 1998); 331–373; Robert V. Remini, *Andrew Jackson: The Course of American Democracy, 1833–1845* (Baltimore, MD: Johns Hopkins University Press, 1998), 1–115.

38. Louis McLane, *Report on the Finances*, December 1831, in *Reports of the Secretary of the Treasury of the United States* (Washington, DC: Blair & Rives, 1837), 3: 224–225.

39. Andrew Jackson to Martin Van Buren, June 14, 1832, and Andrew Jackson to Allan Ditchfield Campbell, May 13, 1832, *The Papers of Andrew Jackson*, ed. Daniel Feller et al. (Knoxville: University of Tennessee Press, 2016).

40. Remini, *Jackson, 1833–1845*, 92.

41. On the two charters, see Holdsworth, *First Bank*, 58–59; Davis R. Dewey, *The Second United States Bank* (Washington, DC: Government Printing Office, 1910), 174–175.

42. Remini, *Jackson, 1833–1845*, 103; James F. Simon, *Lincoln and Chief Justice Taney: Slavery Succession, and the President's War Powers* (New York: Simon & Schuster, 2006), 23.

43. Thomas Jefferson to Albert Gallatin, December 13, 1803, *Works of Thomas Jefferson*.

44. For studies that highlight one or more of these instruments from the perspective of the president, including studies that do not employ an explicit principal-agent framework, see Neustadt, *Presidential Power*; Richard P. Nathan, *The Administrative Presidency* (New York: John Wiley & Sons, 1983); Terry M. Moe, "The Politicized Presidency," in *The New Direction in American Politics*, ed. John E. Chubb and Paul E. Peterson (Washington, DC: Brookings Institution, 1985), 235–272; B. Dan Wood and Richard W. Waterman, "The Dynamics of Political Control of the Bureaucracy," *American Political Science Review* 85, no. 3 (1991): 801–828; Peri E. Arnold, *Making the Managerial Presidency: Comprehensive Reorganization Planning, 1905–1996*, 2nd ed. (Lawrence: University Press of Kansas, 1998); Lewis, *Presidents and Politics*; David E. Lewis, *The Politics of Presidential Appointments: Political Control and Bureaucratic Performance* (Princeton, NJ: Princeton University Press, 2008). For an overview of the principal-agent literature more generally, see Sean Gailmard, "Accountability and Principal-Agent Theory," in *The Oxford Handbook of Public Accountability*, ed. Mark Bovens, Robert E. Goodin, and Thomas Schillemans (New York: Oxford University Press, 2014), 90–105.

45. Lewis, *Presidents and Politics*, 3 and 6.

46. Nathan, *Administrative Presidency*, 88.

47. Wood and Waterman, "Dynamics of Political Control," 804–805.

48. Moe, "Politicized Presidency," 240.

49. Moe, 245.

50. Moe, 261.

51. Moe, 235, 261.

52. Alexander Hamilton, James Madison, and John Jay, *The Federalist Papers*, ed. Clinton Rossiter (New York: Signet Classic, 2003), 434.

53. David A. Stockman, *The Triumph of Politics: Why the Reagan Revolution Failed* (New York: Harper & Row, 1986), 353.

54. Philip G. Joyce, *The Congressional Budget Office: Honest Numbers, Power, and Policymaking* (Washington, DC: Georgetown University Press, 2011), 58.

55. William Greider, *Secret of the Temple: How the Federal Reserve Runs the Country* (New York: Simon & Schuster, 1987), 424.

56. Richard Darman, *Who's in Control?* (New York: Simon & Schuster, 1996), 202.

57. Darman, 228–229.

58. Interview with Robert Reischauer, 2011, Bancroft Library at the University of California, Berkeley, 5, http://bancroft.berkeley.edu/ROHO/projects/debt/reischauer_robert.html.

59. George H. W. Bush, "Address on Administration Goals," February 9, 1989, American Presidency Project, https://www.presidency.ucsb.edu/; Bill Clinton, "Presidential Debate in St. Louis," October 11, 1992, American Presidency Project, https://www.presidency.ucsb.edu/. On Clinton's budget program, see Woodward, *Agenda: Inside the Clinton White House* (New York: Simon & Schuster, 1994).

60. Woodward, *Agenda*, 84.

61. Woodward, 166.

62. Bill Clinton, *My Life* (New York: Alfred A. Knopf, 2004), 521.

63. Simmons, "Obama and Simmons," emphasis added.

64. Stephen Skowronek, *The Politics Presidents Make: Leadership from John Adams to George Bush* (Cambridge, MA: Harvard University Press, 1993). For other studies that incorporate the political time framework, see David A. Crockett, *The Opposition Presidency: Leadership and the Constraints of History* (College Station: Texas A&M University Press, 2002); Kevin J. McMahon, *Reconsidering Roosevelt on Race: How the Presidency Paved the Road to Brown* (Chicago: University of Chicago Press, 2004); Keith E. Whittington, *Political Foundations of Judicial Supremacy: The Presidency, the Supreme Court, and Constitutional Leadership in U.S. History* (Princeton, NJ: Princeton University Press, 2007); Curt Nichols and Adam S. Myers, "Exploiting the Opportunity for Reconstructive Leadership: Presidential Responses to Enervated Political Regimes," *American Politics Research* 38 (2010): 806–841.

65. Skowronek, *Politics Presidents Make*, 34–35.

66. Skowronek, 34–45.

67. Skowronek, 61, 129.

68. Albert Gallatin, "Bank of the United States," *American State Papers, Finance*, 2: 351–353, https://memory.loc.gov/ammem/amlaw/lwsplink.html; Walters, *Albert Gallatin*, 237–240.

69. Bray Hammond, *Banks and Politics in America: From the Revolution to the Civil War* (Princeton, NJ: Princeton University Press, 1957), 114–118 and 197–250.

70. Richard Rush, "Report on the Finances, December 1828," in *Reports of the Secretary of the Treasury of the United States*, 2: 445, https://memory.loc.gov/ammem/amlaw/lwsplink .html.

71. Max M. Edling, *A Hercules in the Cradle: War, Money, and the American State, 1783–1867* (Chicago: University of Chicago Press, 2014), 1–107.

72. Albert Gallatin, "Bank of United States," 2: 481; Holdsworth, *First Bank*, 80–83.

73. Thomas Jefferson to P. S. Dupont de Nemours, January 18, 1802, *Works of Thomas Jefferson*, emphasis added.

74. Thomas Jefferson to John Adams, November 7, 1819, *Works of Thomas Jefferson*.

75. William J. Duane, *Narrative and Correspondence Concerning the Removal of the Deposites, And Occurrences Connected Therewith* (Philadelphia, 1838), 19.

76. Remini, *Jackson, 1833–1845*, 111.

77. Andrew Jackson, "Sixth Annual Message," December 1, 1834, *American Presidency Project*, https://www.presidency.ucsb.edu/.

78. Thomas Jefferson to George Washington, September 9, 1792, *Works of Thomas Jefferson*.

CHAPTER 2. A THEORY OF HISTORICAL VARIATION IN PRESIDENTIAL CONTROL

1. George Washington to Count de Moustier, May 25, 1789, *The Writings of George Washington*, ed. Worthington C. Ford (New York: G. P. Putnam's Sons, 1890). See also Leonard D. White, *The Federalists: A Study in Administrative History, 1789–1801* (New York: Free Press, 1965), 27.

2. Alexander Hamilton, James Madison, and John Jay, *The Federalist Papers*, ed. Clinton Rossiter (New York: Signet Classic, 2003), 434. See also White, *Federalists*, 28.

3. Hamilton, Madison, and Jay, *Federalist Papers*, 421–423, emphasis added.

4. Herbert A. Simon, *Administrative Behavior*, 4th ed. (New York: Free Press, 1997), 31–33.

5. See Richard E. Neustadt, *Presidential Power: The Politics of Leadership* (New York: John Wiley and Sons, 1960), 154–156; Paul C. Light, *The President's Agenda: Domestic Policy Choice from Kennedy to Carter* (Baltimore, MD: Johns Hopkins University Press, 1982), 17–18; Terry M. Moe, "The Politicized Presidency," in *The New Direction in American Politics*, ed. John E. Chubb and Paul E. Peterson (Washington, DC: Brookings Institution, 1985), 242–243.

6. Simon, *Administrative Behavior*, 90.

7. Harry S Truman, *Memoirs: Year of Decisions* (Garden City, NY: Doubleday, 1955), 481.

8. Gerald R. Ford, *A Time to Heal: The Autobiography of Gerald R. Ford* (New York: Harper & Row, 1979), 131.

9. Calvin Coolidge, *The Autobiography of Calvin Coolidge* (Honolulu, HI: University Press of the Pacific, 2004), 196 and 200.

10. Herbert Hoover, *The Memoirs of Herbert Hoover: The Cabinet and the Presidency, 1920–1933* (New York: Macmillan, 1952), 326–327.

11. See Neustadt, *Presidential Power*, 152–156; Light, *President's Agenda*, 18–20; Moe, "Politicized Presidency," 241–242; Andrew Rudalevige, *Managing the President's Program: Presidential Leadership and Legislative Policy Formulation* (Princeton, NJ: Princeton University Press, 2002), 25–40.

12. Simon, *Administrative Behavior*, 92.

13. Theodore C. Sorensen, *Kennedy* (New York: Harper and Row, 1965), 394.

14. Simon, *Administrative Behavior*, 142.

15. Truman, *Year of Decisions*, 87.

16. Ford, *Time to Heal*, 272.

17. Rutherford B. Hayes, *Hayes: The Diary of a President, 1875–1881*, ed. T. Harry Williams (New York: David McKay, 1964), 283.

18. Raymond Moley, *After Seven Years: A Political Analysis of the New Deal* (Lincoln: University of Nebraska Press, 1971), 110, emphasis added.

19. Simon, *Administrative Behavior*, 13.

20. Charles G. Dawes, *The First Year of the Budget of the United States* (New York: Harper & Brothers, 1923), 185. See also Simon, *Administrative Behavior*, 140–150.

21. Richard P. Nathan, *The Plot That Failed: Nixon and the Administrative Presidency* (New York: John Wiley & Sons, 1975), 40.

22. Martin Anderson, *Revolution* (New York: Harcourt Brace Jovanovich, 1988), 197.

23. See Neustadt, *Presidential Power*, 33–57; Light, *President's Agenda*, 53–56; Moe, "Politicized Presidency," 240–241; Charles O. Jones, *The Presidency in a Separated System* (Washington, DC: Brookings Institution, 1994), 52–111 and 182–280.

24. Coolidge, *Autobiography*, 234.

25. Richard Nixon, *The Memoirs of Richard Nixon* (New York: Grosset and Dunlap, 1978), 761–762.

26. On the cycles of decreasing and increasing influence, see Light, *President's Agenda*, 36–38.

27. William H. Taft, *Our Chief Magistrate and His Powers* (New York: Columbia University Press, 1916), 55.

28. "This Week Transcript: President Barack Obama," *ABC News*, January 8, 2017.

29. On the president's incentives more generally, see Light, *President's Agenda*, 62–74; Moe, "Politicized Presidency," 238–239; Rudalevige, *Managing the President's Program*, 26.

30. William G. McAdoo, *Crowded Years: The Reminiscences of William G. McAdoo* (New York: Houghton Mifflin, 1931), 194 and 198.

31. Nixon, *Memoirs*, 533.

32. Nixon, 520–521. See also Allen J. Matusow, *Nixon's Economy: Booms, Busts, Dollars, and Votes* (Lawrence: University Press of Kansas, 1998).

33. George W. Bush, *Decision Points* (New York: Crown Publishers, 2010), 440.

34. Bush, *Decision Points*, 389.

35. Henry M. Paulson, Jr., *On the Brink: Inside the Race to Stop the Collapse of the Global Financial System* (New York: Business Plus, 2010), 237.

36. Bush, *Decision Points*, 458–459.

37. Simon, *Administrative Behavior*, 112.

38. For the theoretical argument that "power may be, and often is, exercised by confining the scope of decision-making," see Peter Bachrach and Morton S. Baratz, "Two Faces of Power," *American Political Science Review* 56, no. 4 (1962): 947–952. And for an empirical analysis of institutional power as agenda control—in this case, applied to Congress—see Gary W. Cox and Mathew D. McCubbins, *Setting the Agenda: Responsible Party Government in the U.S. House of Representatives* (New York: Cambridge University Press, 2005).

39. Jimmy Carter, *Keeping Faith: Memoirs of a President* (New York: Bantam Books, 1982), 89.

40. Bush, *Decision Points*, 367.

41. For studies of policymaking that emphasize "problems" or "events" as much or more than conventional political factors, see Stephen Skowronek, *The Politics Presidents Make: Leadership from John Adams to George Bush* (Cambridge: Harvard University Press, 1993), 34–45; John W. Kingdon, *Agendas, Alternatives, and Public Policies*, 2nd ed. (New York: Longman, 2003), 90–115; David R. Mayhew, "Events as Causes: The Case of American Politics," in *Parties and Policies: How the American Government Works* (New Haven, CT: Yale University Press, 2008), 328–357; Frank R. Baumgartner and Bryan D. Jones, *Agendas and Instability in American Politics*, 2nd ed. (Chicago: University of Chicago Press, 2009), 25–38.

42. Moley, *After Seven Years*, 110.

43. Hamilton, Madison, and Jay, *Federalist Papers*, 318.

44. Lyndon B. Johnson, *The Vantage Point: Perspectives of the Presidency, 1963–1969* (New York: Holt, Rinehart & Winston, 1971), 443.

45. *Annual Report of the Secretary of the Treasury on the State of Finances for the Year 1893* (Washington: Government Printing Office, 1893), LXXI. See also James A. Barnes, *John G. Carlisle: Financial Statesman* (New York: Dodd, Mead, 1931), 307.

46. Grover Cleveland, "Second Annual Message (Second Term)," December 3, 1984, *American Presidency Project*, https://www.presidency.ucsb.edu/. See also Barnes, *Carlisle*, 360.

47. Melvin Small, *The Presidency of Richard Nixon* (Lawrence: University Press of Kansas, 1999), 59; Bush, *Decision Points*, 367.

48. Peter Baker, *Days of Fire: Bush and Cheney in the White House* (New York: Doubleday, 2013), 507–532.

49. Bush, *Decision Points*, 355–394, quote on 364.

50. Bush, 392.

51. Comment made by Rahm Emanuel at the *Wall Street Journal* conference of corporate chief executives on November 19, 2008, http://www.factcheck.org/2011/01/bum-rap-for-rahm/.

52. On "durable shift[s] in governing authority," see Karen Orren and Stephen Skowronek, *The Search for American Political Development* (New York: Cambridge University Press, 2004). On presidents reconstructing the "established regime," see Skowronek, *Politics Presidents Make*. On "durable victories" in policy and the "reconfiguration of governance," see Jacob S. Hacker and Paul Pierson, "After the 'Master Theory': Downs, Schattschneider, and the Rebirth of Policy-Focused Analysis," *Perspectives on Politics* 12, no. 3 (2014): 643–662. And on institutional change more generally, see Douglass C. North, *Institutions, Institutional Change and Economic Performance* (New York: Cambridge University Press, 1990); Jacob S. Hacker, "Privatizing Risk without Privatizing the Welfare State: The Hidden Politics of Social Policy Retrenchment in the United States," *American Political Science Review* 98, no. 2 (June 21, 2004): 243–260; Paul Pierson, *Politics in Time: History, Institutions, and Social Analysis* (Princeton, NJ: Princeton University Press, 2004); James Mahoney and Kathleen Thelen, "A Theory of Gradual Institutional Change," in *Explaining Institutional Change: Ambiguity, Agency, and Power*, ed. James Mahoney and Kathleen Thelen (New York: Cambridge University Press, 2010), 1–37.

53. Herbert Stein, "Oral History Interview," in *The President and the Council of Economic Advisers: Interviews with CEA Chairmen*, ed. Erwin C. Hargrove and Samuel A. Morley (Boulder, CO: Westview Press, 1984), 374.

54. See Jared P. Cole and Daniel T. Shedd, Congressional Research Service, R43562, "Administrative Law Primer: Statutory Definitions of 'Agency' and Characteristics of Agency Independence" (2014), 1–17, https://fas.org/sgp/crs/misc/R43562.pdf.

55. Orren and Skowronek, *American Political Development*, 113.

56. See Skowronek, *Politics Presidents Make*, 41–43; Stephen Skowronek, *Presidential Leadership in Political Time* (Lawrence: University Press of Kansas, 2008), 99–104.

57. Hamilton, Madison, and Jay, *Federalist Papers*, 434–435.

58. Hoover, *Cabinet and Presidency*, 217.

59. David McCullough, *John Adams* (New York: Simon & Schuster, 2004), 471.

60. See Skowronek, *Politics Presidents Make*, 41–43; Skowronek, *Presidential Leadership*, 99–104.

61. William Howard Taft, "Inaugural Address," March 4, 1909, *American Presidency Project*.

CHAPTER 3. PUBLIC-FINANCE PROBLEMS, PRIORITIZATION, ADMINISTRATION, AND POLICY

1. Lida R. Weinstock, Congressional Research Service, IF0443, "Introduction to U.S. Economy: Unemployment" (2020); Marc Labonte, Congressional Research Service, IF10477, "Introduction to U.S. Economy: Inflation" (2019).

2. Weinstock, "Unemployment."

3. Labonte, "Inflation."

4. Marc Labonte, Congressional Research Service, R44663, "Unemployment and Inflation: Implications for Policymaking" (2016).

5. Employment Act of 1946, Pub. L. No. 304, *U.S. Statutes at Large* (1946), 60: 23–26; Full Employment and Balanced Growth Act of 1978, Pub. L. No. 95–523, *U.S. Statutes at Large* (1978), 92: 1887–1908.

6. US Department of the Treasury, "Role of the Treasury," https://home.treasury.gov /about/general-information/role-of-the-treasury.

7. Board of Governors of the Federal Reserve System, "About the Fed," https://www.fed eralreserve.gov/aboutthefed.htm.

8. White House, "Office of Management and Budget," https://www.whitehouse.gov/omb/.

9. White House, "Council of Economic Advisers," https://www.whitehouse.gov/cea/.

10. Congressional Budget Office, "Introduction to CBO," https://www.cbo.gov/about /overview.

11. White House, "National Economic Council," https://obamawhitehouse.archives.gov /administration/eop/nec.

12. Alexander Hamilton, James Madison, and John Jay, *The Federalist Papers*, ed. Clinton Rossiter (New York: Signet Classic, 2003), 434.

13. The *New York Times* is a long-accepted source for creating data sets in political science, particularly in the fields of presidential studies and policymaking. See David R. Mayhew, *Divided We Govern: Party Control, Lawmaking, and Investigations, 1946–1990* (New Haven, CT: Yale University Press, 1991); William G. Howell, *Power without Persuasion: The Politics of Direct Presidential Action* (Princeton, NJ: Princeton University Press, 2003); Brandice Canes-Wrone, *Who Leads Whom? Presidents, Policy, and the Public* (Chicago: University of Chicago Press, 2006).

14. Andrew Rudalevige, *Managing the President's Program: Presidential Leadership and Legislative Policy Formulation* (Princeton, NJ: Princeton University Press, 2002), especially 73–76.

15. On independent agencies, see Marshal J. Breger and Gary J. Edles, *Independent Agencies in the United States: Law, Structure, and Politics* (New York: Oxford University Press, 2015).

16. Marc Labonte, Congressional Research Service, RL30354, "Monetary Policy and the Federal Reserve: Current Policy and Conditions" (2020).

17. Harold D. Lasswell, *Politics: Who Gets What, When, How* (Cleveland: Meridian Books, 1936).

18. "Are Federal Taxes Progressive?" *Tax Policy Center* (May 2020), https://www.taxpol icycenter.org/briefing-book/are-federal-taxes-progressive.

19. Thomas L. Hungerford, Congressional Research Service, R42729, "Taxes and the Economy: An Economic Analysis of the Top Tax Rates since 1945 (Updated)" (2012).

20. Jane G. Gravelle and Donald J. Marples, Congressional Research Service, R45736, "The Economic Effects of the 2017 Tax Revision: Preliminary Observations" (2019).

21. Megan Suzanne Lynch, Congressional Research Service, R41901, "Statutory Budget Controls in Effect Between 1985 and 2002" (2011).

22. Congressional Budget Office, "Economic and Budget Issue Brief: Is Social Security Progressive?" (2006).

23. Congressional Budget Office, "The Distribution of Household Income, 2016" (2019), https://www.cbo.gov/publication/55413.

24. Board of Governors of the Federal Reserve System, "Changes in U.S. Family Finances from 2013 to 2016: Evidence from the Survey of Consumer Finances" (2017), https://www.federalreserve.gov/publications/2017-September-changes-in-us-family-finances-from-2013-to-2016.htm.

25. Hungerford, "An Economic Analysis of the Top Tax Rates since 1945 (Updated)."

26. Marc Labonte, Congressional Research Service, RL31416, "Monetary Aggregates: Their Use in the Conduct of Monetary Policy" (2009).

27. Labonte, "Inflation."

28. Board of Governors of the Federal Reserve System, "Policy Tools: The Discount Window and Discount Rate," https://www.federalreserve.gov/monetarypolicy/discountrate.htm.

29. Congressional Research Service, RS21204, "Gold: Uses of U.S. Official Holdings" (2002); Craig K. Elwell, Congressional Research Service, R41887, "Brief History of the Gold Standard in the United States" (2011).

30. Hugh Rockoff, *Drastic Measures: A History of Wage and Price Controls in the United States* (New York: Cambridge University Press, 1984), 4–5.

31. Marc Labonte, Congressional Research Service, RL 30354, "Monetary Policy and the Federal Reserve; Current Policy and Conditions" (2020); Jeffrey M. Stupak, Congressional Research Service, R45723, "Fiscal Policy: Economic Effects" (2019).

CHAPTER 4. COLLAPSE: THE FAILING NEW ERA APPARATUS LIMITS HOOVER'S CONTROL

1. Herbert Hoover, *The Memoirs of Herbert Hoover: The Great Depression, 1929–1941* (New York: Macmillan, 1952), 5.

2. An Act to Establish the Treasury Department, *U.S. Statutes at Large* (1789), 1: 65–67, see § 2.

3. Andrew W. Mellon, *Taxation: The People's Business* (New York: Macmillan, 1924), 25.

4. Federal Reserve Act, Pub. L. No. 43, *U.S. Statutes at Large* (1913), 38: 251–275, see title and § 13.

5. On the creation and early operations of the Fed, see Allan H. Meltzer, *A History of the Federal Reserve: Vol. 1, 1913–1951* (Chicago: University of Chicago Press, 2003), 65–270. On the real-bills doctrine and the gold standard, see Richard H. Timberlake, "Gold Standards and the Real Bills Doctrine in U.S. Monetary Policy," *Econ Journal Watch* 2, no. 2 (2005): 196–233; Craig K. Elwell, Congressional Research Service Report, R41887, "Brief History of the Gold Standard in the United States" (2011).

6. Federal Reserve Act, § 4.

7. Federal Reserve Act, § 11.

8. Budget and Accounting Act, 1921, Pub. L. No. 13, *U.S. Statutes at Large* (1921), 42: 20–27, § 209.

9. Budget and Accounting Act, §§ 213 and 214.

10. On the creation and early operations of the Bureau of the Budget, see Larry Berman, *The Office of Management and Budget and the Presidency, 1921–1979* (Princeton, NJ: Princeton University Press, 1979), 3–15; Frederick C. Mosher, *A Tale of Two Agencies: A Comparative Analysis of the General Accounting Office and the Office of Management and Budget* (Baton Rouge: Louisiana State University Press, 1984), 35–47.

11. Budget and Accounting Act, § 201.

12. Budget and Accounting Act, § 202.

13. Charles G. Dawes, *The First Year of the Budget of the United States* (New York: Harper & Brothers, 1923), 63.

14. Meltzer, *Federal Reserve*, 65–270.

15. Dawes, *First Year Budget*, 25.

16. Report to the President of the United States by the Director of the Bureau of the Budget (Washington, DC: Government Printing Office, 1922), 91.

17. Richard E. Neustadt, "Presidency and Legislation: The Growth of Central Clearance," *American Political Science Review* 48, no. 3 (1954): 641–671, see 643–647.

18. Herbert Hoover, "Inaugural Address," March 4, 1929, American Presidency Project, https://www.presidency.ucsb.edu/.

19. David Cannadine, *Mellon: An American Life* (New York: Alfred A. Knopf, 2006), 390.

20. Herbert Hoover, *The Memoirs of Herbert Hoover: The Cabinet and the Presidency, 1920–1933* (New York: Macmillan, 1952), 218.

21. Eugene P. Trani and David L. Wilson, *The Presidency of Warren G. Harding* (Lawrence: University Press of Kansas, 1977), 40.

22. Herbert Hoover, *Report on the President's Conference on Unemployment* (Washington, DC: Government Printing Office, 1921); Hoover, *Cabinet and Presidency*, 44–46; William J. Barber, *From New Era to New Deal: Herbert Hoover, the Economists, and American Economic Policy, 1921–1933* (New York: Cambridge University Press, 1985), 16.

23. Hoover, *Cabinet and Presidency*, 58.

24. Hoover, *Great Depression*, 30.

25. Herbert Hoover, "Annual Budget Message," December 4, 1929, American Presidency Project.

26. Barber, *New Era to New Deal*, 80–86, quote on 80.

27. Barber, 118; Meltzer, *Federal Reserve*, 305–306 and 318–320.

28. This price decline measure is from October 1929 to May 1931, when the New York Federal Reserve lowered the discount rate to 1.5 percent. On failing to distinguish between real and nominal interests, see Meltzer, *Federal Reserve*, 322.

29. Hoover, *Great Depression*, 11.

30. Herbert Hoover, "Message to the Special Session of the Congress," April 16, 1929, American Presidency Project, https://www.presidency.ucsb.edu/; Douglas A. Irwin, *Clashing over Commerce: A History of US Trade Policy* (Chicago: University of Chicago Press, 2017), 371–410.

31. Irwin, Clashing over Commerce, 381.

32. Hoover, Cabinet and Presidency, 299.

33. Barber, *New Era to New Deal*, 118–120.

34. Hoover, *Great Depression*, 84.

35. Hoover, 98; Herbert Hoover, "Annual Message," December 8, 1931, American Presidency Project, https://www.presidency.ucsb.edu/.

36. Barber, *New Era to New Deal*, 125–138; Herbert Stein, *The Fiscal Revolution in America* (Chicago: University of Chicago Press, 1969), 31–38.

37. Herbert Hoover, "Statement on Signing the Revenue Act of 1932," June 6, 1932, American Presidency Project, https://www.presidency.ucsb.edu/; W. Elliot Brownlee, *Federal Taxation in America: A Short History* (New York: Cambridge University Press, 2004), 83–84.

38. Hoover, *Great Depression*, 135.

39. Hoover, 30–31.

40. Barry Eichengreen, Hall of Mirrors: The Great Depression, the Great Recession, and the Uses—and Misuses—of History (New York: Oxford University Press, 2015), 157–158; Hoover, Great Depression, 81–120.

41. Donald F. Kettl, *Leadership at the Fed* (New Haven, CT: Yale University Press, 1986), 40.

42. Charles W. Calomiris and David C. Wheelock, "Was the Great Depression a Watershed for American Monetary Policy?" in *The Defining Moment: The Great Depression and the American Economy in the Twentieth Century*, ed. Michael D. Bordo, Claudia Goldin, and Eugene N. White (Chicago: University of Chicago Press, 1998), 27–28; Meltzer, *Federal Reserve*, 358–375.

43. Kettl, *Leadership at the Fed*, 39.

44. Hoover, *Great Depression*, 199.

45. Susan E. Kennedy, *The Banking Crisis of 1933* (Lexington: University Press of Kentucky, 1973).

46. Hoover, *Great Depression*, 210–216, quote on 210.

47. Hoover, 212.

48. Hoover, 205.

49. Hoover, 210 and 212.

CHAPTER 5. INNOVATION: ROOSEVELT STRENGTHENS HIS CONTROL IN RESTRUCTURING THE POLICY DOMAIN

1. Raymond Moley, *The First New Deal* (New York: Harcourt, Brace & World, 1966), 80–85, quote on 80.

2. Moley, 81.

3. Raymond Moley, *After Seven Years: A Political Analysis of the New Deal* (Lincoln: University of Nebraska Press, 1971), 118–123, quote on 119.

4. Moley, 122.

5. Rixey Smith and Norman Beasley, *Carter Glass: A Biography* (New York: Longmans, Green, 1939), 339–342, quote on 341.

6. Franklin Roosevelt, "Proclamation 2039" March 6, 1933, American Presidency Project, https://www.presidency.ucsb.edu/; "Emergency Banking Relief; Bank Conservation Act," Pub. L. 1, *U.S. Statutes at Large* (1933), 48: 1–7; Barry Eichengreen, *Hall of Mirrors: The Great Depression, the Great Recession, and the Uses—and Misuses—of History* (New York: Oxford University Press, 2015), 228–229.

7. Moley, *After Seven Years*, 155.

8. Franklin Roosevelt, *F.D.R.: His Personal Letters, 1928–1945*, ed. Elliott Roosevelt (New York: Duell, Sloan & Pearce, 1950), 342.

9. Moley, *After Seven Years*, 159-160; "Agricultural Adjustment Act," Pub. L. 10, *U.S. Statutes at Large* (1933), 48: 31-54; William J. Barber, *Designs within Disorder: Franklin D. Roosevelt, the Economists, and the Shaping of American Economic Policy, 1933-1945* (New York: Cambridge University Press, 1996), 28-32.

10. Moley, *After Seven Years*, 159.

11. Arthur M. Schlesinger, Jr., *The Age of Roosevelt: The Coming of the New Deal* (Boston: Houghton Mifflin, 1959), 220; Herbert Hoover, *The Memoirs of Herbert Hoover: The Great Depression, 1929-1941* (New York: Macmillan, 1952), 363-368; Moley, *First New Deal*, 196-269.

12. Franklin Roosevelt, "Wireless to the London Conference," July 3, 1933, American Presidency Project, https://www.presidency.ucsb.edu/.

13. "Frederick T. Birchall, "London Gets Message," *New York Times*, July 4, 1933.

14. Barber, *Designs within Disorder*, 24-26 and 45-49; Dean Acheson, *Morning and Noon* (Boston: Houghton Mifflin, 1965), 174-175.

15. Roosevelt, *Personal Letters*, 360-361.

16. Roosevelt, 360-361.

17. Barber, *Designs within Disorder*, 47; Roosevelt, *Personal Letters*, 364.

18. John M. Blum, *From the Morgenthau Diaries: Years of Crisis, 1928-1938* (Boston: Houghton Mifflin, 1959), 67

19. Acheson, *Morning and Noon*, 187.

20. Blum, *Years of Crisis*, 66.

21. Blum, 66-77, quote on 70.

22. "Text of Dr. Sprague's Letter to President," *New York Times*, November 22, 1933; "J. P. Warburg Calls for Gold Standard," *New York Times*, November 23, 1933; Acheson, *Morning and Noon*, 190-194.

23. Blum, *Years of Crisis*, 68.

24. Barber, *Designs within Disorder*, 81-82.

25. "Gold Reserve Act of 1934," Pub. L. 86, *U.S. Statutes at Large* (1934), 48: 337-344.

26. Blum, *Years of Crisis*, 352; Allan H. Meltzer, *A History of the Federal Reserve: Volume 1, 1913-1951* (Chicago: University of Chicago Press, 2003), 415-577.

27. Marriner S. Eccles, *Beckoning Frontiers: Public and Personal Recollections*, ed. Hyman Sidney (New York: Alfred A. Knopf, 1951), 83-84.

28. Marriner S. Eccles, "Desirable Changes in the Administration of the Federal Reserve System," 1934, https://fraser.stlouisfed.org/.

29. Eccles, "Desirable Changes"; Eccles, *Beckoning Frontiers*, 175.

30. "Banking Act of 1935," Pub. L. 308, *U.S. Statutes at Large* (1935), 49: 684-723; Meltzer, *Federal Reserve*, 1: 484-486.

31. Eccles, *Beckoning Frontiers*, 230-248.

32. Allan H. Meltzer, *A History of the Federal Reserve: Volume 2, Book 1, 1951-1969* (Chicago: University of Chicago Press, 2009), 19, note 15.

33. Eccles, *Beckoning Frontiers*, 289.

34. Hoover, *Great Depression*, 393 and 395.

35. "Budget and Accounting Act, 1921," Pub. L. 13, *U.S. Statutes at Large* (1921), 42: 20-27.

36. Robert P. Browder and Thomas G. Smith, *Independent: A Biography of Lewis W. Douglas* (New York: Alfred A. Knopf, 1986), 82.

37. Eccles, *Beckoning Frontiers*, 133-134.

38. "Roosevelt Plans a Budget Surplus," *New York Times*, March 24, 1933; Browder and Smith, *Independent*, 89.

39. Browder and Smith, 92–115.

40. Browder and Smith, 115; Blum, *Years of Crisis*, 231.

41. Blum, 231–238.

42. Franklin Roosevelt, "Annual Message to Congress," January 3, 1934, American Presidency Project, https://www.presidency.ucsb.edu/.

43. Franklin Roosevelt, "Message to Congress," March 2, 1934, American Presidency Project, https://www.presidency.ucsb.edu/.

44. "Trade Agreements Act," Pub. L. 316, *U.S. Statutes at Large* (1934), 48: 943–945; Douglas A. Irwin, *Clashing over Commerce: A History of US Trade Policy* (Chicago: University of Chicago Press, 2017), 413–508.

45. *Annual Report of the Secretary of the Treasury* (Washington, DC: Government Printing Office, 1947), 370.

46. Cordell Hull, *The Memoirs of Cordell Hull* (New York: Macmillan, 1948), 352–377, quote on 375.

47. Franklin Roosevelt, "Message to Congress," June 8, 1934, American Presidency Project, https://www.presidency.ucsb.edu/.

48. Franklin Roosevelt, "Statement on Signing the Social Security Act," August 14, 1935, American Presidency Project, https://www.presidency.ucsb.edu/.

49. Roosevelt, "Message to Congress," June 8, 1934; Schlesinger, *Age of Roosevelt*, 297–315; Mark H. Leff, "Taxing the 'Forgotten Man': The Politics of Social Security Finance in the New Deal," *Journal of American History* 70, no. 2 (1983): 359–381.

50. Schlesinger, Jr., *Age of Roosevelt*, 308–309.

51. Mark H. Leff, *The Limits of Symbolic Reform: The New Deal and Taxation, 1933–1939* (New York: Cambridge University Press, 1984), 93–168, quotes on 130 and 134; Blum, *Years of Crisis*, 297–305; Lewis W. Douglas, *The Liberal Tradition: A Free People and a Free Economy* (New York: Da Capo Press, 1972); Franklin Roosevelt, "Message to Congress on Tax Revision," June 19, 1935, American Presidency Project, https://www.presidency.ucsb.edu/.

52. W. Elliot Brownlee, *Federal Taxation In America: A Short History* (New York: Cambridge University Press, 2004), 92.

53. Moley, *After Seven Years*, 367.

54. Franklin Roosevelt, "Annual Message to Congress," January 6, 1937, American Presidency Project, https://www.presidency.ucsb.edu/.

55. Herbert Stein, *The Fiscal Revolution in America* (Chicago: University of Chicago Press, 1969), 43–102; Alan Brinkley, *The End of Reform: New Deal Liberalism in Recession and War* (New York: Vintage Books, 1996), 28–34.

56. Lauchlin Currie, "Lauchlin Currie's Memoirs: Chapter III: The New Deal," *Journal of Economic Studies* 31, no. 3/4 (2004): 201–234, see 201–203.

57. Lauchlin Currie, "Memorandum on Confidence," 1934, https://fraser.stlouisfed.org/.

58. Lauchlin Currie, "Comments on Pump Priming," 1934, https://fraser.stlouisfed.org/.

59. Lauchlin Currie and Martin Krost, "Federal Income-Increasing Expenditures," 1935, https://fraser.stlouisfed.org/.

60. Currie, "Memoirs," 209.

61. Lauchlin Currie, "Recent Tendency toward a Marking up of Commodity Prices," 1936, https://fraser.stlouisfed.org/.

62. Lauchlin Currie, "Causes of the Recession," 1937, https://fraser.stlouisfed.org/.

63. Eccles, *Beckoning Frontiers*, 304.

64. Lauchlin Currie, "Causes of the Recession," 1938, https://fraser.stlouisfed.org/.

65. Stein, *Fiscal Revolution*, 91–130; Barber, *Designs within Disorder*, 102–115.

66. Blum, *Years of Crisis*, 417–426, quote on 424.

67. Franklin Roosevelt, "Message to Congress on Stimulating Recovery," April 14, 1938, American Presidency Project, https://www.presidency.ucsb.edu/.

68. Franklin Roosevelt, "Excerpts from the Press Conference," November 18, 1938, American Presidency Project, https://www.presidency.ucsb.edu/; John M. Blum, *From the Morgenthau Diaries: Years of Urgency, 1938–1941* (Boston: Houghton Mifflin, 1965), 17 and 38–39.

69. Franklin Roosevelt, "Message to Congress," January 12, 1937, American Presidency Project, https://www.presidency.ucsb.edu/; "Reorganization Act of 1939," Pub. L. 19, *U.S. Statutes at Large* (1939), 54: 561–565; Stephen Hess, *Organizing the Presidency*, 3rd ed. (Washington, DC: Brookings Institution Press, 2002), 30–31.

70. Currie, "Memoirs," 228.

71. Franklin Roosevelt, "Executive Order 8248," September 8, 1939, American Presidency Project, https://www.presidency.ucsb.edu/.

72. Stein, *Fiscal Revolution*, 168 and 204; Larry Berman, *The Office of Management and Budget and the Presidency, 1921–1979* (Princeton, NJ: Princeton University Press, 1979), 14–15.

73. Harold D. Smith, "The Bureau of the Budget," *Public Administration Review* 1, no. 2 (1941): 106–115.

74. Richard E. Neustadt, "Presidency and Legislation: The Growth of Central Clearance," *American Political Science Review* 48, no. 3 (1954): 641–671.

75. Harold D. Smith, *The Management of Your Government* (New York: McGraw-Hill, 1945), 65.

76. Douglas, *Liberal Tradition*, 76 and 131–132; Smith, *Management of Your Government*, 63.

77. Charles G. Dawes, *The First Year of the Budget of the United States* (New York: Harper & Brothers, 1923), 63; John M. Blum, *From the Morgenthau Diaries: Years of War, 1941–1945* (Boston: Houghton Mifflin, 1967), 38.

78. Franklin Roosevelt, "Annual Budget Message," January 3, 1940, American Presidency Project, https://www.presidency.ucsb.edu/.

79. Smith, *Management of Your Government*, 165.

80. John H. Wood, *A History of Central Banking in Great Britain and the United States* (New York Cambridge University Press, 2005), 231; Meltzer, *Federal Reserve*, 1: 415–724.

81. Board of Governors of the Federal Reserve System, *Twenty-Fifth Annual Report* (Washington, DC: Government Printing Office, 1939), 4–5.

82. Franklin Roosevelt, "E.O. 8734," April 11, 1941, American Presidency Project, https://www.presidency.ucsb.edu/; Hugh Rockoff, *Drastic Measures: A History of Wage and Price Controls in the United States* (New York: Cambridge University Press, 1984), 85–98.

83. "Stabilization of Prices," Pub. L. 729, *U.S. Statutes at Large* (1942), 56: 765–768, see sec. 1.

84. Meltzer, *Federal Reserve*, 1: 579–724, especially 594.

85. Eccles, *Beckoning Frontiers*, 382.

86. Franklin Roosevelt, "Annual Budget Message," January 3, 1945, American Presidency Project, https://www.presidency.ucsb.edu/; Stein, *Fiscal Revolution*, 169–196.

87. John F. Witte, *The Politics and Development of the Federal Income Tax* (Madison: University of Wisconsin Press, 1985), 110–130; Brownlee, *Federal Taxation*, 107–121.

88. William H. Cooper, Congressional Research Service Report, RL33743, "Trade Promotion Authority (TPA)" (2014).

89. Franklin Roosevelt, "State of the Union," January 11, 1944, American Presidency Project, https://www.presidency.ucsb.edu/.

CHAPTER 6. STABILIZATION: TRUMAN RELINQUISHES HIS CONTROL IN SECURING THE POLICY DOMAIN

1. Harry Truman, "News Conference," May 2, 1945, American Presidency Project, https://www.presidency.ucsb.edu/. See also Stephen K. Bailey, *Congress Makes a Law: The Story behind the Employment Act of 1946* (New York: Columbia University Press, 1950).

2. Harry S Truman, *Memoirs: Year of Decisions* (Garden City, NY: Doubleday, 1955), 494.

3. Franklin Roosevelt, "State of the Union Message," January 11, 1944, American Presidency Project, https://www.presidency.ucsb.edu/; Employment Act of 1946, Pub. L. 304, *U.S. Statutes at Large* (1946), 60: 23–26, see § 2.

4. Employment Act, § 4. See also Stephen Hess, *Organizing the Presidency*, 3rd ed. (Washington, DC: Brookings Institution Press, 2002), 43–46.

5. Employment Act, § 4.

6. Leon Keyserling, "Oral History Interview," in Erwin C. Hargrove and Samuel A. Morley, *The President and the Council of Economic Advisers: Interviews with CEA Chairmen* (Boulder, CO: Westview Press, 1984), 63.

7. Employment Act, § 3.

8. Edwin G. Nourse, *Economics in the Public Service: Administrative Aspects of the Employment Act* (New York: Harcourt, Brace, 1953), 67–75, quote on 67.

9. Marriner S. Eccles, *Beckoning Frontiers: Public and Personal Recollections*, ed. Hyman Sidney (New York: Alfred A. Knopf, 1951), 228.

10. Nourse, *Economics*, 76–121, quote on 118. See also Bailey, *Congress Makes a Law*, 25 and 167–168.

11. Gerhard Colm, "The Executive Office and Fiscal and Economic Policy," *Law and Contemporary Problems* (1956): 710–723, quote on 715.

12. Richard E. Neustadt, "Presidency and Legislation: The Growth of Central Clearance," *American Political Science Review* 48, no. 3 (1954): 641–671.

13. "Oral History Interview with Roger Jones," Harry S Truman Library, 13, https://www.trumanlibrary.gov/library/oral-histories/jonesrw.

14. Harry Truman, "Message," January 21, 1946, American Presidency Project, https://www.presidency.ucsb.edu/. See also Richard E. Neustadt, "Presidency and Legislation: Planning the President's Program," *American Political Science Review* 49, no. 4 (1955): 980–1021.

15. Employment Act, § 3.

16. Neustadt, "Planning the President's Program," 997.

17. Neustadt, 1003.

18. Neustadt, 1004–1006.

19. Neustadt, 1006–1007.

20. "The 'Fair Deal,'" *New York Times*, January 9, 1949.

21. Neustadt, "Presidency and Legislation," 657–671.

22. "Oral History Interview with Frank Pace, Jr.," Harry S Truman Library, 18, https://www.trumanlibrary.gov/library/oral-histories/pacefj1.

23. Douglas A. Irwin, *Clashing over Commerce: A History of US Trade Policy* (Chicago: University of Chicago Press, 2017), 455–508.

24. Harry Truman, "Statement by the President," August 28, 1950, American Presidency Project, https://www.presidency.ucsb.edu/; Edward D. Berkowitz, "Social Security and the Financing of the American State," in *Funding the Modern American State, 1941–1995: The Rise and Fall of the Era of Easy Finance*, ed. W. Elliot Brownlee (New York: Cambridge University Press, 1996), 148–193, especially 159–169.

25. "Oral History Interview with Leon H. Keyserling," Harry S Truman Library, 160, https://www.trumanlibrary.gov/library/oral-histories/keyserl3.

26. Nourse, *Economics*, 104.

27. "Interview with Keyserling," in Hargrove and Morley, *President and Advisers*, 82.

28. "Interview with Frank Pace, Jr.," 27.

29. "Oral History Interview with John W. Snyder," Harry S Truman Library, 1923, https://www.trumanlibrary.gov/library/oral-histories/snyder47.

30. "Interview with Frank Pace, Jr.," 64–65.

31. "Interview with Frank Pace, Jr.," 33.

32. Larry Berman, *The Office of Management and Budget and the Presidency, 1921–1979* (Princeton, NJ: Princeton University Press, 1979), 48.

33. "Interview with Keyserling," in Hargrove and Morley, *President and Advisers*, 74.

34. Harry S Truman, "News Conference," October 16, 1948, American Presidency Project, https://www.presidency.ucsb.edu/.

35. S. Nelson Drew, ed., *NSC 68: Forging the Strategy of Containment* (Washington, DC: National Defense University Press, 1994), 18.

36. Francis H. Heller, ed., *The Truman White House: The Administration of the Presidency, 1945–1953* (Lawrence: Regents Press of Kansas, 1980), 217.

37. Drew, *NSC 68*, 110.

38. Harry Truman, "Special Message," December 1, 1950, American Presidency Project, https://www.presidency.ucsb.edu/.

39. Harry S Truman, *Memoirs: Years of Trial and Hope* (Garden City, NY: Doubleday, 1956), 31–32.

40. Council of Economic Advisers, *The Economics of National Defense* (Washington DC: Government Printing Office, 1950), 15.

41. John F. Witte, *The Politics and Development of the Federal Income Tax* (Madison: University of Wisconsin Press, 1985), 137–144.

42. "Interview with Keyserling," 167.

43. Harry S Truman, "Special Message," January 23, 1950, American Presidency Project, https://www.presidency.ucsb.edu/.

44. "Interview with Keyserling," 134.

45. Truman, *Year of Decisions*, 483; "Interview with John W. Snyder," 1288–1289.

46. "Interview with Keyserling," 156.

47. Truman, *Year of Decisions*, 482 and 491.

48. Bretton Woods Agreement Act, Pub. L. 171, *U.S. Statutes at Large* (1945), 59: 512–517.

49. Treasury Department, *Annual Report of the Secretary of the Treasury* (Washington, DC: Government Printing Office, 1948), 432; Michael Bordo and Anna J. Schwartz, *NBER* Working Paper 8100, "From the Exchange Stabilization Fund to the International Monetary Fund" (2001): 1–27.

50. James W. Hurst, *A Legal History of Money in the United States, 1774–1970* (Lincoln: University of Nebraska Press, 1973), 83–84 and 125, note 211.

51. Truman, *Year of Decisions*, 487. See also Hugh Rockoff, *Drastic Measures: A History of Wage and Price Controls in the United States* (New York: Cambridge University Press, 1984), 127–176.

52. Harry S Truman, "Radio Report to the American People," January 3, 1946, American Presidency Project, https://www.presidency.ucsb.edu/.

53. Truman, *Years of Trial*, 27.

54. Truman, 27.

55. Eccles, *Beckoning Frontiers*, 434.

56. Eccles, 421.

57. Robert P. Bremner, *Chairman of the Fed: William McChesney Martin Jr. and the Creation of the Modern American Financial System* (New Haven, CT: Yale University Press, 2004), 74.

58. Defense Production Act, *U.S. Statutes at Large* (1950), 64: 798–822, see title IV, §§ 401 and 402.

59. Bremner, *Chairman*, 74–80.

60. Truman, *Years of Trial*, 45.

61. Bremner, *Chairman*, 77–79.

62. Allan H. Meltzer, *A History of the Federal Reserve: Volume 1, 1913–1951* (Chicago: University of Chicago Press, 2003), 711.

63. Bremner, *Chairman*, 80.

64. Bremner, 81–91.

65. Meltzer, *Federal Reserve*, 1: 610–612; Allan H. Meltzer, *A History of the Federal Reserve: Volume 2, Book 1, 1951–1969* (Chicago: University of Chicago Press, 2009), 93–94.

66. "Interview with Keyserling," 164–165.

67. "Interview with Keyserling," 84.

68. Board of Governors of the Federal Reserve System, "Meeting of the FOMC, January 31, 1951," 24.

69. Meltzer, *Federal Reserve*, 2.1: 41–266, quote on 48.

70. Truman, *Years of Trial*, 45; Truman, *Year of Decisions*, 42.

CHAPTER 7. CONSTRAINT: THE NEW DEAL-ERA APPARATUS LIMITS EISENHOWER'S CONTROL

1. Dwight D. Eisenhower, *The White House Years: Mandate for Change, 1953–1956* (Garden City, NY: Doubleday, 1963), 120 and 131.

2. Dwight D. Eisenhower, *The Eisenhower Diaries*, ed. Robert H. Ferrell (New York: W. W. Norton, 1981), 226.

3. Eisenhower, *Mandate for Change*, 201; Iwan W. Morgan, *Eisenhower versus the Spenders: The Eisenhower Administration, The Democrats and the Budget, 1953–60* (London: Pinter, 1990), 56–58; John W. Sloan, *Eisenhower and the Management of Prosperity* (Lawrence: University Press of Kansas, 1991), 20–25.

4. Dwight Eisenhower, "Special Message," May 20, 1953, American Presidency Project, https://www.presidency.ucsb.edu/.

5. Eisenhower, *Mandate for Change*, 202.

6. Eisenhower, 201.

7. Eisenhower, *Diaries*, 250.

8. George M. Humphrey, *The Basic Papers of George M. Humphrey as Secretary of the Treasury, 1953–1957*, ed. Nathaniel R. Howard (Cleveland: Western Reserve Historical Society, 1965), 50.

9. Eisenhower, *Mandate for Change*, 304–307, quote on 304.

10. Sherman Adams, *First-Hand Report: The Story of the Eisenhower Administration* (New York: Harper & Brothers, 1961), 156.

11. Arthur F. Burns, "Oral History Interview," in Erwin C. Hargrove and Samuel A. Morley, *The President and the Council of Economic Advisers: Interviews with CEA Chairmen* (Boulder: Westview Press, 1984), 95.

12. Sloan, *Management of Prosperity*, 133–143; Raymond J. Saulnier, *Constructive Years: The U.S. Economy under Eisenhower* (New York: University Press of America, 1991), 63–75.

13. Humphrey, *Basic Papers*, 248.

14. Burns, "Oral History Interview," 116.

15. Edward S. Flash, Jr., *Economic Advice and Presidential Leadership: The Council of Economic Advisers* (New York: Columbia University Press, 1965), 115.

16. Burns, "Oral History Interview," 98.

17. Flash, *Economic Advice*, 115.

18. Eisenhower, *Mandate for Change*, 305.

19. Herbert Stein, *The Fiscal Revolution in America* (Chicago: University of Chicago Press, 1969), 304.

20. Dwight Eisenhower, "News Conference," March 31, 1954, American Presidency Project, https://www.presidency.ucsb.edu/.

21. Sloan, *Management of Prosperity*, 85.

22. Adams, *First-Hand Report*, 154.

23. Sloan, *Management of Prosperity*, 139.

24. Eisenhower, *Mandate for Change*, 84.

25. John D. Morris, "Dodge Begins Budget Study; Stresses He Is Observer Only," *New York Times*, November 13, 1952; Larry Berman, *The Office of Management and Budget and the Presidency, 1921–1979* (Princeton, NJ: Princeton University Press, 1979), 48–50.

26. "Oral History Interview with Roger Jones," Harry S Truman Library, 101, https://www.trumanlibrary.gov/library/oral-histories/jonesrw; Richard E. Neustadt, "Presidency and Legislation: Planning the President's Program," *American Political Science Review* 49, no. 4 (1955): 980–1021, see 985.

27. Neustadt, "Planning the President's Program," 981–991.

28. Eisenhower, *Mandate for Change*, 285 and 298.

29. Neustadt, "Planning the President's Program," 991–996; Eisenhower, *Mandate for Change*, 298–304.

30. "Program for '54," *New York Times*, January 10, 1954.

31. Eisenhower, *Mandate for Change*, 286–287.

32. "Interview with Mr. Roger Jones," November 8, 1976, Dwight D. Eisenhower Library, 13–14, https://www.eisenhowerlibrary.gov/sites/default/files/research/oral-histories/oral-history-transcripts/jones-roger-497.pdf.

33. Burns, "Oral History Interview," 106.

34. Eisenhower, *Mandate for Change*, 128.

35. Burns, "Oral History Interview," 104.

36. Dwight D. Eisenhower, *The White House Years: Waging Peace, 1956–1961* (Garden City, NY: Doubleday, 1965), 309.

37. Sloan, *Management of Prosperity*, 98–101, quote on 100.

38. Sloan, 70; Edwin L. Dale, Jr., "President Asks 71.8 Billon Budget, A Peacetime High," *New York Times*, January 17, 1957.

39. Humphrey, *Basic Papers*, 238.

40. Eisenhower, *Waging Peace*, 128.

41. Humphrey, *Basic Papers*, 252.

42. Arthur Larson, *Eisenhower: The President Nobody Knew* (New York: Charles Scribner's Sons, 1968), 141; Morgan, *Eisenhower versus Spenders*, 83–98.

43. Eisenhower, *Waging Peace*, 309.

44. Sloan, *Management of Prosperity*, 143–149, quote on 147.

45. Eisenhower, *Diaries*, 352–353.

46. "Economic Report of the President," *Council of Economic Advisers* (1955), 7, https://fraser.stlouisfed.org/title/economic-report-president-45/1955-8126.

47. Walter W. Heller, "Oral History Interview," in *The President and the Council of Economic Advisers: Interviews with CEA Chairmen*, ed. Erwin C. Hargrove and Samuel A. Morley. Boulder, CO: Westview Press, 1984, 199 and 201–202.

48. Joseph A. Loftus, "Dr. Burns Favors Kennedy Tax Cut," *New York Times*, February 5, 1963.

49. Lyndon B. Johnson, "Special Message," May 17, 1965, American Presidency Project, https://www.presidency.ucsb.edu/.

50. Council of Economic Advisers, "Economic Report of the President," (1962), 46, https://fraser.stlouisfed.org/title/economic-report-president-45/1962-8133; Stein, *Fiscal Revolution*, 372–453.

51. Sloan, *Management of Prosperity*, 69–104, quote on 85.

52. Morgan, *Eisenhower versus Spenders*, 127–151, quote on 132.

53. "The 1959–60 Budget," *New York Times*, July 1, 1960.

54. Theodore C. Sorensen, *Kennedy* (New York: Harper & Row, 1965), 238–239.

55. Lyndon B. Johnson, *The Vantage Point: Perspectives of the Presidency, 1963–1969* (New York: Holt, Rinehart & Winston, 1971), 69–71.

56. "Text of Eisenhower's Budget Letter," *New York Times*, March 30, 1963.

57. Eisenhower, *Mandate for Change*, 131.

58. Eisenhower, *Mandate for Change*, 194; "Republican Party Platform of 1952," American Presidency Project, https://www.presidency.ucsb.edu/.

59. Eisenhower, "Annual Message," February 2, 1953, https://www.presidency.ucsb.ed documents/annual-message-the-congress-the-state-the-union-16.

60. Robert P. Bremner, *Chairman of the Fed: William McChesney Martin Jr. and the Creation of the Modern American Financial System* (New Haven: Yale University Press, 2004), 97.

61. Sloan, *Management of Prosperity*, 119.

62. Eisenhower, "Annual Message," February 2, 1953, https://www.presidency.ucsb.ed documents/annual-message-the-congress-the-state-the-union-16.

63. Eisenhower, *Mandate for Change*, 125–126, quote on 126.

64. Robert P. Bremner, *Chairman of the Fed: William McChesney Martin Jr. and the Creation of the Modern American Financial System* (New Haven, CT: Yale University Press, 2004), 98.

65. Bremner, *Chairman*, 93–105.

66. Paul Heffernan, "Reserve Stage Set to Get More Funds," *New York Times*, June 28, 1953.

67. Bremner, *Chairman*, 106.

68. Bremner, 107.

69. Daniel Vencill, "William McChesney Martin, Jr." in *Biographical Dictionary of the Board of Governors of the Federal Reserve*, ed. Bernard S. Katz (New York: Greenwood Press, 1992), 192–210, quote on 196. See also Allan H. Meltzer, *A History of the Federal Reserve: Volume 2, Book 1, 1951–1969* (Chicago: University of Chicago Press, 2009), 41–266.

70. Eisenhower, *Diaries*, 278. See also Meltzer, *Federal Reserve*, 2.1: 41–266.

71. Bremner, *Chairman*, 113.

72. Bremner, 110–115, quote on 115.

73. William P. Yohe and Louis C. Gasper, "The 'Even Keel' Decisions of the Federal Open Market Committee," *Financial Analysts Journal* 26, no. 6 (1970): 105–117, see 107.

74. Meltzer, *Federal Reserve*, 2.1: 244.

75. Joint Economic Committee of the United States Congress, "Hearings: Employment, Growth, and Price Levels: Answers to Questions on Monetary Policy and Debt Management" (1959), 1739–1740, https://books.google.com/books?id=DDk4AAAAIAAJ&printsec=frontcover#v=onepage&q&f=false.

76. Bremner, *Chairman*, 120–136, quote on 121.

77. Sloan, *Management of Prosperity*, 122.

78. Eisenhower, *Waging Peace*, 379.

79. Dwight Eisenhower, "Annual Message," January 9, 1959, American Presidency Project, https://www.presidency.ucsb.edu/; Stein, *Fiscal Revolution*, 354.

80. Board of Governors of the Federal Reserve System, "Board of Governor Members, 1914–Present," https://www.federalreserve.gov/aboutthefed/bios/board/boardmembership.htm.

81. Sloan, *Management of Prosperity*, 105–106.

82. Eisenhower, *Waging Peace*, 387.

83. Yohe and Gasper, "Even Keel," 107; Owen F. Humpage and Sanchita Mukherjee, "Even Keel and the Great Inflation," (Federal Reserve Bank of Atlanta: 2013), 1–23, see 8.

84. Board of Governors of the Federal Reserve System, "Meeting of the [FOMC], October 24, 1967," 34, https://www.federalreserve.gov/monetarypolicy/files/fomcmod19671024.pdf; Meltzer, *Federal Reserve*, 2.1: 523.

85. Bremner, *Chairman*, 151.

86. Allen J. Matusow, *Nixon's Economy: Booms, Busts, Dollars, and Votes* (Lawrence: University Press of Kansas, 1998), 20.

87. Craig K. Elwell, Congressional Research Service, R41887, "Brief History of the Gold Standard in the United States" (2011), 1–15, see 12–13, https://fas.org/sgp/crs/misc/R41887.pdf.

88. Richard Nixon, "Address to the Nation," August 15, 1971, American Presidency Project, https://www.presidency.ucsb.edu/; Richard Nixon, *The Memoirs of Richard Nixon* (New York: Grosset & Dunlap, 1978), 515–522.

89. Bremner, *Chairman*, 276–277.

90. Eisenhower, *Waging Peace*, 654.

CHAPTER 8. COLLAPSE: THE FAILING NEW DEAL-ERA APPARATUS LIMITS CARTER'S CONTROL

1. Richard Nixon, "Annual Message," January 22, 1971, American Presidency Project, https://www.presidency.ucsb.edu/documents/annual-message-the-congress-the-state-the-union-1. See also Herbert Stein, "The Fiscal Revolution in America, Part II: 1964–1994," in

Funding the Modern American State, 1941–1995: The Rise and Fall of the Era of Easy Finance, ed. by W. Elliot Brownlee (New York: Cambridge University Press, 1996), 194–286, especially 209–256; Herbert Stein, *Presidential Economics: The Making of Economic Policy from Roosevelt to Clinton*, 3rd ed. (Washington, DC: American Enterprise Institute, 1994), 133–207.

2. Stein, *Presidential Economics*, 147.

3. Stein, "Revolution in America," 243.

4. Richard Nixon, "Statement Announcing Measures to Be Taken Under Phase IV of the Economic Stabilization Program," July 18, 1973, American Presidency Project, https://www.presidency.ucsb.edu/.

5. There is no consensus regarding the time period of the Great Inflation. Here, I use 1973 through 1986 based on the thirteen-year-long run of a double-digit problem index. This end date matches that of Allan H. Meltzer in *A History of the Federal Reserve: Volume 2, Book 2, 1970–1986* (Chicago: University of Chicago Press, 2009), 1133.

6. Yanek Mieczkowski, *Gerald Ford and the Challenges of the 1970s* (Lexington: University Press of Kentucky, 2005), 66–67.

7. Congressional Budget and Impoundment Control Act of 1974, Pub. L. 93-344, *U.S. Statutes at Large* (1974), 88: 297–339.

8. Congressional Budget and Impoundment Control Act of 1974, § 201.

9. Congressional Budget and Impoundment Control Act of 1974, § 202.

10. Congressional Budget and Impoundment Control Act of 1974, § 201.

11. Congressional Budget and Impoundment Control Act of 1974, § 603. See also Allen Schick, *The Federal Budget: Politics, Policy, Process*, revised ed. (Washington, DC: Brookings Institution Press, 2000), 18–20.

12. Larry Berman, *The Office of Management and Budget and the Presidency, 1921–1979* (Princeton, NJ: Princeton University Press, 1979), 108.

13. Berman, *OMB and Presidency*, 108–116.

14. Berman, 118; An Act to Amend the Budget and Accounting Act, Pub. L. 93-250, *U.S. Statutes at Large* (1974), 88: 11.

15. Kenneth D. Garbade, "The Institutionalization of Treasury Note and Bond Auctions, 1970–75," *FRBNY Economic Policy Review* (May 2004): 29–45; Meltzer, *Federal Reserve*, 2.2: 831–832.

16. Richard Nixon, *The Memoirs of Richard Nixon* (New York: Grosset & Dunlap, 1978), 520–521.

17. Board of Governors of the Federal Reserve System, "Meeting of the [FOMC], August 21, 1973," 39.

18. Board of Governors of the Federal Reserve System, "Meeting of the [FOMC], October 10, 1973," 4–5.

19. Stein, *Presidential Economics*, 206. See also Allen J. Matusow, *Nixon's Economy: Booms, Busts, Dollars, and Votes* (Lawrence: University Press of Kansas, 1998), 9.

20. Stein, "Revolution in America," 237.

21. Stein, 249.

22. Gerald Ford, "News Conference," August 28, 1974, American Presidency Project, https://www.presidency.ucsb.edu/; Mieczkowski, *Gerald Ford*, 112.

23. Gerald Ford, "Address to a Joint Session of the Congress," October 8, 1974, American Presidency Project, https://www.presidency.ucsb.edu/.

24. Gerald Ford, "Address to the Nation," January 13, 1975, American Presidency Project, https://www.presidency.ucsb.edu/; Mieczkowski, *Gerald Ford*, 154–160.

25. Gerald R. Ford, *A Time to Heal: The Autobiography of Gerald R. Ford* (New York: Harper & Row, 1979), 202.

26. Ford, *Time to Heal*, 202.

27. Arthur F. Burns, "The Anguish of Central Banking," The 1979 Per Jacobsson Lecture, 691, https://fraser.stlouisfed.org/files/docs/publications/FRB/pages/1985-1989/32252 _1985-1989.pdf; Meltzer, *Federal Reserve*, 2.2: 895–900.

28. Craig K. Elwell, Congressional Research Service, "Brief History of the Gold Standard" (2011): 9–13, https://fas.org/sgp/crs/misc/R41887.pdf.

29. Ford, *Time to Heal*, 151–152.

30. Ford, 125–126.

31. Jimmy Carter, "Economic Recovery Program," January 31, 1977, American Presidency Project, https://www.presidency.ucsb.edu/.

32. W. Carl Biven, *Jimmy Carter's Economy: Policy in an Age of Limits* (Chapel Hill: University of North Carolina Press, 2002), 49.

33. Jimmy Carter, *Keeping Faith: Memoirs of a President* (New York: Bantam Books, 1982), 78.

34. Jimmy Carter, "The State of the Union," January 19, 1978, American Presidency Project, https://www.presidency.ucsb.edu/.

35. Biven, *Carter's Economy*, 199.

36. Edward Cowan, "Carter Now Seeks a Smaller Tax Cut and 3-Month Delay," *New York Times*, May 13, 1978; Stein, "Revolution in America," 263.

37. Board of Governors of the Federal Reserve System, "Meeting of the [FOMC], January 17–18, 1977," 41.

38. Meltzer, *Federal Reserve*, 2.2: 918.

39. Biven, *Carter's Economy*, 92; Meltzer, *Federal Reserve*, 2.2: 910–925.

40. Biven, *Carter's Economy*, 141.

41. Charles Schultze, "Oral History Interview," in *The President and the Council of Economic Advisers: Interviews with CEA Chairmen*, ed. Erwin C. Hargrove and Samuel A. Morley (Boulder, CO: Westview Press, 1984), 485.

42. Biven, *Carter's Economy*, 238–239.

43. Federal Reserve Reform Act of 1977, Pub. L. 95–188, *U.S. Statutes at Large* (1977), 91: 1387–1391, quote on 1387.

44. Full Employment and Balanced Growth Act of 1978, Pub. L. 95–523, *U.S. Statutes at Large*, (1978), 92: 1887–1908, quote on 1889. See also Board of Governors of the Federal Reserve System, "The Federal Reserve System: Purposes and Functions," 9th ed. (2005), 2.

45. Stein, *Presidential Economics*, 217–218.

46. Meltzer, *Federal Reserve*, 2.2: 1034.

47. Paul Volcker and Toyoo Gyohten, *Changing Fortunes: The World's Money and the Threat to American Leadership* (New York: Times Books, 1992), 166–170, quote on 167. See also William L. Silber, *Volcker: The Triumph of Persistence* (New York: Bloomsbury Press, 2012), 165–177.

48. Volcker and Gyohten, *Changing Fortunes*, 169–171; Meltzer, *Federal Reserve*, 2.2: 1037–1042.

49. Biven, *Carter's Economy*, 247.

50. Jimmy Carter, "Anti-Inflation Program Remarks," March 14, 1980, American Presidency Project, https://www.presidency.ucsb.edu/.

51. Meltzer, *Federal Reserve*, 2.2: 1049–1057.

52. Jimmy Carter, "Budget Message to the Congress," January 28, 1980, American Presidency Project, https://www.presidency.ucsb.edu/.

53. Carter, "Anti-Inflation Program Remarks."

54. Steven Rattner, "Bid to Widen Voter Support," *New York Times*, August 29, 1980; Stein, "Revolution in America," 263.

55. Biven, *Carter's Economy*, 245.

56. Michael Quint, "Volcker's 'Strict' Monetarism," *New York Times*, October 5, 1980.

57. Paul A. Volcker, "Monetary Policy," in *American Economic Policy in the 1980s*, ed. Martin Feldstein (Chicago: University of Chicago Press, 1994), 148.

58. Biven, *Carter's Economy*, 11.

59. Schultze, "Oral History Interview," 478–479.

60. Volcker and Gyohten, *Changing Fortunes*, 172.

CHAPTER 9. INNOVATION: REAGAN STRENGTHENS HIS CONTROL IN RESTRUCTURING THE POLICY DOMAIN

1. Martin Anderson, *Revolution* (New York: Harcourt Brace Jovanovich, 1988), 114–116.

2. Anderson, 116–120.

3. Anderson, 114.

4. Anderson, 124–139, quote on 125.

5. Paul C. Light, *The President's Agenda: Domestic Policy Choice from Kennedy to Clinton*, 3rd ed. (Baltimore: Johns Hopkins University Press, 1999), 234.

6. David. A. Stockman, *The Triumph of Politics: Why the Reagan Revolution Failed* (New York: Harper & Row, 1986), 2.

7. Stockman, 56.

8. Stockman, 81–99, quote on 84; Murray Weidenbaum, *Advising Reagan: Making Economic Policy, 1981–82* (St. Louis, MO: Washington University, 2005), 13–15. The CEA chair eventually contributed to the economic forecast but his influence was diminished due to the lateness of his appointment.

9. Stockman, *Triumph of Politics*, 96–97.

10. Stockman, 100–134, quote on 124.

11. Stockman, 159–178, quote on 159.

12. Stockman, 160.

13. Stockman, 223.

14. Martin Tolchin, "Reagan Challenges Report by Congress on Budget for 1982," *New York Times*, March 18, 1981.

15. Stockman, *Triumph of Politics*, 164–165.

16. Paul C. Roberts, *The Supply-Side Revolution: An Insider's Account of Policymaking in Washington* (Cambridge, MA: Harvard University Press, 1984), 1–33, quote on 5.

17. Roberts, 32.

18. Roberts, 25.

19. Ronald Reagan, *An American Life* (New York: Simon & Schuster, 1990), 231–232.

20. Stockman, *Triumph of Politics*, 84–85; Donald T. Regan, *For the Record: From Wall Street to Washington* (New York: Harcourt Brace Jovanovich, 1988), 139–162.

21. Stockman, *Triumph of Politics*, 229–230; Reagan, *American Life*, 279.

22. Ronald Reagan, "Address to the Nation on the Economy," February 5, 1981, American Presidency Project, https://www.presidency.ucsb.edu/.

23. Ronald Reagan, "Address to the Nation on Federal Tax Reduction Legislation," July 27, 1981, American Presidency Project, https://www.presidency.ucsb.edu/.

24. Dennis S. Ippolito, *Deficits, Debt, and the New Politics of Tax Policy* (New York: Cambridge University Press, 2012), 117–118.

25. Edward Cowan, "Reagan's 3-Year, 25% Cut in Tax Rate Voted by Wide Margins in the House and Senate," *New York Times*, July 30, 1981.

26. John W. Sloan, *The Reagan Effect: Economics and Presidential Leadership* (Lawrence: University Press of Kansas, 1999), 138–139 and 145–146; Iwan Morgan, *The Age of Deficits: Presidents and Unbalanced Budgets from Jimmy Carter to George W. Bush* (Lawrence: University Press of Kansas, 2009), 84; Jerry Tempalski, Department of Treasury, Office of Tax Analysis, WP 81, "Revenue Effects of Major Tax Bills" (2013), https://www.treasury.gov/resource-center/tax-policy/tax-analysis/documents/wp81-table2013.pdf.

27. This analysis is based on the data from Tempalski, "Revenue Effects of Major Tax Bills." I use the only GDP estimate provided for bills between 1940 and 1968 and the revenue effect in year four for bills after 1968.

28. Ronald Reagan, "Remarks on Signing the Economic Recovery Tax Act of 1981," August 13, 1981, American Presidency Project, https://www.presidency.ucsb.edu/.

29. Sloan, *Reagan Effect*, 148–151.

30. Stockman, *Triumph of Politics*, 353.

31. Philip G. Joyce, *The Congressional Budget Office: Honest Numbers, Power, and Policymaking* (Washington, DC: Georgetown University Press, 2011), 58.

32. Ippolito, *Deficits, Debt*, 121–125, quote on 124.

33. Regan, *For the Record*, 178.

34. Weidenbaum, *Advising Reagan*, 51.

35. Ronald Reagan, *The Reagan Diaries*, ed. Douglas Brinkley (New York: HarperCollins, 2007), 210.

36. William A. Niskanen, *Reaganomics: An Insider's Account of the Policies and the People* (New York: Oxford University Press, 1988), 296.

37. Ronald Reagan, "Statement Announcing the Establishment of the National Commission on Social Security Reform," December 16, 1981, American Presidency Project, https://www.presidency.ucsb.edu/.

38. W. Andrew Achenbaum, *Social Security: Visions and Revisions* (New York: Cambridge University Press, 1986); Edward D. Berkowitz, "Social Security and the Financing of the American State," in *Funding the Modern American State, 1941–1995: The Rise and Fall of the Era of Easy Finance*, ed. W. Elliot Brownlee (New York: Cambridge University Press, 1996), 148–193.

39. Ronald Reagan, "Remarks on Signing the Social Security Amendments," April 20, 1983, American Presidency Project, https://www.presidency.ucsb.edu/.

40. Balanced Budget and Emergency Deficit Control Act of 1985, Pub. L. 99–177, *U.S. Statutes at Large* (1985), 99: 1037–1101; Megan Suzanne Lynch, Congressional Research Service, R41901, "Statutory Budget Controls in Effect between 1985 and 2002" (2011), https://fas.org/sgp/crs/misc/R41901.pdf.

41. James C. Miller, III, *Fix the U.S. Budget! Urgings of an "Abominable No-Man"* (Stanford, CA: Hoover Institution Press, 1994), 30–50, quote on 35.

42. Balanced Budget and Emergency Deficit Control Reaffirmation Act of 1987, Pub. L. 100–119 *U.S. Statutes at Large* (1987), 101: 754–788; Lynch, "Statutory Budget Controls," 6–8.

43. Miller, *Fix the U.S. Budget*, 53.

44. Joyce, *Congressional Budget Office*, 59.

45. Ronald Reagan, "Address before a Joint Session of the Congress," February 6, 1985, American Presidency Project, https://www.presidency.ucsb.edu/. See also Jeffrey H. Birnbaum and Alan S. Murray, *Showdown at Gucci Gulch: Lawmakers, Lobbyists, and the Unlikely Triumph of Tax Reform* (New York: Random House, 1987).

46. Regan, *For the Record*, 194.

47. Stockman, *Triumph of Politics*, 235.

48. Morgan, *Age of Deficits*, 113–114.

49. Reagan, *American Life*, 335.

50. Reagan, 333–335.

51. Anderson, *Revolution*, 119–120.

52. Reagan, "Address before a Joint Session of the Congress," February 18, 1981, https://www.presidency.ucsb.edu/documents/address-before-joint-session-the-congress-the-program-for-economic-recovery-0.

53. William Greider, *Secret of the Temple: How the Federal Reserve Runs the Country* (New York: Simon & Schuster, 1987), 379.

54. Milton Friedman, "The Role of Monetary Policy," *American Economic Review* 58, no. 1 (1968): 1–17.

55. Board of Governors of the Federal Reserve, "Meeting of the FOMC, December 18–19, 1980," 61, https://www.federalreserve.gov/monetarypolicy/files/FOMC19801219meeting.pdf; Allan H. Meltzer, *A History of the Federal Reserve: Volume 2, Book 2, 1970–1986* (Chicago: University of Chicago Press, 2009), 1070–1125.

56. Greider, *Secret of the Temple*, 351–449, quote on 426.

57. Paul Volcker and Toyoo Gyohten, *Changing Fortunes: The World's Money and the Threat to American Leadership* (New York: Times Books, 1992), 175.

58. Board of Governors of the Federal Reserve, "Meeting of the FOMC, December 21–22, 1981," 22.

59. Meltzer, *Federal Reserve*, 2.2: 1086–1087.

60. Meltzer, 2.2: 1098–1131, quote on 1099.

61. Greider, *Secret of the Temple*, 478.

62. William L. Silber, *Volcker: The Triumph of Persistence* (New York: Bloomsbury Press, 2012), 215.

63. Donald F. Kettl, *Leadership at the Fed* (New Haven, CT: Yale University Press, 1986), 160, 185–186; Greider, *Secret of the Temple*, 333.

64. Volcker and Gyohten, *Changing Fortunes*, 164 and 235.

65. Kettl, *Leadership at the Fed*, 183–84; Meltzer, *Federal Reserve*, 2.2: 1068 and 1104–1025.

66. Board of Governors of the Federal Reserve, "Meeting of the FOMC, October 5, 1982," 50.

67. Peter T. Kilborn, "Volcker Suggests Federal Reserve May Shift Tactics," *New York Times*, October 10, 1982.

68. Board of Governors of the Federal Reserve, "Meeting of the FOMC, February 8–9, 1983," 32.

69. Silber, *Volcker*, 239–242, quote on 240; Greider, *Secret of the Temple*, 616–620.

70. Peter T. Kilborn, "Reagan Refuses to Join Critics of Fed," *New York Times*, May 15, 1984.

71. Board of Governors of the Federal Reserve, "Meeting of the FOMC, December 17–18, 1984," 21; Meltzer, *Federal Reserve*, 2.2: 1154–1155 and 1170–1172.

72. For a discussion of "fine tuning," see, for example, Board of Governors of the Federal Reserve, "Meeting of the FOMC, February 12–13, 1985," 44–45.

73. Paul A. Volcker, "The Triumph of Central Banking?" *The 1990 Per Jacobsson Lecture*, 3, http://www.perjacobsson.org/lectures/1990.pdf; Silber, *Volcker*, 266.

74. Volcker, "Triumph of Central Banking," 17.

75. Paul A. Volcker and Christine Harper, *Keeping at It: The Quest for Sound Money and Good Government* (New York: Public Affairs, 2018), 113.

76. Alan Greenspan, *The Age of Turbulence: Adventures in a New World* (New York: Penguin Press, 2007), 94.

77. Board of Governors of the Federal Reserve, "Membership of the Board of Governors, 1914–Present"; Meltzer, *Federal Reserve*, 2.2: 1141–1143.

78. Peter T. Kilborn, "Fed Nominee Announced by President," *New York Times*, May 24, 1988.

79. Ronald Reagan, "Remarks at the Swearing-In Ceremony for Alan Greenspan," August 11, 1987, American Presidency Project, https://www.presidency.ucsb.edu/documents/remarks -the-swearing-ceremony-for-alan-greenspan-chairman-the-board-governors-the-federal.

80. Reagan, "Remarks at Ceremony for Greenspan."

CHAPTER 10. STABILIZATION: BUSH RELINQUISHES HIS CONTROL IN SECURING THE POLICY DOMAIN

1. John H. Sununu, *The Quiet Man: The Indispensable Presidency of George H. W. Bush* (New York: Broadside Books, 2015), 47.

2. Bob Woodward, "The President's Key Men: Splintered Trio, Splintered Policy," *Washington Post*, October 7, 1992.

3. "Interview with Michael Boskin," July 30–31, 2001, Miller Center: George H. W. Bush Oral History Project, 44–45, https://millercenter.org/the-presidency/presidential-oral-histories /michael-boskin-oral-history.

4. "Official at Brookings Picked by Congress for Its Budget Post," *New York Times*, March 3, 1989.

5. David E. Rosenbaum, "Of Freezes and Squeezes: Bush's Call for Flexible Budget Procedure Is Step That Is More Political than Fiscal," *New York Times*, February 16, 1989.

6. Richard Darman, *Who's in Control?* (New York: Simon & Schuster, 1996), 206.

7. Darman, *Who's in Control*, 206–207.

8. Darman, 207.

9. Darman, 204–205.

10. Darman, 201–202.

11. George Bush, "Address Accepting the Presidential Nomination," August 18, 1988, American Presidency Project, https://www.presidency.ucsb.edu/documents/address-accepting-the -presidential-nomination-the-republican-national-convention-new.

12. Darman, *Who's in Control*, 209.

13. Darman, 214–215.

14. Darman, 217–218.

15. David E. Rosenbaum, "Bush and Leaders Reach Agreement on Budget Outline," *New York Times*, April 15, 1989.

16. Louis Uchitelle, "Bush, Like Reagan in 1980, Seeks Tax Cuts to Stimulate the Economy," *New York Times*, September 22, 1988.

17. Iwan Morgan, *The Age of Deficits: Presidents and Unbalanced Budgets from Jimmy Carter to George W. Bush* (Lawrence: University Press of Kansas, 2009), 135–136; Dennis S. Ippolito, *Deficits, Debt, and the New Politics of Tax Policy* (New York: Cambridge University Press, 2012), 159–161.

18. George Bush, "Statement on Deficit Reduction," November 2, 1989, American Presidency Project, https://www.presidency.ucsb.edu/.

19. George Bush, "Address on Administration Goals," February 9, 1989, American Presidency Project, https://www.presidency.ucsb.edu/.

20. George Bush, "Message to the Congress Transmitting the Fiscal Year 1991 Budget," January 29, 1990, American Presidency Project, https://www.presidency.ucsb.edu/.

21. Darman, *Who's in Control*, 237.

22. Congressional Budget Office, "An Analysis of the President's Budgetary Proposal for Fiscal Year 1991" (March 1990), summary, https://www.cbo.gov/sites/default/files/101st-congress-1989-1990/reports/90-cbo-008.pdf.

23. Darman, *Who's in Control*, 228–229.

24. "Interview with Robert Reischauer," 2011, Bancroft Library at the University of California, Berkeley, 5, https://digitalassets.lib.berkeley.edu/roho/ucb/text/reischauer_robert.pdf.

25. Darman, *Who's in Control*, 243.

26. Darman, 246.

27. Darman, 251.

28. Darman, 257.

29. Congressional Budget Office, "The Economic and Budget Outlook: An Update," (July 1990), x.

30. George Bush, "Address before a Joint Session of the Congress," September 11, 1990, American Presidency Project, https://www.presidency.ucsb.edu/.

31. Darman, *Who's in Control*, 276–277.

32. George Bush and Brent Scowcroft, *A World Transformed* (New York: Alfred A. Knopf, 1998), 380.

33. George Bush, "Address to the Nation," October 2, 1990, American Presidency Project, https://www.presidency.ucsb.edu/.

34. Darman, *Who's in Control*, 272–287, quote on 273; Morgan, *Age of Deficits*, 144–145.

35. Alan Greenspan, *The Age of Turbulence: Adventures in a New World* (New York: Penguin Press, 2007), 120.

36. David E. Rosenbaum, "Greenspan Calls Budget Proposal a 'Credible Plan,'" *New York Times*, October 4, 1990.

37. Ippolito, *Deficits, Debt*, 164–165.

38. George Bush, "Memorandum of Disapproval," October 11, 1991, American Presidency Project, https://www.presidency.ucsb.edu/; Morgan, *Age of Deficits*, 151.

39. George Bush, "Remarks Accepting the Presidential Nomination," August 20, 1992, American Presidency Project, https://www.presidency.ucsb.edu/; Ippolito, *Deficits, Debt*, 166–167.

40. Bush, "Remarks Accepting the Presidential Nomination."

41. George Bush, "Remarks at a Welcome Rally in Anaheim, California," September 13, 1992, American Presidency Project, https://www.presidency.ucsb.edu/.

42. Sebastian Mallaby, *The Man Who Knew: The Life and Times of Alan Greenspan* (New York: Penguin Press, 2016), 379.

43. George Bush, "The President's News Conference," February 6, 1989, American Presidency Project, https://www.presidency.ucsb.edu/.

44. Board of Governors of the Federal Reserve System, "Meeting of the [FOMC], February 9–10, 1988," 43.

45. Daniel L. Thornton and David C. Wheelock, "A History of the Asymmetric Policy Directive," *Review–Federal Reserve Bank of St. Louis* 82, no. 5 (2000): 116.

46. Board of Governors of the Federal Reserve System, "Meeting of the [FOMC], February 9–10, 1988," 74.

47. Mallaby, *Man Who Knew*, 381–384.

48. Board of Governors of the Federal Reserve System, "Meeting of the [FOMC], July 5–6, 1989," 38. For other discussion of a "soft landing," see meetings of May 16, 1989, at 19; August 22, 1989, at 29–35; December 18–19, 1989, at 78 and 94.

49. Board of Governors of the Federal Reserve System, "Meeting of the [FOMC], August 21, 1990," 36 and 44; Mallaby, *Man Who Knew*, 395–396.

50. Board of Governors of the Federal Reserve System, "Meeting of the [FOMC], October 2, 1990," 53.

51. Robert D. Hershey, Jr., "The Budget Agreement: Politics Denied in Greenspan Support," *New York Times*, October 5, 1990.

52. Board of Governors of the Federal Reserve System, "[FOMC] Conference Call, January 9, 1991," 1; Bob Woodward, *Maestro: Greenspan's Fed and the American Boom* (New York: Simon & Schuster, 2000), 75–77.

53. Board of Governors of the Federal Reserve System, "[FOMC] Conference Call, February 1, 1991," 2.

54. Board of Governors of the Federal Reserve System, "Meeting of the [FOMC], March 26, 1991," 2–3.

55. "Meeting of the [FOMC], March 26, 1991," 7.

56. Greenspan, *Age of Turbulence*, 99–100.

57. George Bush, "Remarks Announcing the Nomination of Alan Greenspan," July 10, 1991, American Presidency Project, https://www.presidency.ucsb.edu/.

58. Bush, "Remarks Announcing the Nomination of Alan Greenspan."

59. David E. Rosenbaum, "Greenspan Named for New Term as Chairman of Federal Reserve," *New York Times*, July 11, 1991.

60. Woodward, *Maestro*, 84.

61. Steven Greenhouse, "Bush Calls on Fed for Another Drop in Interest Rate," *New York Times*, June 24, 1982. See also Mallaby, *Man Who Knew*, 415–416.

62. Board of Governors of the Federal Reserve System, "Meeting of the [FOMC], June 30–July 1, 1992," 32–33.

63. Steven Greenhouse, "Greenspan Backed for Another Term," *New York Times*, February 27, 1992.

64. Mallaby, *Man Who Knew*, 416.

65. David Hoffman, "Bush Becomes Pragmatic Champion of the Reagan Revolution," *Washington Post*, March 5, 1988.

CHAPTER 11. CONSTRAINT: THE REAGAN-ERA APPARATUS LIMITS CLINTON'S CONTROL

1. "1992 Democratic Party Platform," July 13, 1992, American Presidency Project, https://www.presidency.ucsb.edu/documents/1992-democratic-party-platform.

2. Bill Clinton, "Presidential Debate in St. Louis," October 11, 1992, American Presidency Project, https://www.presidency.ucsb.edu/documents/presidential-debate-st-louis.

3. Bill Clinton and Al Gore, *Putting People First: How We Can All Change America* (New York: Times Books, 1992), 7 and 15.

4. John F. Harris, *The Survivor: Bill Clinton in the White House* (New York: Random House, 2005), 23.

5. Bob Woodward, *The Agenda: Inside the Clinton White House* (New York: Simon & Schuster, 1994), 60–76.

6. Bill Clinton, "Executive Order 12835," January 25, 1993, American Presidency Project, https://www.presidency.ucsb.edu/; Robert E. Rubin and Jacob Weisberg, *In an Uncertain World: Tough Choices from Wall Street to Washington* (New York: Random House, 2003), 115.

7. "Interview with Alan Blinder," June 27, 2003, William J. Clinton Presidential History Project, 35–36, https://millercenter.org/the-presidency/presidential-oral-histories/alan-blinder-oral-history.

8. Rubin and Weisberg, *Uncertain World*, 118.

9. Alan Greenspan, *The Age of Turbulence: Adventures in a New World* (New York: Penguin Press, 2007), 143–144.

10. Woodward, *Agenda*, 80–92, quotes on 84 and 91.

11. Woodward, 80–92.

12. Woodward, 94.

13. Greenspan, *Age of Turbulence*, 147.

14. Woodward, *Agenda*, 120–121.

15. Greenspan, *Age of Turbulence*, 147.

16. Woodward, *Agenda*, 124 and 128.

17. Woodward, 130.

18. Woodward, 132.

19. Robert B. Reich, *Locked in the Cabinet* (New York: Alfred A. Knopf, 1997), 64–65.

20. Richard L. Berke, "Clinton Tells Middle Class It Now Faces a Tax Increase Because Deficit Has Grown," *New York Times*, February 16, 1993.

21. Bill Clinton, "Address Before a Joint Session of Congress," February 17, 1993, American Presidency Project, https://www.presidency.ucsb.edu/documents/address-before-joint-session-congress-administration-goals.

22. Steven Greenhouse, "Clinton's Program Gets Endorsement of Fed's Chairman," *New York Times*, February 20, 1993.

23. Iwan Morgan, *The Age of Deficits: Presidents and Unbalanced Budgets from Jimmy Carter to George W. Bush* (Lawrence: University Press of Kansas, 2009), 173.

24. Reich, *Locked in the Cabinet*, 104–105.

25. Woodward, *Agenda*, 165–166.

26. Woodward, 198, 200, and 224–225.

27. David E. Rosenbaum, "A Fading Call to Arms," *New York Times*, August 3, 1993.

28. Dennis S. Ippolito, *Deficits, Debt, and the New Politics of Tax Policy* (New York: Cambridge University Press, 2012), 171–173; Morgan, *Age of Deficits*, 175–176; Megan S. Lynch, Congressional Research Service, R41901, "Statutory Budget Controls in Effect Between 1985 and 2002" (2011): 11.

29. Jerry Tempalski, Department of Treasury, Office of Tax Analysis ,WP 81, "Revenue Effects of Major Tax Bills" (2013), https://www.treasury.gov/resource-center/tax-policy /tax-analysis/documents/wp81-table2013.pdf. I compare the revenue effect as a percentage of GDP in year four.

30. Woodward, *Agenda*, 214.

31. Bill Clinton, "Address to a Joint Session of the Congress," September 22, 1993, American Presidency Project, https://www.presidency.ucsb.edu/.

32. Haynes Johnson and David S. Broder, *The System: The American Way of Politics at the Breaking Point* (Boston: Little, Brown, 1996), 116–136, quote on 127–128.

33. Philip G. Joyce, *The Congressional Budget Office: Honest Numbers, Power, and Policymaking* (Washington, DC: Georgetown University Press, 2011), 162–163.

34. Robert D. Reischauer, Congressional Budget Office, "An Analysis of the Administration's Health Proposal" (February 1994), xiii, https://www.cbo.gov/sites/default/files/103rd -congress-1993-1994/reports/doc07.pdf.

35. Reischauer, "Analysis," xv.

36. Robert Pear, "Congress Asserts Health Proposals Understate Costs," *New York Times*, February 9, 1994.

37. Pear, "Congress Asserts."

38. David E. Rosenbaum, "About-Face by Clinton," *New York Times*, December 16, 1994; Bill Clinton, "Address to the Nation," December 15, 1994, American Presidency Project, https://www.presidency.ucsb.edu/.

39. Morgan, *Age of Deficits*, 179; Elizabeth Drew, *Showdown: The Struggle Between the Gingrich Congress and the Clinton White House* (New York: Simon & Schuster, 1996), 13–58 and 203–212.

40. Dick Morris, *Behind the Oval Office: Winning the Presidency in the Nineties* (New York: Random House, 1997), 158–183, quote on 162.

41. Bill Clinton, "The President's News Conference," April 18, 1995, American Presidency Project, https://www.presidency.ucsb.edu/.

42. Todd S. Purdum, "President Offers Plan to Balance Federal Budget," *New York Times*, June 14, 1995; Bill Clinton, "Address to the Nation," June 13, 1995, American Presidency Project, https://www.presidency.ucsb.edu/.

43. Bill Clinton, "Message to the Congress," January 6, 1996, American Presidency Project, https://www.presidency.ucsb.edu/; Adam Clymer, "Clinton Meets Challenge by Offering Budget Plan," *New York Times*, January 7, 1996.

44. Ippolito, *Deficits, Debt*, 187–190; Morgan, *Age of Deficits*, 194–195.

45. Jerry Gray, "Clinton and GOP Spell Out Details for Balanced Budget," *New York Times*, May 16, 1997.

46. Bill Clinton, "Farewell Address to the Nation," January 18, 2001, American Presidency Project, https://www.presidency.ucsb.edu/.

47. George W. Bush, "Address Before a Joint Session of Congress," February 27, 2001, American Presidency Project, https://www.presidency.ucsb.edu/.

48. Greenspan, *Age of Turbulence*, 214.

49. Greenspan, 220; "Excerpts from Fed Chairman's Testimony," *New York Times*, January 26, 2001; Richard W. Stevenson, "In Policy Change, Greenspan Backs a Broad Tax Cut," *New York Times*, January 26, 2001.

50. Congressional Budget Office, "The Budget and Economic Outlook: Fiscal Years 2002–2011" (January 2001), summary, https://www.cbo.gov/sites/default/files/107th-congress -2001-2002/reports/entire-report.pdf.

51. David E. Rosenbaum, "Slowdown Doesn't Discourage Rosy Forecast for Economy," *New York Times*, February 1, 2001.

52. Tempalski, "Revenue Effects of Major Tax Bills"; Morgan, *Age of Deficits*, 214–226.

53. Greenspan, *Age of Turbulence*, 226–248, quote on 228–229.

54. Greenspan, 241–242.

55. Bill Clinton, *Back to Work: Why We Need Smart Government for a Strong Economy* (New York: Alfred A. Knopf, 2011), 15.

56. Clinton and Gore, *Putting People First*, 5–7 and 23.

57. Clinton, "Address before a Joint Session of Congress," February 17, 1993.

58. Reich, *Locked in the Cabinet*, 177.

59. "Interview with Alan Blinder," 80.

60. Woodward, *Agenda*, 313.

61. Keith Bradsher, "2 Economists Nominated to Fed," *New York Times*, April 23, 1994.

62. Alan S. Blinder, *Hard Heads, Soft Hearts: Tough-Minded Economics for a Just Society* (Cambridge: Perseus Books, 1987), 33 and 51.

63. Sebastian Mallaby, *The Man Who Knew: The Life and Times of Alan Greenspan* (New York: Penguin Press, 2016), 447.

64. Board of Governors of the Federal Reserve System, "Meeting of the [FOMC], November 15, 1994," 42–43; Bob Woodward. *Maestro: Greenspan's Fed and the American Boom* (New York: Simon & Schuster, 2000), 125–137.

65. Alan Blinder, "Comments," in *American Economic Policy in the 1990s*, ed. by Jeffrey A. Frankel and Peter R. Orszar (Cambridge: MIT Press, 2002), 46.

66. Greenspan, *Age of Turbulence*, 156.

67. "Interview with Alan Blinder," 80 and 86.

68. Greenspan, *Age of Turbulence*, 161.

69. David E. Sanger, "Facing Foes, Rohatyn Ready to Withdraw as Fed Choice," *New York Times*, February 13, 1996; Mallaby, *Man Who Knew*, 484–487.

70. Bill Clinton, "Remarks at a Democratic Dinner," February 15, 1996, American Presidency Project, https://www.presidency.ucsb.edu/documents/remarks-democratic-dinner -new-york-city.

71. Greenspan, *Age of Turbulence*, 162.

72. Alison Mitchell, "Two New Faces Join Greenspan as Fed Choices," *New York Times*, February 23, 1996.

73. Board of Governors of the Federal Reserve System, "Meeting of the [FOMC]," January 31–February 1, 1995, 43.

74. Mallaby, *Man Who Knew*, 487–491.

75. Laurence H. Meyer, *A Term at the Fed: An Insider's View* (New York: Harper Business, 2004), 203.

76. Board of Governors of the Federal Reserve System, "Meeting of the [FOMC]," July 2–3, 1996, 50 and 72; Meyer, *Term at the Fed*, 40–43.

77. Greenspan, *Age of Turbulence*, 182.

78. Bill Clinton, "Remarks Announcing the Nominations for . . . the Federal Reserve," February 22, 1996, American Presidency Project, https://www.presidency.ucsb.edu/.

79. Ben S. Bernanke, *The Courage to Act: A Memoir of a Crisis and Its Aftermath* (New York: W. W. Norton, 2015), 43–81, quote on 71–72.

80. Greenspan, *Age of Turbulence*, 241–242.

81. Bernanke, *Courage to Act*, 39.

82. Bernanke, 321.

83. Neil Irwin, "Of Kiwis and Currencies: How a 2% Inflation Target Became Global Economic Gospel," *New York Times*, December 19, 2014.

84. Clinton, *Back to Work*, 16–17.

85. Bill Clinton, *My Life* (New York: Alfred A. Knopf, 2004), 521.

CHAPTER 12. THE REAGAN-ERA APPARATUS LIMITS OBAMA'S CONTROL IN MANAGING THE GREAT RECESSION

1. This section builds upon a critique of the unitary executive framework and a historical analysis presented in Patrick R. O'Brien, "A Theoretical Critique of the Unitary Executive Framework: Rethinking the First-Mover Advantage, Collective-Action Advantage, and Informational Advantage," *Presidential Studies Quarterly* 47 (2017): 169–185.

2. "2008 Democratic Party Platform," August 25, 2008, American Presidency Project, https://www.presidency.ucsb.edu/.

3. Barack Obama, "Address Accepting the Presidential Nomination," August 28, 2008, American Presidency Project, https://www.presidency.ucsb.edu/.

4. Barack Obama, "Remarks in Columbia, Missouri," October 30, 2008, American Presidency Project, https://www.presidency.ucsb.edu/.

5. Barack Obama, "Inaugural Address," January 20, 2009, American Presidency Project, https://www.presidency.ucsb.edu/.

6. Barack Obama, *A Promised Land* (New York: Crown, 2020), 211; Noam Scheiber, *The Escape Artists: How Obama's Team Fumbled the Recovery* (New York: Simon & Schuster, 2011), 1–12.

7. Brian Stelter, "No Question We're in a Financial Pickle. What Do We Call It?" *New York Times*, December 11, 2008.

8. Larry Summers to Barack Obama, December 15, 2008, "Economic Recovery Plan," 1, https://delong.typepad.com/20091215-obama-economic-policy-memo.pdf.

9. Noam Scheiber, "The Memo That Larry Summers Didn't Want Obama to See," *New Republic*, February 22, 2012.

10. Ron Suskind, *Confidence Men: Wall Street, Washington, and the Education of a President* (New York: Harper, 2011), 153.

11. Summers, "Economic Recovery Plan," 6.

12. Summers, 10–12.

13. Barry Eichengreen, *Hall of Mirrors: The Great Depression, the Great Recession, and the Uses—and Misuses—of History* (New York: Oxford University Press, 2015), 329.

14. Ben S. Bernanke, *The Courage to Act: A Memoir of a Crisis and Its Aftermath* (New York: W. W. Norton, 2015), 387

15. Michael Grunwald, *The New New Deal: The Hidden Story of Change in the Obama Era* (New York: Simon & Schuster, 2012), 118.

16. Robert M. Gates, *Duty: Memoirs of a Secretary at War* (New York: Alfred A. Knopf, 2014), 281–282.

17. Bob Woodward, *Obama's Wars* (New York: Simon & Schuster, 2010), 35.

18. Scheiber, *Escape Artists*, 61.

19. Scheiber, 61–62.

20. Suskind, *Confidence Men*, 154.

21. Obama, *Promised Land*, 239.

22. Obama, 239.

23. Jeff Zeleny and David M. Herszenhorn, "Obama Seeks Wide Support in Congress for Stimulus," *New York Times*, January 5, 2009.

24. Christina Romer and Jared Bernstein, "The Job Impact of the American Recovery and Reinvestment Plan" (January 9, 2009), 3–4, https://www.economy.com/mark-zandi/documents/The_Job_Impact_of_the_American_Recovery_and_Reinvestment_Plan.pdf.

25. Iwan Morgan, *The Age of Deficits: Presidents and Unbalanced Budgets from Jimmy Carter to George W. Bush* (Lawrence: University Press of Kansas, 2009), 251.

26. Stephen Labaton, "Fed Chief Says Recession Is 'Very Likely Over,'" *New York Times*, September 15, 2009.

27. Jerry Tempalski, Department of Treasury, Office of Tax Analysis, WP 81, "Revenue Effects of Major Tax Bills" (2013).

28. Timothy F. Geithner, *Stress Test: Reflections on Financial Crises* (New York: Crown, 2014), 372–373.

29. Geithner, 336.

30. Obama, *Promised Land*, 240.

31. Philip G. Joyce, *The Congressional Budget Office: Honest Numbers, Power, and Policymaking* (Washington, DC: Georgetown University Press, 2011), 179–206.

32. Suskind, *Confidence Men*, 140–141.

33. Barack Obama, "News Conference," July 22, 2009, American Presidency Project, https://www.presidency.ucsb.edu/.

34. Barack Obama, "Address before a Joint Session of the Congress," September 9, 2009, American Presidency Project, https://www.presidency.ucsb.edu/.

35. Joyce, *Congressional Budget Office*, 192–197.

36. Barack Obama, "Remarks following a Meeting with Senate Democrats," December 15, 2009, American Presidency Project, https://www.presidency.ucsb.edu/.

37. Dennis S. Ippolito, *Deficits, Debt, and the New Politics of Tax Policy* (New York: Cambridge University Press, 2012), 233–234; "Key Elements of the U.S. Tax System: What Tax Changes Did the Affordable Care Act Make?" Tax Policy Center, https://www.taxpolicycenter.org/sites/default/files/briefing-book/what_tax_changes_did_the_affordable_care_act_make_3.pdf.

38. Tempalski, "Revenue Effects," 81.

39. Bob Woodward, *The Price of Politics* (New York: Simon & Schuster, 2012), 31 and 33.

40. Barack Obama, "Budget Message," February 1, 2010, American Presidency Project, https://www.presidency.ucsb.edu/; Woodward, *Price of Politics*, 41–42.

41. Jackie Calmes, "$100 Billion Increase in Deficit Is Forecast," *New York Times*, February 1, 2010.

42. Bernanke, *Courage to Act*, 504.

43. Woodward, *Price of Politics*, 79; Ippolito, *Deficits, Debt*, 236–237.

44. Woodward, 77.

45. Woodward, 218–219.

46. Woodward, 245.

47. Woodward, 326–327 and 339–341.

48. Jackie Calmes, "Fault-Finding Grows Intense as Cuts Near," *New York Times*, February 23, 2013.

49. Ippolito, *Deficits, Debt*, 240–42; Grant A. Driessen and Marc Labonte, Congressional Research Service, R42506, "The Budget Control Act of 2011 as Amended: Budgetary Effects" 2015), 1–21.

50. Woodward, *Price of Politics*, 355.

51. Congressional Budget Office, "Economic Effects of Reducing the Fiscal Restraint That Is Scheduled to Occur in 2013" (May 2012), 1–2, https://www.cbo.gov/publication/43262.

52. Geithner, *Stress Test*, 487–488.

53. Barack Obama, "Remarks on Congressional Passage of Tax Reform Legislation," January 1, 2013, American Presidency Project, https://www.presidency.ucsb.edu/.

54. Barack Obama, "Remarks at the Town Hall Education Arts Recreation Campus," December 4, 2013, American Presidency Project, https://www.presidency.ucsb.edu/.

55. Jonathan Weisman, "Parties Focus on the Positive as Budget Cuts Draw Near," *New York Times*, February 27, 2013.

56. Driessen and Labonte, "Budget Control Act."

57. "President Obama's News Conference on the Sequester," *Washington Post*, March 1, 2013.

58. Bernanke, *Courage to Act*, 379.

59. Bernanke, 356.

60. Board of Governors of the Federal Reserve System, "Press Release," March 18, 2009.

61. Board of Governors, "Press Release," March 18, 2009.

62. Bernanke, *Courage to Act*, 398.

63. Bernanke, 409.

64. Geithner, *Stress Test*, 261–262.

65. Geithner, 286–287.

66. Suskind, *Confidence Men*, 249.

67. Geithner, *Stress Test*, 293–294.

68. Suskind, *Confidence Men*, 458.

69. David Axelrod, *Believer: My Forty Years in Politics* (New York: Penguin Press, 2015), 360.

70. Suskind, *Confidence Men*, 378.

71. Bernanke, *Courage to Act*, 426–427.

72. Barack Obama, "Remarks on the Reappointment of Ben S. Bernanke," August 25, 2009, American Presidency Project, https://www.presidency.ucsb.edu/.

73. Geithner, *Stress Test*, 398.

74. Geithner, 401–403.

75. Barack Obama, "Remarks on Financial Regulatory Reform," June 17, 2009, American Presidency Project, https://www.presidency.ucsb.edu/.

76. Geithner, *Stress Test*, 427.

77. David H. Carpenter, Congressional Research Service, R42572, "The Consumer Financial Protection Bureau (CFPB): A Legal Analysis" (2014).

78. Barack Obama, "Remarks on the Appointment of Elizabeth Warren as Assistant to the President," September 17, 2010, American Presidency Project, https://www.presidency.ucsb.edu/.

79. Geithner, *Stress Test*, 434.

80. Board of Governors of the Federal Reserve System, "Credit and Liquidity Programs and the Balance Sheet"; Eichengreen, *Hall of Mirrors*, 304–306.

81. Bernanke, *Courage to Act*, 483.

82. Bernanke, 382.

83. Board of Governors of the Federal Reserve System, "Press Release," November 3, 2010.

84. Bernanke, *Courage to Act*, 432–433.

85. Bernanke, 503.

86. Board of Governors of the Federal Reserve System, "Statement of Longer-Run Goals," January 25, 2012.

87. Bernanke, *Courage to Act*, 39–40.

88. Binyamin Applebaum, "Fed Signals That a Full Recovery Is Years Away," *New York Times*, January 25, 2012.

89. Bernanke, *Courage to Act*, 520–521.

90. Bernanke, 519.

91. Board of Governors of the Federal Reserve System, "Press Release," September 13, 2012.

92. Board of Governors of the Federal Reserve System, "Press Release," December 12, 2012.

93. Bernanke, *Courage to Act*, 529.

94. Bernanke, 540–542.

95. Board of Governors of the Federal Reserve System, "Press Release," December 18, 2013.

96. Bernanke, *Courage to Act*, 565–566.

97. Neil Irwin, "The Most Important Least-Noticed Economic Event of the Decade," *New York Times*, September 29, 2018.

98. Ben Bernanke, "Japanese Monetary Policy: A Case of Self-Induced Paralysis" (December 1999), 25–26, https://www.princeton.edu/~pkrugman/bernanke_paralysis.pdf.

99. Bill Simmons, "Obama and Bill Simmons: The GQ Interview," *GQ*, November 17, 2015.

100. Bernanke, *Courage to Act*, 567.

101. Obama, *Promised Land*, 524–525.

102. Obama, 304–305.

CHAPTER 13. A PRELIMINARY EXAMINATION OF TRUMP'S CONTROL

1. Congressional Budget Office, "The Distribution of Household Income, 2016" (2019), https://www.cbo.gov/publication/55413.

2. Board of Governors of the Federal Reserve System, "Changes in U.S. Family Finances from 2013 to 2016: Evidence from the Survey of Consumer Finances" (2017), https://www.federalreserve.gov/publications/2017-September-changes-in-us-family-finances-from-2013-to-2016.htm.

3. Ezra Klein, "Read Bernie Sander's Populist, Policy-Heavy Speech Kicking off His Campaign, *Vox*, May 26, 2015.

4. "Transcript for Meet the Press," *NBC News*, May 8, 2016.

5. Donald Trump, "Address Accepting the Presidential Nomination at the Republican National Convention," July 21, 2016, American Presidency Project, https://www.presidency.ucsb.edu/.

6. Bernie Sanders, "To Rein in Wall Street, Fix the Fed," *New York Times*, December 23, 2015.

7. Donald Trump, "Presidential Debate," October 19, 2016, American Presidency Project, https://www.presidency.ucsb.edu/.

8. "Republican Party Platform," July 18, 2016, American Presidency Project, https://www.presidency.ucsb.edu/.

9. Transcript for "Meet the Press," *NBC News*, May 8, 2016.

10. Trump, "Address Accepting the Presidential Nomination at the Republican National Convention," July 21, 2016.

11. Trump, "Address Accepting the Presidential Nomination at the Republican National Convention," July 21, 2016.

12. Michael Lewis, *The Fifth Risk* (New York: W. W. Norton, 2018), 22.

13. Lewis, 32.

14. Bob Woodward, *Fear: Trump in the White House* (New York: Simon & Schuster, 2018), 59 and 249; Donald J. Trump, @realDonaldTrump, Twitter, March 30, 2017.

15. Michael Wolff, *Fire and Fury: Inside the Trump White House* (New York: Henry Holt, 2018), 116.

16. "Donald Trump's Contract with the American Voter," *Washington Post*, October 22, 2016.

17. Jim Tankersley and Julie Hirschfeld Davis, "Trump's $1.5 Trillion Infrastructure Plan Is Light on Federal Funds, and Details," *New York Times*, January 31, 2018.

18. Carl Hulse, "Republicans Will Reject Trump's Budget, but Still Try to Impose Austerity," *New York Times*, May 23, 2017.

19. Julie Hirschfeld Davis and Emily Cochrane, "Government Shuts Down as Talks Fail to Break Impasse," *New York Times*, December 21, 2018.

20. Alan Rappeport and Mark Landler, "With New Budget Deal, Trump Surrenders to the Administrative State," *New York Times*, February 9, 2018.

21. "18 Confusing Things Donald Trump Has Said about Health Care," *Politico*, July 20, 2017.

22. Robert Pear and Kate Kelly, "Trump Concedes Health Law Overhaul Is 'Unbelievably Complex,'" *New York Times*, February 27, 2017.

23. Thomas Kaplan and Robert Pear, "Health Bill Would Add 24 Million Uninsured but Save $337 Billion, Report Says," *New York Times*, March 13, 2017; Thomas Kaplan and Robert Pear, "Senate Health Bill in Peril as CBO Predicts 22 Million More Uninsured," *New York Times*, June 26, 2017.

24. Susan Collins, @SenatorCollins, Twitter, June 26, 2017.

25. "Press Release: Senator John McCain on Health Care Reform," September 22, 2017, https://www.mccain.senate.gov.

26. Julie Hirschfeld Davis and Alan Rappeport, "Trump Proposes the Most Sweeping Tax Overhaul in Decades," *New York Times*, September 27, 2017.

27. Peter Nicholas, Richard Rubin, and Siobhan Hugues, "Over Golf and an Airport Chat, Trump and GOP Hashed Out a Historic Tax Plan," *Wall Street Journal*, December 20, 2017.

28. Woodward, *Fear*, 290.

29. Donald Trump, "Remarks by President Trump on Tax Reform," November 29, 2017, American Presidency Project, https://www.presidency.ucsb.edu/.

30. "Preliminary Details and Analysis of the Tax Cuts and Jobs Act," Tax Foundation (December 2017), https://files.taxfoundation.org/20171220113959/TaxFoundation-SR241-TCJA-3.pdf.

31. Donald Trump, "Remarks on Signing Legislation on Tax Reform," December 22, 2017, American Presidency Project, https://www.presidency.ucsb.edu/.

32. Jerry Tempalski, Department of Treasury, WP 81, "Revenue Effects of Major Tax Bills"

(2013). The calculation for the TCJA is based on dividing the estimated FY 2021 total revenue effect from the JCT by the estimated FY 2021 GDP from the CBO. See Joint Committee on Taxation, "Estimated Revenue Effects of the 'Tax Cuts and Jobs Act'" (December 6, 2017); Congressional Budget Office, "The Budget and Economic Outlook: 2018 to 2028" (April 9, 2018).

33. Tax Policy Center, "Distributional Analysis of the Conference Agreement for the Tax Cut and Jobs Act" (December 2017).

34. Stephen J. Adler, Jeff Mason, and Steve Holland, "Exclusive: Trump Says He Thought Being President Would Be Easier Than His Old Life," *Reuters*, April 27, 2017.

35. Douglas A. Irwin, *Clashing Over Commerce: A History of US Trade Policy* (Chicago: University of Chicago Press, 2017), 371–564; J. F. Hornbeck and William H. Cooper, Congressional Research Service, RL33743 "Trade Promotion Authority (TPA) and the Role of Congress in Trade Policy" (2011), 1–20.

36. Annie Lowrey, "The 'Madman' Behind Trump's Trade Theory," *Atlantic*, December 2018; Andrew Restuccia and Megan Cassella, "'Ideological Soulmates': How a China Skeptic Sold Trump on a Trade War," *Politico*, December 26, 2018.

37. Robert E. Lighthizer, "The Venerable History of Protectionism," *New York Times*, March 6, 2008.

38. Woodward, *Fear*, 55–60, quote on 60.

39. Woodward, 140.

40. Jonathan Swan, "Exclusive: Trump Vents in Oval Office," *Axios*, August 27, 2017.

41. Woodward, *Fear*, 158.

42. Donald Trump, "Press Release—President-Elect Donald J. Trump Appoints Dr. Peter Navarro to Head the White House National Trade Council," December 21, 2016, American Presidency Project, https://www.presidency.ucsb.edu/.

43. Woodward, *Fear*, 140.

44. Andrew Restuccia, Nahal Toosi, and Tara Palmeri, "John Kelly Folds Navarro's Trade Shop into National Economic Council," *Politico*, September 29, 2017.

45. Kate Kelly and Maggie Haberman, "Gary Cohn Says He Will Resign as Trump's Top Economic Adviser," *New York Times*, March 6, 2018.

46. Woodward, *Fear*, 249.

47. Congressional Research Service, R45529, "Trump Administration Tariff Actions (Sections 201, 232, and 301): Frequently Asked Questions," (2019), 1–49.

48. US Department of the Treasury, Bureau of the Fiscal Service, "Monthly Treasury Statement: Receipts and Outlays of the United States Government For Fiscal Year 2019 through March 31, 2019, and Other Periods" (March 2019), 10, https://fiscal.treasury.gov/files/reports-statements/mts/mts0319.pdf.

49. Donald J. Trump, @realDonaldTrump, Twitter, November 29, 2018.

50. Jim Tankersley, "Trump's Tariffs Could Nullify Tax Cut, Clouding Economic Picture," *New York Times*, June 3, 2019.

51. Jason Lemon, "Trump's Former Economic Adviser Slams Administration over Trade War," *Newsweek*, March 14, 2019.

52. Felicia Sonmez, "Kudlow Acknowledges U.S. Consumers, Not China, Pay for tariffs on Imports," *Washington Post*, May 12, 2019.

53. "Republican Party Platform," July 18, 2016, American Presidency Project, https://www.presidency.ucsb.edu/.

54. Donald Trump, "Presidential Debate," October 19, 2016, American Presidency Project, https://www.presidency.ucsb.edu/.

55. Jeff Mason, "Clinton Slams Trump for Commenting on Fed Policies," *Reuters*, September 6, 2016.

56. Ylan Q. Mui, "Donald Trump Says Federal Reserve Chair Janet Yellen 'Should Be Ashamed of Herself,'" *Washington Post*, September 12, 2016.

57. Ken Thomas, "Donald Trump Names Jerome Powell as Federal Reserve Chair Nominee," *PBS NewsHour*, November 2, 2017.

58. Binyamin Applebaum, "Randal Quarles Confirmed as Federal Reserve Governor," *New York Times*, October 5, 2017.

59. Ana Swanson and Binyamin Appelbaum, "Trump Announces Jerome Powell as New Fed Chairman," *New York Times*, November 2, 2017.

60. Nick Timiraos, "Fed Chairman Powell Taps Two Advisers," *Wall Street Journal*, February 18, 2018.

61. Binyamin Appelbaum, "Trump Wants Faster Growth. The Fed Isn't So Sure," *New York Times*, March 12, 2017.

62. Jim Tankersley, "Trump Picks Monetary Expert for No. 2 Job at Federal Reserve," *New York Times*, April 16, 2018.

63. Binyamin Appelbaum, "Fed Predicts Modest Economic Growth from Tax Cut," *New York Times*, December 13, 2017.

64. Jeanna Smialek, "Trump Redoubles Attacks on Fed Chair, Saying 'I Made Him,'" *New York Times*, June 26, 2019.

65. Board of Governors of the Federal Reserve System, "Transcript of Chairman Powell's Press Conference," March 21, 2018.

66. Jim Tankersley, "Trump Takes a Rare Presidential Swipe at the Fed," *New York Times*, July 19, 2018.

67. Board of Governors of the Federal Reserve System, "Transcript of Chairman Powell's Press Conference," September 26, 2018.

68. Thomas Franck, "Trump Says the Federal Reserve Has 'Gone Crazy' by Continuing to Raise Interest Rates," *CNBC*, October 10, 2018.

69. Board of Governors of the Federal Reserve System, "Transcript of Chairman Powell's Press Conference," December 19, 2018.

70. Matt Phillips, "Stocks Tumble after Fed Signals More Rate Rises in 2019," *New York Times*, December 19, 2018.

71. Binyamin Appelbaum, "Stock Market Rout Has Trump Fixated on Fed Chair Powell," *New York Times*, December 23, 2018; Jeanna Smialek, "Trump's Feud with the Fed Is Escalating, and Has a Precedent," *New York Times*, June 24, 2019; Donald J. Trump, @realDonaldTrump, Twitter, December 24, 2018.

72. David Beavers, "Mnuchin: Trump 'Absolutely Respects' Fed's Independence," *Politico*, July 29, 2018.

73. Binyamin Appelbaum, "Trump Attacks the Fed as Stocks Fall and the Midterms Loom," *New York Times*, October 11, 2018.

74. Kris Schneider, "Trump Recognizes He Doesn't Have the Authority to Fire Fed Chairman: Mulvaney," *ABC News*, December 23, 2018.

75. Jeanna Smialek, "Trump Renews Attacks on Fed, Putting Central Bank in a Bind," *New York Times*, June 10, 2019.

76. Caitlin Oprysko, "Trump Accuses the Fed of Making a 'Big Mistake' with Its Interest Rate Hikes," *Politico*, June 10, 2019.

77. Philip Rucker and Robert Costa, "Bannon Vows a Daily Fight for 'Deconstruction of the Administrative State,'" *Washington Post*, February 23, 2017; "Breitbart's Bannon Declares War on the GOP," *60 Minutes*, September 10, 2017.

78. "Transcript for Meet the Press," *NBC News*, June 23, 2019.

CHAPTER 14. CONCLUSION

1. Board of Governors of the Federal Reserve System, "2020 Statement on Longer-Run Goals and Monetary Policy Strategy," August 27, 2020, emphasis added.

2. Jeanna Smialek, "Fed Chair Sets Stage for Longer Periods of Lower Rates," *New York Times*, August 27, 2020.

3. Jeanna Smialek and Jim Tankersley, "One Thing America Might Buy With All the Spending? Less Inequality," *New York Times*, April 23, 2021.

4. Andrew Davis, "Summers Sees 'Least Responsible' Fiscal Policy in 40 Years," *Bloomberg*, March 20, 2021.

5. Joseph R. Biden, "Remarks on the National Economy in Cleveland, Ohio," May 27, 2021, American Presidency Project, https://www.presidency.ucsb.edu/.

6. For an overview of the varying independence of independent agencies and commissions, see Marshall J. Breger and Gary J. Edles, *Independent Agencies in the United States: Law, Structure, and Politics* (New York: Oxford University Press, 2015).

7. George W. Bush, *Decision Points* (New York: Crown Publishers, 2010), 191.

8. Leon Panetta, *Worthy Fights: A Memoir of Leadership in War and Peace* (New York: Penguin Press, 2014), 252–255.

9. Bob Woodward, *Obama's Wars* (New York: Simon & Schuster, 2010), 278.

10. Meghan Keneally, "What Trump Has Said about Afghanistan," *ABC News*, August 21, 2017.

11. Donald J. Trump, "Address to the Nation on United States Strategy in Afghanistan and South Asia," August 21, 2017, American Presidency Project, https://www.presidency.ucsb.edu/.

12. Bob Woodward, *Fear: Trump in the White House* (New York: Simon & Schuster, 2018), 256 and 314–315.

INDEX